D1690227

Also in the Variorum Collected Studies Series:

PETER HARMAN
After Newton: Essays on Natural Philosophy

ROBERT FOX
The Culture of Science in France, 1770-1900

R.W. HOME
Electricity and Experimental Physics in Eighteenth-Century Europe

ROSHDI RASHED
Optique et mathématiques
Recherches sur l'histoire de la pensée scientifique en arabe

JOHN M. RIDDLE
Quid Pro Quo:
Studies in the History of Drugs

GUY BEAUJOUAN
Science médiévale d'Espagne et d'alentour

GUY BEAUJOUAN
'Par raison de nombres'
L'art du calcul et les savoirs scientifiques médiévaux

CURTIS WILSON
Astronomy from Keplar to Newton

ALLEN G. DEBUS
Chemistry, Alchemy and the New Philosophy, 1550-1700

GERARD L'E. TURNER
Scientific Instruments and Experimental Philosophy, 1500-1850

BRUCE S. EASTWOOD
Astronomy and Optics from Pliny to Decartes

WALTER PAGEL
From Paracelsus to Van Helmont
Studies in Renaissance Medicine and Science

WILLIAM A. WALLACE
Galileo, the Jesuits, and the Medieval Aristotle

Newton, his Friends
and his Foes

Professor A. Rupert Hall

A. Rupert Hall

Newton, his Friends and his Foes

VARIORUM

This edition copyright © 1993 by A. Rupert Hall.

Published by VARIORUM

Ashgate Publishing Limited
Gower House, Croft Road,
Aldershot, Hampshire GU11 3HR
Great Britain

Ashgate Publishing Company
Old Post Road,
Brookfield, Vermont 05036
USA

ISBN 0-86078-347-2

A CIP catalogue record for this book is available from the British Library.

This Variorum edition is printed on acid-free paper.

Printed by   Galliard (Printers) Ltd
             Great Yarmouth, Norfolk
             Great Britain

COLLECTED STUDIES SERIES CS390

CONTENTS

An Autobiographical Introduction   ix–xi

Acknowledgements   xii

THE RE-DISCOVERY OF NEWTON'S MANUSCRIPTS

I   Sir Isaac Newton's Note-book, 1661–1665   239–250
The Cambridge Historical Journal 9. Cambridge: Cambridge University Press, 1948

II   Further Optical Experiments of Isaac Newton   27–43
Annals of Science 11. London: Taylor & Francis, 1955

III   Newton on the Calculation of Central Forces   62–71
Annals of Science 13. London: Taylor & Francis, 1957

IV   Newton's Chemical Experiments   113–152

(In collaboration with Marie Boas Hall)

Archives Internationales d'Histoire des Sciences 11. Paris: Hermann, 1958

PAPERS ON THE PRINCIPIA

V   Correcting the *Principia*   291–326
Osiris 13. Philadelphia, Pa., 1958

VI   Newton's 'Mechanical Principles'   167–178

(In collaboration with Marie Boas Hall)

Journal of the History of Ideas 20. Lancaster, Pa., 1959

VII	Newton's Theory of Matter *(In collaboration with Marie Boas Hall)* Isis 51. Philadelphia, Pa., 1960	131–144
VIII	Newton and his Editors Notes and Records of the Royal Society 29. London, 1974	397–417
IX	Beyond the Fringe: Diffraction as Seen by Grimaldi, Fabri, Hooke and Newton Notes and Records of the Royal Society 44. London, 1990	13–23

NEWTON AND THE ROYAL SOCIETY

X	Two Unpublished Lectures of Robert Hooke Isis 42. Philadelphia, Pa., 1951	219–230
XI	Newton's First Book Archives Internationales d'Histoire des Sciences 13. Paris: Hermann, 1961	39–61
XII	Horology and Criticism: Robert Hooke Studia Copernicana 16 – Science and History: Studies in Honor of Edward Rosen. Ossolinskich, Poland, 1978	261–281
XIII	Henry More and the Scientific Revolution Henry Moore (1614–1687). Tercentenary Studies, ed. S. Hutton. Dordrecht: Kluwer Academic Publishers, 1990	37–54

NEWTON AND EUROPE

XIV	Huygens and Newton The Anglo-Dutch Contribution to the Civilization of Early Modern Society: An Anglo-Netherlands Symposium, 27–28 June (1974). London: British Academy/ Oxford University Press, 1976	45–59

XV	Le problème de la vitesse de la lumière dans l' oeuvre de Newton	179–194
	L'Histoire des Sciences: Textes et Etudes. Roemer et la Vitesse de la Lumière. Paris: Librairie J. Vrin, 1978	
XVI	Leibniz and the British Mathematicians, (1673–1676)	131–152
	Studia Leibnitiana Supplementa 17 – Les Sciences. Wiesbaden: Franz Steiner Verlag, 1978	
XVII	Newton in France: A New View	233–250
	History of Science 13. Chalfont St Giles: Science History Publications Ltd., 1975	
Index		1–4

This volume contains xii + 330 pages

PUBLISHER'S NOTE

The articles in this volume, as in all others in the Collected Studies Series, have not been given a new, continuous pagination. In order to avoid confusion, and to facilitate their use where these same studies have been referred to elsewhere, the original pagination has been maintained wherever possible.

Each article has been given a Roman number in order of appearance, as listed in the Contents. This number is repeated on each page and quoted in the index entries.

AN AUTOBIOGRAPHICAL INTRODUCTION

During the first half of the present century our knowledge of England's greatest scientist, Isaac Newton, advanced little. There appeared no new edition of his published writings, though the last 'complete' text had been printed between 1779 and 1785; suggestions for the publication of Newton's correspondence came to nothing; and though a new biography by Louis Trenchard More (1934) drew on some fresh documentation, it followed the lines of Sir David Brewster's pioneering *Memoirs* (1855). True, two useful sets of interpretive essays commemorated the bicentenary of Newton's death in 1727 but they too followed well-worn paths and perpetuated erroneous, if well established traditions. Perhaps the first hint of a change came in 1947 with the publication of the Royal Society's (delayed) tercentenary essays, including Vavilov's on Newton's atomism, and Keynes's view of Newton drawn from his own collection of manuscripts. Since then, an enormous change in Newtonian scholarship has taken place in the second half of this century; the papers here reprinted chart one man's passage through this epoch of great achievement by a band of scholars — I. Bernard Cohen, J.W. Herivel, Alexandre Koyré (a giant in his time), J.E. McGuire, H.W. Turnbull, R.S. Westfall, D.T. Whiteside, and many more.

About forty-five years ago, when I was looking into the history of ballistics, I read Boris Hessen's imaginative essay on 'The social and economic roots of Newton's *Principia*' (1931). His positive assertions about the social and technological objectives of the second book of Newton's classical work prompted me to examine earlier writers, from whom I learned nothing to the point, if we except W.W.R. Ball, who had printed in his *Essay on Newton's Principia* (1893) the correspondence between Newton and Halley about the publication of that book. These letters are still our major source of information. I therefore decided to look into Newton's own manuscripts in the Cambridge University Library to see if they threw any light upon his choice of topics in Book II.

In the Introduction to his monumental *Mathematical Papers of Isaac Newton*, D.T. Whiteside has traced the history of this vast legacy that came to Cambridge in the late nineteenth century, and of the few (besides W.W.R. Ball) who turned over its pages. There, I found no further enlightenment upon Book II, beyond its presence (as was to be expected) in the manuscripts preceding the printer's text sent to the Royal Society; indeed, Newton discussed resisted and projectile motion in a short essay on the motion of bodies that he prepared immediately before the *Principia* family of texts. But what caught my imagination much more than this essentially fruitless enquiry into Newton's purposes was the wealth of information I encountered bearing upon the earliest phases of Newton's great discoveries in mathematics and science. I *think* I was the first person to be excited by the historical significance of Newton's October 1666 tract 'On resolving problems by Motion' (that is, fluxions); I certainly appreciated the significance of his student notebooks, and especially of the record of his experiments on light carried out with a prism, which securely take such investigations back to the sixteen-sixties. It was at once apparent to me, among other things, that Newton's own spare statements about his early optical researches, which all subsequent writers had copied, were insufficient and indeed (perhaps wilfully) misleading. Newton's path to a 'New Theory of Light and Colours' had been neither so straight nor so swift as he made out. That many of the subtleties involved in reconstructing this path then escaped me is natural enough.

This was the background to my first two short papers on Newton's optics here reprinted. The pages noting his first sketchy thoughts on mechanics were discovered by Professor H.W. Turnbull, and their elucidation was much improved by Mr J.W. Herivel, some years after my account (Paper III). In the late nineteen-fifties (if I remember rightly) he, and several of the scholars I have already named, began to interest themselves in Newton's manuscripts. New researches were now proceeding so rapidly that Professor Cohen was able (at Chicago in 1960) to deliver an account of 'Newton in the light of recent scholarship'.

Other papers in this volume have followed more or less directly from my first interest in Newton as a man who might be revealed through his manuscripts — as I had convinced myself in 1947. The notion may seem trite now, but it had not occurred to such men as Florian Cajori and Louis Trenchard More. More than ten years later, in 1958–59, when my wife and I studied Newton's chemical experiments, we were fortunate in that a critical notebook had recently been restored to the University Library, after lodging in the University Archives since the eighteen-eighties. No one had noticed its absence! As for documentary studies upon Robert Hooke (Papers X, XII) I was led to these by his claims with respect to both Henry Oldenburg and Isaac Newton. (I had begun preliminary work on the former's correspondence in 1949.) Perhaps no one since Richard Waller had read those of Hooke's manuscripts which in some devious way had found a home in that Newtonian stronghold, Trinity College, Cambridge.

Some of the later papers in this volume were written as contributions to symposia at the request of various bodies, all of whom I thank for the honour of their invitation. I mention two only, the British Academy and the *Centre de Synthèse*, Paris; to successive Directors of the *Centre*, Mademoiselle Suzanne Delorme and Monsieur Jacques Roger, I am much indebted for the participation I have enjoyed in French intellectual life. Finally, my gratitude goes to the Royal Society of London, many of whose Fellows and all of whose Librarians have encouraged, promoted and made pleasant my life as an historian.

My wife, Marie Boas Hall, has generously permitted reproduction in this volume of three of our joint papers (Papers IV, VI and VII), for which my affectionate thanks.

A. RUPERT HALL

Tackley, Oxon
1992

ACKNOWLEDGEMENTS

I am grateful to the following publishers, institutions and journals for their generous permission to reproduce the papers included in this volume: Cambridge University Press, Cambridge (for paper I); *Annals of Science* (II, III); Hermann, Paris (IV, XI); *Osiris* (V); *Journal of the History of Ideas* (VI); *Isis* (VII, X); The Royal Society of London (VIII, IX); *Studia Copernica* (XII); Kluwer Academic Publishers, Dordrecht (XIII); The British Academy, London (XIV); Librairie J. Vrin, Paris (XV); Franz Steiner Verlag, Wiesbaden (XVI); Science History Publications Ltd., Chalfont St Giles (XVII).

Full bibliographic details of the original publications are given in the Contents page.

I

1. SIR ISAAC NEWTON'S NOTE-BOOK, 1661–65

Preserved in the portion of the former Portsmouth Collection of Newton's books and papers deposited in the University Library, Cambridge, is a commonplace book begun by him in his first year at Trinity College and used until about the time of his retreat to Lincolnshire when the plague visited Cambridge in 1665. In this small volume, 9·5 × 14·2 cm. (now pressmarked Add. 3996), consisting of 140 leaves bound in worn leather, Newton commenced writing his student notes at both ends in accordance with a custom not unusual when paper was dear, having recorded his ownership with the inscription 'Isaac Newton Trin. Coll. Cant. 1661'. It is curious that although this book has been available for examination for sixty years and has been described in the Catalogue to the Collection[1] it has never received the attention which should be accorded to any source which can throw light on the most obscure portion of Newton's career, the years of preparation under Isaac Barrow preceding the great period of discovery in 1665–66.[2]

Newton arrived in Cambridge in the early days of June 1661. Of the formal education he had received up to his nineteenth year very little is known; the anecdotes in which Sanderson's *Logic*, Kepler's *Optics*, *Euclid* and a book of judicial astrology purchased at Stourbridge Fair figured have been rejected as unreliable by his latest biographers.[3] For an account of Newton's studies during his early years at Cambridge more material is available in the history of education at the University, in Newton's own statements, and in his notes. It is by a fuller exploration of this last source, the most valuable of all since it is least subject to error, that an attempt can be made to assess Newton's knowledge and promise as a young man, and to remove some of the obscurity about his earliest discoveries.[4] As an undergraduate he studied elementary mathematics, astronomy, optics, and natural philosophy, probably under the direction of Isaac Barrow.[5] He was not sufficiently advanced to study Oughtred's standard text-book on algebra or Cartesian geometry until early in 1664, that is when he was

---

[1] *A Catalogue of the Portsmouth Collection of Books and Papers written by or belonging to Sir Isaac Newton* (Cambridge, 1888), 47, no. 8.

[2] This is not a unique note-book. Another dated 1659 has been described by D. E. Smith in the Mathematical Association's Memorial Volume (ed. W. J. Greenstreet), *Isaac Newton 1642–1727* (London, 1927), pp. 16 seq. Others which have still not been minutely examined are in the Cambridge University Library; that now pressmarked Add. 4000 (see below, p. 240) is later than the one discussed here.

[3] [Sir David] Brewster, [*Memoirs of the Life, Writings and Discoveries of Sir Isaac Newton*] (Edinburgh, 1855), I, 21. [L. T.] More, [*Isaac Newton, a biography*] (London, 1934), pp. 31 seq.

[4] Although Professor More writes that 'From Newton's note-books, some of his letters and conversations, and from our knowledge of the course of study then in vogue, we can give a reasonably accurate and full statement of his undergraduate work' (op. cit. p. 35), he has not quoted directly from Add. 3996, and the quotation from Add. 4000 is transcribed from Brewster.

[5] More, p. 35. Brewster's remark 'No friendly counsel regulated his youthful studies, and no work of a scientific character guided him in his course' is nonsense. Books were available, Newton was encouraged to read them and did. He received a wider and more scientific training than he would have had as a public schoolboy in the nineteenth century.

twenty-two and half-way through his third year at the University. But from this point his progress was rapid. More than thirty years later, when his mathematical innovations were being challenged, he satisfied himself that it was late in 1664 that he had purchased the mathematical works of Van Schooten and Descartes and borrowed those of John Wallis. The annotations then made, the discovery of the method of infinite series which followed, and the computation of the area of a hyperbolic sector, were recorded in a later note-book (Add. 4000) on a blank leaf of which the autobiographical note in question was written in 1699.[6] This second volume, not discussed here (it has already been slightly drawn upon by Newton's biographers) gives an account of his progress in mathematics after the end of 1663, and points directly to the early months of 1665 as the time of his first mathematical discovery, itself an extension of Wallis' method. In the summer of that year he left Cambridge for his Lincolnshire home. Precisely when this move occurred is not known; all that is certain is that he graduated in January 1664/5 and went down between May and 8 August when Trinity College was closed on account of the plague which had become dangerous in the town;[7] the holding of Stourbridge Fair was prohibited, and by a Grace of 12 October teaching and the University sermons were discontinued. Only on 5 March 1665/6 was Cambridge pronounced free from infection. As the plague revived again in the following summer the University was dispersed for the greater part of the two years 1665–66 which were critical in the development of Newton's intellect.[8] During the four years at Trinity a rather ill-educated freshman had developed into a graduate of no very obvious promise; his note-books support the tradition that when he left the University in the summer of 1665 Newton had created no ripple in the quiet academic pool, and apparently had neither read more widely nor thought more profoundly than his fellows.

Yet, in fact, Newton had already gathered all the material he required, he had already profited to the full from his university years, and genius was on the point of bursting into exuberant discovery. In the next two years, when he had little contact with the world of learning outside the few books in his own possession, Newton laid the foundations of his greatness as a natural philosopher, for it was at this time that he grasped the essential point for his optics and mechanics while he was already developing it in mathematics.[9] This was the period of Newton's originality: the rest of his life (when he could be persuaded to devote himself to science) was spent in the expansion, confirmation and defence of the ideas which began to take shape in

[6] Brewster, I, 23; More, p. 36. As a textually accurate version of this famous passage has never, I think, appeared in print, it may be worth giving here. 'July 4th 1699. By consulting an accompt of my expenses at Cambridge in the years 1663 & 1664 I find that in ye year 1664, a little before Christmas I being then senior Sophister, I bought Schooten's Miscellanies & Cartes's Geometry (having read this geometry & Oughtred's Clavis above half a year before) & borrowed Wallis's works & by consequence made these Annotations out of Schooten & Wallis in winter between the years 1664 & 1665. At which time I found the method of Infinite series. And in summer 1665 being forced from Cambridge by the Plague I computed ye area of ye Hyperbola at Boothby in Lincolnshire to two & fifty figures by the same method. Is. Newton.' (Add. 4000, f. 14.) Brewster's misreading of 'clean over' for 'above', copied by subsequent writers, considerably changes the sense of the passage. This note-book was begun December–January 1663 (O.S.).

[7] Brewster, I, 24–5; More, pp. 40–1.

[8] C. H. Cooper, *Annals of Cambridge* (1842–53), III, 517–18.

[9] There is little evidence of an interest in chemistry in his early notes. This may perhaps explain why Newton contributed less to the refoundation of this science, to which later he diverted so much of his attention, than to the physical sciences which were in the forefront of his mind during the critical period.

SIR ISAAC NEWTON'S NOTE-BOOK, 1661–65

his mind during the Lincolnshire exile. Newton himself was well aware of the significance of these years:

> In the beginning of the year 1665 [he wrote] I found the Method of approximating series & the rule for reducing any dignity of any Binomial into such a series. The same year in May I found the method of Tangents of Gregory and Slusius, & in November had the direct method of fluxions, & the next year in January had the Theory of Colours & in May following I had entrance into ye inverse method of fluxions. And the same year I began to think of gravity extending to ye orb of the Moon, & (having found out how to estimate the force with which a globe revolving within a sphere presses the surface of the sphere), from Kepler's rule...I deduced that the forces which keep the Planets in their Orbs must [be] reciprocally as the squares of their distances from the centers about which they revolve: & thereby compared the force requisite to keep the Moon in her Orb with the force of gravity at the surface of the earth & found them answer pretty nearly. All this was in the two plague years 1665 & 1666 for in those days I was in the prime of my age for invention and minded Mathematics and Philosophy more than at any time since.[10]

It was at this time too that Newton's best-known experimental work was done, leading to the work on light which he reported to the Royal Society in 1672, and which earned for him on the one hand election as a Fellow and on the other hand a not altogether favourable European reputation.

Thus one great problem which faces any student of Newton's work is the explanation of the metamorphosis of the inventive but by no means precocious schoolboy who contrived mechanical toys and sundials into the brilliant natural philosopher of ten years later. Any knowledge of Newton's reading and thought from his first arrival in Cambridge to his departure in the summer of 1665 is precious. Clearly discoveries of such weight as Newton's were not fortuitous nor spontaneous, but were preceded by a period of study and reflexion on existing knowledge, concentrated perhaps in 1664 and early in 1665, of which all too little is known because the foundations upon which he based a magnificent edifice have been almost completely hidden. The masterly ease with which Newton explained the experiments on the refrangibility of the sun's rays by his theory of colour, developing a veritable treatise on light in his letters to the Royal Society, is made more comprehensible by the knowledge that these were not his first experiments or very recent thoughts. Similarly, when testing the hypothesis of universal gravitation a system of the universe and the mathematics of astronomy were already present in Newton's mind; more familiar indeed than the accurate measure of the earth itself. Any study of Newton which seeks to work backwards from the author of the *Principia* to the young Fellow of Trinity ends inevitably in 1665–6; it is impossible to proceed through these crucial years to the prehistory of his philosophy. Instead one must take the other road, begin with the freshman and work forward to discover the unfolding of his ideas. To do this it is necessary to turn to the note-books.

The second of those in the Cambridge Library (Add. 4000) tells comparatively little of his work outside mathematics, where, as has been said, he is shown to have extended Wallis's method of series early in 1665, and to have begun the method of fluxions in May of the same year, before leaving Cambridge. The volume with which we are here concerned, however, was begun in 1661, and is far more informative. Naturally in a private commonplace book there is little record of dates by which the

---

[10] Add. 3968, no. 41, bundle 2. Newton was dissatisfied with the draft—perhaps because the dates do not seem to be entirely correct—and struck it out.

sequence of the entries can be established, and it is rarely possible to guess when a particular note was written. The latest date I have found is that of the observation of a comet on 5 April 1665.[11] The script, the pen and the ink vary as remarks were added at different times, sometimes on the same page; the epitomes of books he read, on the other hand, are much more uniform in appearance but form the least interesting part of the volume. Probably the earliest entry made by Newton was in taking notes headed: 'Aristotelis Stagiritae Peripateticorum principis Organo. Definitiorum, summarumque sententiarum recollectio.' The following ten pages are covered with extracts from Porphyry's Introduction and the 'Categories'; in each case Newton copied out in Greek the first sentence of each paragraph.[12] The leaves 16 to 26 are taken up with notes under the title 'Johannis Magiri Phisiologiae Peripateticae Contractio'.[13] Newton carefully summarized in Latin the chapters of this lengthy exposition of the conventional philosophy, but omitted the commentaries of the author which are longer than the chapters to which they refer. This abstract breaks off at book IV, chapter V of the original. The next entries were probably made a year or two after these elementary studies as they consist of astronomical notes: on the diameters of the stars and planets, on the equation of time, on the sun's parallax, etc. (Folios 27–30.)

Turning to the other end of the volume, again it is probable that the first pages were written during Newton's early terms at Trinity. They begin with some phrases and sentences in Greek copied from the *Nicomachean Ethics* of Aristotle, annotations of a work by Eustachius *a Sancto Paulo, Ethica sive summa moralis disciplinae, in tres partes divisa* (of which an edition was published in Cambridge in 1654), and some pages of *Axiomata* under such headings as 'Circa Doctrinam Essentiae, Entis & non entis', 'Circa Doctrinam Actus & potentiae', 'Circa Doctrinam Causae & causati'. These long and detailed metaphysical notes, an integral part of the university course of the period, extend from fol. 43 to fol. 71. Next Newton approached the subject of rhetoric, with the work of Geraldus Vossius, canon of Canterbury, *Rhetorices contractae, sive partionum oratoriarum Libri V* (Oxford, 1631, 1655, 1666, etc.) as his text-book. This summary is followed by a note in English of the connotation of the word 'idea'.

The remaining pages of the commonplace book are more interesting as yielding information, not only on Newton's course of reading, but on the growth of his own ideas. By their writer they were considered so important that he compiled an index to them. They consist of scattered notes, principally on scientific subjects, collected under the title 'Quaestiones quaedam Philosophicae',[14] and were written in the course of three or four years at least, as the changes in calligraphy and ink indicate, as well as the development of those topics in science which will always be associated with Newton's name. The notes are of various types; some appear to be transcripts,

---

[11] 'Of ye Sunn Starrs & Plannets & Comets.' Fol. 116.

[12] This should dispose of the suggestion that Newton was almost ignorant of Greek, while his knowledge of written French at least is demonstrated by proof corrections in his own hand to Des Maizeau's, *Recueil de diverses pièces sur la philosophie, la religion naturelle, l'histoire, les mathématiques, &c. Par Mrs. Leibniz, Clarke, Newton & autres auteurs célèbres* (Amsterdam, 1720). These corrections are to be found in the Cambridge University Library copy, pressmark Adv. d. 39. 2.

[13] *Johannis Magiri Physiologiae Peripateticae Libri sex, cum commentariis*. An edition was published in Cambridge in 1642.

[14] At the top of the page in a fainter ink is written the tag 'Amicus Plato amicus Aristotelis sed magis amica veritas'. (Fol. 88.)

SIR ISAAC NEWTON'S NOTE-BOOK, 1661–65

more or less direct, from his reading; others reveal considerable originality. Some are records of the opinions of others, some the results of his own observations and experiments. Occasionally, but not always, the source of the idea is indicated; the distinction between what is Newton's own and what he has borrowed is often vague and difficult to determine.[15] One point at least is beyond doubt on the evidence of this note-book, the two writers who exercised the greatest influence on Newton at this time were Descartes and Boyle. Descartes' conceptions of the structure of matter and of the rotation of the heavenly bodies by a vortex of 'First Matter' were very familiar to Newton, and already, tentatively, he was critical of them. The *Principia Philosophiae* of Descartes is referred to several times as are the writings of Boyle and a famous work of the Cambridge Platonist and later friend of Newton, Henry More.[16]

Many of the entries in this miniature reference and memorandum book which Newton compiled for himself are discussions of the prevailing hypotheses after a fashion which he later considered unworthy. The first note reads:

Of ye first mater.

Whither it be mathematicall points: or mathematicall points & parts: or a simple entity before division indistinct: or individually or Atomes. 1. Not of Mathematicall points since w^t wants dimentions cannot constitute a body in theire conjunction because they will sinke into ye same point.

The second hypothesis is rejected for the same reason:

2. Not of simple entity before division indistinct for this must be an union of ye parts into wch a body is divisible since those parts may againe bee united & become one body as they were before at the creation.

Newton continues the discussion of the hypothesis he favours under a separate head.

Of Attomes.

It remaines therefore y^t ye first matter must be attoms And y^t Matter may be so small as to be indiscerpible the excellent Dr. Moore in his booke of ye soules imortality hath proved beyond all controversie yet I shall use one argument to shew y^t it cannot be divisible in infinitum & y^t is this: Nothing can be divided into more parts y^n it can possibly be constituted of. But matter (i.e. finite) cannot be constituted of infinite parts....

The entry continues at some length; the writer was dissatisfied with it and ran his pen through it.[17]

Of greater interest in the formation of Newton's ideas are the following passages on the solar system. Descartes was the great authority and in criticism of his philosophy Newton, in his early twenties, wrote with moderation.[18] But his interest

---

[15] I surmise that Newton went through his book writing at the head of each page a likely heading under which to collect his notes, classified by subjects; then filled up the spaces as his reading and thinking offered material. In several instances the spaces allotted to a subject were too small, so that he had to continue in another place with a cross-reference; in others no entry was made under the page-heading (i.e. 'Of ffluidity, Stability, humidity, Siccity', 'Of ffigure, subtility, hebetude, smothnes, asperity', 'Of Odours & Vapors'). (Fols. 95, 96, 106.)

[16] *The Immortality of the Soul, so farre forth as it is demonstrable from the knowledge of its nature and the light of reason* (London, 1659).

[17] Fols. 88–9.

[18] Even in 1713 Newton was careful to dissociate himself from Roger Cotes' attack on the Cartesian system in the Preface to the second edition of the *Principia*.

in the passage of comets taught him that they might move across the Cartesian vortex.

Of ye Celestiall matter & orbes.

Whither Cartes his first element can turne about ye vortex & yet drive ye matter of it continually from y^e ☉ [sun] to produce light & spend most of its motion in filling up ye chinks betwixt ye Globes. Whither ye least globuli can continue always next y^e ☉ & yet come always from it & cause light & whither when y^e ☉ is obscured ye motion of ye first Element must cease (& so whither by his hypothesis y^e ☉ can be obscured) & whither upon ye ceasing of ye first elements motion ye Vortex must move slower. Whither some of ye first Elements comeing (as he confesseth y^t he might find out a way to turne ye Globuli about their one [own?] axes to grate ye 3rd El. into wrathes like screws or cockle-shells) immediately from ye poles & other vortexes into all ye parts of o^e [our] vortex would not impel ye Globuli so as to cause a light from the poles and those places whence they come.[19]

This suggests an attempted explanation of the Northern Lights.

Of ye Sunn Starrs & Plannets & Comets.

Whither ☉ move ye vortex about (as Des-Cartes will) by his beames. pag. 54 Princip. Philos. partis 3^e. Whither ye vortex can carry a comet towards ye poles & whence 'tis y^t y^e ☉ is turned about upon his axis. Whither Cartes his reflexion will unriddle ye mistery of a comets bird. [I.e. beard or tail.]

Newton's notes go on to refer to the comets of 26 October 1618; on 10 December 1664 he observed a comet whose altitude was 3° 40′ or 4° at a distance of 9° 48′ from the moon. Another was observed at 4.30 on the morning of Saturday 17 December 1664 and was watched until 23 January 1664/5. A third was seen in Andromeda on 1–5 April 1665.[20]

The ebb and flow of the sea, a perennial problem of science, which Newton solved in Prop. XXIV of Book II of the *Principia*, had already aroused his interest. Under the heading 'Of Water & Salt' he wrote:

To try whither ye Moone pressing ye Atmosphere cause ye flux and reflux of ye sea. Take a tube of above 30 inches filled with quicksilver or else take a tube with water wch is so much longer y^n 30 inches as ye quicksilver is weightier y^n water & ye top being stopped ye liquor will sink 3 or 4 inches below it leaving a vacuum (perhaps) then as ye air is more or less pressed without by ☾ [moon] so will ye water rise or fall as it doth in a witherglasse by heate or cold. The same may be done by comparing ye motions of ye water of 2 weatherglasses one whereof is within a vessell of water ye other not. [In another hand.] Observe if ye sea water rise not in days & fall at nights by reason of ye earth pressing from ☉ upon ye night water etc. Try also whither ye water is higher in mornings or evenings to know whither ☉ or its vortex press forward most in its annual motion.[21]

Another note which appears to be of late date and which almost certainly relates to the construction of his reflecting telescope, is given under the head 'Of minerals'.

Metall for reflection may bee thus made. Melt throughly 3 pounds of Copper then take 4 ounces of white Arsenick 6 ounces of Tartar & 3 ounces of Saltpeter finely powdered together & put y^m into ye melted copper & stir y^m well together with a rod of iron until they have done smoaking (but beware of ye pernicious fume for ye Arsenick is poison). Then after a little blowing ye fire to make it as hot as before, put in 6 ounces of Tinglass 2 ounces of Regulus of Antimony & after another blast or two

---

[19] Fol. 93.   [20] Fol. 93; continued on fols. 114–16.   [21] Fols. 111–12.

SIR ISAAC NEWTON'S NOTE-BOOK, 1661–65

put in a pound of Tin & stir it a very little & immediately cast it. The Tinglass makes ye mettall tough & ye Antimony makes it fine & of a steell colour too much of [it] will make it bleaw. The Saltpeter opens ye pores of ye mettal to let ye filth evaporate & ye Tartar helpeth to carry it away. [A different hand.] If this mettall must be cast smooth line the sand mold with the smoak of a linke.[22]

The notes on physics, like those on astronomy, are partly borrowed and partly original; sometimes jejune and sometimes penetrating. What Newton wrote on the subject of violent motion might have come straight from the pen of Jean Buridan or Nicolas Oresme—the very illustrations he uses are theirs. Of 'Attraction Magneticall' he wrote:

1. The motion of any magneticall ray may bee knowne by attracting a needle in a corke on water.

Whither a magneticall pendulum is perpendicular to ye Horizon or not, & whither iron is heaviest w^n is impregnated, or when ye north pole or south pole is upmost. Coroll. a perpetual motion.

3. Whither magneticall rays will blow a candle move a red-hot copper or iron needle or passe through a red-hot plate of copper or iron.

5. Whither a loadstone will not turne round a red-hot iron fashioned like windmill sailes, as ye wind doth y^m. Perhaps cold iron may reflect ye magn: rays wth ye pole wch shuns ye loadstone.[23]

It will come as no surprise that Newton made several sketches of possible ways of applying magnetic effects to obtain a perpetual motion. Under 'Of Gravity and Levity' he suggests:

Try whither ye weight of a body may be altered by heate or cold, by dilatation or condensation, beating, powdering, transferring to severall places or several heights, or placing a hot or heavy body over it or under it or by magnetisme, whither lead or its dust spread abroade, whither a plate flat ways or edg ways is heaviest. Whither ye rays of gravity may bee stopped by reflecting or refracting y^m if so a perpetuall motion may be made one of these two ways.[24]

The most profound as well as the most original writing in this commonplace book is undoubtedly that on optics. This is to be expected, for the first discoveries which Newton deemed worthy of publication were made in this science, and approximately at the time when he was using this note-book. The passages in which he described his early work on light and colours, preparing the way for the great series of experiments communicated to the Royal Society in his celebrated letter of 6 February 1671/2, deserve quotation at some length. The dates of these notes are unfixed. Although the latest date in the volume is 5 April 1665, it is possible that Newton continued his records in it for some time and, therefore, that the optical experiments were made after the spring of 1665. But it is not necessary that it should be so. Consideration of the notes in this volume suggests to me that they cannot represent the thought of the Newton of the great Lincolnshire period of discovery. According to Conduitt, Newton bought a prism at the Stourbridge Fair in August 1665 to test Descartes' theory of light; but (according to Cooper) Stourbridge Fair was not held because of the outbreak of plague, and all authorities agree that Newton must have left Cambridge before the beginning of August.[25] Perhaps his first interest in optics

[22] Fol. 111. [23] Fol. 102.
[24] Fol. 121. Galileo is quoted as saying that an iron ball falls 100 braccia ('perhaps 66 yards') in 5 seconds.
[25] More, p. 40.

should be referred to the previous year; Professor More writes: 'He had, as early as 1664, bought a prism and had made some observations on the refraction of light.'[26] Sir David Brewster was of the opposite opinion: 'There is no evidence...that he used it [the Stourbridge prism] for this purpose [the study of light], and there is every reason to believe that he was not acquainted with the true composition of light when Dr Barrow completed his Optical Lectures, published in 1669.'[27] Whatever Newton's reasons for not telling Barrow of his discoveries (not at all the same thing as failing to make any) Newton's words and his note-books, showing that his discovery of the nature of light was made at least as early as 1665–6, completely contradict Brewster's statement. Apart from the passage already quoted (above p. 241) Newton declared in his letter to the Royal Society of February 1672: 'in the beginning of the year 1666 (at which time I applied myself to the grinding of optic glasses of other figure than spherical) I procured a triangular glass prism, to try therewith the celebrated phenomena of colours.' He then described his surprise on finding the spectrum oblong and not round like the hole through which the beam of light was admitted.[28] Now Newton's notes on methods and instruments for grinding parabolic and hyperbolic lenses are in Add. 4000 immediately following the calculations of the summer of 1665. Consequently, there are two good reasons for thinking that, in his letter, Newton wrote '1666' for 1665, and that his note of 1699 (verified with his own records by himself) is more accurate, the definitive theory of colours being obtained in January 1666, as a result of experiments on the refraction of a beam of light, carried out either with a new prism or one bought in 1664. Therefore the notes in Add. 3996 on prismatic experiments must have been entered between (August?) 1664 and the end of 1665, for one conclusion at least seems beyond doubt, the notes now published represent Newton's first serious thought on the problems of light and colour. The observations on the refraction of a beam of light in a dark room which cleared up the whole matter for him were made later and obscured these earlier trials.

Of Light.

Light cannot be by pressure &c for wee should see in ye night as well or better y^n in ye day we should see a bright light above us because we are pressed downwards... ther could be no refraction since ye same matter cannot presse 2 wayes, ye sun could not be quite eclipsed ye Moone & planetts would shine like sunns. A man goeing or running would see in ye night....Also ye Vortex is Ellipticall therefore light cannot come from ye sunn directly &c....[29]

Of Colours.

That darke colours seeme further of y^n light ones may be from hence y^t the beames loose little of their force in reflecting from a white body because they are powerfully resisted thereby but a darke body by reason of ye looseness of its parts give[s] some admission to ye light & reflects it but weakly & so ye reflection from whiteness will be sooner at ye eye or else because ye white sends beams wth more force to ye eye & gives it a feircer knock.

Colours arise either from shaddows intermixed wth light or stronger & weaker reflection or parts of ye body mixed with & carried away by light.

[26] Ibid. p. 43. No reference is given to support this statement.
[27] Brewster, I, 27.
[28] Quoted by More, p. 73.
[29] Fol. 103.

SIR ISAAC NEWTON'S NOTE-BOOK, 1661–65

From some of these ariseth splendor & dulnesse.
No colours will arise out of ye mixture of pure black and white....[30]
Try if two prisms ye one casting blew upon y^e other's red doe not produce a white.

Newton then drew a sketch of the manner in which the reflection of light from two differently coloured surfaces through a prism reaches the eye, showing the different angles of refraction.

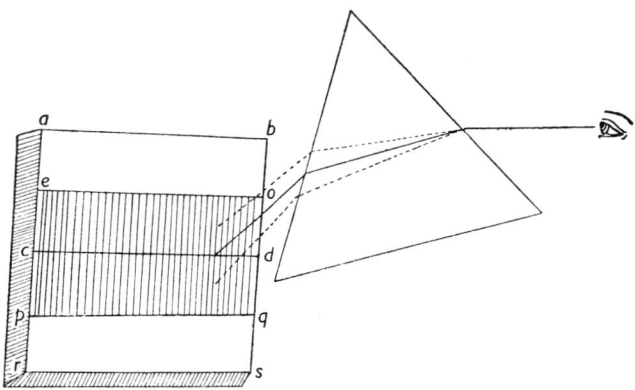

If *abdc* be white & *cdsr* black y^n *eodc* is red.
If *abdc* be black & *cdsr* white y^n *eodc* is blew.
If *abdc* be blew & *cdsr* white[r] y^n *eodc* is blewer.

	white		blew		Red
	black		blew		blewer
	blew		black		Greene, or Red [31]
	black		red		blew
	red		black		redder
If *abdc* be	red	& *cdsr* be	white	y^n *eodc* is	blew
	white		red		redder
	white		whiter		blew
	whiter		white		redd
	black		blacker		Greene or dark rd.
	blacker		black		blew

1. Note y^t slowly moved rays are refracted more then swift ones.

2^{ndly} If *abdc* be shaddow and *cdsr* white then ye slowly moved rays coming from *cdqp* will be refracted as if they had come from *eodc* soe y^t ye slowly moved rays being separated from ye swift ones by refraction there ariseth 2 kinds of colours viz. from ye slow ones blew, sky colour, & purple from ye swift ones red yellow [32] & from them wch are neither moved very swift nor slow greene but from ye slow & swiftly moved rays mingled ariseth white grey and black. Whence it is y^t *cdqp* will not appear red unless *qsrp* be dark because as many slow rays as come from *cdqp* & are refracted as if they came from *eodc*; soe many sloe rays come from *qsrp* & are refracted as if they came from *dqpc* unless *qsrp* be darker y^n *dqpc*.

3^{rdly} That ye rays which make blew are refracted more y^n ye rays which make red appears from this experiment. If one halfe of ye thred *abc* be blew & ye other red &

---

[30] Fol. 105. Cf. Antonius de Dominis, *De Radiis Visis*: 'If some darkness be mingled with the light, which yet permits it a passage and is not completely absorbed, there then occur the intermediate colours.' Quoted by More, p. 63.

[31] Added in a later hand.   [32] Blank in original.

a shade or black body be put behind it then looking on ye thred through a prism one halfe of ye thred shall appear higher y^n ye other, not both in one direct line, by reason of unequal refractions in ye differing colours.

4. Hence redness, yellowness &c are made in bodys by stoping ye slowly moved rays wthout much hindering of ye motion of ye swifter rays, & blew, greene & purple by diminishing ye motion of ye swifter rays & not of ye slower. Or in some bodys all these colours may arise by diminishing ye motion of all ye rays in a greater or less geometricall proportion, for y^n there will be less difference in their motions y^n otherwise.

5. If ye particles in a body have not so greate an elastick power as to return back ye whole motion of a ray then y^t body may be lighter or darker coloured according as ye elastick virtue of that bodys parts is more or less.

6 and 7. Colours also arise from the size of the pores in the surface of the body.

8. Though 2 rays be equally swift yet if one ray be lesse y^n ye other that ray shall have so much lesse effect on y^e sensorium as it has lesse motion y^n y^e others &c.

Whence supposing y^t there are loose particles in y^e pores of a body bearing proportion to y^e greater rays, as 9 : 12 & y^e less globules is in proportion to y^e greater as 2 : 9, ye greater globulus by impinging on such a particle will loose $\frac{6}{7}$ parts of its motion y^e less glob. will loose $\frac{2}{7}$ parts of its motion & y^e remaining motion of y^e glob. will have almost such a proportion to one another as their quantity have viz. $\frac{5}{7} : \frac{1}{7} :: 9 : 1\frac{4}{5}$ wch is almost 2 y^e lesse glob. & such a body may produce blews and purples. But if y^e particles on wch y^e globuli reflect are equal to y^e lesse globulus it shall loose its motion & y^e greater glob. shall loose $\frac{2}{11}$ parts of its motion and such a body may be red or yellow.

9. How an impression of colour is produced by pressure on the eyeball.

10. Of the succession of colours when red-hot steel is quenched in water and tempered. Newton notes that when the yellow is reached in tempering the steel is fit for gravers or drills, at the blue it is suitable for springs for watches.

12. Combination of colours.
Red and blue make purple.
Yellow and red make orange.
Purple and red make scarlet.
Red and green make a dark tawny orange.
Yellow from a prism falling upon blue gives green.
Blue from a prism falling upon red gives green.

Newton also observed the colours produced by diffraction:

26. A feather or black riband put betwixt my eye and ye setting sunne makes glorious colours.[33]

There are altogether fifty-one articles on colours of which the later and larger group deals with the formation or loss of colour in chemical reactions. For example:

47. Take Lignum Nephriticum (ye infusion of wch in fair water is good against ye stone of ye kidneys) put a handfull of thin slices of it into 3 or 4 pounds of pure spring water after it hath infused there a night put ye water into a clean violl & if you see ye light through it it appears of a golden colour (excepting sometimes a skycoloured circle at ye top). But if ye infusion was too strong ye liquor will then appeare dark and reddish. But if your eye is 'twixt ye liquor & light it appeares ceruleous &c. Acid salts destroy ye blew colour & sulphureous restore it againe wthout making any change

---

[33] Fols. 122–5, 133. Variants of the experiments noted are described in Newton's *Optics* (1704), Part I, Proposition I.

in ye golden colour, which may be usefull to ye finding whither bodys abound more in wth acid or sulphureous salts.[34]

From these notes of Newton's it is obvious that he had at this time only a small part of the knowledge gained by later work, but that even his early conclusions were by no means insignificant. He had found that the apparent colour of an object is related both to the structure of its surface and the composition of the light falling on it. He guessed that the colour of the refracted ray was dependent on its velocity; as most of the mathematical work in optics had been done in terms of the velocity of the ray, and Newton apparently believed already that light was the result of the motion of globules or corpuscles, it was natural that he should seek a first explanation of the different refrangibility of rays in difference in their velocities. The prism or grating acted as a filter to distinguish the slow-moving corpuscles from the fast. He had observed the colours produced by diffraction. Above all, he had discovered the varying refrangibility of light—that the rays which 'make blue' are more bent than those which make red. This has always been accepted as the core of the Lincolnshire discoveries, made by passing a beam of light through a prism, from which all else followed. This note-book shows that Newton first became aware of the effect when looking at reflected light through the glass. Professor More has written:

We know definitely that in 1664, he made some observations with a prism and was interested in the subject of improving the refracting telescope, and the question is, which of the two lines of work led to his discovery of the nature of light. It is generally stated that it followed from his observation that the image of the sun through a prism was oblong instead of circular. The serious objection to this belief is that he continued to work on lenses for at least a year and if, as he believed, their chromatic aberration was unavoidable then all this labour was useless.[35]

The evidence is that both these opinions are mistaken. Newton himself has explained very simply how he discovered the fact that rays of different-coloured light are not equally refracted, by looking at a parti-coloured thread. The probability is that he did this before trying the effect of passing a narrow beam through the prism, and before attempting to improve the telescope by removing spherical aberration.[36] A revised time-scale for Newton's discoveries might run as follows:

1664 to spring 1665.	Early prismatic experiments. Discovery of varying refrangibility of coloured light.
	Observations of comets.
Summer 1665.	Mathematical discoveries.
Autumn 1665.	Attempts to grind lenses of more complex curvature. Further prismatic experiments.
Winter 1666.	Completion of the theory of colours. Making of the reflecting telescope.

If the hypothesis that Newton made two separate series of optical experiments is accepted, the importance of the earlier is seen to lie in the interpretation it suggested for the later and more famous series. The explanation of his continued attempts to improve the refracting telescope may then be that Newton did not realize from his early experiments that varying refrangibility is the cause of chromatic aberration.

[34] Fol. 134.
[35] More, p. 67. I have been able to discover nothing to relate the first optical experiments *definitely* to 1664.
[36] Assuming either that the formula for a speculum metal is later than the notes on colour or that it has no direct connexion with the reflecting telescope.

This only became apparent when his former discovery was confirmed by a different experimental method. An observation made in looking at coloured surfaces might not at once appear to be of immense significance for astronomy.

In conclusion it will not be out of place to quote the rather pompously phrased opinion of Brewster: 'The history of science affords many examples where the young aspirant had been early initiated into her mysteries, and had even exercised his powers of invention and discovery before he was admitted within the walls of a college, but he who was to give Philosophy her laws, did not exhibit such early talent.'[37] One must confess, after examining such juvenilia of Newton as remain, that this judgement of Newton as an undergraduate is not unfair. There is little evidence in the passages quoted (and in many more omitted) of precocity, of remarkable industry, or of exceptional ability, until the notes on light appear, which cannot nave been written before his third year at the University and possibly only just before the acknowledged epoch of his greatest inventiveness. The quick intelligence, the wide grasp are much less striking in Newton at twenty-two than in the 'young Archimedes', Christian Huygens, at seventeen. The mystery of Newton's sudden growth in mental stature from plodding student to brilliant innovator is heightened if it must be restricted to a period of one, or at most two, years.

[37] Brewster, I, 19.

II

FURTHER OPTICAL EXPERIMENTS OF ISAAC NEWTON.

SOME years ago the present writer published a brief description of one of Newton's early scientific note-books, in which the immature stages of his work in optics may be partially traced [1]. From other unpublished sources a good deal more can be learnt, though it would be impossible to reconstruct the whole story without a very lengthy discussion.

The extent to which Newton drew his first ideas in optics and chemistry from the writings of Robert Boyle has hardly been sufficiently appreciated. The two major biographers, Brewster and More, seem to have missed this early influence of Boyle on Newton almost completely, though their later relations are well known [2]. As regards Newton's theory of colours, it is generally agreed that the awakening of his interest is to be attributed to the years 1665–6, not in any case to a period before the latter part of 1664. Now it was in that year that Boyle printed his *Experiments and Considerations touching Colours*, a book which of course demonstrated a scientific method very different from that of Newton in his maturity, and which is far from being a treatise on optics in the ordinary sense [3]. It can only be a conjecture that when Newton bought a prism to " to try the celebrated phaenomena of Colours " he was inspired by the passage in the book where Boyle had written:

> "The Triangular Prismaticall Glass being the Instrument upon whose Effects we may the most Commodiously speculate the Nature of Emphatical Colours, (and perhaps that of Others too ;) we thought it might be usefull to observe the several Reflections and Refractions which the Incident Beams of Light suffer in Rebounding from it, and passing through it." [4]

But it is no conjecture that Newton was powerfully influenced by Boyle, in the undertaking if not the interpretation of his experiments.

In a note-book probably begun about this time, and continuing in use until at least 1693, Newton took a page of notes from Boyle on colours [5]:

> 1. The rays reflected from Leafe Gold are Yellow, but those transmitted are blew, as appears by holding a leafe of Gold twixt yo^e eye & a Candle. [Boyle, *op. cit.*, pp. 198–9.]

---

[1] *Cambridge Historical Journal*, 1949, **9**, 239 seq.

[2] Sir D. Brewster, *Memoirs of Sir Isaac Newton*, Edinburgh, 1855; L. T. More, *Isaac Newton*, New York and London, 1934.

[3] Boyle's book was entered in the Registers of the Company of Stationers (ed. Roxburghe Club, London, 1913, **2**, 335) on 11 December 1663.

[4] *Experiments and Considerations touching Colours*, London, 1664, 191.

[5] Cambridge University Library, MS. Add. 3975, *f.* 2r. Cf. *Catalogue of the Portsmouth Collection*, Cambridge, 1888, 21.

2. Lignum Nephriticum sliced & . . . infused . . . reflects blew rays & transmits yellow ones. . . . [Boyle, pp. 199–212.]
3. The flat peices of some kinds of Glase will exhibit ye same Phaenomena wth Lignum nephriticum. [Boyle, pp. 216–9.]

Newton also refers to Boyle's 22nd, 24th, and 27th experiments:

4. But Generally bodys wch appeare of any colour to ye eye, appeare of ye same colour in all positions. . . .
5. The tincture of Lignum Nephriticum may bee deprived of its blew colour wthout any alteration made in ye yellow by putting a little of any acid Salt into it. And Sulphureous Salts (whither Urinous . . . or Lixiviate . . .) doe restore ye blew colour wthout making any change in the yellow. [Boyle, p. 204 *seq.*]

At the point where one might expect that Newton would annotate Boyle's remarks on the 'emphaticall' colours, he begins instead to describe the results of his own experiments with prisms, in which he had so much greater success than Boyle:

Experiments wth y^e Prisme.
6. On a black peice of paper I drew a line *opq*^{6} [Fig. 1], whereof one halfe *op* was a good blew y^e other *pq* a good deepe red (chosen by Prob of Colours). And looking on it through y^e Prisme *adf*, it

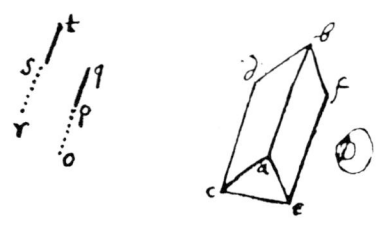

FIG. 1.

appeared broken in two betwixt y^e colours, as at *rst*, y^e blew parte *rs* being nearer y^e vertex *ab* of y^e Prisme y^n y^e red parte *st*. Soe y^t blew rays suffer a greater refraction y^n red ones.
Note [I call those blew or red rays &c, wch make ye Phantome of such colours]
The same experiment may bee tryed wth a thred of two colours held against ye darke.
7. Taking a Prisme, (whose angle *fbd* was about 60^{gr}) into a darke roome into wch ye sun shone only at one little round hole *k* And laying it close to ye hole *k* in such manner y^t ye rays, being equally refracted at (*n* & *h*) [Fig. 2] their going in & out of it cast colours *rstv* on y opposite wall. The colours should have beene in a round circle were all y^e rays alike refracted, but their forme was oblong

---

[6] I have italicized the labels for convenience.

Further Optical Experiments of Isaac Newton

terminated at theire sides r & s wth streight lines; theire bredth rs being $2\frac{1}{3}$ inches, theire length tv about 7 or eight inches, & y^e centers

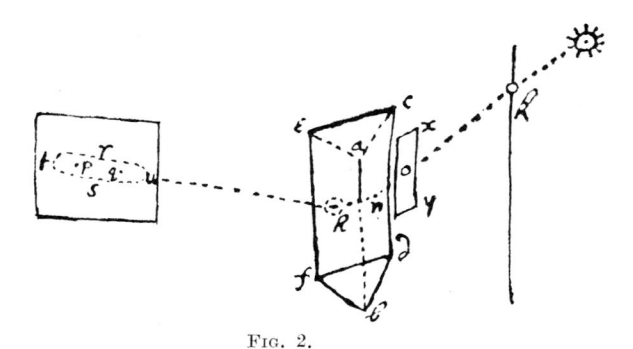

FIG. 2.

of y^e red & blew, (q & p) being distant about $2\frac{3}{4}$ or 3 inches. The distance of y^e wall $irsv$ from y^e Prisme being 260 inches.

8. Setting y^e Prisme in y^e midst twixt y^e hole k & y^e opposite wall, in y^e same posture, & laying a boarde twixt y^e hole k & y^e Prisme close to y^e Prisme, in wch board there was a small hole as big as y^e hole k (viz. $\frac{1}{8}$ of an inch in Diameter) soe y^t y^e rays passing through both those holes to y^e Prisme might all bee almost parallell (wanting lesse y^n 7 minutes, whereas in y^e former experiment some rays were inclined 31 min). Then was the length & breadth of y^e colours on y^e wall every way lesse y^n halfe y^e former by about 2 inches viz $rs=\frac{3}{8}$ inch, $tv=2\frac{3}{4}$ inch, & $pq=1\frac{1}{4}$ inch. Soe y^t y^e Red & blew rays wch were parallel before refraction may bee esteemed to bee generally inclined one to another after refraction (some more some lesse y^n) 34 min. And y^t some of them are inclined more y^n a degree, in this case. And therefore if theire sines of incidence (out of glasse into aire) be ye same, theire sines of refraction will generally bee in ye proportion of 225 to 226, & for ye most extreamely red & blew rays, they will be as 130 to 131 For by ye experiment if their angle of incidence out of ye glasse into ye aire bee 30^d. The angle [of] refraction of ye red rays being 48gr 35′ : ye angle of refraction of ye blew rays will bee 48gr 52′ generally ; but if ye rays be extreamely red & blew ye angle of refraction of ye blew rays may be more y^n 49gr 5′.

These notes, and the ones that immediately follow them, were obviously the bases for the printed accounts which appeared later in the *Philosophical Transactions* and the *Opticks*. Yet it is curious that the length of the spectrum given in no. 7 as seven or eight inches appears in the *Philosophical Transactions* as $13\frac{1}{4}$ inches, the other dimensions being much the same. Nor is there any record at this point of the *experimentum crucis*. On the other hand, Newton had made measurements of the relative refrangibility of red and blue light which he did not use in print.

Notes 15 and 16 contain an interesting observation bearing on the result derived from the *experimentum crucis*, and note 44 describes an experiment which may in fact be a version of it :

> 15. If a foure square vessell *abcd* bee made wth two parallell sides of well polished glasse AC, BD, & bee filled with water ; And if ye sunns rays passing into a darke roome through y^e hole k doe fall very obliquely on y^e glasse sides of y^e vessell y^e rays at their egresse shall paint colours on y^e paper Eff on wch they fall [The blew & red rays being separated by y^e first refraction] [Fig. 3].

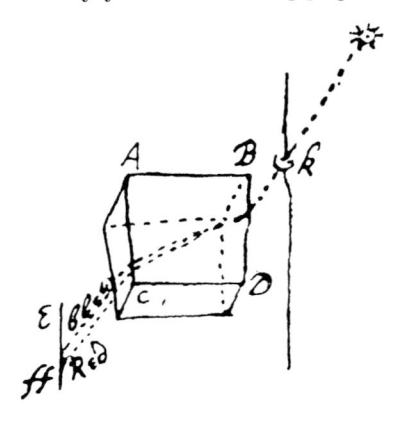

FIG. 3.

> 16. The colours are not made broader (as they would be were y^e prisme triangular) by removing y^e paper farther from y^e vessell [becaus y^e blew & red rays become parallel againe after y^e second refraction]. [*Note in another ink*] if the rays pass through two holes neare or close to ye vessell on either side, ye colours div ... [7].

It is not quite clear that Newton had attempted this experiment. The wording would almost suggest that the effect described had been deduced rather than witnessed. Further experiments with prisms led to the observation of what are now called interference effects. The discovery was made in quite a different way from Robert Hooke's, apparently independently, and not impossibly even before the publication of *Micrographia*. The various stages in Newton's observations are recorded in the following notes :

> 23. If in ye open aire you looke at ye Image of ye Sky reflected from ye basis of ye Prism *ef*, holding yo^e eye O almost perpendicular to ye basis you will see one part of ye sky *ep* (being as it were shaded wth a thin curtaine) to appeare darker y^n ye other *qf*. [For all ye rays wch can come to ye eye from *qf*, fall soe obliquely on ye basis

---

[7] MS. Add. 3975, *f*. 3*v*. The rest of the addition is illegible.

as to bee all reflected to ye eye. Whereas those wch can come to ye eye from *ep* are so direct to ye basis as to bee most of y^m transmitted to *g* :] & ye partition of those two parts of ye Sky, *pq*, appears blew ; [For y^e rays wch can come to y^e eye from *pq*, are so inclined to y^e basis y^t all y^e blew rays are reflected to y^e eye whilst most of y^e red rays are transmitted through to *g* . . .] [Fig. 4].

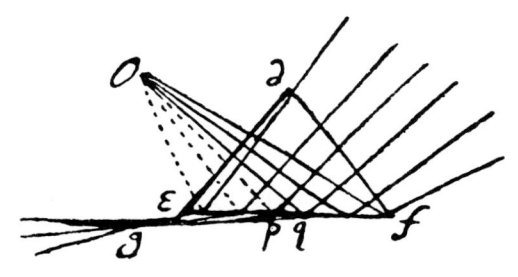

FIG. 4.

24. Tying two Prismes basis to basis *def* & *bef* together : I so held y^m in y^e sun beames, transmitted through a hole into a darke roome, y^t they falling pretty directly upon y^e basis *ef* [Fig. 5] were most of y^m transmitted to *B* on y^e paper *CB* ; though some of y^m were reflected to *C* by y^e filme of aire betwixt y^e Prismes. But both *C* & *B* were white. Then I inclined y^e Basis (*ef*) of y^e Prismes more

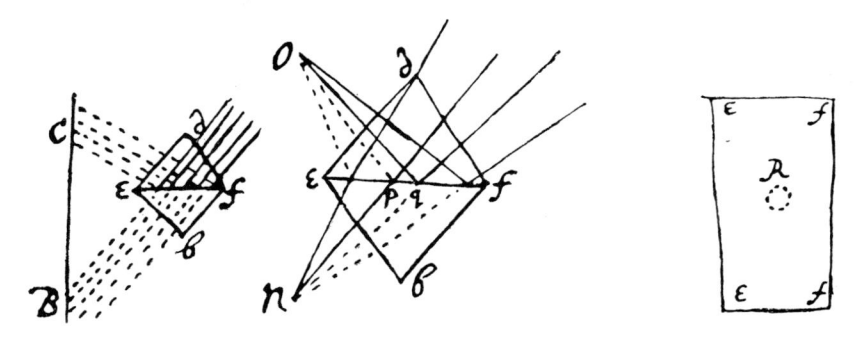

FIG. 5.   FIG. 6.

& more to y^e rays untill *B* changed from white to Red, & y^e white at *C* became blewish ; & inclining y^e Prisme a little more y^e Red at *B* vanished & y^e blewish colour at *C* became white againe.

27. The two Prismes being tyed hard together then in trying ye 24th Experiment, there appeared a white spot in ye midst of ye red colour *B*, & a darke spot in ye blewish colour *C*. And after ye base *ef* of ye Prismes was more [&] more inclined to ye rays, so y^t ye red colour vanished & y^t (by ye laws of Refraction) noe light could penetrate ye filme of aire *ef*, Yet ye white spot remained at *B* & ye darke one in ye midst of ye light at *C*.

28. Holding my eye at O or N [Fig. 5] very obliquely to ye basis ef; to my eye at O appeared a black spot (R) [Fig. 6] in ye midst of ye white basis (or filme of aire) ef, & to my eye at N appeared a white spot (R) in ye midst of ye black basis (or plate of aire) ef, th[r]ough wch spot (as through a hole in ye midst of a black body) I could distinctly see any object, but could discern nothing through any other parte of ye appearingly black basis ef.

29. By variously pressing ye Prismes together at one end more y^n at another I could make ye said spot R run from one place to another; & ye harder I pressed ye prismes together, ye greater ye spot would appeare to bee [Soe y^t I conceive ye Prismes (their sides being a little convex & not perfectly plaine) pressed away ye interjacent aire at R & becoming contiguous in y^t spot, transmitted ye Rays in y^t place as if they had become one continuous piece of glasse; whereas ye plate of aire (ef) is a very reflecting body; soe y^t ye spot R may bee called a hole made in ye plate of aire (ef).

30. In ye 27th Experiment when ye colour white or red was trajected on B, there would appear severall circles of colours about ye white spot at B & also about ye darke one at C. But these colours vanished together wth ye red colour at B: Growing greater & distincter untill they vanished.

31. Likewise in ye 28th exper: when ye spot was on y^t side [of] ye partition pq next ye eye, it appeared to my eye both at O & N encompassed wth divers circles of colours. W^{ch} circles would grow greater & distincter by how much ye coloured partition pq came nearer & nearer to y^m (y^t is by how much ye base ef was more & more oblique to ye rays) & soe vanished by degrees as ye said limb pq came to y^m. Before they began to vanish they appeared round or Ellipticall thus [Fig. 7a]. But in their vanishing (especially if looked on through a hole much smaller than my pupill) they appeared incurved thus [Fig. 7b].

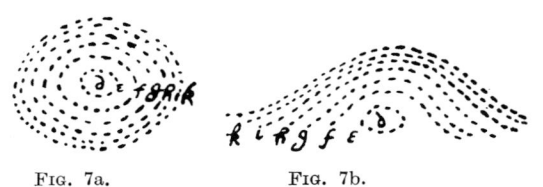

FIG. 7a.   FIG. 7b.

Succeeding notes show that Newton examined these rings of colour with considerable care. He found that they became most conspicuous when viewed through a narrow slit; in this way he counted 25 alternations of red and blue, and there were many other rings so close together that he could not number them. On illuminating the pair of prisms with monochromatic light derived from a third prism the rings were seen to be all of that colour, but alternating in intensity. Newton observed that the rings were broader towards the centre of the spot and decreased in width as their radius increased; therefore he judged "by y^e exactest measure I could make" that they increased in number in the same proportion as the layer of air between the glass surfaces increased in thickness [Fig. 8]:

FIG. 8.

[33]. (sit $cd=$ radio curvitatis vitri; $efghik$ circuli colorum; & $el = \dfrac{fm}{2} = \dfrac{gn}{3} = \dfrac{hp}{4} = \dfrac{iq}{5} = \dfrac{kr}{6} =$ crassitiei aeris). And this I observed by a sphericall object glasse of a Prospective tyed fast to a plaine glasse, so as to make y^e said spot wth y^e circles of colours appeare.

[35]. When y^e rays were perpendicular to y^e aire ef, y^e diameter of 5 of y^e circles was one parte, whereof 400 was y^e radius dC of y^e glasses curvity. The said ra[d]ius being 25 inches. Soe y^t (el) y^e thicknesse of y^e aire for one circle was $\frac{1}{64000}$ inch, or 0,000015625 [wch is y^e space of a pulse of y^e vibrating medium]

[*Later note.*] By measuring it since more exactly I find $\frac{1}{83000}$ =to y^e said thicknesse [8].

The thirty-seventh experiment gives the order of the colours as seen in different ways:

37. The circles of colour appear in this order from y^e center of y^e eye O Or on y^e paper at C viz Darke (or pellucid), white, yellow, greene, blew, purple, Red, yellow, greene blew purple, Red, yellow Greene, Blew &c. But to ye eye N or ye paper at B they appear in this order Light (or pellucid) black, blew, Greene, yellow, Red, purple, blew, greene.

In the forty-third experiment water was included between the prisms in place of air and the colours appeared as before, exhibiting " such phaenomena as it ought to doe were it a spot of aire ". But since the air was excluded it must be that " ye water cannot nimbly enough follow ye spot R, but leaves ye space S empty to be possessed by Aether alone until ye water have time to creepe into it ".

It is obvious from the *Opticks*, Book II, Part I, Observations 1–6, that the published work was closely based on these experiments and others like them. Some of the phrasing is almost identical. Yet from the expansion of the treatment in the *Opticks*, even on the points covered by these notes, and from the references in the book to telescope lenses of different curvatures, it can be seen that a good deal more experimental

[8] MS. Add. 3975, *f. 6r*.

work had been done before Newton began to prepare a proper account of his discoveries, by which time also he had learnt of Hooke's parallel observations. It is interesting to note that though Newton had, characteristically, begun to make measurements and computations at a very early stage of his inquiry—which contrasts, in this way, with the purely qualitative discussion in *Micrographia*—this quantitative aspect was very much elaborated when he came to write for the public. Newton's two theoretical remarks are difficult to interpret. Later, of course, he was equally prepared to admit that the aether filled vacuities in matter (as in *Opticks*, Query 19), and that it was capable of transmitting light. But he did not develop the idea that there might be a relationship between the spatial periodicity of the coloured rings and the dimensions of luminous pulses. Conversely there is no hint in these notes of the hypothesis of 'Fits' of reflection and transmission, which confirms a natural expectation that this hypothesis was the product of a late stage in Newton's thought on optics. In fact, whereas in these notes and correspondingly in Part I of Book II of the *Opticks* he seems to be approaching a theory of interference-colours which would relate them directly and simply to the dimensions of the interval between two surfaces, in the hypothesis of 'Fits' Newton insists rather on the obliquity of the rays to the surfaces :

> " And as the reason why a thin Plate appeared of several Colours in several Obliquities of the Rays, was, that the Rays of one and the same sort are reflected by the thin Plate at one obliquity and transmitted at another, and those of other sorts transmitted where these are reflected, and reflected where these are transmitted : So the reason why the thick Plate of Glass . . . did appear of various Colours in various Obliquities, and in those Obliquities propagated those Colours to the Chart, was, that the Rays of one and the same sort did at one Obliquity emerge out of the Glass, at another did not emerge, but were reflected back . . . by the hither Surface of the Glass, and accordingly as the Obliquity became greater and greater, emerged and were reflected alternately for many Successions ; and that in one and the same Obliquity the Rays of one sort were reflected, and those of another transmitted ".[9]

Thus Newton attached great importance to the variation of the critical angle with the colour of the light striking the interface remarked on in note 23 above.

Farther on in the note-book he wrote down a few more observations on these colours in terms of a vibratory theory of light, without apparently developing any firm hypothesis :

> If rays be incident out of glasse upon a filme of air terminated twixt two glasses, the thicknesse of a vibration is $\frac{1}{81,000}$ or $\frac{1}{80,000}$ part of an inch.

[9] *Opticks*, Bk. II, Pt. IV, Obs. 7. It is curious that in very different ways both Hooke and Newton make great play with obliquity in discussing the formation of colours ; cf. *Micrographia*, 57–8.

Further Optical Experiments of Isaac Newton

If water was put twixt the glasses the thickness of a vibration was $\frac{1}{100,000}$ inch, or $\frac{3}{4}$ of its former dimensions, viz as y^e densitys of the interjected mediums.
If y^e rays were incident obliquely, the circles increased so that their diameters are as y^e secants of the rays obliquity wthin the film of air, or reciprocally as their celerity wthin the said film.
And the thicknesse belonging to each vibration is as the squares of these secants of celeritys, And ye lengths of ye rays belonging to each vibration as their cubes.
The first pulse ends at the first dark circle.
The thicknesse of a pulse of extreme rubiform rays to that of purpuriform ones perpendicularly incident is greater than 3 to 2 & lesse than 5 to 3. viz as 9 to 14 or 13 to 20. And the thicknesse belonging to each colour is 13, 14, $14\frac{1}{2}$, $15\frac{1}{2}$, $16\frac{1}{2}$, $17\frac{1}{2}$, $18\frac{1}{2}$, 19 for extreame purple, intense purple, Indico, blew, green, y^e terminus of green & yellow, yellow, orang, red, extream red [10].

If 'thicknesse' means the distance between the two surfaces, and gives the measure of the 'space' or length of the pulse (note 35), then we have here a statement of a hypothetical correspondence between the colour of light and the length of its pulsations or vibrations.

The same page of the note-book is completed, in a slightly different script, with notes on the effect of disease upon vision, taken from Boyle's *Essays of Effluviums* (1673). A few pages farther on there are more notes from Boyle, *New Experiments and Observations touching Cold* (1665) and *The Origine of Formes and Qualities* (1666). It would seem likely therefore that the last entry on interference colours was written some time before 1673, perhaps (from the difference in the writing) as early as 1669 or 1670.

After discussing interference, Newton returns to his prismatic experiments. The most interesting is perhaps the *experimentum crucis*:

44. Refracting ye Rays through a Prisme into a darke roome (as in ye 7th Experiment) And holding another Prisme about 5 or 6 yards from ye former to refract ye rays againe I found First y^t ye blew rays did suffer a greater Refraction by ye second Prisme than ye Red ones.
45. And secondly y^t ye purely Red rays refracted by ye second Prisme made noe other colours but Red & ye purely blew ones noe other colours but blew ones.[11]

The disposition of the prisms, including the second diaphragm, if used, is not described. The notes also record study of the combinations of colours from which white light could be reconstituted by casting the colours from three prisms upon one another.

Notes 51 to 53 deal with the multiple reflection and refraction of light in spheres of water and the formation of the colours of the rainbow, with references to Descartes's *Meteors*.

[10] MS. Add. 3975, *f.* 15*v*.
[11] *Ibid.*, *f.* 7*v*.

Then, as in the *Opticks*, consideration of the reflection of light from opaque bodies suggests some ideas on the relationship of this reflection to their corpuscular structure :

> 56. The pouders of Pellucid bodys is white soe is a cluster of small bubles of aire, ye scrapings of black or cleare horne, &c : [because of ye multitude of refracting surfaces] soe are bodys wch are full of flaws, or those whose parts lye not very close together (as Metalls, Marble, ye Oculus Mundi Stone &c) [whose pores betwixt their parts admit a grosser Aether into y^m y^n ye pores in their parts] hence
> 57. Most Bodys (viz : those into which water will soake as paper, wood, Marble, ye Oculus Mundi Stone &c) become more darke & transparent by being soaked in water [for ye water fills up ye reflecting pores].

The next group of notes describes the sensations of colours aroused in Newton's eye by pressing on the exterior of the eyeball near the retina ; this dangerous experiment was performed by putting a bodkin " betwixt my eye & ye bone as neere to ye backside of my eye as I could : & pressing my eye wth ye end of it ". This leads on to the long discussion of the physiology of vision, printed by Brewster from Harris [12]. The last paragraph, omitted by them, reads as follows :

> From ye whiteness of the brain & marrow the thicknesse of its vessells may be determined & their cavitys guessed at. And its pretty to consider how they agree wth the utmost distinctnesse in vision. As also wth ye extent of nature in conveying distinctly ye motions of the Aether.[13]

The observations on colour in this note-book break off here. In another volume, however, press-marked MS. Add. 4000 in the Cambridge University Library, there is evidence of Newton's attention to the practical part of optics. This is interesting as confirming the stories about his mechanical bent in youth, manifested here in sketches of a variety of machines for lens-grinding. According to his own account it was in the year 1666 that he applied himself to " the Grinding of Optick Glasses of other figures than Spherical ", but this statement was apparently not quite accurate. For the date " 166$\frac{3}{4}$ January " is written near to one end of the volume, and the " Annotations out of Schooten & Wallis made in winter between the years 1664 & 1665 " appear at the other. After them follows the section " Of refractions " which is quoted below. It would be more plausible, therefore, to suppose that Newton's interest in Descartes's suggestions for the use of lenses of non-spherical curvatures was greatest at some period about the middle of 1665. At this time he was clearly something more than a beginner in optics. He had read Descartes's *Dioptrique* and probably Boyle's

---
[12] Brewster, *op. cit.*, vol. i, p. 432.
[13] MS. 3975, *f.* 11*v*.

Further Optical Experiments of Isaac Newton 37

Experiments . . . touching Colours. Probably he had begun his own experiments on refraction—but unfortunately it is impossible to relate these notes on lens-grinding into a chronological sequence with others on optics. However, he was not yet so confident in his understanding of the formation of colours by refraction that he had come to believe that the chief defect of lenses—chromatic aberration—was intrinsic and incapable of remedy. I have suggested elsewhere that there was no long interval between Newton's discovery of the true nature of white light and the abandonment, enforced by his new theory, of his attempts to work corrected lenses. Yet one may well suppose that the interval between Newton's first steps towards his theory (arising from his observations on the displacement of parti-coloured images seen through a prism) and his full realization that red and blue rays could not be brought to the same focus by any curvature of the lens, was sufficient for the investigations described below. Contrary to the general impression, it seems fairly certain that Newton's interest in the grinding of non-spherical lenses was chiefly speculative. There is no suggestion in the notes that he had succeeded in grinding such a lens, or had even fabricated any of his rather implausible machines. In fact his application to the subject can hardly have survived for more than a very few weeks.

Of Refractions.

1. If y^e ray ac bee refracted at the center of y^e circle $acdg$ towards d & $ab \perp be \perp gc \parallel ed$. Then suppose $ab : ed :: d : e$. See Cartes Dioptricks [Fig. 9].

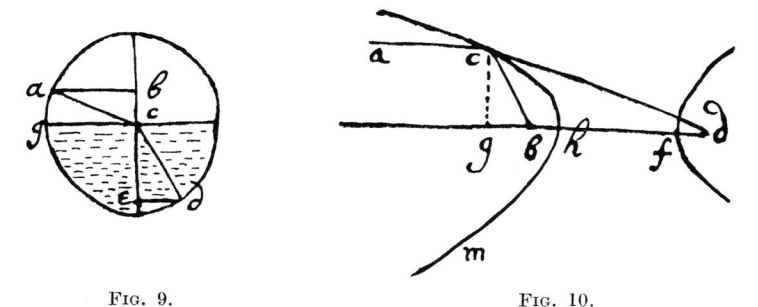

Fig. 9. Fig. 10.

It should be remarked that as the sketch suggests the line gc represents the interface between two media at which the ray is refracted according to the law stated, which supposes (following Descartes) that the refractive indices of the media are as the sines of the angles of incidence and refraction, ab, de.

    2. If there be an hyperbola the distance of whose foci bd are to its transverse axis hf as d to e. Then y^e ray $ac \parallel bd$ is refracted to y^e exterior focus (d). See C. Dioptr. [Fig. 10] [14].

[14] René Descartes, *La Dioptrique*, Leyde, 1637, pp. 103-4.

3. Having y^e proportion of d to e, or $bd : hf$. The Hyperbola may bee thus described [Fig. 11].

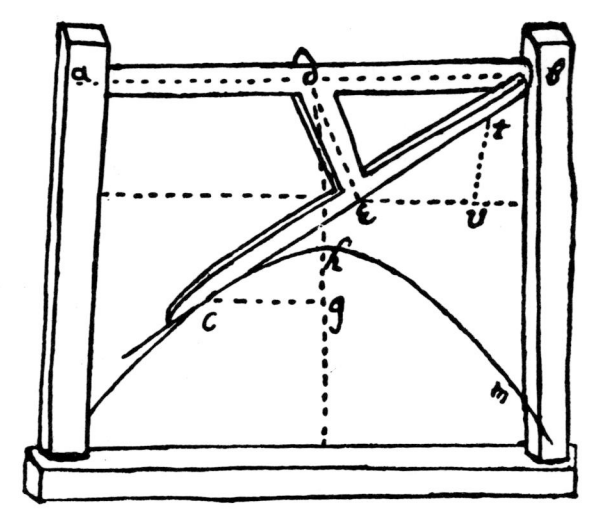

FIG. 11.

1. Upon y^e centers a, b, let y^e instrument $adbtec$ bee moved in wch instrument observe y^t $ad \perp de \perp cet$ & y^t the beame cet is not in y^e same plane wth $adbe$ but intersects it at y^e angle tev soe y^t if $tv \perp ev$, then $d : e :: et : tv$. Or $d : e ::$ Rad : sine of $\angle tev$. Also make $de = \frac{q}{2}$ ie half y^e transverse diameter.

   Then place the fiduciall side of y^e plate chm in the same plaine wth ab & moving y^e instrument $adbect$ to & fro its edge cet shall cut or weare it in y^e shape of y^e desired Parabola [sic]. . . .

2. By the same proceeding Des=Cartes concave Hyperbolicall wheele may bee described by beeing turned wth a chissel $dtec$ [Fig. 12] whose edge is a streight line inclined to the axis of the mandrill by y^e $\angle tev$ wch angle is found by making $d : e :: et : tv ::$ Rad : sine of etv.[15]

In his *Dioptrique*, Chap. X, Descartes had described one machine for drawing a hyperbola mechanically, or cutting the figure out of sheet metal, and another for shaping a wheel to a hyperbolical profile so that it could be used for grinding lenses. Newton's machines are considerably simpler and more practicable. Their accuracy is established by geometrical demonstration.

[15] MS. Add. 4000 *f.* 26*r*.

Newton first shows that in an upright hyperbola, such as *chm* [Fig. 10], if d is the distance between the foci and e the vertical axis,

$$x^2 \frac{(d^2-e^2)}{e^2} + x \frac{(d^2-e^2)}{e} = y^2.$$

Then examining the curve *chm* cut or ground on the edge of the plate by the tool *cet* in the first machine [Fig. 11], he makes *cg*, *gh* the co-ordinates of any point *c* on this curve, at which *cet* is a tangent. Let $gh = x$, $cg = y$, and the angle of inclination of *cet* to *ab* be θ. It follows from the construction of the machine that $de = dh = \frac{e}{2}$, and $\tan \theta = \frac{e}{\sqrt{d^2-e^2}}$. Further, $dg = dh + gh = x + \frac{e}{2} = \sqrt{\frac{e^2}{4} + y^2 \tan^2 \theta}$. Therefore,

$$x^2 + ex = y^2 \frac{e^2}{(d^2-e^2)}, \quad \text{i.e.} \quad x^2 \frac{(d^2-e^2)}{e^2} + x \frac{(d^2-e^2)}{e} = y^2,$$

Fig. 12.

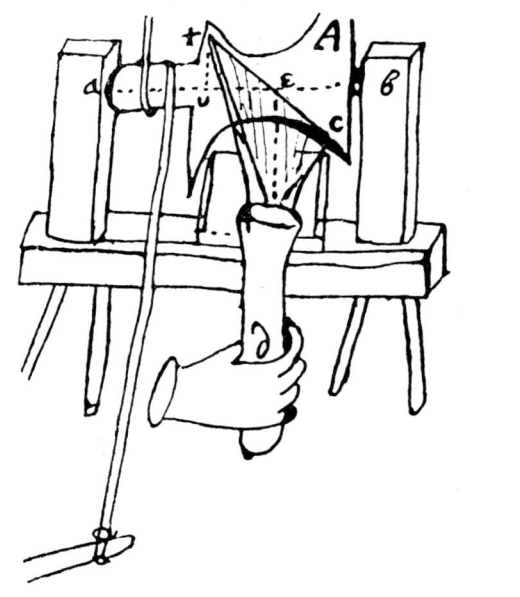

Fig. 13.

as before and the curve produced is the required hyperbola. Newton's geometry is slightly more diffuse but proceeds essentially through the same steps.

[3] 3. By the same reason a wheele may be turned Hyperbolically concave y^e Hyperbola being convex. . . .

II

40

4. Also Des=Cartes his Convex wheele B may be turned or ground trew a concave wheele A being made use of instead of a patterne.

5. In turning the concave wheele A [Fig. 13] it will perhaps bee best to weare it wth a stone p & let the streight edged chissel d serve for a patterne. And it may bee convenient to grind ye stone (or irons) p into ye fashion of a cone. . . . That it may fit ye hollow of the wheele A The angle of wch cone being a right one or something greater it will almost grind the wheele to the same figure.

The next two notes purport to demonstrate these procedures geometrically. They are false and have been crossed out; the correct demonstration occurs a little later.

[3] 9. Having such a cone smoothly pollished wthin & wthout, by the helpe of a square set y^e plate perpendicular to one side hae the fiduciall edge being distant from y^e vertex the length of $ae = \dfrac{edd - e^3}{dd - ee}$ & if y^e edge of y^e plaine everywhere touch the cone, tis trew [figure omitted].

10. The exact distance (ae) of y^e plate from the vertex of y^e cone neede not bee much regarded for that changeth onely the bignesse not y^e shape of y^e figure.

[By y^e broken lookinglasse I find in glasse refraction, y^t $d : e : : 43 : 28 : : 1000 : 651 : : 1536 : 1000$[16]. These are almost insensibly different from truth $d : e : : 20 : 13 : : 100 : 65 : : 153 - : 1000$. Or $d : e : : 23 : 15 : : 100 : 652+$. Or $d : e : : 66 : 43 : : 1000 : 651,5151+$. Or [*sic*].

After the geometrical demonstrations already reproduced above, the notes go on to relate various ways of producing a parabola " (& other figures after y^e same manner) pretty exactly ". Various devices for forming a small curved surface from a larger pattern are also described. One shows how a non-spherical surface, such as that of a lens, can be derived from the appropriate plane curve.

On f. 30r there are some remarks on the design of optical instruments:

In both telescopes & microscopes tis most convenient to have a convex glasse next ye eye for by that meanes ye angle of vision will bee much greater y^n it will be wth a concave one (though both doe magnifie alike). If ye convex glasse be Hyperbolicall (&c) make it soe bigge y^t ye penecilli may crosse in ye pupill; y^t is, ye exterior focus will be as far distant from y^e vertex as y^e eye is. Let y^e glasse bee as thinn as may bee y^t y^e eye bee not too farr from y^e vertex yet it should bee about as thick as y^e distance of y^e interior focus from y^e vertex.

[*Written in a different script and ink.*] And by this meanes also, (y^e focus of y^e object=glasse being wthin y^e telescope twixt y^e glasses) there may bee placed at that focus y^e edge of a steele ruler accurately divided into equall parts (to measure y^e diameters or distances of starrs &c) wch should bee soe made y^t by a pinne or handle it may bee placed

[16] The ' broken Looking-glass ' is mentioned in *Opticks* (4th Ed., 177).

Further Optical Experiments of Isaac Newton

in any posture & in any parte of ye focus, wthout otherwise altering ye Telescope in observations.

[*Written as the last entry but one.*] Note that were not ye glasses faulty they would not onely magnify objects but render vision more distinct : each of the penicilli passing through (perhaps but) the 10th, 20th or 100th parte of ye pupill must be more exactly refracted to one point of ye Tunica Retina y^n in ordinary vision in wch each of ye penicilli spreads over all the pupill.

Note also y^t ye glasse *a* [Fig. 14] may be ground Hyperbolicall by ye line *cb*, if it turns on ye Mandrill *E* whilst *cb* turns on ye axis *rd* being inclined to it as was showed before. If the Edge (*cb*) bee not durable enough, inough instead thereof use a long small cilinder : wch I conceive to bee the best way of all. For a Cilinder of all Sollids is most easily made exact (being turned, as in the figure [Fig. 15], by a gage untill its thicknesse bee everywhere equall. 2 the Cilinder may be made to slip up & downe & turn round whereby it will not onely grinde y^e glasse crosse wise to take of all hubbes, but also y^e glasse & cilinder

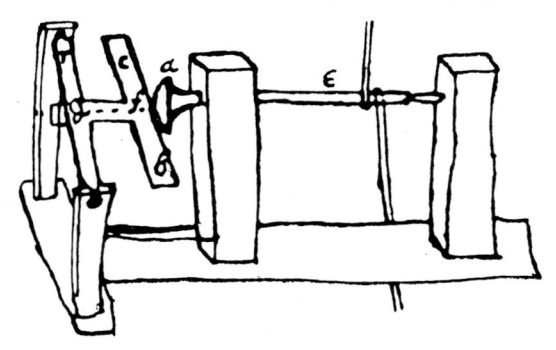

FIG. 14.

will grinde y^e one y^e other truer & truer. All y^e difficulty is in placing y^e axis *rd* perpendicular to the Mandrill *ae* & vertex to vertex wch may yet bee done exactly severall ways & untill y^n the glasse & Cilinder will not fit. & should y^e axes not intersect y^e glasse would bee still

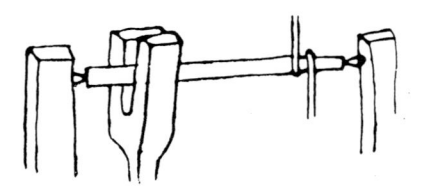

FIG. 15.

Hyperbollical except a point at the vertex of it. The same instrument may also serve for severall glasses only making *df* longer or shorter. Let the Cilinder hang over the glasse.

[*f.* 31r. Another change of script and ink.]

To Grinde Sphericall optick Glasses

If ye glasse (*bc*) is to bee ground sphaerically hollow : Naile a steele plate to ye beame (*fg*), on ye upper side : In wch make a center hole for ye steele pointe (*f*) of ye shaft (*def*) : to wch shaft fasten a plugg (*a*) of stone or leade or leather &c : (wth wch you intend to grinde ye glasse (*bc*) : wch shaft & plugg being swung to & fro upon ye center *f* will grind ye glasse *bc* sphaerically hollow [figure omitted].

The manner whereby glasse may be ground sphaerically convex may appeare by ye annexed figure (being ye former way inverted). . . . But if this way bee not exact enough yet hereby may bee grownd plates of metall well nigh sphaericall, And by these plates may bee ground glasses after ye usuall manner. . . .

But the best way of all will bee to turn ye glasse circularly upon a mandrill whilst ye plate is steadily rubbed upon it or else to turne ye plate upon a mandrill whilest ye glasse is rubbed upon it or let sometimes ye one, sometimes ye other be turned : & by this means they will either of them weare the other to a truly sphericall forme. but however let there bee a hoope of some mettall wch weares more difficultly then glasse to defend ye glasse from weareing more at its edges then in ye middle. . . .

Let not an object glasse bee ground sphaerically convex on both sides, but sphaerically convex on one side & plane or but a little convex on ye other, & turne ye convexest side towards ye object.

The final entry on *f*. 32*v* is a second draft. The first has been struck out with two strokes of the pen.

If ye Glasses of a Telescope bee not truely ground. Theire errors may bee thus found.

Because an error is much more easily discernable in ye object glasse y^n in ye eye glasse let us first suppose ye eye glasse to bee ground true towards its center, (tis exact enough if it be sphericall, & not Hyperbolicall), & so wee may find & rectifie ye errors of ye object glasse.

First make a thin plate (A) [Fig. 16] of brasse & in the center of it a small hole (whose diameter perhaps may bee about y^e 50th or 100th parte of an inch. With wch plate cover y^e eye glasse y^e center of it respecting y^e center of y^e glasse.

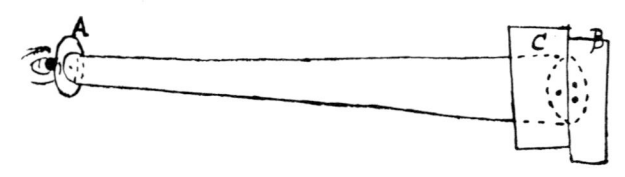

Fig. 16.

Secondly make two other plates the one (B) wth two holes as neare to its edge as may bee theire distance being about y^e 5th parte of an inch or lesse, & y^e other C wth one hole close to y^e midst of its edge. Let y^e Diameters of these 3 holes bee about a 20th pte of an inch or lesse. And their edges [i.e. the edges of the plates] must bee true that they may slide one upon another, & yet not let ye suns rays passe through, to wch purpose make y^m oblique. Wth these two plates

Further Optical Experiments of Isaac Newton 43

cover ye object glasse (first stopping ye hole of C) ye holes of ye other plate [B] respecting the center of ye glasse & looke at a stare (or ye edge of ye sunne &c) & if ye object appeare double (like two starrs &c) make ye Tube longer or shorter untill it appeare single. Then open ye hole of C, & ye plate B being fixed, slide ye plate C up & downe still looking at ye starre. When there appeares but one starre y^t part of ye glasse under ye hole of C is truely ground in respect of ye parte of ye glasse under ye two holes of B. But not when ye starre appeares double. And ye position of ye starre caused by ye hole of C in respect of ye starre caused by ye holes of B shews wch way ye glasse under ye hole of C is erroneously inclined ; the distance of ye two starrs giving ye quantity of ye error.

Thus ye errors of ye object glasse being found in every place of it they may be all rectified, & found againe, & againe rectified, untill they almost or altogether vanish.

Then may ye eye-glasse bee rectified much after ye same manner in every parte of it, & if it bee necessary ye object glasse may bee againe rectified & againe ye eye-glasse untill ye Telescope bee as perfect as ye worke-man can make : whome perhaps experience may teach by this & ye former rules to make telescopes as perfect as men can hope to make them.

[Final paragraph written with a different pen and ink.]

These Glasses may also bee rectified on ye Mandrill by observing ye Images made by reflection from ye vertex & all other pts of the glasse w^t proportion they have one to another & how much they are longer y^n broader in one place then another &c.

This concludes the optical section in this note-book. It is clear that following this page two leaves are missing, and their contents are unknown. The entry on the correction of lenses appears in places untypical of Newton's style, and possibly it is derived from some printed book.

From this evidence, Newton's early study of lenses was not of great profundity. He had more than enough mathematics for geometrical optics, and he had read Descartes, by far the best treatise of the age. He shows signs, like Descartes, of being inclined to over-geometrize what was in large part a technical problem, ultimately solved by the practical men Chester Moor Hall and John Dollond. There are signs too of the mathematical precision in experiment which is so significant a feature of the *Opticks*. Yet, as Newton had no practical success, one could not say at this stage that his study of the aberrations of lenses had gone much beyond what Descartes had done.

Finally, it is once more demonstrated that Newton's biographical reminiscences, if not meticulous in their chronology, are reliable in essentials. It is certain that he had worked—largely theoretically— on non-spherical lenses before he discovered the cause of chromatic aberration, which he was to regard as their chief and irreparable **imperfection**.

III

NEWTON ON THE CALCULATION OF CENTRAL FORCES

To Professor H. W. Turnbull, F.R.S., principal director of the edition of Newton's correspondence sponsored by the Royal Society, must be ascribed the credit for the first description of the documents discussed in this note.[1] While examining papers in the Portsmouth Collection in the Cambridge University Library for a different purpose, I happened to notice a paper in Newton's hand dealing with the calculation of centrifugal accelerations.[2] From a reference in Dugas its connexion with a mysterious passage in a letter which Newton claimed to have written to Huygens on 12 June 1673 (o.s.) was readily apparent[3].

At this point I turned back to Professor Turnbull's article, and so found that this paper, and another, were already known to him. He has generously concurred in the publication of this note.

In a letter to Halley of 27 July 1686, Newton quoted himself as having written to Huygens on 23 June 1673 as follows:

> " Sir, I receiv'd your letters, with Mr. Hugen's kind present[4], which I have viewed with great satisfaction, finding it full of very subtile and useful speculations very worthy of the author. I am glad that we are to expect another discourse of the vis Centrifuga, which speculation may prove of good use in Natural Philosophy and Astronomy, as well as Mechanics. *Thus for instance if the reason, why the same side of the moon is ever towards the earth, be the greater conatus of the other side to recede from it, it will follow (upon supposition of the earth's motion about the sun), that the greatest distance of the sun from the earth is to the greatest distance of the moon from the earth, not greater than 10000 to 56: and therefore the parallax of the sun not less than 56/10000 of the parallax of the moon, because were the sun's distance less in proportion to that of the moon, she would have a greater conatus from the sun than*

---

[1] " Isaac Newton's Letters ". *Manchester Guardian*, Saturday, 3 October 1953, p. 4. Professor Turnbull here announced his intention of printing the longer document in the *Correspondence*; but he has kindly consented to a preliminary publication in this form.

[2] *A Catalogue of the Portsmouth Collection of Books and Papers written by or belonging to Sir Isaac Newton*, Cambridge, 1888, p. 1, section I, I, 5. Present pressmark MS Add 3958 (5), fol. 87. The papers are not ' unsorted ', as Professor Turnbull stated, but they were imperfectly analysed by the cataloguers of 1888.

[3] René Dugas, *La Mécanique au XVIIe siècle*, Paris, 1954, pp. 359–360. *Œuvres Complètes de Christiaan Huygens*, viii, pp. 325–332.

[4] A copy of *Horologium Oscillatorium*.

> *from the earth. I thought also some time that the moon's libration might depend upon her conatus from the sun and earth compared together till I apprehended a better cause*"[5].

In fact, as the wording indicates, the letter was written to Oldenburg, not to Huygens direct ; and for an unknown reason the copy of the letter actually received by the latter did not contain the italicized sentences. That, as the editors of Huygens works suggest, they were omitted on later instructions from Newton, is pure conjecture.

As Professor Turnbull remarked in his article, the document printed below " incidentally contains the working out of a numerical result which is baldly stated without explanation in the letter " [or rather, in Newton's later transcript of his original letter] ; " it concerned the reason why the Moon turns her face steadily towards the Earth rather than towards the Sun ". Indeed, we might well go further and state that it is apparent that, in this paper, Newton's interest was in the calculation of centrifugal accelerations for the sake of their application to astronomical problems ; it shows little concern with the exploration of pure dynamics in the manner of Huygens. Indeed, according to Newton's own statements, in other letters to Halley, the paper was written some time before 1673, and independently of Newton's own reading of the *Horologium Oscillatorium*. In the well-known letter (20 June 1686) in which Newton rebuffed Hooke's claim to the discovery of the inverse square law of gravitation, the former declared :

> " That, in one of my papers writ (I cannot say in what year, but I am sure some time before I had any correspondence with Mr. Oldenburgh, and that's) above fifteen years ago, the proportion of the forces of the planets from the sun, reciprocally duplicate of their distances from him, is expressed, and the proportion of our gravity to the moon's conatus recedendi a centro terrae is calculated, though not accurately enough. That when Hugenius put out his Horol. Oscil., a copy being presented to me, in my letter of thanks to him, I gave those rules in the end thereof a particular commendation for their usefulness in Philosophy, and added out of my aforesaid paper an instance of their usefulness, in comparing the forces of the moon from the earth, and earth from the sun ; in determining a problem about the moon's phase, and putting a limit to the sun's parallax, which shews I had then my eye upon comparing the forces of the planets arising from their circular motion, and understood it".

And in a further letter to Halley (14 July 1686) Newton pushes the period of the composition of the document even further back :

> . . . in that very paper, which I told you was writ some time above fifteen years ago, and to the best of my memory was writ eighteen or nineteen years ago, I calculated the force of ascent at the equator, arising from the earth's diurnal motion, in order to know what would be

---

[5] Sir David Brewster, *Memoirs . . . of Sir Isaac Newton*, Edinburgh, 1855, vol. i, p. 451 ; Huygens, *Œuvres Complètes*, vii, p. 326n.

the diminution of gravity thereby. But yet to do this business right, is a thing of far greater difficulty than I was aware of"[6].

It is clear that the paper Newton consulted, and which he asserted was written between 1667 and 1671, is that printed below: although in fact it contains no mention of universal gravitation. It is solely concerned with centrifugal, and not with centripetal, accelerations.

Florian Cajori, in his article on Newton's 'delay' in announcing the law of gravitation, supposed that Newton made his famous comparison of the Earth's gravitational force on the Moon, with the centrifugal force arising from the Moon's motion in its orbit, on two separate occasions, that is, in 1666 and at some later date between 1667 and 1672[7]. His argument that a calculation said by Newton to have been made 15, 18 or 19 years ago could not have been the same as that which Newton, on a separate occasion, attributed to a time 20 years ago, is hardly convincing. Newton himself nowhere clearly states that he made two separate attacks on the same problem before the time when he returned to it, through his communication with Hooke and Halley, from 1679 onwards. Indeed his recollections seem more consistent with the view that he went into these questions during some single, fairly extended period of time, since there is no hint of a repetition of calculations with changed values for the size of the Earth's radius. If Newton was correct in attributing the commencement of such studies to 1666, then it would be reasonable to assume that the present document belongs to about 1667 or 1668, certainly earlier than 1671, the upper limit suggested by Newton himself. Cajori's discussion is indeed largely invalidated by the content of the present document, of which he was ignorant, which shows (as the quotation from the second letter to Halley indicates) that Newton's idea of the size of the Earth was by no means as accurate, even in 1673, as Cajori thought.

The paper is a single folded sheet, without title, and the text begins abruptly:

"1. Corporis A in circulo AD versus D gyrantis, conatus a centro tantus est quantus in tempore AD (quod pono minutissimum esse) deferret a circumferentia ad distantiam DB: siquidem eam distantiam in eo tempore acquireret si modo conatu non impedito libere moveret in tangente AB.

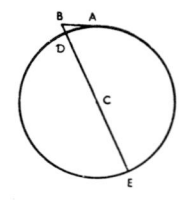

Jam cum hic conatus corpora, si modo in directum

---

[6] S. P. Rigaud, *Historical Essay on the first publication of Sir Isaac Newton's Principia*, Oxford, 1838; Appendix, pp. 28, 40. Cf. also the discussion of Florian Cajori in "Newton's Twenty Years' Delay in Announcing the Law of Gravitation", *Sir Isaac Newton, 1727–1927*, London, 1928, pp. 172–175.

[7] Cajori, *op. cit.*, pp. 173, 175.

1 Corporis A in circulo AD versus D gyrantis, conatus a centro tantus est quantus in tempore AD (quod pono minutissimum esse) deferret a circumferentia ad distantiam DB: siquidem eam distantiam in eo tempore acquireret si modo conatui non impedito moveretur in tangente AB.

Jam cum hic conatus corpora, sic modo in directum ad modum gravitatis continuo urgeret, impelleret per spatia quæ forent ut quadrata temporum: ut noscatur per quantum spatium in tempore unius revolutionis impellerent, quæro lineam quæ sit ad BD ut est quadratum peripheriæ ADEA ad AD^q. Scilicet est BE . BA :: BA . BD (per 3 elem). Vel cum inter BE ac DE et inter BA ac DA differentia supposita infinite parva, substituo pro se invicem et emergit DE . DA :: DA . DB. ~~...~~ faciendo deniq DA^q (sive DE×DB) . ADEA^q :: DB . $\frac{ADEA^q}{DE}$, obtineo lineam quæsitam (nempe ~~quadr Periphiæ~~ tertiam proportionalem in ratione peripheriæ ad diam in directum constanter applicatus etiam) per quam conatus recedendi a centro, propelleret corpus in tempore unius revolutionis.

Verbi gratia cum ista tertia proportionalis æquet 19,7392 semidiametros si conatus recedendi ad centrum ea virtute gravitatis tantus esset quantus est conatus in æquatore recedendi a centro propter motum terræ diurnum: in die periodico propelleret gravia per 19¾ semidiametros terrestres sive per 69087 milliaria, et in hora per $\frac{120}{1}$ mill. Et in minuto primo per $\frac{1}{30}$ mill sive per 100 passus, id est 500 pedes. Et in minuto secdo per $\frac{5}{106}$ ped, sive per 5/9 digit. Ut reperta tanta est vis gravitatis ut gravia decorsum prolet 16 pedes circiter in 1″. Hoc ut 0350 vicibus longius in eodem tempore quam conatus e centro circiter. Adeoq vis gravitati est toties major, ut se terra convertendo faciat corpora recedere et in aera prosilire.

2 Corol. Hine in diversis circulis conatus a centro, est ut diametri applicata quadrata temporum revolutionum, sive ut diametri ductæ in numerum revolutionum factarum in eodem quovis tempore. Sic cum Luna revolvit 27 dies 7 horis 43′ sive in 27,3216 diebus (cujus quadratum est 746½) ac distat 59 vel 60 semidiametris terrestribus a terra. Duco distantiam ☽ 60 in quadratum revolutionis lunaris 1; ac distantiam superficiei terrestris a centro 1 in quadratum revolutionum 746½, et sic habeo proportionem 60 ad

ad modum gravitatis continuo urgeret, impelleret per spatia quae forent ut quadrata temporum: ut noscatur per quantum spatium in tempore unius revolutionis ADEA impellerent, quaero lineam quae sit ad BD ut est quadratum periferiae ADEA ad AD^q. Scilicet est BE. BA :: BA. BD (per 3 elem). Vel cum inter BE ac DE ut et inter BA ac DA differentia supponitur infinitè parva, substituo pro se invicem et emergit DE. DA :: DA. DB. Faciendo denique DA^q (sive DE x DB). $ADEA^q$ :: DB. $\dfrac{ADEA^q}{DE}$, obtineo lineam quaesitam (nempe tertiam proportionalem in ratione periferiae ad diametrum) per quam conatus recedendi a centro in directum constantur applicatus propelleret corpus in tempore unius revolutionis.

Verbi gratia cum ista tertia proportionalis aequat 19,7392 semidiametros si conatus accedendi ad centrum virtute gravitatis tantus esset quantus est conatus in aequatore recedendi a centro propter motum terrae diurnum: in die periodico propelleret grave per $19\frac{3}{4}$ semidiametros terrestres sive per 69087 milliaria. Et in hora per 120^{mill}. Et in minuto primo per $1/30^{mill}$ sive per 100/3 passus, id est 500/3 pedes. Et in minuto se[cun]do per $5/108^{ped}$, sive per 5/9 digit. At revera tanta est vis gravitatis ut gravia deorsum pellat 16 pedes circiter in 1", hoc est 350 vicibus longius in eodem tempore quam conatus a centro circiter, adeoque vis gravitatis est toties major, ut ne terra convertendo faciat corpora recedere et in aere prosilire.

2. Coroll. Hinc in diversis circulis conatus a centris sunt ut diametri applicato ad quadrata temporum revolutionis, sive ut diametri ductae in numerum revolutionum factarum in eodem quovis tempore. Sic sum Luna revolvit in 27 diebus 7 horis & 43' sive in 27,3216 diebus (cujus quadratum est $746\frac{1}{2}$) ac distat 59 vel 60 semidiametris terrestribus a terra. Duco distantiam ☽ 60 in quadratum revolutionis Lunaris 1; ac distantiam superficiei terrestris a centro 1, in quadratum revolutionum $746\frac{1}{2}$, et sic habeo proportionalem 60 ad $746\frac{1}{2}$, quae est inter conatum Lunae et superficiei terrestris recedendi a centro terrae. Itaque conatus superficiei terrestris sub aequatore est $12\frac{1}{2}$ vicibus circiter major quam conatus Lunae recedendi a centro terrae. Adeoque vis gravitatis est 4000 vicibus major conatu lunae recedendi a centro terrae, et amplius. Et si conatus ejus a terra efficit ut cum eodem facie terram semper respiciat; Hujus Lunaris et terrestris systematis conatus recedendi a sole debet esse minor quam conatus Lunae recedendi a Terra, aliter luna respiceret solem, potius quam terram.

Sed ut de hâc re justiorem aestimationem faciam sit 100000 distantia systematis Lunaris a sole, & y distantia lunae a terra. Et cum conficit 13^{revol} 4^{sig} 12^{gr} 52' in anno stellari, sive 13,369 revolutiones

III

(cujus quadratum est 178,73) : duco distantiam solis 100000 in quadratum ejus revolutionis 1, et distantiam Lunae y in quadratum ejus revolutionum 178.73 et fit 100000 ad 178.73y, ita conatus terrae a sole ad conatum Lunae a terrâ. Unde constat quod distantia lunae a Terra debet esse major quam 100000/178.73 sive $559\frac{1}{2}$ respectu distantiae solis 100000. Et inde Solis maxima parallaxis in orbita lunari non erit minor 19′ et solis horizontalis parallaxis in terra non minor 19″ puta cum ☉ et ☽ distant 90^{gr} ab Apogaeis. Pone vero parallaxim esse 24″ et erit distantia lunae a terra $706\frac{3}{4}$, et conatus ejus recedendi a terra ad conatum terrae recedendi a sole ut 5 ad 4 circiter. Et sic vis gravitatis erit 5000 vicibus major conatu terrae recedendi a Sole. Sit Magni orbis $\frac{1}{2}$diam 100000, terrae $\frac{1}{2}$diam. Eritque $365\frac{1}{4} \times 365\frac{1}{4} \, x$ (sive 132408 ita conatus hominis a terra, ad conatum ejus a sole.

Denique in Planetis primariis cum cubi distantiarum a sole reciproce sunt ut quadrati numeri periodorum in dato tempore : conatus a sole recedendi reciproce erunt ut quadrata distantiarum a sole. Verbi gratia est in ☿, ♀, ⊕, ♂, ♃, ♄, ut 4/27, 10/19, 1, 2 5/16, 27 1/8, 90 5/6, sive ut 1, 3 5/9, $6\frac{3}{4}$, 15 2/3, $183\frac{1}{2}$, $614\frac{1}{2}$, reciproce. Vel directe ut 614, 173, 91, 39, 31/3, 1."

This may be somewhat freely translated as follows :

" 1. The tendency away from the centre [C] of the body A, revolving in the circle AD towards D, is as great as the distance DB which the body would deviate from the circumference in the time AD (which I take to be very short); for it would traverse that distance if the tendency were not restrained, and if the body were free to move along the tangent AB.

Now this tendency in the body, if it acted continually in a straight line in the manner of gravity, would impel the body through spaces which would be as the squares of the times ; in order to know the space [from C] through which the body is impelled in the time of one revolution ADEA, I seek that line which is to BD, as the square of the periphery ADEA is to AD^2. Now $\dfrac{BE}{BA}=\dfrac{BA}{BD}$; or (since the differences between BE and DE, and between BA and DA, are by supposition infinitely small) substituting one for the other respectively gives $\dfrac{DE}{DA}=\dfrac{DA}{DB}$. Then lastly by making DA^2 (that is, DE . DB) to $ADEA^2$, as DB to $\dfrac{ADEA^2}{DE}$, I obtain the line sought, namely the third proportional in the ratio of the periphery to the diameter [and this is the distance] through which the tendency to recede from the centre in a straight line, acting constantly, would propel the body during the time of one revolution.

For example, since this third proportional is [invariably] equal to 19.7392 [i.e. $2\pi^2$] radii, if the tendency towards the centre caused by gravity were of the same magnitude as the tendency to recede from the centre at the Equator arising from the diurnal motion of the Earth, in one day a heavy body would move through $19\frac{3}{4}$ terrestrial radii, or 69087 *millaria* [i.e. 65423 English miles]. And in an hour through 120 *millaria*. And in a minute through $\frac{1}{30}$ *millaria* or $\frac{100}{3}$ paces, that is, $\frac{500}{3}$ feet. And in a second through $\frac{5}{108}$ feet, or $\frac{5}{9}$ inch. But indeed such is the force of gravity that heavy bodies fall downwards 16 feet in one second approximately, that is, about 350 [*read* 346] times further in the same time than [they would by] the tendency from the centre, and thus the force of gravity is so many times the greater, lest the earth in its rotation should cause bodies to fly from it and leap into the air.

2. Corollary. Thus in different circles the tendencies from their centres are as the diameters divided by the squares of the periods of revolution, or as the diameters multiplied by the numbers of revolutions completed in any given time. Thus since the Moon completes a revolution in 27 days 7 hours and 43 minutes or in 27.3216 days (of which the square is $746\frac{1}{2}$), and is distant 59 or 60 terrestrial radii from the Earth, I multiply the distance of the Moon, 60, by the square of [the number of] revolutions, 1; and the distance of the Earth's surface from its centre, 1, by the square [of the number] of its revolutions, $746\frac{1}{2}$, and thus I have the ratio of 60 to $746\frac{1}{2}$, which is the ratio between the tendency from the centre of the Earth at the Moon, and that at the surface of the Earth. And thus the tendency at the Earth's surface on the Equator is $12\frac{1}{2}$ times greater than the tendency of the Moon to recede from the centre of the Earth. And so the force of gravity is 4000 times greater than the tendency of the Moon to recede from the centre of the Earth, and more [$346 \times 12\frac{1}{2} = 4325$]. And if its tendency to recede acts so that [the Moon] always faces the Earth with the same aspect, the tendency of this system of Earth and Moon to recede from the Sun ought to be less than the tendency of the Moon to recede from the Earth: otherwise the Moon would face towards the Sun, rather than towards the Earth.

But, so that I may make a more accurate calculation, let 100,000 be the distance of the system of the Moon from the Sun, and y the distance of the Moon from the Earth. And as the Moon completes

13 revolutions, 4 signs, 12 degrees and 52 minutes in one sidereal year, or 13.369 revolutions (of which the square is 178.73), I multiply the distance of the Sun, 100,000, by the square [of the number] of [the Earth's] revolutions, 1, and the distance of the Moon, y, by the square [of the number] of its revolutions, 178.73, and as 100,000 to 178,73y, so is the tendency of the Earth from the Sun to the tendency of the Moon from the Earth. Whence it follows that the distance of the Moon from the Earth should be greater than $\dfrac{100{,}000}{178.73}$ ($=559\frac{1}{2}$), as compared with the distance of the Sun, 100,000. And hence the maximum parallax of the Sun with respect to the orbit of the Moon should be not less than 19′, and the horizontal parallax of the Sun at the Earth not less than 19″. I suppose that the Sun and Moon are 90° distant from the Apogees. Take the parallax to be 24″, and the distance of the Moon from the Earth will be 706$\frac{3}{4}$, and its tendency to recede from the Earth, to the tendency of the Earth to recede from the Sun [will be] as about 5 to 4. And so the force of gravity will be about 5000 times greater than the tendency of the Earth to recede from the Sun. Let the radius of the great orb be 100,000, the radius of the Earth x. And the tendency of a man away from the Earth, is to his tendency away from the Sun, as $365\frac{1}{4} \times 365\frac{1}{4}x$ (132,408) [to 1].

Lastly, for the Planets, as the cubes of their distances from the Sun are reciprocally as the squares of the numbers of their revolutions in a given time, the tendency to recede from the Sun will be reciprocally as the squares of their distances from the Sun. For example in Mercury Venus, the Earth, Mars, Jupiter and Saturn it is as 4/27, 10/19, 1, 2 5/16, 27$\frac{1}{8}$, 90$\frac{5}{6}$ or as 1, 3 5/9, 6$\frac{3}{4}$, 15$\frac{2}{3}$, 183$\frac{1}{2}$, 614$\frac{1}{2}$ reciprocally. Or directly as 614, 173, 91, 39, 3$\frac{1}{3}$, 1."

What conclusions may be drawn from this paper ?

(1) The calculations are evidently those described in the letters to Huygens and Halley.

(2) Newton could calculate centrifugal accelerations by a method independent of Huygens's discoveries. Thus a conjecture of M. Dugas, " que Newton ait pu atteindre dès cette époque [1666] *l'accélération centripète* d'un mobile décrivant une circonference d'un mouvement uniforme, sans avoir à connâitre de la *vis centrifuga* du sens de Huygens" seems to be confirmed[8]. In the paper Newton never speaks of a central *force*, but only of a *conatus*, or tendency towards or away from a centre of revolution ; he uses the word *force* only in relation to gravity. (In another document

---

[8] Dugas, *op. cit.*, p. 360.

69 Newton on the Calculation of Central Forces

considered below, he does however speak of 'vis terrae a sole ....', 'vis terrae a centro ...'). His calculations are limited to accelerations, not extending to the forces producing them.

(3) A simple computation shows that Newton here takes the length of the Earth's radius to be 3313 miles, substantially less than the true value. There is no indication that he saw fit to revise this estimate even as late as 1673, and thus Cajori's long discussion of this question is rendered fruitless. It is now a matter of fact, not of inference (as will be seen again below), that Newton was deceived in this matter, and could not have calculated the Moon's centripetal acceleration correctly. This of course does not weaken the obvious conclusion that no man of Newton's temperament would have announced a 'law of universal gravitation' on the evidence available to him in 1666, or even in 1673.

In fact, if a more correct approximation of 4000 miles is substituted for Newton's figure of 3313, the centrifugal acceleration at the Earth's surface, on the equator, becomes 1·32 inches/sec², instead of 1·11 ; thus the ratio of the force required to produce this acceleration to the force of gravity is 1/288. Multiplying this by 12·5, Newton's second ratio, the centripetal acceleration of the Moon in its orbit becomes $\frac{1}{3600}$ g. This is exactly what is required to demonstrate the inverse square law.

From the value of 3313 miles, however, the value of g would be about 27, instead of 32 ft/sec², a notable discrepancy. Even more remarkable is the concealment of the significance of the number $(60)^2$ in Newton's ratio of 'more than 4000' to one. Hence it may be that Newton's mistake had some real effect in persuading him to lay aside work of this kind.

(4) Finally, and unfortunately for the historian, this document offers no direct and conclusive evidence that Newton had yet entertained the conception of universal gravitation, nor does it contain a formulation of the inverse square law. Nothing in it is incompatible with either of these ideas, and the calculations, especially those relating to the successive planets and showing that their centrifugal accelerations are inversely as the squares of their distances from the Sun (a ratio established with the aid of Kepler's Third Law, as Newton elsewhere recorded) could have been used to confirm the square-law hypothesis. It might indeed be inferred that the object of making these calculations with respect to the planets was precisely the confirmation of this law : that it would be difficult to imagine any other purpose they could serve[9]. But

the fact remains that the obvious correlation between the decrease of the centripetal acceleration due to gravity, and that of the centrifugal acceleration due to the planet's revolution in an orbit, is not here noted by Newton; it is surely curious that, after explaining why bodies adhere to the surface of a rotating Earth (a problem treated by Galileo in his *Dialogues*) and why the Moon always turns the same face to the Earth, he should have omitted to record the reason for the planets' stability in their orbits. With Newton, however, the argument from silence is never strong; and the present paper certainly could not be taken to exclude the possibility that Newton was familiar with the elements of the theory of universal gravitation already, even though there is no direct reference to such a theory.

The other notes, already mentioned by Professor Turnbull, are found on the verso of a piece of vellum on which a lease was engrossed[10]. A note in Newton's hand reads "15^s for a post fine of w^t hath past twixt my uncle Ayscough & Mrs Oliver". The notes are scattered in disorder, along with numerical computations: I have tried simply to follow them down the sheet.

7000 diam. 22000 miliar.=circumf. terrae.

y^e force from gravity is 159·5 times greater y^n y^e force from y^e Earth's motion at y^e Equator.

3000^{cub}=mil. 5500^{mil}=◊ terrae=16500000 cubit

Terra sub Equatore movet 16500000 cubit in 6 horis

Et tantem velocitatem grave cadendo in $1436'',14=23',9357=23' 56'',14$ acquiret,

gravitas movebit corpus per 28·64 inches in 0,00021013709 hours

yt is in $\dfrac{0{,}0126082253'}{2} = \dfrac{0{,}75649352''}{2}$ or $\dfrac{45''',389611}{2} = 22''',6958$

as 1 : 4000 :: vis terrae a Sole ad vim gravitatis

3000 Brace=Mile. 3500 Miles=$\frac{1}{2}$ diamiter of y^e Earth

5000 $\frac{1}{2}$ diamiters of y^e Earth=Solar distance=$3000 \times 3500 \times 5000$ = 52500000000 braces

The Earth in about $\begin{cases} 58^{\text{days}} \ 2^{\text{ho}} \ 36' \text{ or } 37' \text{ moves } y^e \text{ length of } y^e \\ \text{solar distance} \\ 83677' = 1394^h \ 37' = 58^d 2^{\text{ho}} \ 37' \end{cases}$

vis gravitatis in 83677' movebit corpus per distantiam 100826500737600 braces

Vis terrae a sole movebit corpus per distantiam 26250000000 braces in 83677'

---

[9] Professor Turnbull writes privately that he would prefer to interpret these calculations in such a manner, and thus as evidence for Newton's possession of the square law.

[10] C.U.L., MS. Add. 3958 (2).

71   Newton on the Calculation of Central Forces

Vis gravitatis in 60″ movebit corpus per distantium 14400 braces

Vis terrae a sole in 60″ movebit corpus per distantiam $\dfrac{26250000000}{7001840329}$

$= 3{,}7490143544$

Soe y^t y^e force of a body from y^e Sun is to y^e force of its gravity as one to 3749 or there abouts

Vis terrae a centro movebit corpus in 229′,090909 per distantiam 5250000 braces

Vis gravitatis in 229′,090909 movet corpus per 755747081 ^{braces}

Soe y^t y^e force of y^e Earth from its center is to ye force of Gravity as one to 144 or there abouts.

        1 : 300 :: vis a centro terrae : vim Gravitatis
        1 : 7500 :: vis terrae a sole : vim Gravitatis[11]

It seems unnecessary to elaborate on these rough and inconsistent computations, which are naturally to be presumed to be earlier than those of the fully written paper. They would seem to represent an attempt to work out Newton's ideas at a very primitive stage, at what date it is impossible to determine.

Besides their computations of centrifugal accelerations, both documents contain some much briefer notes on mechanics, dealing with the motion of pendulums. Thus it may be judged that at the time of their composition Newton's thoughts were directed fairly steadily towards this science. Doubtless when more material of the same kind has been studied—and Professor Turnbull is engaged on bringing it to light—a clearer picture will emerge. We can be confident that Newton's recollection "(having found out how to estimate the force with which a globe revolving within a sphere presses the surface of the sphere) from Kepler's rule . . I deduced that the forces which keep the Planets in their Orbs must [be] reciprocally as the squares of their distances from the centers about which they revolve" was faithful, even though the dates of this discovery, and of its subsequent development, remain obscure. Newton certainly did little to facilitate the historian's task.

[11] It seems that here a cubit and a brace (*bracchia*) are taken as equal, and as 1/3000 of a 'mile', 3,500 'miles' ($= 3313$ English miles) constituting the terrestrial radius. Hence both are equal to 1·67 English feet. Yet it can be computed from the relations given above that Newton has taken g variously as 16 cubits/sec.^{2}, 400 'inches', and 8 braces. I have not attempted to reconcile these discordances.

IV

Newton's Chemical Experiments

By Marie Boas and Rupert Hall

Since Newton's interest in chemical matters began to receive serious attention, various writers have attempted interpretations of the rather discordant materials available in print. Because Newton's only specifically chemical publication was *De Natura Acidorum* (which appeared in John Harris' *Lexicon Technicum*), the earlier accounts were otherwise based on such hearsay reports as those of Humphrey Newton and Conduitt, on the more incidental chemical references in the *Quaeries* to the *Opticks,* and on letters whose exact status as representative of Newton's real thought is somewhat controversial. Few later writers have added substance to the materials discussed by Newall in 1928 and McKie in 1942, though the same ground has been traversed more than once since (1). The only fresh evidence drawn into the discussion has come from the sale of Newton's papers in 1936, of which, as Messrs. Sotheby's excellent catalogue then made it clear, a large proportion was concerned with alchemy (2). Lord Keynes, who purchased heavily at the sale, during the Royal Society celebrations of 1946 drew a picture of Newton the alchemist in strong colours, from which he was led to declare in an unfortunately memorable phrase that Newton was « the last of the magicians ». Of the alchemical papers (now at King's College, Cambridge) he wrote that they were « wholly magical and wholly devoid of scientific value » yet it was « also impossible not to admit that Newton had devoted years of work to [them] » (3). This picture was not unfamiliar, but since Brewster's time no one had had the oppor-

---

(1) Most early writers on Newton seem to have treated his chemical interests as detracting from his genius. In his biography of 1934 L. T. MORE still seemed to consider them an eccentricity. Newton's chemistry is discussed as a serious historical problem by Lyman C. NEWALL in « Newton's work in Alchemy and Chemistry », *Sir Isaac Newton, 1727-1927*, History of Science Society, London, 1928, 203-255; by Douglas McKIE in « Some Notes on Newton's Chemical Philosophy written upon the Occasion of the Tercentenary of his Birth », *Philosophical Magazine,* VIIth series, vol. 33, 1942, 847-870; by S. I. VAVILOV in « Newton and the Atomic Theory », *Newton Tercentenary Celebrations,* Cambridge, 1947, 43-55; and by R. J. FORBES in « Was Newton an Alchemist? », *Chymia,* vol. 2, 1949, 27-36.

(2) Sotheby and Co., « Catalogue of the Newton Papers sold by Order of the Viscount Lymington », 1936, section I.

(3) J. M. KEYNES, « Newton, the Man », in *Newton Tercentenary Celebrations,* Cambridge, 1947, 27-34.

tunity of reading Newton's notes; few have seized it since, for the very good reason that they are very largely transcriptions from printed books (4). Newton never wrote an alchemical treatise; nor did he ever declare his opinion of alchemy, except to comment on a few well-publicized alchemical processes.

Inevitably, students of Newton have reached opposite but equally unimpugnable conclusions, depending on whether they identify « Newton » with the author of the *Quaeries* and other printed fragments, or whether they identify him with the ardent reader of Basil Valentine, Kerkringius, Ashmole, *The Marrow of Alchemy*, the *Musaeum Hermeticum*, and so on. The first is a sober natural philosopher, whose ultimate concern (as with all the natural philosophers of the seventeenth century) is to discover the structure and basic properties of matter. This Newton uses the evidence of chemical phenomena in support of the mechanical philosophy in the manner initiated by Boyle and probably in imitation of Boyle. It is in this light that Newall summarizes *De Natura Acidorum* and passages in the *Quæries* as speculations on affinity (5); while McKie attaches them to Newton's atomism :

> Newton had elaborated a coherent chemical philosophy. Its fundamental basis was the ancient atomic theory in which the transmutability of matter was implied. ... But Newton had made his own characteristic contribution in arguing from phenomena (and he insisted that his conclusions were so derived) that, between the particles of bodies, there was an exceedingly strong force of attraction reaching only to a short distance from the particles and producing the phenomena of chemistry (6).

In short Newton, like Boyle, was both a physical and chemical corpuscularian, and as Forbes puts it :

> What he tried to achieve was really an extension of his synthesis in mechanics. He believed that some atomic theory

---

(4) The King's College papers have been utilised by F. Sherwood Taylor in « An Alchemical Work of Sir Isaac Newton », *Ambix*, vol. V, 1956, 59-84; and by D. Geoghegan in « Some Indications of Newton's Attitude towards Alchemy », *Ambix*, vol. VI, 1957, 102-106.
(5) Newall, *Sir Isaac Newton, 1727-1927*, 216, 218.
(6) McKie, *Philosophical Magazine*, VIIth series, vol. 33, 1942, 866.

could be found in which the variety of elements was explained by geometrical groupings of a universal atomic substance (7).

This is a logical and plausible presentation of the *use* that Newton made, in cold print, of chemical experiments. There was no necessity for him to have made these experiments himself, since they are common in the literature; it is worth remembering that in the *Principia,* and elsewhere in the *Opticks,* Newton frequently refers to experiments made by others. This presentation shows us Newton adding his own conception of attractive force to the chemical corpuscularianism of Boyle — a comprehensible step forward. McKie's picture of Newton as the chemical philosopher, excellently drawn, stands by itself — until one thinks of the Oak, and the Green Lion, and the Star. Was it the chemical philosopher whose fire in the laboratory « well furnished with chymical materials as bodyes, receivers, heads, crucibles, etc., which was made very little use of, ye crucibles excepted, in which he fused his metals » scarce went out for six weeks at spring and fall? What was Newton doing with his incessant fires and melting of metals, if he was repeating the kind of reactions mentioned in the *Quæries?*

The furnace-man, who ran up and down the steps leading from his first floor room next the Great Gate of Trinity to the little garden by the street, was Lord Keynes' magician. Forbes qualifies Newton's alchemical library as « astonishing ». Sherwood Taylor, like Keynes, uncompromisingly calls him an alchemist :

> that Newton was studying alchemy over a long period has already been demonstrated, and is confirmed by a preliminary survey of these [King's College] MSS some of which are of dates as early as 1676, and others as late as 1696.

Further,

> even a preliminary perusal of Newton's alchemical papers will leave no doubt in any mind familiar with alchemical literature,

---

(7) FORBES, *Chymia,* vol. 2, 1949, 32. The somewhat anachronistic phrasing of the second sentence is Forbes's rather than Newton's. Cf. McKIE's suggestion that Newton's « object was to arrive at some general law of chemical attraction corresponding to his law of gravitational attraction », *loc. cit.,* 867.

IV

> that Newton was in the fullest sense an alchemist. He conducted alchemical experiments, he read widely and universally in alchemical treatises of all types, and he wrote alchemy, not like Newton, but like an alchemist (8).

That the overwhelming bulk of Newton's alchemical papers consists of transcripts from books was remarked upon by Sherwood Taylor, and is evident from the Sotheby Catalogue. In fact Newton was one of those who are able to work only with pen in hand; he copiously annotated everything he read — Descartes, More, Boyle, Hooke as well as the alchemists — and it is difficult to explain Newton's extraction of alchemical books that stood on his own shelves save as the result of a psychological compulsion, which also led him to draft any important document several times over. All that the alchemical papers prove is that Newton read those authors attentively; it is difficult, and may be impossible, to find anything among them of Newton's own composition. Sherwood Taylor seems to have misled himself in this respect, in speaking of Newton as writing on alchemy; for the document he prints in *Ambix* is clearly, as its content and Sherwood Taylor's footnotes reveal, not as he claims Newton's own but an anthology from chemical authors designed to illustrate the progress of the Work. Newton is no more its author than Palgrave was author of the *Golden Treasury,* though as Palgrave's anthology is indicative of a conception of poetry, so Newton's compilation is indicative of a conception of alchemy. If the distinction between a « student of alchemy » and an « alchemist » is not too fine a one to be drawn (and without it, might not all historians of alchemy be called alchemists?), it would appear from his papers that Newton was indeed an engrossed student, but not a practitioner of alchemy — they contain no evidence that he ever attempted the Work. They hint neither at the experiments we know he made, nor at those which he described in print.

Justifiably, therefore, McKie has protested that

> too much emphasis is put upon these [alchemical] extracts... We might also ask what man of science would care to be judged by what he had copied out of books. ... Until we know what Newton's own opinion was about the material that he

(8) Sherwood TAYLOR, *Ambix,* V, 1956, 61.

copied out from alchemical works, we have no warrant, however extensive that material may be, for concluding that it reflected his own views on chemistry, especially when the chemical thought set forth in his published writings shows an advance towards modern chemistry rather than a reversion to the already discredited pursuit of gold-making (9).

Yet if copying out Ripley and Starkey no more makes a man an alchemist than copying out Wordsworth makes him a poet, the act is reasonably capable of supporting the inference of an interest in alchemy or poetry. It would be untrue to suppose that Newton read alchemists only for their descriptions of such processes as might be enlightening to a chemical philosopher (as it seems that Boyle did) : Newton also copied out that which was symbolical, allegorical, mystical and esoteric. In *this*, too, he hoped to find meaning of some kind. That he could cherish this hope seems to stretch his character as a chemical philosopher.

Sherwood Taylor tries to find a bridge between the *Theatrum Chemicum Brittanicum* and the *Principia* in the more obscure aspects of Newton's natural philosophy :

> At one point at least, alchemy fitted into Newton's cosmology. He was convinced of the need for a universal medium which should explain gravitation, electrical and magnetic forces, and animal motion. The explanation of these, in terms of various aetherial substances, was natural enough to any man of the age; and a great part of alchemy is concerned with that universal medium, the philosopher's mercury (10).

Conversely Forbes, while recognising Newton's interest in alchemy, and his long-continued experimentation, argues that no « sharp division marked the cleft between those imaginative conceptions we call alchemy and the more rational discussion of chemical facts, now called chemistry ». Newton, writes Forbes, was not a gold-maker like the worst types of medieval and later alchemists, « he was an adept like Boyle, Locke, and any of his contemporaries interested in chemistry » (11).

---

(9) McKie, *loc. cit.*, 867.
(10) Sherwood Taylor, *loc. cit.*, 63.
(11) Forbes, *loc. cit.*, 30-32.

This will hardly do. The identification of the « spirit » of the General Scholium with the philosophers' mercury does not make Newton's thinking more comprehensible: it makes it less so. Nor does it help to say that if Boyle and Locke and Newton were alchemists, at least they were not bad ones! What is an alchemist if he is not a would-be gold-maker? The seventeenth century alchemists, whose works Newton annotated, were sure there was a certain process for making gold (at the least) and most alleged confidently that they possessed it. Alchemy was never disinterested chemical research, nor was it a variant form of natural philosophy. It had one object, though many ill-defined processes, and it had no philosophy other than that of transmutability. Alchemy, which assumed a theory of metals as its premise, had no need to search for such a theory: its *raison d'être* was the realization of the theory through chemical operations, and its end-product was a lump of gold. The alchemical writers whom Newton studied understood this; if Newton was at one with them, then his object also was the making of gold (not necessarily from avaricious motives only) — or at least the attainment of some intermediate sign that he was on the right track to a workable process.

However one regards Newton's chemical work, nothing is to be gained by obscuring the difference between alchemy and chemistry as both flourished in Newton's time. It would be absurd to suggest that the writings of Boyle and Lemery, or of Newton himself in the chemical passages of the *Quaeries,* are barely distinguishable from the matter of Newton's alchemical notes. Is it then necessary to suppose that Newton's attitude to chemical phenomena was not merely enigmatic, but Janus-like? Was he both adept and philosopher, as Albertus Magnus and Roger Bacon were popularly reputed to be? Admittedly there was nothing in his chemical philosophy, or in the mechanical philosophy, to suggest that the transmutation of metals was inherently impossible. Newton no more held the modern conception of a chemical element than Boyle did. Since it was possible that there was a grain of truth in alchemical boasts, hardly more surprising than the acknowledged transmutations of tradesmen, it was a reasonable task for the chemical philosopher to attempt to discover how far, if at all, the structure of a metal might be permanently modified in chemical reactions. There was no *a priori* reason known to Newton and Boyle for supposing that such modifications were impossible (12). On the other hand, there is no evidence that either was confident that a process for affecting the very structure of metals would ever be attained, still less that it ever had been. *Pace* Sherwood Taylor, it seems plausible to agree with McKie and Forbes that whatever Newton's views on transmutation were, he could not have thought of metallurgical chemistry simply and solely in the manner of Starkey, Yarworth and their predecessors. He might read the alchemists for clues to the experiments he should make, but his own interpretation of them would be that of the rational mechanical philosopher, not that of the alchemist.

What these experiments were, no recent writer has been able to declare. This is curious, since Newall in 1928 printed extracts from the *Catalogue of the Portsmouth Collection* (13) which summarize two important documents now in the Cambridge University Library. Newall did not examine the originals : indeed, at the time when he wrote one of them was lying unrecognized in the University archives, to which it had found its way by mistake in 1887.

This is a notebook, now pressmarked MS Add 3975. Like Newton's other notebooks, it is a small calf-bound volume containing notes of reading, experiments and hypotheses on a variety of subjects, arranged under topical headings (14). The notes made under any single heading seem to follow in chronological sequence as they were added from time to time. At folio 49 there is the heading « Of fire, flame, ye heate & ebullition of ye hearte & Divers mixed liquors, & Respiration »; at folio 61 we have « Of Formes & Transmutations wrought in them »; and at folio 71 « Of Salts, & Sulphureous bodyes, & Mercury & Metals ». The two first of these sections, and the third as far as folio 80, consists of notes from Boyle (the *New Experiments Physico-Mechanical,* and especially the *Origin of Forms and Qualities*); there is, however, a

---

(12) McKie makes the extremely interesting point (*loc. cit.*, 853) that Newton in the *Principia* appears to accept the doctrine of Van Helmont and Boyle on the conversion of water and « humid spirits » to earth and solid matter; cf. *Sir Isaac Newton's Mathematical Principles of Natural Philosophy,* ed. Florian Cajori, Berkeley, 1946, 529-530, 542.

(13) *Catalogue of the Portsmouth Collection of Books and Papers written by or Belonging to Sir Isaac Newton,* Cambridge, 1888. Section II, Divisions IV and VI.

(14) Optical notes in this volume have been discussed by A. R. Hall in « Further Optical Experiments of Isaac Newton », *Annals of Science,* vol. XI, 1955, 27-43.

reference on folio 65 to Starkey's *Pyrotechny Asserted*. Notes on his own experiments begin on folio 80, and extend to folio 84; they continue again from folio 267 to folio 283. Very similar experiments, sometimes identical with those of the notebook but not invariably so, are recorded on loose folded sheets (MS Add 3973). When the notebook duplicates the sheets its account is fuller and more detailed, and it seems that the sheets were written out first. The two records complement each other and clearly relate to the same experimental programme, so they may be considered together.

The earliest date found in any of these chemical notes is 10 December 1678. Newton had by this time been interested in chemistry for at least three years, if Collins is to be believed in his report (29 June 1675) that « Mr Newton intends not to publish anything, as he affirmed to me, but intends to give in his lectures yearly to the public library, & prosecutes his chemical matters and experiments » (15). The first reference in Newton's own letters to chemical matters is his comment on Boyle's « uncommon experiment about the incalescence of gold and mercury » (April 26, 1676) in which, as in the well-known letter to Boyle himself (February 28, 1678/9) Newton makes free use of the mechanical, corpuscular hypothesis (16). The latest date is February 1696, and it would seem that with his removal from Trinity Newton abandoned his chemical experiments for ever. Many intermediate dates are recorded, but by no means every experiment has a date attached, and it is not always possible to tell when a particular burst of activity at the furnace begins or ends. Over the period of 18 years there is no mention of chemical research in 1680, possibly 1683, and 1694, while there is a long gap between 1686 and 1690. But since the dated entries are scattered no certain inferences can be drawn; moreover, many pages of the notebook

---

(15) Collins to James Gregory, 29 June 1675, in H. W. TURNBULL, ed. *James Gregory Tercentenary Memorial Volume*, London, 1939, 310-311. Cf. the same to the same, 19 October 1675 : « ... Mr. Newton (whom I have not writ to or seen these eleven or twelve months, not troubling him as being intent upon chemical studies and practices, and both he and Dr. BARROW beginning to think mathematical speculations to grow at least dry, if not somewhat barren) is not of the same mind... »; S. J. RIGAUD, *Correspondence of Scientific Men of the Seventeenth Century... in the Collection of the... Earl of Macclesfield*, Oxford, 1841, II, 280. However, Newton wrote mathematical letters to Collins on July 24 and August 27, 1675 (*ibid.*, II, 370-373) and their correspondence was resumed later.

(16) RIGAUD, *Ibid.*, II, 395-97, 407-419.

are filled before the first date occurs (May 10, 1681) and again after the last (May 16, 1686). Some periods of intense activity are indicated, for example in December 1678 and January 1679; in May and June 1681; from May to August in 1682; in April and May 1686. One might guess that Newton would relight his fire when the coming of better weather coincided with the end of his formal lectures; but there are dates in December, January and February in the experimental records. For one day (« Munday June 26, 1682 ») Newton records nine experiments; this is his account of the day's work :

Munday June 26 Reg[ulus of] copper 8, serpens non destil-[lata] 1, destil. 1. Of this without being melted 15 parts, sal ammoniac 20 parts, there remained in the bottom 3 parts. The subl[imate] was white and with water gave a very white precipitate not readily dissolvable in A[qua] F[ortis], fusible in a great heat like antimony and something more volatile. Out of the water nothing more was precipitated by salt of tartar so that all that sublimed besides sal ammoniac was precipitated before by water alone. The white sublimate 18 parts, salt of iron 9, left in the bottom 7 parts, so that it carries up but 2/7, and perhaps the salt was not thoroughly dried before.

Reg[ulus of] copper 10 or 12 parts, serpens non destil 1 part dried and melted. There sank a Reg[ulus] of copper and swam on it a scoria with stiriae like the scoria of other Reg[ulus]'s of a dull metallic colour but cleaner. The scoria was in proportion to the Reg[ulus] as 5 to 4. 12 gr of the scoria sublimed with 12 of sal ammoniac left 5 gr in the bottom. These 5 gr I sublimed again with 6 gr and there remained 3 1/12 gr in the bottom, so that the matter is more fixed by melting then without melting. This sublimate was white and with water gave a white precipitate as the former.

Reg[ulus] of copper 4 or 4 1/2 parts serpens non destil 1 part in fusion ran thick like bird lime, made no Regulus, and when cold was very hard and looked of a dull metallic colour. There was therefore too much of the serp[ent]. About 1 to 6 of Reg[ulus] may be a good proportion to let fall no Regulus just.

Bismuth ore and Tin ore melted together with antimony equal quantities of each and sublimed gave a sublimate dirty :

IV

Lead ore impregnated with salt of iron and copper and this sublimate together ana [equal quantities] did not melt so much as with salt of iron and copper alone nor was made more volatile then with salt of iron alone. But iron, Le[ad] o[re] and antimony 1 melted together and sublimed with sal ammoniac this sublimate and the sublimed salt of iron and copper ana did make the lead ore some thing [more] fusible and volatile then the salt of iron and copper alone. Yet of 16 parts of Lead ore after evaporation in a glass laid on a red hot sand there remained 6 parts fixed. So then tin and bismuth are not to be used this way for volatilizing lead but rather sublimate of iron or at least some thing better which that may lead to.

Munday, June 26, 1682 I melted Tinglass 1, lead ore 2, antimony 4, and had a little Reg[ulus]. Item bismuth 1, lead ore 2, antimony 2 and had more Reg[ulus]. Item Tinglas 1, lead ore 3, antimony 2 and had as much more Reg[ulus] as I put in lead ore more than before, that is increased by almost 1/2. Item bismuth 1, lead ore 4, antimony 2 and had the Reg[ulus] increased almost 1/3 that is made double almost to what it was in the 2d exp[erimen]t but the Reg[ulus] was not so pure as when there was less Lead, nor separated so well from the scoria, and therefore I added 1/2 of salt peter to the metal in fusion. And thus an ounce of bismuth two ounces of antimony four ounces of lead ore gave me 1 1/2 ounce of Reg[ulus]. If I had added as much more niter I believe it would have done better. In refining this Regulus did not melt well (17).

Newton's chemical notes are far from easy to understand. Besides the ordinary symbols of the day (here expanded into the contemporary names of the substances) he used non-standard symbols. An « o » attached to the usual symbol for a metal appears to indicate the ore of the metal; thus he sometimes refers to « Lead ore », sometimes to « Le. o. », sometimes to ♄₀ , all presumably the same material, perhaps galena (PbS). Other symbols appear to indicate the salt of a metal; ☿ may be interpreted ;s « salt of antimony ». In addition, he uses esoteric terms (the serpent, Diana, *Leo viridis*, philosophical sal ammoniac, etc.)

(17) MS Add. 3975, fol. 125-127.

some of which may be understood from their context, while others defy translation (18). The notes are chiefly in English, with the exception of some of the more esoteric passages; the following is perhaps the extreme example:

> Dissolve Leonem vir[idem] volat[ilem] in sale centrale Veneris et destill[at]a hic spiritus est Leonis vir[idis]. Sanguis Leonis viridis Venus, Draco Babylonicus omnia veneno suo interficiens, a columbis tamen Dianæ mulcendo victus, Vinculum mercurii.
>
> Neptunus cum tridenta inducit Ph[ilosoph]os in hort[o] soph[istico]. Ergo Neptunus est menstruum aqueum minerale ac tridens fermentum aquæ simile caduceus mercurii quovem mercurius fermentatur, vizt Columbæ, duæ aridæ, cum venere arida martiali.
>
> Certe mercurii Caduceus est vitriolum duplex fermentans

---

(18) As already indicated, various assumptions have been made in quoting from the MSS. Besides the common symbols and names for the metals and other materials, it has been possible to conjecture at Newton's meaning for less usual symbols and terms. For the aid of the reader these are given below:

♂ iron ore; ♀ copper ore; ♄ lead ore; ♃ tin ore; ♅ bismuth ore; ⚚ salt of antimony (perhaps antimony sulphate); ⚛ vinegar of antimony; ⚜ sublimate of antimony; ⚝ salt of sublimate of antimony; ☿ copper antimoniate (SbCu₂); ⚹ salt of copper antimoniate; ⚘ sublimate of salt of copper; ⚵ sublimate of copper.

Acetum antimonii	: vinegar of antimony.
ana	: equal quantities.
Cadaceus	: « double vitriol fermenting crude white antimony ».
Diana	: bismuth ore, tin and bismuth in the proportion 1 : 9 : 30.
Le. o.	: lead ore.
Leo viridis	: possibly the green salt formed when cuprous chloride stands in moist air (cupric oxychloride).
Net (rete)	: Antimony alloy containing iron and copper.
Oak	: regulus of iron, copper and antimony.
Salt of iron	: probably a volatile chloride of iron.
Serpent	: vinegar of antimony.
Spar	: probably fluorspar, calcium fluoride.
Spirit of antimony	: perhaps one of the antimony acids.
Venus volans (ven. vol.; ve. vo.)	: sublimate of copper i. e. copper heated with sal ammoniac, perhaps cuprous chloride.

There are other non-standard symbols and various names of substances occurring in the notes to which it has not yet proved possible to attach a definite significance.

antimonium crudum album. Hæc enim principia metallica tenere non fusa sunt, et affinia tam sibi ipsis (ut ex reg[ulo] martis et reti patet) quam mercurio (ut ex fermentatione Reg[uli] cum mercurio patet) (19).

Probably this represents Newton's own « translation » into alchemical language of a comprehensible chemical idea, which he thought he had deciphered in alchemical literature and his own experiments; but we have not ventured to effect the « reverse translation » ourselves. Latin is not invariably used in esoteric contexts, however; sometimes it is used without any intention of distinction :

Lead ore 240 gr, antimony sub[limata] and praecip[itata] 240 gr, Rete sub[limata] and præcip[itata] 60 gr, Reg tin 1 + Bism[uth] 1 confusa subl[imata] and præcip[itata] 80 gr; hæc omnia confusa et contrita et pulveris hujus 8 gr subl[imata] cum sale copper antimoniate [$SbCu_2$] 2 gr and sal ammoniac 8 gr [re]linquebatur in fundo 4 gr : quæ resus sub[limatæ] cum sale copper antimoniate 1 1/4 and sal ammoniac 5 gr [re]linquebatur in fundo 3 1/2. Nequit igitur plumbum hoc modo (facta cum metallis volatilibus colliquefactiona) elevari (20).

The use of alchemical terms gives an air of esoteric mystery to Newton's chemical pursuits as recorded in these notes which seems, in fact, not to be wholly warranted. Sometimes, it is true, he uses such terms where they have (to us) little concrete meaning. He does not explain what he understands by « our » or « the philosophers » sal ammoniac, for instance, and his very first entries in the notebook relate obscurely to the mercury-sulphur theory of metals :

In Aqua fortis 2 oz dissolve mercury 1 oz or as much as it will dissolve. Then put an ounce of Lead laminated or filed into it by degrees and the lead will bee corroded dissolving by degrees into mercury and besides there will fall downe a white præcipitate like a limus being the mercury præcipitated by the sulphur of lead. Out of an ounce of lead may bee got 1/3 oz of mercury. If the remaining liquor bee evaporated there

(19) MS Add. 3973, fol. 12.
(20) MS Add. 3975, fol. 147.

remains a reddish matter tasting keene like sublimate. The same liquor will extract the mercury of tin (21).

Yet he notes immediately, in connection with the solution of copper in the same liquid, « I know not whither that mercury came out of the liquor or of [the] copper, for the liquor dissolves copper ». Often, as well, alchemical terms as Newton uses them have a precise and definite meaning — *his* meaning, if not that of his alchemical authors. Thus « diana » is a tin-bismuth alloy, made with one part of bismuth ore, nine parts of tin, and 30 parts of bismuth, very probably named from its silvery appearance; the « net » (or « rete ») is an antimony alloy containing iron and copper; the « oak » is another such alloy, or as Newton puts it « Reg[ulus of] iron, copper, antimony »; the « serpent » is another name for vinegar of antimony. One may with good reason suppose that Lion's blood, the eagle of tin, Neptune, the Caduceus, the Green Lion (Leo viridis) and so forth equally had a concrete meaning for Newton (whatever they may have meant to the alchemists whose works he read so avidly), even though it has not been so far possible to identify with certainty from his notes the substances to which he assigned these esoteric names. The influence of the alchemical metallurgists is also discernible in the importance he attached to the visible appearance of a cast regulus (22). At one point he melted various proportions of « regulus of iron » with copper, examining the structure of the solidified alloy : 9 1/4 of the former to 4 of the latter « gave a substance with a pit hemisphericall and wrought like a net with hollow work as twere cut in »; 8 1/2 to 4 « gave noe pit but a net worke forme spread all over the top, yet more impressed in the middle »; 2 parts of

---

(21) *Ibid.*, fol. 80.

(22) The preparation of the regulus of any metal is thus described by Newton : « To make Regulus of Antimony, Iron, Lead, Copper, etc. Take of antimony twelve oz, of iron 4 1/2 or 5 1/4 or copper 6,6 1/4 or of lead 8 1/2 or proportionably more to the antimony if it will beare it. When they are melted pour them of and you will have a Reg[ulus]. You may when they are molten throw two or three oz of nitre on them which having done working them pour of. If the scoria of lead bee full of small eaven rays there is two little lead in proportion. If any reg[ulus] swell much in the midst of the upper surface it argues two much antimony. If it bee flat it argues two little. The better your proportions are the brighter and britler will the Reg[ulus] bee and the darker the scoria and the easier will they part. And also the more perfect the star, unlesse the salts on the top worke and bubble in the cooling to disturbe the said superficies. The work succeeds best in least quantitys » (*Ibid.*, fol. 81).

regulus to one of copper « gave a net work but not so Notable as the former, and so did R[egulus] iron 5, copper 2 ». Hence Newton judged that the proportion of 9 or 8 1/2 to 4 was the best (23). Sometimes he referred to the « star » conspicuously associated with metallic antimony and its alloys : he noted that a complicated regulus made with antimony, iron and ores of iron, copper, tin, lead and bismuth, purified with saltpetre, « had a glorious Star », and described it as « wrought with network » (24).

Newton seems to have believed that it was possible — and profitable — to decipher alchemical terminology (at least in so far as this was used in a genuine experimental context), and that he had succeeded in doing so. This by no means makes him an alchemist. It was no more inherently improbable that the alchemical « flying eagle » should be a metallic compound than that the « sal mirabile » of Glauber should be anything as definite as sodium sulphate (or vitriol of potash, as Glauber might have termed it, if he had not tried to conceal its true nature while still boasting of its virtues). While Newton was struggling with the compounds of antimony, Boyle was isolating and studying phosphorus from even more tenuous clues than Newton thought he possessed. Chemistry and chemical nomenclature were still at a stage where such procedure was inevitable. Indeed, at about the time that Newton concluded these experiments, the first of a series of *Hermetic Dictionaries* appeared : designed to enable the rational eighteenth-century chemist to read the mystic alchemical literature of the preceding century, these usually leave the worst obscurities still obscure. One need not believe that Newton was correct in his interpretation of alchemical terms, but it seems eminently reasonable to suppose that even in his most esoteric alchemical language he intended to speak chemical sense.

From their nature it can hardly be doubted that the notes represent the results of Newton's own chemical experiments. They included almost nothing attributable to his indefatigable instinct to summarize or extract from other writers (except for those places already noted). There are two contrary instances to this rule, both in the notebook. At folios 83 and 84 he refers to vitriol of tartar and sal ammoniac :

(23) *Ibid.*, fol. 83.
(24) *Ibid.*, fol. 151-2; Apr. 26, 1686.

If Tartarum Vitriolatum (which is commonly known & to be had in shops being a præcipitate made by dropping oyle of vitriol upon salt of Tartar) be put into oyle of Tartar per deliquium it makes a great effervescence, and an earthy sediment is præcipitated out of the salt of Tartar by the acting of the acid spirit of the vitriol upon it. This præcipitate some fools call Magisterium Tartari Vitriolati.

Sal Armoniack consists of an acid and urinous salt both which are severally volatile enough but together they fix one another yet not so much but that the whole salt will rise with a round heat, there ascending first white flowers and then gradually yellowi ones but the yellow being more sluggish will scarce ascend so high as the white and settle into a harder mass (25).

And he goes on to say that « David Vonder Becke ad Joelem Langelottum saith that volatilised salt of Tartar may be again fixed by addition of another volatile [salt], and again made volatile by an easy labour »; there follows a quotation from von der Becke, and another from Boyle on salt of urine. The two paragraphs first quoted clearly derive from von der Becke, who states that some call the precipitate formed when salt of tartar is dissolved in oil of vitriol « magistery of vitriolated tartar », and foolishly prefer it to the genuine vitriolated tartar (26). The source of the second quotation or paraphrase has not been identified : it is so unlike the rest of the notes, and is so casually interpolated among experiments on antimony, that its character is easily recognizable :

There is a liquor as insipid as water of which a man may drink a pint without the least offence or injury. Tis got and prepared in three days and may be made at any time of the year, but best in September or the end of August the air being then well impregnated and perhaps for the same reason in Spring about April or May. For tis a general Menstrue more general then that of sp[iri]t of salt or sp[iri]t of wine. This Menstrue digested with the calx of gold or silver for 30 days

(25) *Ibid.*, fol. 83-4.
(26) *Ibid.*, fol. 83-4. Cf. *Davidis von der Becke Epistola ad... Joelem Langelottum... qua salis tartari aliorumque salium fixorum...* VOLATISATIO... *demonstratur*. Hamburg, 1672.

in a due heat extracts their tinctures and leaves the rest of the body like white ashes not any more reducible by fusion to a metal nor perhaps fusible. It extracts 12 gr of sulphur out of an ounce of gold and 10 gr of sulphur out of an ounce of silver and leaves the rest of the body in a white calx as above. It extracts also the tinctures of other metals. Tis prepared with an easy heat without trouble or labour and all the art and difficulty is in the degrees of heat and modus of working (27).

The influence of other books is discernible (notably the *Triumphal Chariot of Antimony*, which though not specifically mentioned in the notebook describes many experiments similar to those he actually performed and in fact he copied out long extracts of this and other works by Basil Valentine at various times on other sheets), but these is nothing else in these notes suggestive of direct quotation.

There are several notes of preparations set out in perfectly straightforward terms, which presumably derive from his chemical reading, and conversations with experienced chemists like Boyle and (later) Vigani. Thus,

Venetian sublimate is made of mercury 2 p[ar]ts, refined silver 2 p[ar]ts, vitriol calcined to red 1 p[ar]t and salt decrapitated 1 p[ar]t. The Hollanders sophisticate it with Arsnic. The sophisticated is in long splinters and turns black with oyle of tartar dropt on it. But the true turns yellow and is in little grains like hempseed (28).

A note on the preparation of butter of antimony (the chloride) is characteristically worded in quantitative form :

Antimony [sulphide] 1 lb, mercury sublimate 1 lb gives butter of antimony 1/2 lb, which precipitated with water gives 1/4 lb or oz 4 1/4 of white precipitate. But the mercury sublimate dissolves not all the metalline part of the antimony for by the addition of fresh mercury sublimate more butter may be got out of it (29).

(27) MS Add. 3975, fol. 267-8.
(28) *Ibid.*, fol. 80.
(29) *Ibid.*, fol. 101.

There are besides reflections of the contemporary chemical literature and its doctrines in scattered remarks on non-metallic preparations. For example,

> Salt or oyle of Tartar put into Aqua fortis gradually till it be satiated after ebullition becomes saltpeter by incorporating the acid spirit yet without any præcipitation of earth in the action.
>
> If Sal Armoniack be put into Oyle of Tartar per deliquium, its acid salt will let go the urinous and work upon the Alcaly. And the urinous thus let loos becomes very volatile so as to strike the nose with a strong scent and fly all away if it be not soon inclosed in a vessel.
>
> So if to a solution of crude Tartar in water be put by degrees Salt of Tartar, or Tartar calcined suppose to black, the acid spirit of the Tartar will forsake the alcalisate (or urinous) to work upon the fixt Salt of Tartar. And the Alcalisate (or urinous) salt thus let loos becomes very volatile so as to fly suddenly away. And in the remaining solution will bee a salt compounded of the acid sp[iri]t of Tartar and sulphureous or volatile part of the Alcaly, which salt is volatile but not more volatile then Sal-armoniack or its flowers. But by the addition of new salt of Tartar (perhaps after it hath been sublimed) on which the acid may work the urinous will be let loos and become exceding volatile as before and in the action the earthy parts of the fixt salt will be precipitated (30).

In the midst of metallurgical experiments a record of the preparation of ether seems to have no obvious relevance to anything else that Newton was doing :

> Ol[eum] vitriol well rectified from flegm, grows hot by mixing with water or sp[iri]t of wine or of mercury or perhaps with any liquor. This and sp[iri]t of wine mixed ana and digested together for ten days in destillation there ascended a sp[iri]t more fragrant then the sp[iri]t of wine (viz sp[iri]t of wine and sp[iri]t of mercury mixed) and on this sp[iri]t there swam an oyle which in a few days was dissolved by the sp[iri]t and became one with it. The caput mort[uum] was black and in the air resolved (a good part of it) into a black

(30) *Ibid.*, fol. 83.

IV

liquor. The sp[iri]t towards the latter end was more acid then towards the beginning (31).

Shortly before this he had described one experiment on the preparation of *mercurius dulcis* (mercurous chloride) from the sublimate (mercuric chloride) as follows :

> Mercury sublimate 4, mercury 4, sublimed together into mercury dulcis and a little mercury adhered to the top of the glas. This mercury dulcis put in with its weight of fresh mercury would imbibe none of it but left the mercury running : So that mercury sublimate 4 will imbibe but mercury 3 or 3 1/2. Note that mercury dulcis is much less volatile then mercury sublimate (32).

which is reflected in Quæry 31 of the *Opticks* :

> Mercury sublimate... re-sublimed with fresh Mercury,... becomes *Mercurius Dulcis*, which is a white tasteless Earth scarce dissolvable in Water, and *Mercurius Dulcis* re-sublimed with Spirit of Salt returns into Mercury sublimate (33).

For the most part, however, there is little in these notes to parallel the printed observations in the *Opticks*, except the discussion of fixity and volatility (see below, p. 22), for they are almost purely experimental, and embody very little in the way of theoretical speculation. Interspersed with accounts of experiments (which often include some crude statement of temperature used : in sublimation experiments Newton often notes that the heat was barely equal to that required to sublime sal ammoniac, i. e. c. 350 degrees centigrade) are more personal notes on technique or method, such as this observation :

> In subliming crude antimony the yellow and red flowers in a tall still ascend all into the head and there fall into the cavity. Some little brimstone sticks to the upper part of the body and there melts into drops which take fire like other brimstone. The main and good part of the antimony settles below an inch or two above the sand. If the flours in the head be sublimed again per se in a gentle heat, there first arises a

(31) *Ibid.*, fol. 103-4.
(32) *Ibid.*, fol. 103.
(33) *Opticks*, London, 1931, 385.

yellow sulphureous substance which burns like brimstone, and the matter below turns black when about 1/4th thereof is sublimed and when 1/3d therof is sublimed tis as black as the good sublimate in the lower part of the body but not of so much virtue (34).

What Newton calls the « sublimate of antimony » however was prepared with the aid of sal ammoniac, and he carefully notes that

> The sublimate of antimony for this use [i. e. subliming other metals such as copper or iron] must be drawn from antimony dry. For if water be added to dissolve the sal ammoniac, it works more on the antimony then it should, and separates a copious red light sublimate from the heavier dark grey sublimate neither of which are of that virtue the sublimate in ando has. And the light red sublimate is of no virtue at all (35).

Some of the accounts of experiments are filled out into a rather vivid description of what was seen to happen at different stages; very often the fire was raised until the glass vessel was so hot that it began to collapse or run : after this Newton would test the *caput mortuum* remaining in it by heating a portion on a red-hot fire-shovel to see if it still contained any volatile matter. In one of these operations related in more detail he began by subliming a mixture of prepared sal ammoniac and vitriol in various stated proportions. He stated (for what reason is not clear) that he preferred the fifth proportion (sal ammoniac 18, vitriol 12 parts). Having examined the *caput mortuum*, he proceeded to submit the sublimate (5-3/5 parts) to various reactions :

> To the volatized part therefore I poured its weight of A[qua] F[ortis]. Being urged with too much heat it boyled over into a glass vessel it stood in. Then in a boyling heat I put in antimony till the A[qua] F[ortis] was satiated. Another time I put in A[qua] F[ortis] by degrees but that did not so well. Let the A[qua] F[ortis] be put in all at once and a gradual heat be gently administered till the matter be almost boyling hot or boyling hot, then put in antimony till it be

(34) MS Add. 3975, fol. 148-9.
(35) *Ibid.*, fol. 111.

IV

satiated. To this I poured water till all the mercury vitæ was præcipitated. It took 8 or 12 times its quantity of water to cleare it well. Then I evaporated till the salt was ready to crystallise and put it in a retort and made it boyle till the flegm was distilled. At another time I dryed it before I put it in the retort and then using too big a heat the salt arose before all the acid spirit was come over. Wherefore I washed back the salt with warm water and distilled it of with a boyling heat and continued that heat till all the acid flegm and sp[iri]t of antimony was come over, for it came over almost all before the salt rose, which it would not have done if I had increased the heat too soon. Then I increased the heat and the salt sublimed into the neck of the retort white, and tasting almost like sea salt but more pungent. There rose with it a small quantity of sp[iri]t of antimony which I conceive may be separated by rectification, or by boyling the salt with a little spar and filtring it (36).

This demonstrates well enough the complexity of the operations on which Newton was engaged. Unfortunately there are no remarks to elucidate the design of such experiments as these.

Writing only for himself, Newton was under no obligation to explain what he intended to do, or what in fact he thought he had succeeded in doing. Since the notes are primarily records of experiments performed they contain a very few general remarks about the plan of attack which Newton must have had in mind. So slight is the interpretative content of these notes, indeed, that Newton did not scruple to enter random experiments and notes often far removed in topic from the series with which he was at the moment chiefly concerned. This is one of the reasons why it is impossible to identify some of the compounds used by Newton, for many of the more strangely named ingredients appear suddenly with no previous warning; as often in experimental notebooks, the crucial ideas suggesting some new procedure were not written down, because the experimenter was too absorbed in them to need a reminder, or perhaps to realize how much he was omitting. Yet on occasion Newton, even here, interpolates a brief conclusion or comment, and from these it is possible to separate the experiments into two general groups : first and foremost, a long series on the

(36) *Ibid.*, fol. 142-3.

IV

NEWTON'S CHEMICAL EXPERIMENTS ☆ 133

volatilization and fusibility of metallic alloys; and secondly a less coherent series dealing with the composition of a number of chemical compounds.

It would appear that the majority of Newton's experiments on metals was intended to discover ways by which individual metals could be rendered more volatile or to prepare alloys of low melting and boiling points, in other words to alter the *physical* characteristics of metals and alloys. The object of these procedures, and the procedures themselves, are alike obscure, not only because Newton had no eye for the reader he never expected, but also because his terminology is somewhat careless. Since the materials on which he operated had often been prepared with the aid of sal ammoniac, he tended to assume that every process was a sublimation when, in fact, it was frequently a fractional distillation. If this is borne in mind it is easier to follow what was happening. That it is never possible to be completely certain about what happened is obvious : most of the materials with which Newton worked were impure, especially the indeterminate ores he was fond of employing. (Presumably the ores were used with the idea that the metallic mineral was alive and fertile, whereas a smelted metal was dead and inert; besides, the gangue was commonly thought to contain some of the « sulphur » of the metal). Moreover, Newton only rarely took much trouble to ascertain whether the substance he thought he was following through a series of reactions actually passed over in each of the various distillations to which he subjected his materials. (This might be called the « Beguin » error of early chemistry : his « burning spirit of Saturn » (acetone) containing, as Boyle pointed out, no lead at all.) Yet Newton was capable, on occasion, of checking both *caput mortuum* and distillate for the presence of, say, copper; so that it is possible that his checks on chemical identities were more careful than he indicates. For just when, after following a series of reactions, one is tempted to conclude that the supposed sublimate of a metal is in fact nothing but sal ammoniac, there comes a second set of processes at the end of which Newton reaches just that conclusion — which suggests that one's suspicion of the first metallic sublimate may be false. It seems not at all unreasonable to allow that not all of Newton's laboratory procedure was noted down scrupulously.

His greatest interest appears to have been in the volatilization of metals and their alloys. In the various processes attempted sal ammoniac was an essential ingredient. This he bought (according to a memorandum at the end of the notebook) from « Mr Stonestreet Druggist by Bow Church on the same side the street towards Pauls at the sign of the Queens head with a rose in her breast », at two shillings per pound. Other materials frequently figuring in the processes are antimony (stibnite) at fourpence the pound, mercury sublimate at five shillings and fourpence and double aqua fortis at the same price, crucibles at five pence the nest, and oil of vitriol at three shillings. « Jallap » must have had a more personal use. When Mr Timothy Langley took over in 1693 prices were a little lower, but quicksilver still cost five shillings per pound. Modern chemical textbooks (for the most part deplorably unhelpful on the subjects that Newton explored) note that sal ammoniac mixed with iron filings and heated will give a sublimate containing ferric chloride. Newton seems to have achieved this with other metals as well, or at least he thought he had. Thus he made much use of an antimony sublimate, prepared from stibnite and sal ammoniac (37) and the mysterious « ven[us] vol[ans] » (or « ve, vo. ») is apparently a volatile chloride of copper, a sublimate obtained by heating sal ammoniac and copper. These experiments on metallic sublimates afford one of the few instances of Newton's using the results for a published statement; in Quæry 31 of the *Opticks* he asks :

> And is it not also from a mutual attraction that the Spirits of Soot and Sea-salt unite and compose the Particles of Sal-ammoniac, which are less volatile than before, because grosser and freer from Water; and that the Particles of Sal-ammoniac in Sublimation carry up the Particles of Antimony, which will not sublime alone; ... and that when Mercury sublimate is sublimed from Antimony, or from Regulus of Antimony, the Spirit of Salt lets go the Mercury, and unites with the antimonial metal which attracts it more strongly, and stays with it till the Heat be great enough to make them both ascend together, and then carries up the Metal with it in the form of a very fusible Salt, called Butter of Antimony, although the

---

(37) Sublimate of antimony is also referred to in the *Opticks*, Quaery 31 (ed. London, 1931, 383).

Spirit of Salt alone be almost as volatile as Water, and the Antimony alone as fix'd as Lead? (38).

One cannot but wonder whether Newton had any such theoretical conclusions in mind when designing and performing these experiments or whether, as seems more probable, he merely used the results of the experiments when writing a theoretical discussion of the role of affinity in chemistry many years later. There is very little trace of the concept of intra-corpuscularian attraction, or of affinity, in the experimental notes.

Combined with this broad interest in the sublimation of metals was the desire to determine what individual entities could be made to « rise » with various conditions. There are many examples of this; for instance :

Le[ad] o[re] 12 gr, Ore of Tinglas [bismuth] ground fine 8 gr, sal ammoniac 12 gr sublimed together, the matter boyled but little, and rose more heavily, then without Ore of Tinglas and after in a red heat in the open air it had done fuming there remain'd 16 gr in the bottom. So that the Tinglas ore fixed part of the Le[ad] o[re] (39).

There are experiments on various kinds of regulus combined with sal ammoniac and sublimed; in these experiments Newton was carefully quantitative in order to be able to evaluate the advantages and disadvantages of adding various compounds. Thus he sublimed regulus of antimony with tin, bismuth, and sal ammoniac, weighed the result, and compared this with the amount obtained when « red antimonial precipitate » (a mixture of oxides and sulphides of antimony) was added; in the latter case he collected less sublimate and concluded : « so that the precipitate holds down the tin » (40). Or again, after a number of similar experiments, he concluded : « So then tin and bismuth are not to be used this way for volatizing lead but rather sublimate of iron or at least something better which that may lead to » (41). In spite of this, he was slow to be convinced and performed many more experiments all leading to the conclusion that bismuth and

(38) *Opticks*, 382.
(39) MS Add. 3975, fol. 124.
(40) *Ibid.*
(41) *Ibid.*, fol. 126-7. See above, p. 10.

tin did not render other metals more easily volatile (42). On the other hand he believed that antimony did render other metals more volatile; as he wrote :

> Reg[ulus] iron, reg[ulus] iron ore + copper ore ana, Reg[ulus] iron ore + copper ore ana 1 with copper 1/4, Reg[ulus] iron ore + copper ore ana 1 with copper 1/2, Reg[ulus] tin, Reg[ulus] made with antimony 2, tin ore 1, Reg[ulus] lead ore 2 in 10 hours in a gentle heat grew hard with the undistilled spirit [of antimony]. Reg[ulus] made with tin ore 1, antimony 2 and Reg[ulus] lead 2 was almost as hard as Reg[ulus] tin. Reg[ulus] lead vulg[ar] made with antimony 3 lead 2 and unrefined was soft and by further digestion hardened not but afterwards in cold ran per deliquium. Reg[ulus] made with antimony 2, lead ore 1, Reg[ulus] tin 2 was almost as soft as Reg[ulus] lead and so was Reg[ulus] of antimony alone but these by 4 or 5 hours digestion more grew hard and did not any more run per deliquium. Reg[ulus] of iron vulgar seemed to harden the soonest and grow most tastless. Reg[ulus] of iron ore and copper ore with 1/4 or 1/2 of copper was not so hard as Reg[ulus] iron being at first a little more moistened. Reg[ulus] of iron ore and copper ore with out copper was as hard as any and tastless. These Reguli with out copper did better then with copper the hardning coming from the antimony. Reg[ulus] iron, Reg[ulus] iron ore and copper ore, Reg[ulus] tin vulg[ar] were all three tastless. The rest not altogether tastless. These things were remarkable that Reg[ulus] of lead vulg[ar] did not harden, that Reg[ulus] of antimony and tin did harden, and that Reg[ulus] of iron vulg[ar] and of iron ore and copper ore did harden more with out copper than with her. I tryed also the white precipitate of antimony dissolved in A[qua] R[egia] [i. e. antimony pentachloride] but it did not harden the spirit either distilled or undestilled (43).

Though in the course of Newton's study of volatile compounds which (as he believed, at least) contained various metals there seems to be much random experimentation, there is in fact a

(42) *Ibid.*, *esp.* fol. 129-30; also 136-8, 147.
(43) *Ibid.*, fol. 130-31.

discernible theoretical pattern in his procedures. These may originate (as the quotation from the *Opticks,* above p. 22 suggests) from the earliest method — that of Paracelsus — for making butter of antimony (antimony trichloride, boiling point 223.5° C.) : metallic antimony was distilled with mercury sublimate. In this case, clearly, one had first rendered mercury « volatile » by preparing the sublimate, and then as it were transferred the volatility from the mercury to the antimony. It was not unreasonable to suppose that other metals could similarly acquire volatility (as we might say, if chlorides of two metals are known to be volatile, it would be worth while to try whether other metallic chlorides would be volatile too — as indeed some are). Moreover, it seemed from the preparation of butter of antimony that one metal could replace another in a « volatile salt » in a simple heat-process; experiments of this kind could suggest the idea of, and provide the empirical basis for, a replacement series, such as Newton published in *Quæry* 31, where it is noted that the « attraction » of Mercury is weak. Similarly, if it was found that the volatility of sal ammoniac could be *directly* transferred to antimony by subliming the two substances together (the product, presumably, being an impure butter of antimony), it was a fair supposition that other metals (or metallic compounds) might also become volatile by sublimation with sal ammoniac. Thus there were two possible procedures for procuring the volatile salt of a metal (it would seem that Newton always worked with a chloride) : it might be obtained directly, by sublimation with sal ammoniac, or it might be obtained by replacement, one metal succeeding another in the « salt ». Apparently Newton's experiments on volatilization exploited both of these methods, and certainly he directed many trials to discovering the order in which one metal would replace another; thus he starts with a volatile antimony « salt » which he heats with iron compounds to make a volatile iron « salt »; having obtained this he takes the iron « salt » with copper to make a volatile copper « salt »; and then with this he goes on to yet other metals. (Whether Newton really had the volatile metallic compounds he thought he had prepared is another question). Whatever the ultimate aim of this study of volatility — and the art of changing volatile to fixed and *vice versa* had apparently some alchemical significance — it is perhaps in the light of a theory of successive replacement, rather than as purely empirical tests to determine the most volatile form of regulus, that one should view Newton's elaborate and complex series of attempts to sublime metals with the aid of sal ammoniac and mercury sublimate.

There is another — and in some ways more interesting, because more comprehensible — type of experiment scattered through the notebook though less apparent in the loose sheets. This is concerned with the actual progress of a reaction and involves consideration of various reaction products. Thus, after a series of experiments on the volatilization of alloys, there is a paragraph beginning:

> Three parts of sublimate of crude antimony sublimed from 2 of antimoniate vitriol of copper carried up one part of the vitriol and being dissolved in water let fall one part of precipitate. Quære what remains in the sublimate? (44)

This seems like a promising beginning but Newton goes on:

> Of this sublimate with its precipitate one part, distilled liquor of antimony 1 part, A[qua] F[ortis] 3 parts, Iron ore 1 1/2 parts gave a fat yellowish salt which would run per deliquium and not flow on a red hot iron. Six grains of this salt by the fuming away of the sal ammoniac in heat became five. And of these five, half a grain only was carried up by 12 grains of sublimate of antimony.

which may have been intended as the start of an investigation of composition, but which to the modern reader if not to Newton throws very little light on the problem. Again, Newton writes:

> Sublimate of Venus made with sublimate of antimony, dissolved and philtred to separate the antimony and dried and mixed either with iron filings or with spar would not rise in a second sublimation but stayed behind with the iron or spar and made the spar of a keen tast. The design was to separate the sal ammoniac from the salt of copper but the sal ammoniac did not fasten on the spar nor much on the iron, but rose alone without the copper. And if Spar and sal ammoniac were taken alone, the sal ammoniac rose from the spar without being destroyed by it.

(44) *Ibid.*, fol. 115.

Salt of tartar, as it destroyed the sal ammoniac, so it precipitates Venus in a blew form and holds it down and therefore is no fit medium to separate the salt of copper and sal ammoniac.

Sublimate of copper antimoniate 5 parts, iron antimoniate 1 part, Venus ore antimoniate Vitriol 1 part, Antimonial Sublimate 7 parts, dissolved in A[qua] F[ortis] 20 parts and antimony ground 10 parts being added for the A[qua] F[ortis] to work on and destroy the sal ammoniac. Then filtered and distilled, there rose first a substance like sal ammoniac in view but not in tast, being keener. This fell to the lower part of the neck of the retort. Then with a greater heat rose a very white salt much of which stuck to the top of the neck. This last salt was all dissolvable in water, the first salt some of it indissolvable setling to the bottom of the water like a white curd. When dissolved the water smelt strong, I suppose by reason of the spirit of sal ammoniac much volatised and altered by the operation. The matter in the bottom during the distillation was fluid almost till the latter end of the distillation and the salt which rose last was fusible. There remained much matter in the bottom which upon effusion of water let go a saline solution of a blew colour and vitriolick tast. So then a good part of the vitriol was fixed by the fixed salt or dissolved spar of the antimony and consequently antimony which had been sublimed and precipitated ought to have been used, or else regulus of antimony. That part of the salt which stuck loosely to the neck of the glass being rubbed off did not in the air run per deliquium (45).

Such experiments suggest that Newton was not content merely to volatilize metals, but that at the same time he was investigating the volatilizing power of sal ammoniac. It is as if, even with his attention fixed on a problem posed by the writers on alchemy, he could not help glancing aside to pursue a problem suggested by Boyle who would, for example, have been glad to read of the experiment on mixed metals and ores from which various salts resulted. This Boyle would have found enlightening in his attempt to examine the cohesion and separation of corpuscles in reaction and distillation.

(45) *Ibid.*, fol. 115-17.

IV

After dropping one group of experiments about July 19th (either 1682 or 1683) when Newton resumed the work again in the winter (February 29, 1683/4) he began with an experiment on which he commented more fully than usual :

> To mercury 20 gr I added by degrees fullers earth grinding them together till the earth drank up all the mercury, which was almost done with twice as much earth, and very well with thrice as much, that is with 60 gr. The whole weighed 75 gr there being lost 5 gr in the grinding. Perhaps some moisture might exhale from the earth. To this I poured sp[iri]t of antimony 19 gr. In a gentle heat of digestion for a day or two some moisture came over. Then distilling in naked fire there came over first much moisture then some mercury running. No sp[iri]t of antimony arose. At length almost in a red heat arose a white salt. And increasing the fire to a red heat and continuing it 3 or 4 hours there arose fumes continually but at last more slowly then at first by much.
>
> This salt (some of it) stood melted in the neck for some time, and I am apt to think it dissolved some of the mercury there. In a while it coagulated and some of it next the fire sublimed before it melted again. Perhaps it was incrassated by the dissolution of some mercury. The matter in the bottom looked redder then fullers earth and weighed 43 gr and on a red hot iron did not smoak. The sublimed salt and mercury together weighed 26 gr besides a grain or two left in the retort neck. Fullers earth 60 gr after being well dryed in the fire in a fireshovel not red hot weighed 43 1/2 gr. The salt was very pouderous. Its tast strong sourish ungrateful and tasting something like sublimate. Part of it did not dissolve in water. Probably the tasting and dissolvable part is analogous to sublimate the undissolvable part to mercurius dulcis. Quaere? (46).

One cannot but agree with Newton's conclusion — and regret that he did not stay for an answer.

On experiment only, of those easily intelligible, sounds like Newtonian chemistry as the eighteenth century thought of it, that is chemistry in terms of attraction and affinity. It is one of

---

(46) *Ibid.*, fol. 135-36.

a group dealing with the sublimation of metals, and very like them, apart from the closing sentence:

> Spelter [zinc] 2 and reg[ulus] antimony 1 or spelter 2 and reg[ulus] tin 1 melted together flamed and much of the spelter sublimed in white fumes adhering to the sides of the crucible. The metal in the bottom being ground, and Acet[um] antimonij poured on it, the Acet[um] worked vehement with a smart ebullition and extracted a salt. Three parts of this matter took up above 2 of acet[um] (if not 3) and left 1/3 in the bottom. The matter dryed before the separation of the salt from it did not sublime with sal ammoniac but the salt extracted did sublime with sal ammoniac prepared, as freely as salt of copper if not more freely for it left a less remainder. Nonne sal iste mercurio affinior quam sal venusij? Nonne mediator est inter utrumque ad cad[uceus] comp[ositum]? (47)

This is tantalizing, but again merely a reflection tossed out for further consideration — which this experiment at least seems never to have received. But it is sufficient to establish the fact that the idea and term « affinity » were present already in Newton's mind.

That he reflected more deeply on what passed in a chemical reaction than appears at first sight of the real paucity of theoretical discussion in these notes is fairly deducible from the passages quoted above, to which a few others might be added. The clearest theoretical discussion of all is a comment upon that omnipresent Newtonian reagent, sal ammoniac; as usual the discussion appears in a paragraph quite unrelated to the experiments which precede and follow it:

> If sal ammoniac be dissolved in aqua fortis to make aqua regis, and the menstruum distilled, the aqua fortis in a gentle heat comes over first and leaves the sal ammoniac behind, the same in weight and vertue as before: so that the sal ammoniac is not altered or destroyed by the A[qua] F[ortis] until the menstruum be imployed in dissolving gold or some other body (48).

(47) *Ibid.*, fol. 148.
(48) *Ibid.*, fol. 154.

An admirable conclusion, if only Newton had indicated what use it was to either chemical theory or practice!

A very striking feature of all these experiments is the careful nature of the manipulative technique and, above all, a keen interest in and comprehension of the niceties of precisely measuring the quantities involved. Historians of chemistry are slowly growing aware of the gross injustice done to earlier chemists by the common but fallacious statement that quantitative chemistry began with Lavoisier; from Helmont on, seventeenth-century chemists were eager to weigh and measure — especially as the easiest method of determining whether or not a reaction had taken place was to weigh starting materials and end-products. Newton often uses this method, but it was not his only reason for weighing. Every reaction set down by Newton is in the form of an exact recipe (even if we cannot always identify all the ingredients); from his earliest record, dated December 10, 1678, which reads :

> Crude unmelted and finely poudered antimony 240 gr sal ammoniac as much well mixed, by sublimation left 130 gr below. The sublimate looked very red (49).

to one of his last, dated 1 April 1695, in which he melted antimony 10 oz, iron ore well powdered and sifted very fine 5 oz, copper ore ground fine 1/4 oz, tin ore ground fine 1/4 oz, bismuth ore ground fine 1/8 oz; the matter after cooling will be « very spongy and brittle so as to break easily in your hand and grind easily with little or no grittiness » (50), Newton weighed his reagents and the resultant products in which he was interested. Sometimes, but not invariably, the equation is complete. When he used gain of weight as evidence that a reaction had occurred, Newton was careful to consider all possible variations in weight because of the conditions of the reaction; the best example of this is an experiment involving spar and « volatile copper » :

> Sp[a]r 8 gr, ve[nus] vo[lans] 10 gr sublimed together in a gentle heat sufficient to make the sal ammoniac all rise left a white pouder weighing 10 gr in the bottom. To this 4 gr or more of Ve vo [was]added and sublimed again in a heat a

(49) MS Add. 3973, fol. 1.
(50) *Ibid.*, fol. 29.

little bigger by accident : there were only 9 gr left in the bottom. This put into a new glass and urged with a red heat the matter began to melt so soon as the glass began to be red hot, but the glass being stopt the rarified air within it made it soon burst in the bottom so soon as it was so hot as to be soft. The matter had then let go a little fume which gave the inside of the glass a faint soile but scarce amounted to half a grain, nor tasted much. The matter did not melt so as to flow but only to be soft like stiff birdlime. Nor did it bubble. Of the remaining matter in the bottom I took five grains and laid them on a glass plate and set it on live coales so as to be red hot for almost half an hour. The glas with the matter I weighed together before I set it on the fire and also when I took it of and found it did not loose in the heat above 1/4 of a grain, no not though the glass was so hot as to bend of it self on the coales. Nor did the matter bubble at all or run, but only grow soft like stiff birdlime. That which was next the glass was as soft as melted glass, or almost, but that which was further from the glass was not so soft as to sink down or change its figure. Whence sp[a]r is not to be spiritualized immediately by Ven. vol. (51).

It is fair to say that in these experiments Newton is rigidly quantitative, for if he does not specify the amount of each reactant to be used (which may vary from a few grains to nearly a pound) he specifies the proportion by weight of each. In this lies one of the more original aspects of his work. Other chemists commonly used weights in recipes; but few if any besides Newton were interested in proportions, or recognized as he did that different proportions gave different yields of the desired product. Newton by contrast was extremely interested in proportions, especially in connection with the preparation of alloys. He remarks that the properties of an alloy depend as much upon the proportions of the metals as upon the metals themselves. Thus the mysterious sounding « Diana » is an alloy of bismuth ore, tin and

(51) MS Add. 3975, fol. 118-119. Spar is perhaps calcium fluoride (Derbyshire spar, fluorspar) widely used as a flux in metallurgy. It is not, however, easy to reconcile this with Newton's reference in the *Opticks* (Quaery 31, London, 1931, p. 385) to « Spar of Lead » except that this may come from association in the Derbyshire mines, where galena was also found.

bismuth in the proportion of 1 : 9 : 30 and it is in terms of parts, not quantities, that Newton defines it. So too in the preparation of regulus of antimony he sometimes goes into great detail; for example,

> Antimony 2 parts Lead Oar 1 part melted together with 1/2, 1/4 or 1/6 of Iron filings put in afterward gives about as much Regulus as the Iron filings weighed.
> Antimony 12, lead vulg[ar] 6 or 7, iron 1, salt duplex 1 gives 3 2/3 Reg[ulus] pure and at one purging with nitre very pure.
> Antimony 6, lead ore 6, salt duplex 1 boyle so as almost to run over in fusion. Melt the antimony and put in the ore and salt mixed.
> Antimony 1, lead ore 4 became thickish in fusion, the lead being put in by degrees.
> Antimony 12, lead ore 6, 7, 8 or 9 gave a very little Reg[ulus].
> Antimony 1, mercury vit[ae] 3 gave a substance like Amber (52).

A more complex example is the following :

> Another sort of antimony which came from the straits and looked like the foot of good antimony having all over the loaf little and very short veins running every way across bedded in a matter of the same colour which brake almost like steel without veins but coarser and in some postures looked yellowish in others blewish in certain places and was made into very large loafes, of above a foot in length and breadth and brake every way alike. Of this 4 gr nitre 4 gr, 5 1/3 gr, 6 2/3 gr beaten and mixed together gave 15 gr, 93 gr, 3 gr of Reg[ulus]. Whence antimony : nitre :: 12 : 15 1/2 or 7 to 9 is the best proportion to get most Reg[ulus] in proportion to the summ of the matters (53).

And again,

> Reg[ulus] copper 2, copper 4 (Tinglas/Spelter) 1, melted together gave a substance sufficiently brittle, even as brittle as

---

(52) MS Add. 3975, fol. 101.
(53) *Ibid.*, fol. 269-71.

the former. It brake smooth like glass all over the lower half. In the upper half were many glittering granulae of Reg[ulus] of antimony and between them it brake rough like fine steel. This being melted again and stirred well brake rough with granulae of Reg[ulus] of antimony all over it. It seems the copper by mixing with the spelter lets go some of the Regulus and the glassiness was now lost by the avolation of some of the Spelter. In other trials with the same proportion of materials the mixture became glassy all over and without granulae of Reg[ulus]. If at the first fusion there were two of Reg[ulus] copper, 3 of copper and 1 of Spelter, the matter was more brittle and brake all over like fine steel except a very small line at the edges where it brake smooth like glass. In the middle above was a drop of Reg[ulus] of antimony. This melted again with 1/15 more of copper so as to make the proportion of Reg[ulus], copper, spelter as 10, 16, 5 became more glassy and the Reg[ulus] antimony became dispersed all over the metal in little granulae. If at the first fusion there were Reg[ulus] copper 2, copper 6, Spelter 1 the mixture brake all over like steel without any drops or granulae of Reg[ulus] and was very hard and difficulty pulverisable. The best proportion seemed 2 : 4 : 1 (54).

An interesting case where Newton carefully compared the results of a reaction when made with various proportions of the ingredients is that group of experiments in which he saturated a complex regulus of antimony with vinegar of antimony and then sublimed with sal ammoniac. This is particularly remarkable as it looks like a well-designed attempt to determine what had, in fact, occurred in the process. In this case Newton recognized that part of the sublimate was the sal ammoniac with which he had started. It is also worth noting that Newton observed the difference between reactions in closed and open vessels, as he did on a number of other occasions, though there is no indication that he had any interest in the possible role of air, other than the empirical fact of its effect.

The net [regulus of iron and copper] imbibed with 1/7, 1/3, 1/3, 1/2, 2/3, 1 of antimonial vinegar and 8 gr thereof

(54) *Ibid.*, fol. 271-72.

IV

sublimed with 16, 14, 12, 11, 10, 8 of common sal ammoniac there remained 5, 4, 2 8/9, 2 2/3, 2 4/5, 4. The first boyled not. The second melted and boyled and sublimed quickly with an easy heat, the third was still more fusible, the 4th boyled most of all, the fift and third boyled much alike, the sixt boyled little melted difficultly rose heavily, and was thre or 4 times longer in subliming then the fift. The remainder of the fift 2 parts sublimed again with sal ammoniac 3 parts left 1 1/3. The fift 8 parts sublimed with sal ammoniac 8, 10, 12, 16 parts left 3, 2 3/4, 2 8/9, 3 1/2 : of which the last rose heavily and did not flow so much as the three first. This was in an open vessel. In a shut vessel 240 gr of the fift sublimed with 300 gr of sal ammoniac left only 64 gr in the bottom. The sublimate weighed 340 gr whereof I reccon 170 gr melted and 170 sal ammoniac. The rest of the sal ammoniac being destroyed and turned into water in the action. Item 360 gr of the third sublimed with 540 gr of sal ammoniac left 115 gr in the bottom, and in the subliming boyled much. Of the last sublimate but one which weighed 340 gr, 12 sublimed from 12 gr of Le[ad] o[re] melted difficulty rose heavily and left 6 gr in the bottom. The like did 24 gr sublimed from 12 gr of Le.o. (55).

A later and similar example concerns the mixed regulus of lead and bismuth saturated with salt of antimony :

Reg[ulus] lead 10 parts, Reg[ulus] lead 12 + bismuth 1 = 10 parts, Reg[ulus] lead 4 + bismuth 1 = 10 parts. Each imbibed with salt of antimony drunk up 2 parts thereof. The first was 12 or 15 hours in drying, the 2d and 3d dried in an hour or two and the 2d dried more quickly than the 3d. Each of these 10 gr sublimed in the open air with vulgar sal ammoniac 12 gr the 1st and 3d left 2 gr below the 2d 2 1/2 gr. And the 1st in sublimation boiled more than the 2d and the 2d more then the 3d. For the first boiled much the 3d scarce at all.

Item the 2d imbib[ed] 60 gr, and the 3d imbib[ed] 60 gr as above. Each of these 60 gr ground with sal ammoniac vulgar 80 gr and sublimed in retorts : the 2d in sublimation

---

(55) *Ibid.*, fol. 141.

melted more freely then the 3d and part of the sublimate thereof ran down again in transparent drops which that of the 3d did not. After sublimation there remained below 8 gr of the 2d like a sooty matter not melted into drops and 4 gr of the 3d melted into drops : so that 20 gr of sal ammoniac carried up 13 gr of the 2d and 14 gr of the 3d. And therefore the 3d is more volatile then the 2d. The sublimate of the second precipitated sank more readily to the bottom of the water and looked much redder then that of the 3d. For that of the 3d looked pale [like] ashes and when stirred continued longer in the water without subsiding and made a more spongy and light mudd when it did subside : so that it was subtiler then the precipitate of the 3d. The (precipitate/sublimate) of the 2d when dry weighed 45 1/2 gr besides about 1/4 or 1/2 of a grain which was lost : that of the 3d weighed 47 1/8 gr. Perhaps 20 gr of sal ammoniac would carry up more then 14 gr of the 3d. So that in the 2d there sticks about 1/3 of the salt of antimony in the 3d none at all or but 1/10. The 2d and 3d laid upon a red hot iron melted and fumed in some measure away. But if the iron had just lost its red heat before they were laid on it, they fumed without melting (56).

The consideration of proportionality most useful to modern eyes is to be found in Newton's attempt to prepare highly fusible metals. He nowhere states the reason for his interest in alloys of low melting-point, but he performed a number of experiments to discover the alloy that fused most readily. If his own statement is believed his success was remarkable :

Lead two parts, tin 3 parts, tinglass [bismuth] 4 parts melted together make a very fusible metal which in summer will melt in the Sun. Lead 4 + tin 2 + tinglass 4 is as fusible or rather a very little more fusible than lead 4 + tin 3 + tinglass 3, but lead 4 + tin 2 1/2 + tinglass 3 1/2 is still more fusible and lead 2 + tin 2 1/2 + tinglass 3 1/2 still more. Tinglass is more fusible then tin and tin then lead (57).

(56) *Ibid.*, fol. 274-75.
(57) *Ibid.*, fol. 107. For comparison, easily fusible modern alloys are Rose's metal, bismuth 2, lead 1, tin 1, m. p. 93.75° C.; and Lipowitz's metal, bismuth 15, lead 8, tin 4, cadmium 3, m. p. 60-65. Cadmium was, of course, not known to Newton, though it occurs in association with zinc ore. Bismuth metal melts at 271° C., tin at 231.84° C. and lead at 327.4° C., so Newton's order of fusibility is not correct.

IV

He tried many proportions of the most easily fusible metals that he knew (58); it is therefore quite just that an alloy of lead 5 + tin 3 + bismuth 8 with a melting point of 94.5° should be known as « Newton's metal », even though these proportions seem to be different from Newton's.

This interest in alloys of low melting point is very likely to be connected with the vexed question of the mercury of metals. Some chemists of the later seventeenth century — like Boyle — rejected the whole concept implied by the term; yet there was a certain logic in it. The conspicuous attribute of mercury was its liquidity; it carried and was pervaded by the form of fluidity, as the more philosophically inclined chemists said, and one recognised its presence in a compound when out of this matter a running mercury could be produced. If it were ever possible to extract a metal fluid at normal temperatures — a « mercury » — from materials into which ordinary mercury did not enter, this would be (unlike quicksilver itself) the true philosophers' mercury. Quicksilver naturally seemed to contain the highest proportion of this philosophers' mercury, but it was logical enough to imagine that, as the melting point of a metal or alloy was lower, so its content of mercury was greater. Thus an alloy liquid at a temperature less than that of boiling water, and also rather dense, would seem not only to approximate to ordinary mercury, but to be very rich in the philosophers' mercury too. Newton may well have once again taken a rationalist view of what the alchemists meant, and have assumed that they hinted at the production of a normally fluid metal other than quicksilver, and so have attempted to reproduce their experiments or gain the same results : but he does not say what purpose the alloy might serve.

In spite of all their confusions and obscurities these are not the experiments of an adept or an esoteric alchemist. They are rather genuine metallurgical and chemical explorations, which afford much insight into Newton's preoccupation with chemistry. We do not know the theoretical purpose which he had in mind, for it is as if we had only Newton's optical experiments without the *Opticks,* or his astronomical calculations without the *Principia.* Whatever his purpose, presumably he never satisfied himself that he had sufficient evidence for firm conclusions, and so there are

(58) MS Add. 3973, Dec. 12, 1678, fol. 1.

no hints from which to guess at his interpretations. This is hardly surprising, for Newton's notebooks where they deal with other topics than chemistry are equally empirical. We are no more justified in hazarding, from what is available here, a picture of the kind of book on chemical philosophy that Newton might have written, than we would be in deducing the *Principia* and *Opticks* from his experimental and mathematical notes. Conversely, the very fact that we should be extremely unlikely to infer these two classics in science from the extant notebooks, teaches us how rash it would be to infer the poverty of his chemical philosophy from the laconic materials described above, a lesson reinforced by the *Quæries* in the *Opticks*. A study of the chemical notes confirms the knowledge otherwise obtained about Newton's method of working; ideas were firmly contained in his mind, it was above all observational detail and matters of fact that he committed to paper. Thus, here, the connection between his experiments on metallic compounds and his theory of attractive affinity is no more tenuous than that between his measurements of interference rings and his theory of optical « fits ».

Hence we can derive from the notebooks no direct answer to the question : what kind of a chemical philosopher was Newton? The historian seeking to answer it must still look elsewhere. On the other hand the notebooks do reveal much about Newton as a chemical experimenter — the range and great duration of his activity, the careful and exact methods he employed, the patience with which he approached his object (whatever that was) from a variety of different points of attack. No one can read these records and doubt that Newton was a good experimental chemist — as good as he was an experimental physicist. And far, far more experienced; Newton's period of experiment in optics lasted perhaps five years — from 1664 to 1669 — chemical experiment occupied him four times as long, and more constantly.

It is perhaps again typical of Newton that the range of his experiment was limited. Unlike other major scientists of his age Newton did not dabble in the whole range of science — in observation with the telescope and microscope, trials with the air-pump and so on. He left quite large areas even of optics untouched. His serious chemistry never ranged beyond the metals and a few of their compounds; of course the multiplicity and complexity of the reactions he investigated (formation of chlorides, oxychlorides,

IV

ammonium salts, oxides and sulphides, metallic acids and so forth) are quite great enough, bearing in mind the feeble analytic resources available. Even today the nature and composition of some compounds that Newton may have stumbled upon appear to be obscure. Newton never — and this was singular in his time — had the slightest interest in medical chemistry, that great inspiration to chemical research. What led him to study metals so intently? One may guess that his study was stimulated by an accident, and two motives. The accident was his interest, arising from optics, in speculum metals. If it is correct to suppose that the reflecting telescope provided his first introduction to practical metallurgy, these first experiments may have provoked questions in his mind about the structure of metals and alloys. The changes in structure and physical properties of bronzes that result from quite small variations in the composition of the alloy are fairly conspicuous, as Newton himself observed. At any rate, there seems no evidence for Newton's having any interest in chemistry before the speculum metal work, and we know that it was in metallic chemistry — and in similar metals — that he was interested soon afterwards. Again, Newton may well have thought that metals would be highly suitable subjects for a study of structural composition, the thought of which was never far from his mind, as McKie and Forbes have well said. (Though it was a thought which might often be overlaid by other, more immediately exciting topics). It is not so easy to « lose » a metal in a sequence of reactions, and it seems easy to identify as precise body. The metals react freely with numerous reagents, giving a variety of different products. Besides this (as Newton remarks in his notes) metals are the symbol of fixity. How better could one plumb the secrets of material structure through chemical means than by explaining this very problem of the fixity and invulnerability of metals? Was there any way of « opening » them, of making them permanently change their physical characteristics, of destroying (to use the later concept) their elementary nature? If something of this could be done, even if it was only possible, for example, to gain some rational knowledge of a fairly rudimentary point, such as the difference between fixed and volatile metallic compounds, would not this be of the greatest benefit to the theory of chemical structure?

Linked with this one cannot overlook the second motive, the

legacy of the alchemists whose influence tended precisely in the same direction, towards the study of metals. Probably we shall never know what directed Newton to alchemical writings, and what was the development of his attitude towards their content. At present it seems that he had no leanings of this kind in his early years, at the epoch of the great discoveries when he was in the prime of his age for invention. One may plausibly suppose that he turned to the alchemists precisely because he had become interested in metallurgical chemistry : where else should he turn for information at that time? There was a side of Newton's mind receptive to the symbolism, concealment and mysticism of alchemy. Many highly intelligent men love the thrill of unpicking a cipher, unravelling a hidden significance (it is the highest flattery to one's sense of superiority); one can hardly doubt that Newton had this passion, and in gratifying it he at the same time met with much straightforward metallurgical chemistry. He can scarcely have failed to recognize that many alchemical writers were at best but dupes of themselves or of others, and at worst brazen liars and cheats. Nevertheless, he seems to have felt that the profoundly esoteric terminology of alchemy was only an extension of the superficially esoteric language of ordinary chemistry; and similarly that the more recondite experimentation of the former was but an extension of the better-known and clearer experimentation of the latter. Newton was not in any admissible sense of the word an alchemist; there is no evidence that any of his processes are of the kind necessarily preliminary to the Great Work, or that he ever hoped to fabricate a factitious gold. That he did seek to correlate alchemical language with experimental facts is clear : one may instance the triumphant remark : « Vidi sal ammoniacum philosophicum. Hic non præcipitatur per salem tartari » (59). We may infer that he hoped to acquire progressively more remarkable facts as he developed the correlation. But it was *always* facts that he sought; and the correlation between his own experiments and alchemical literature was significant only in so far as it indicated to Newton the direction in which he should pursue the experiments which yielded him

---

(59) *Ibid.*, fol. 17. Newton records that 240 gr of « calx albus » with thrice as much fuller's earth and 60 gr of common sal ammoniac gave 104 gr of « philosophical sal ammoniac » apart from 2 or 3 gr which were lost.

facts. One might say that alchemical writings were for Newton only a means to an end — the end being the elucidation of chemical entity and structure. One may well doubt whether Newton was ever interested in alchemical gold; but certainly he was fascinated by the thought of the knowledge that precise exploration of the alchemical path (exploration in his own rational terms) might yield. It was knowledge that might be of outstanding importance for chemical philosophy — enough gold in itself.

· Newton's experiments read like those of a rational, experimental scientist at a time when alchemy could not be discounted — when, one might say, transmutability was a far less vulnerable concept than the chemical immutability of the modern element. Philosophy would have gained as much — far more indeed — from a resolution of metals into constituent fractions as it gained from the resolution of fixed alkalis at the hands of Davy. This, or something like it, some dent on the smiling, passive resistance of iron, copper, lead and tin to all assaults upon their integrity, seems to have been Newton's object. In this he failed; instead of learning more about the nature of metals, he only learned something of the way in which they enter into compounds — important, but a by-product. Yet it was a discovery that only a scientist, and no alchemist, could have made, a fact that seems to clinch the argument for the status of Newton as a scientific and not an alchemical chemist. Of his work as it is known to us one can only comment in his own phrase : « Whence I knew it to be the shadow of a noble experiment » (60).

Marie BOAS.
A. RUPERT HALL.

---

(60) *Ibid.*, fol. 6. This remark follows the record of an experiment in which antimony sublimate was sublimed with lead antimoniate in the proportion of two to one. This mixture proved almost totally volatisable.

* Dr A. Rupert HALL, Lecturer in the History of Science at Cambridge University and Fellow of Christ's College, Cambridge.
Dr Marie BOAS, Associate Professor of History, University of California, Los Angeles.

V

Correcting the *Principia*

As Professor ALEXANDRE KOYRÉ has pointed out, there has been little detailed study of the text of NEWTON's masterpiece, *Philosophiae Naturalis Principia Mathematica* (1). According to a recent announcement in *Isis*, he and Professor I. BERNARD COHEN of Harvard are engaged upon a variorum edition of the book (2); the object of this paper (for which desultory notes were made ten years ago) is to examine the emendations made in that part of it which is in some sense of greatest mathematical interest, and which was most subjected to criticism by NEWTON's contemporaries —the first four sections of Book II. In remedying numerous errors of the first edition of the *Principia* (1687) these sections were extensively revised. The changes are noted below (pp. 302-309), and the more significant of them elucidated in subsequent notes (pp. 309-326).

It is probable that the first edition of the *Principia* numbered no more than about 300 copies; these were fairly soon dispersed by sale or gift—surprisingly quickly for so forbidding a treatise— so that there was talk of a second edition within a very few years (3). But those who hoped for it were as eager to see the errors of the first corrected, as for the readier availability of the text. In August 1691 CHRISTIAAN HUYGENS, in returning a list of errors in the 1687 printing to FATIO DE DUILLIER (4), hoped that in the new edition "tous ces Errata pourroient estre corrigez, et beaucoup de choses obscures eclaircies" (5). FATIO however replied :

---

(1) "Pour une édition critique des œuvres de Newton," *Revue d'Histoire des Sciences* ,1955, vol. 8, 19-37.

(2) *Isis*, 1958, vol. 49, 81.

(3) A. N. L. MUNBY, "The distribution of the first edition of Newton's *Principia*," *Notes and Records of the Royal Society of London*, 1952, vol. 10, 37-8.

(4) On FATIO, see B. GAGNEBIN, "De la cause de la pesanteur. Mémoire de Nicolas Fatio de Duillier," *Notes and Records of the Royal Society of London*, 1949, vol. 6, 105-160.

(5) HUYGENS, "Œuvres Complètes," vol. 10, 209; 18 Dec. 1691.

© 1958 The University of Chicago Press. Reprinted from *Osiris* XIII, 1958 pp. 291–326. Used by permission.

> Il est assez inutile de prier Monsieur Newton de faire une nouvelle édition de son livre. Je l'ai importuné plusieurs fois sur ce sujet sans l'avoir jamais pu fléchir. Mais il n'est pas impossible que j'entreprenne cette édition; à quoi je me sens d'autant plus porté que je ne crois pas qu'il y ait personne qui entende à fonds une si grande partie de ce livre que moi, graces aux peines que j'ai prises et au temps que j'ai employé pour en surmonter l'obscurité.

He proposed to spend some time at Cambridge seeking enlightenment from the author of the *Principia* himself, and thought it would be the occupation of two or three years to enlarge the work into a folio which would be easier to comprehend than NEWTON's quarto (6). Rumours of the new edition, spread by FATIO, reached the Marquis de l'Hospital: HUYGENS warned him that it would not come speedily, for there was an infinity of errors to correct, many of them due to the author, as he confessed himself (7). LEIBNIZ thought that NEWTON's book was one of those best deserving of perfection and that FATIO would do well to take on the task of revising it; it was not astonishing that mistakes should have been made, in so difficult an investigation (8). Two years later, in 1694, when FATIO had abandoned his ambition, DAVID GREGORY appears briefly in HUYGENS' correspondence as a candidate for the editorship—apparently no one now expected NEWTON himself to undertake so laborious a task, and the news of his nervous breakdown led some to suppose that his intellectual powers had vanished for ever (9). On the contrary, NEWTON seems steadily to have contemplated the issue of a new edition, for he noted corrections in an interleaved copy of the first (10), and continued to seek after fresh astronomical data to illustrate the law of gravitation.

(6) *Ibid.*, 213.
(7) *Ibid.*, 346, 354.
(8) *Ibid.*, 261. (To JOHANN BERNOULLI at this time (1697) NEWTON was 'un des Mathematiciens de nôtre temps que j'estime le plus'; 'Der Briefwechsel von Johann Bernoulli,' Basel, 1955, 430).
(9) 'Œuvres Complètes,' 614, 616, 626. In a letter from Oxford (24 November 1694), after raising some questions on pp. 113-4 of the *Principia*, Gregory writes. 'I am glad to understand you have been at London, and that your design of the new edition of your book is going on and in forwardness' (Cambridge University Library, MS Add, 3980, fol. 8). This does not suggest GREGORY's participation.
(10) Cambridge University Library, pressmark Adv. b.39.1.

Four chief criticisms were directed against the *Principia*, one philosophical and three mathematical. The first was, of course, aimed at the Newtonian concept of gravity with its apparently esoteric idea of attraction. The other three concerned the obscurity of NEWTON's language, the mistakes of principle in certain of his demonstrations, in Book II especially, and the vast number of minor slips, some due to the author's, some to the printer's carelessness. Many points of the last kind were such as would cause little difficulty to readers skilled in both Latin and mathematics (others would be unlikely to perceive them), but they marred the perfection of a great book, while a few were faults of consequence. Soon after receiving the *Principia*, in August 1689, HUYGENS engaged in a discussion with NEWTON of his treatment of motion in a resisting medium, which caused the latter to restate his arguments at some length (11). No doubt with his own care of a revised edition in mind, FATIO DE DUILLIER prepared a long list of emendations, which he was still extending in December 1691, and which was also checked by NEWTON himself (12). FATIO reported to HUYGENS:

> Mr Newton recevra parfaitement bien tout ce que Vous avez dit. Je l'ai trouvé tant de fois pret à corriger son livre sur des choses que je lui disois que je n'ay pû assez admirer sa facilité, particulièrement sur les endroits que Vous attaquez. Il a quelque peine à entendre le François mais il s'en tire pourtant avec un Dictionaire (13).

NEWTON's own attitude to mistakes was rather lofty. As he told COTES on one occasion, "You need not give yourself the trouble of examining all the calculations of the Scholium. Such errors as do not depend upon wrong reasoning can be of no great consequence & may be corrected by the Reader" (14). And COTES

---

(11) 'Œuvres Complètes,' vol. 10, 33-4, 321-332; cf. A. R. HALL. 'Ballistics in the Seventeenth Century,' 1952, 145-7.

(12) 'Œuvres Complètes,' vol. 10, 146-155, 215. The more important emendations in FATIO's list were printed in JOHANN GROENING, 'Bibliotheca Universalis seu codex operum variorum,' Hamburg, 1701, as an addendum entitled *Annotata in Newtonii Philos. Nat. Principia Mathematica* (pp. 105-128) to no. vi, *Historia Cycloeidis* (separately paginated 1-128). On p. 112 attention is drawn to the well-known fallacy of Prop. 37, Book II, probably by HUYGENS. Cf. also 'Œuvres Complètes,' vol. 9, 321 n. 1, 323 n. 2.

(13) 'Œuvres Complètes,' vol. 9, 387; 6 March 1690.

(14) J. EDLESTON, 'Correspondence of Sir Isaac Newton and Professor Cotes,' London and Cambridge, 1850, 31.

in his turn found that there was much to do, to make the text of the first edition accurate and satisfactory. There can be no doubt that much more than a reprint was desired and was necessary. Some of the greatest among NEWTON's contemporaries, among them HUYGENS and LEIBNIZ, seem to have hoped that in his revision NEWTON would tone down certain of his glaring heresies—his hostility to the Cartesian theory of matter, his phraseology of attraction, and his opposition to the undulatory theory of light. But whatever might have happened had the *Principia* been reissued in the calm period of the early 1690s—not that NEWTON would ever have modified his philosophy on any major issue—there was no prospect of any relaxation on his part from 1710 onwards, when the quarrel between the Newtonian and the continental philosophers and mathematicians was growing more bitter.

Among the outstanding anti-Newtonian mathematicians of the early eighteenth century was JOHANN BERNOULLI (1667-1748), a close friend and warm admirer of LEIBNIZ, who formulated important criticisms of NEWTON's treatment of the motion of bodies in resisting fluids (15). His attitude towards the *Principia* may be judged from his letters to LEIBNIZ (16). By April 1710 BERNOULLI had heard that a second edition was in preparation, which he was eager to see and curious also to know whether NEWTON had corrected several errors "of which I was the first to be aware' (17). Later he mentions having formerly read the *Principia* very carefully, and made a list of its mistakes. In two letters to LEIBNIZ (12 August 1710, 10 December 1710) BERNOULLI stated his objections in detail : NEWTON had failed to prove, though he had asserted, the inverse law of centripetal acceleration—that if the force towards the centre is inversely as the square of the distance, a body must describe a conic section in its motion about the centre (18); NEWTON's conclusion in Proposition X, Book II,

---

(15) Cf. HALL, *op. cit.*, 152-6.

(16) Leibnitii et Bernoulli Commercium Philosophicum et Mathematicum,' Lausanne and Geneva, 1745.

(17) *Ibid.*, vol. II, 223. LEIBNIZ replied : 'Velim discere, quos in priore paralogismos notaris, scilicet hanc veniam petimusque damusque vicissim, optimus ille est qui minimis urgetur' (II, 226).

(18) *Ibid.*, vol. II, 229-231. This question was treated by BERNOULLI in the *Mémoires de l'Académie Royale des Sciences*, 1710 (nouvelle édition, Paris, 1732,

was false by a proportion of 3 to 2 (19); NEWTON's demonstration that a vertical jet of water reaches only half of the height of the supply-head was falsified by experiment; his ideas on the friction between the particles composing fluids were misconceived; and finally BERNOULLI rebuffed NEWTON's attacks on the Cartesian theory of vortices (20). LEIBNIZ's advice that his friend should submit his criticisms privately to NEWTON "vel ad emendanda, vel ad explicanda sua" (21) went unheeded, for BERNOULLI had published his chief sources of difference from NEWTON before the revised edition of the *Principia* appeared, and only one of them, it seems, was privately communicated to NEWTON (22). This was the fallacy of Proposition X, Book II.

The fact that NEWTON had made a blunder of some magnitude was a crux in the controversy between the English and the continental mathematicians. It seems that it was JOHANN BERNOULLI who aggravated the claim that NEWTON did not in fact invent the calculus independently to the wounding judgement that he was not capable of having invented it; even in 1687 the *Principia* revealed NEWTON's inept handling of its fundamental principles. For BERNOULLI argued that NEWTON's mathematical discovery had

---

521-533), reprinted in his 'Opera Omnia,' Lausanne and Geneva, 1742, vol. I, 470-480; and thereafter repeated as an instance of NEWTON's incompetence. The charge was strongly resented by the Newtonians (cf. letter of KEILL to NEWTON, 9 Nov. 1713, Cambridge University Library, Add 3985, fol. 2).

(19) 'Commercium Philosophicum,' vol. II, 231-2. This defect was also worked up by BERNOULLI in the Paris *Mémoires* (1711, 47-56), 'Opera Omnia,' vol. I, 502-8, in an article that also discusses adversely Props. XV and XVI of Book II; again in the long paper "De motu corporum, gravium, pendulorum et projectilium" in the *Acta Eruditorum* (February 1713, 77-95; March 1713, 115-132), 'Opera Omnia,' vol. I, 515-558, and was generally used as witness to NEWTON's weakness in the principles of the calculus. See below Note 8, p. 313.

(20) 'Commercium Philosophicum,' vol. II, 331, 374, 376-382.

(21) *Ibid.*, 244. BERNOULLI could indeed write 'Monui Newtonum quorumdam suorum errorum, verbis tamen mollissimis, ne Virum hunc offenderem, mihi alioquin satis benevolum, utpote qui me novissime Societati Regiae Londinensi ultro proposuit, atque cooptari fecit . . .' (*ib.*, 299) but his language in print (see below, p. 317) hardly matched the grace of his sentiment.

(22) According to whom the existence of a mistake (but not the just solution), was pointed out 'in his Unkle's name' by NICHOLAS BERNOULLI 'in Autumn 1712' (C.U.L., Add. 3968, fol. 481). Cf. NEWTON's letter to COTES (below, p. 317), and JOHANN BERNOULLI, 'Opera Omnia,' vol. I, 556. But according to the *Addition* attributed to NICHOLAS ('Opera Omnia,' vol. I, 509-510) it was NICHOLAS himself who discovered the 'cause' of the error.

been a method of solving equations by the use of infinite series; he had not discovered an equivalent to the Leibnizian calculus and it was wrong to suppose that whatever NEWTON had found out and concealed was the same as that which LEIBNIZ had discovered and published openly. Now NEWTON had used the method of series for the solution of Proposition X—and the answer he derived was false; this, argued BERNOULLI, was because he was not mathematician enough to appreciate the difference between his method and that of LEIBNIZ (23).

The English reacted violently (24). NEWTON, in a private memorandum of 7 June 1713 accounted for his lapse thus (after describing the visit paid him by NICHOLAS BERNOULLI):

Mr Newton corrected the error himself, shewed him the correction & told him that the Proposition should be reprinted in the new Edition wch was then coming abroad. The Tangents of the Arcs GH and HI are first moments of the Arcs FG & FH & should have been drawn the same way with the motion describing those arcs, whereas through inadvertency one of them had been drawn the contrary way, & this occasioned the error in the conclusion (25).

To KEILL, who was puzzled to know what BERNOULLI was getting at (26), he wrote of BERNOULLI's article:

It appears thereby that I did not understand ye 2nd fluxions when I wrote that Scholium [i.e. to Prop. X] because (as he thinks) I take

(23) As KEILL wrote later, 'I am almost confident that he wrote that paper [in the *Acta Eruditorum*, 1713] on purpose to show that you did not understand 2nd Fluxions' (to NEWTON, May 19, 1714, C.U.L., Add. 3985, fol. 7).

(24) KEILL to NEWTON, 26 April 1714: 'I have read both the pieces concerning the Commercium [Epistolicum] inserted in the Journal Litéraire [i.e. for November and December 1713; second edition, vol. II, La Haye, 1739, 445-453; the second piece is a French version of the 'Charta Volans'] and I think I never saw any thing writ with so much impudence falshood and slander as they are both I am of opinion that they must be immediatly answered and I am now drawing up an answer wch I will finish as soon as I hear from you . . .' (C.U.L., Add. 3985, fol. 5).

(25) C.U.L., Add. 3968, fol. 481.

(26) KEILL to NEWTON, 26 April 1714: 'I only want to know what he means by saying that their are things in your principia contrary to the Doctrine of Fluxions if it be that where you say the terms of the series for the binome are the first 2nd and 3rd Fluxions &c. But this is not in the Principia but in the book of Quadratures and it is plain you only mean that they are Proportional. I would likewise know who that great Mathematician is who has long ago observed it, and who it is I doe not find in the Acta Lipsiae.'

the second terms of the series for the first fluxions, the third terms for the second fluxions & so on. But he is mightly mistaken when he thinks that I there make use of the method of fluxions. Tis only a branch of ye method of converging series that I there make uses of (27).

KEILL, thus primed by NEWTON (as in many other instances), was now ready to defend the national honour in the *Journal Littéraire*—published at the Hague (28)—in an article read and amended by NEWTON himself. But even KEILL had to admit that NEWTON had never clearly expressed the relations between fluxions and the successive terms of the binomial expansion (29). There, thankfully, we may leave this arid dispute, noting only that NEWTON was able to correct Proposition X while continuing to assert the appropriateness of the form of reasoning he had employed in the first edition (30).

It does not seem to be clear why the *Principia* was not re-issued in the 1690s, nor why in 1708 NEWTON decided to bring it out at last in a revised form. BENTLEY was the successful instigator of a new edition; the story has it that NEWTON allowed him to undertake it for profit "because he was covetous and wanted money." It was RICHARD BENTLEY who decided on the style of

---

(27) EDLESTON, *op. cit.*, 171, 173. Thereby to a certain extent BERNOULLI's view of NEWTON's mathematical invention was justified. NEWTON *had* made use of series, where the followers of LEIBNIZ used differentials. Moreover, there were the awkward passages in the *Tractatus de Quadratura Curvarum* to overcome (below, p. 319).

(28) The same journal had previously published Leibnizian views, above n. 24.

(29) All this is interesting for its bearing on the methods used by NEWTON not in demonstrating but in discovering some of the more recondite propositions of the *Principia*. His own statements indicate that he never used fluxions at any stage in his work on Prop. X (since if he had used an accurate fluxional method in the first instance, he would have recognised the mistake in the demonstration worked out for the book). NEWTON indeed could not claim both the use of fluxions in this particular instance—as BERNOULLI credited him with their use, though not revealed explicitly in the demonstration—and the perfection of the fluxional method itself. He was forced to either to deny that he had used fluxions at all (which seems to be true), or to admit that his use of them had been faulty. It would therefore seem that even in 1687 NEWTON's mathematical method was still highly eclectic, and that a fluxional analytical attack on a problem by no means invariably preceded the working out of a demonstration by the synthetic method.

(30) See below, p. 317. As the unreconstructed form of the fluxions scholium in the second edition serves to remind us, this had been finished shortly before the quarrel between NEWTON and LEIBNIZ reached its height of foolish acerbity.

the new printing and struck off specimen pages; it was BENTLEY who appointed ROGER COTES as editor (". . . he does it at my Orders, to whom he owes more than y^t. And so pray you be easy as to y^t; we will Care y^t no little slip in a Calculation shall pass this fine Edition . . ."); it was BENTLEY who wrote to NEWTON after the book was out "I thank you anew y^t you did me the honour to be its conveyor to ye world" (31). Posterity has been more properly cognizant of the devoted labour COTES applied to his formidable task. Approved by NEWTON in May 1709, it was not until September that he received from him a corrected text extending to Book II, Proposition XXXIII, Corollary II (p. 320) and was able to begin work.

As editor of the second edition COTES seems to have played a more active role than NEWTON originally intended for him. In his first surviving letter to COTES (11 October 1709) NEWTON wrote:

---

(31) BENTLEY to NEWTON, 10 June 1708 : 'By this I hope you have made some progress towards finishing your great work, wch is now expected here with great impatience, & the prospect of it has already lower'd ye price o ye former Edition above half of what it once was. I have here sent you a specimen of ye first sheet, of wch I printed about a Quire : so y^t the whole will not be wrought off, before it have your approbation I bought this week a hundred Ream of this Paper you see; it being impossible to have got so good in a year or two (for it comes from Genoa) . . . I hope you will like it & ye Letter too, wch upon trials we found here to be more suitable to ye volume than a greater, & more pleasant to ye Eye. I have sent you likewise ye proof sheet, y^t you may see what changes of pointing, putting letters Capital, &c I have made, as I hope, much to ye better. This Proof sheet was printed from your former Edition, adjusted by your own corrections and additions. The alterations afterwards are mine : which will shew & justify themselves, if you compare nicely the proof sheet with ye finishd one. The old one was without a running Title upon each page, wch is deformd. Y^e Sections only made wth Def. I. Def. II. which are now made full & in Capitals DEFINITIO. I. &c. Pray look on Hugenius de Oscillatione, wch is a book very masterly printed, & you'll see that is done like this. Compare any period of ye Old & New; & you'l discern in ye latter by ye chang of points and Capitals a clearness and emphasis, y^t the other has not; as all y^t have seen this specimen acknowledg. Our English compositors are ignorant & print Latin Books as they are used to do English ones; if they are not set right by one used to observe the beauties of ye best printing abroad. In a few places I have taken ye liberty to chang some words, either for ye sake of ye Latin, or ye thought it self . . . But all these alterations are submitted to your better judgment; nothing being to be wrought off finally without your approbation . . .' (Trinity College, Cambridge, MS R. 4.47, 19; cf. also nos. 20 and 24; BREWSTER, vol. II, 248-252). Despite BENTLEY's self-praise, few would now agree that the second edition of the *Principia* is typographically so superior to the first. NEWTON's copy of HUYGENS' *Horologium Oscillatorium* is now in private possession in California.

I would not have you be at the trouble of examining all the Demonstrations in the Principia. Its impossible to print the book wthout some faults & if you print by the copy sent you, correcting only such faults as occurr in reading over the sheets to correct them as they are printed off, you will have labour more then it's fit to give you (32).

From the correspondence it is apparent that COTES took a more serious view of his editorial responsibility and had a more meticulous sense of the need to bring the new edition from the press as perfect as possible. He could not but be sensitive to the delicacy of his position : NEWTON was much his senior in years, and had won his deservedly great fame by the very text which COTES was now amending in detail. He must also have been aware of the well-known peculiarities of NEWTON's temperament. Hence he wrote diffidently in the early stages of the revision :

I have ventured to make some little alterations myself whilst I was correcting the Press such as I thought either Elegancy or Perspicuity or Truth sometimes required. I hope I shall have y^r pardon if I be found to have trusted perhaps too much to my own Judgement, it not being possible for me without great inconvenience to ye work & uneasiness to y^r self to have y^r approbation in every particular (33).

As the book progressed, however, COTES did not hesitate to persist when confident of his rectitude; for instance, in dealing with Proposition XV, Book II, he refused to allow that NEWTON's amendments were sufficient, and persuaded NEWTON that his own version was correct. The author of the *Principia* excused himself on the familiar ground that "I have of late years disused myself" from such matters. In revising the Scholium Generale after Proposition XL COTES ignored a certain suggestion of NEWTON's, preferring his own emendation. In the end, as COTES remarked, "besides your own corrections & those I acquainted You with whilst the Book was printing, I may venture to say I made some Hundreds, with which I never acquainted You" (34).

Cordial, if not warm, relations never failed between NEWTON and COTES, for the latter was always a staunch Newtonian, contemptuous of continental critics. When the time came to con-

---

(32) EDLESTON, *op. cit.*, 5.
(33) EDLESTON, *op. cit.*, 9.
(34) *Ibid.*, 168.

sider a preface for the new edition, COTES even proposed an open attack on LEIBNIZ, which was vetoed by both NEWTON and BENTLEY, "else, y^t will be ye reply, (not that its untrue) but y^t its rude & uncivil" (35). NEWTON was reluctant to be "examined" on what COTES might write, and it may be doubted whether a draft of the preface printed by COTES was ever approved by NEWTON.

COTES' attention, throughout the correspondence printed by Edleston, is given to mathematical matters to the almost complete exclusion of other issues until this question of the preface is reached. Only on the subject of attraction was he inclined to cavil at NEWTON's expression of his philosophy and of his mode of inquiry. That all attraction is mutual "I am persuaded, . . . when the Attraction may properly be so called" wrote COTES, obscurely, but he did not believe that the supposition of an attractive force's residing in a central body could be qualified as other than a hypothesis. Moreover it was necessary that the *Principia* should be "cleared from some prejudices which have been industriously laid against it. As that it deserts Mechanical causes, is built upon Miracles, & recurrs to Occult qualitys". (Once again LEIBNIZ was the villain of the piece). In consequence NEWTON drafted some additions to the General Scholium of Book III which he sent to COTES on 28 March 1713 (36). In large part, therefore, such variations between the first and second editions of the *Principia* as have any philosophical interest originated with its author.

COTES was a competent mathematician, but it was beyond his power to remedy the greatest single defect of the *Principia*, its outmoded mathematical texture, even had he wished to do so. By 1713 the ascendancy of the Leibnizian calculus among the mathematicians of the continent was assured; the geometrical demonstration, familiar to HUYGENS and others as well as to NEWTON in 1687, was already obsolete. Given the situation that prevailed in England at the time it was impossible that the obsolete should not be preserved, but that it was preserved was a tragedy for English science. The first and second editions of the *Principia*

---

(35) EDLESTON, *op. cit.*, 149-150.
(36) EDLESTON, 151-6; cf. I. BERNARD COHEN, "Franklin and Newton," Philadelphia 1956, 136-7.

bridge a crisis in the history of mathematics, whose effects are well illustrated by the contrast in mathematical character between the discussions of HUYGENS and LEIBNIZ of NEWTON's treatment of motion in fluids (1691), and JOHANN BERNOULLI's paper in the *Acta Eruditorum* (1713). The *Principia* was to remain a classic fossilized, on the wrong side of the frontier between past and future in the application of mathematics to physics. Thus so far as the future was concerned COTES' laborious correction of the details of mathematical argument was pointless: very soon only English readers would care, or need, to struggle with NEWTONS' ponderous theorems.

Masses of material relevant to the correction of the *Principia* have been preserved in the Portsmouth Collection (Cambridge University Library). These include letters exchanged between NEWTON and GREGORY, COTES, KEILL and others (many still unpublished); the corrected copy of the first edition (Adv. b. 39.1); and numerous drafts for the revision of particular passages, especially in MS. Add. 3965. (There are also many drafts of the revised fluxions scholium for the third edition of the *Principia*). I have been unable to trace the copy from which the second edition was printed—this after passing through the compositor's hands may have been destroyed later by COTES. At Trinity College there are several copies of the first edition of the book (all with the "plures bibliopolas" imprint) bearing emendations in NEWTON's hand: that presented to his College in 1687, which also has "Error" written in the margin in several places; that presented to LOCKE, who noted that NEWTON "errores propria manu correxit"; and that from NEWTON's own library, given to the College by the Pilgrim Trust in 1943 (37). There are also corrections in RICHARD BENTLEY's copy (38). The volume containing the manuscript materials printed by Edleston is pressmarked R 16 38; this also contains drafts by both NEWTON and COTES of their revisions, and includes NEWTON's holograph of the General

---

(37) Pressmark NQ 16 200; Proposition X is uncorrected in this copy, but the equations on p. 268 are corrected.

(38) The copy owned by W. W. ROUSE BALL has written in it all the variants of the second edition, perhaps done by 'Dr Burdell who Communicated His Thoughts to Sr Isaac on ye first edition, on which he made these Corrections and Alterations.'

V

302

Scholium concluding the *Principia* (39). BENTLEY's letters to NEWTON, and others concerning the *Principia*, dispersed at the Lymington sale in 1936, are in MS. R 4 47.

TABLE COMPARING THE READINGS OF THE FIRST AND SECOND EDITIONS OF THE *PRINCIPIA*

BOOK II, SECTIONS I-IV

Page	EDITION I	EDITION II	Page
237	*Si corpori resistitur in ratione velocitatis, & sola vi insita...*	*velocitatis, et idem sola vi...*	212
239	ut Resistentia Medii in principio...	ut resistentiae Medii principio...	213
240	acquisitam, ut vis data gravitatis qua perpetuo urgetur, ad excessum vis hujus supra vim qua in fine temporis illius resistitur.	perpetuo urgetur, ad vim resistentiae qua in fine temporis illius impeditur. *(Note 1)* *†	214
241	Describatur Hyperbola quaevis GTBS secans erecta perpendicula... & rectis GK, DP in *t* & V occurrat;...	Asymptotis DC, CP, describatur Hyperbola quaevis GTBS secans perpendicula... * & rectis EH, GK, DP in I, *t* & V occurrat...*	215
	aequalem $\dfrac{tGT}{N}$, & projectile...	aequalem $\dfrac{tGT}{N}$, vel quod perinde est, cape R*r* aequalem $\dfrac{GTIE}{N}$, & projectile...*	
		Corol. 1. Est igitur R*r* aequalis $\dfrac{DR \times AB}{N} - \dfrac{RDGT}{N}$, ideoque si producatur RT ad X ut sit RX aequalis $\dfrac{DR \times AB}{N}$, (id est, si compleatur parallelogrammum ACPY, jungitur DY secans CP in Z, &	217

---

(39) Of which he wrote to COTES: 'I intended to have said much more about the attraction of the small particles of bodies, but upon second thoughts I have chosen rather to add but one short paragraph about that Part of Philosophy' (2 March 1712/3; EDLESTON, *op. cit.*, 147). Any surviving draft of NEWTON's first thoughts would be invaluable.

† The explanatory notes on this table of variants will be found below, pp. 309 sqq. This symbol * signifies that the emendation is found in the interleaved copy of the first edition of the *Principia*; Cambridge University Library, Portsmouth Collection, Adv. b, 39.1.

producatur RT donec occurrat DY in X;) erit Xr aequalis $\frac{\text{RDGT}}{\text{N}}$, & propterea tempori proportionalis.*
Corol. 2. Unde si capiantur innumerae CR vel, quod perinde est, innumerae ZX, in progressione Geometrica; erunt totidem Xr in progressione Arithmetica. Et hinc Curva DraF per tabulam Logarithmorum facile delineatur.*

242 *Corol. 1.* Hinc si vertice...

Corol. 3. Si vertice D,... *(the remainder is as in I, corols. 1-5.)*

245 longitudinem DP ut modo inventa longitudo DF ad longitudinem eandem per experimentum cognitam, erit vera...

longitudinem DP, ut longitudo DF per experimentum cognita ad longitudinem DF modo inventam, erit vera... 219

245 *Scholium.* Caeterum corpora resisti in...

Scholium. Caeterum, resistentiam corporum esse in...* 219

vacant (uti posthac demonstrabitur) corpora resistuntur in...

vacant resistentiae corporum sunt in...*

Actione corporis...

Etenim actione corporis...

246 & *sola vi insita*...

& *idem sola vi insita*...* 220

proportionales...

proportionalia...*

249 resistentia & corpus conjunctim...

resistentia & tempus conjunctim...* 223

aequivelocia corpora resistuntur...

aequivelocibus corporibus resistitur...

aequivelocia corpore resistuntur...

aequivelocibus corporibus resistitur...

250 Nam tempus augetur in ratione resistentiae diminutae, & spatium augetur in ratione temporis.

(Sentence omitted) (Note 2)

aequivelocia corpora resistuntur...

aequivelocibus corporibus resistitur...

applicata...

applicati...

resistentiae sint ut D^n & E^n...

resistentiae, ubi velocitates aequales ponuntur, sint ut D^n & E^n...

spatia quibus amittent...

spatia quibus Globi, quibuscunque cum velocitatibus moti, amittent.

resistentiae, &...

resistentiae auctae, &... 224

Lemma II. aequatur momentis Terminorum...

Lemma II. aequatur Momentis laterum singulorum...*

ex Terminis...

ex lateribus vel terminis...*

251 Cave tamen intellexeris particulas finitas. Momenta, quam primum finitae sunt magnitudinis, desinunt esse momenta. Finiri enim repugnat aliquatenus perpetuo eorum incremento vel decremento. Intelligenda sunt principia...

particulas finitas. Particulae finitae non sunt momenta, sed quantitates ipsae ex momentis genitae. Intelligenda sunt... *(Note 3)**

Termini... hunc Terminum... & contenti ABC... & dignitatum

Lateris... hoc latus... & geniti contenti ABC... genitarum dignitarum...*

252 Ponatur AB aequale... Ponantur A, B, C, aequalia; & ipsius...

253 $2aA^{-\frac{1}{2}}$ ... id est $maA^{m-1} + nbB^{n-1}$;

254 & notarum formulis. Utriusque fundamentum... dimidiata ratione...

256 dimidiata ratione...

Corol. 4. Sed & particula temporis, quo spatii particula quam minima NKLO in descensu describitur, est ut rectangulum KN × PQ. Nam quoniam spatium NKLO est ut velocitas ducta in particulam temporis; erit particula temporis ut spatium illud applicatum ad velocitatem, id est ut rectangulum quam minimum KN × KL applicatum ad AP. Erat supra KL ut AP × PQ. Ergo particula temporis est ut KN × PQ, vel quod perinde est, ut $\frac{PQ}{CK}$. Q.E.D.

Corol. 5. Eodem argumento particula temporis, quo spatii particula nklo in ascensu describitur, est ut $\frac{pq}{Ck}$.

257 ut tempus descensus omnis praeteriti.

ut $\frac{pq}{Ck}$, id est, per Corol. 5, Prop. VIII. ut particula temporis.

258 ut $\frac{PQ}{CK}$; & propterea per Corol. 5. Prop. VIII. Lib. II. ut particula temporis incremento velocitatis PQ respondens.

259 spatium ABRP, quod corpus tempore quovis... ABKN & AVD ut spatia tota ab initio descensus descripta.

Ponatur AB semper aequale... Ponantur latera A, B, C, sibi mutuo semper aequalia; & ipsius...* 225

$\frac{1}{2}aA^{-\frac{1}{2}}$ ... id est $maA^{m-1} B^n + nbB^{n-1} A^m;$* 226

notarum formulis, & Idea generationis quantitatum. Utriusque fundamentum... 227

subduplicate ratione...*
subduplicata ratione... *(Note 4)** 228
(These two corollaries are omitted.)
(Note 5)

ut tempus descensus omnis praeteriti. Si modo sectorum Tangentes Ap, AP sint ut velocitates.* 229

ut $\frac{pq}{CK}$, id est ut velocitatis decrementum quam minimum pq directe & vis illa Ck quae velocitatem diminuit inverse, atque adeo ut particula temporis decremento respondens. *(Note 5)*

ut $\frac{PQ}{CK}$, id est, ut incrementum velocitatis directe utque vis generans incrementum inverse, atque adeo ut particula temporis incremento respondens. *(Note 5)* 230

spatium quod corpus... ab initio genitae ABNK & ATD ut spatia tota ab initio descensus descripta. *(Note 6)* 231

260 indeque datur & spatium quod semisse velocitatis illius dato tempore describi potest, & tempus quo corpus velocitatem... in ratione temporum; dabitur... quae est ad Sectorem ut spatium quaesitum ad spatium jam ante inventum.	indeque datur tempus quo corpus... 232 *(Note 7)* in ratione tempus dati ad tempus modo inventum, dabitur... quae est ad sectorum ADT vel AD*t* ut spatium quaesitum ad spatium quod tempore dato, cum velocitate illa maxima jam ante inventa, uniformiter describi potest.
260 *tum corporis velocitas in iisdem locis.* Sit AK planum illud plano Schematis perpendiculare; ACK linea curva... *(through to p. 263, end of Corol. 2.)*... ut rectangulum CF in FG—kl ad 4FG *quad.*	*tum corporis velocitas & Medii re-* 232 *sistentia in locis singulis.* Sit PQ planum illud plano Schematis perpendiculare;... *(through to p. 234, end of Corol. 1.)*... & Medii densitas erit ut $\dfrac{S \times AC}{R \times HT}$. *(Note 8)*
263 *Corol. 3.* ... linea definiatur... AB... BC... *(In Exempl. 1. also the notation of the points in the figure is different, but I have not noted these variations.)* secundum in quo quantitas illa extat unius dimensionis;... insistentis ad indefinitae quantitatis initium B;...	*Corol. 2.* ... linea PFHQ definia- 234 tur... AC... CH... secundum in quo quantitas illa est 235 unius... insistentis ad initium indefinitae quantitatis *o*...
264 Terminus quartus, qui hic est $\dfrac{anno^3}{2e^5}$, exhibet variationem...	Terminus quartus determinat va- 236 riationem...
Praeterea CF est latus quadratum... *(continuing to p. 265)*... corpus illud describet circuli quadrantem LCK. Q.E.I.	Conferatur jam series... *(continuing to)* ... corpus illud describet Circuli quadrantem FHQ.Q.E.I.
266 per]pendicularem egrederetur, sumenda esset OB seu *a* ...	perpendicularem egrederetur, & in arcu semicirculi PFQ moveri inciperet, sumenda esset AC seu *a*...
terminus $\dfrac{c-2a}{b}$ *o* pro Q*o*, & ejus coefficiens $\dfrac{c-2a}{b}$ pro Q; tertius item terminus $\dfrac{oo}{b}$ pro R*oo*, & ejus coefficiens $\dfrac{1}{b}$ pro R. quarti termini S*o*³ coefficiens S evanescere,...	terminus $\dfrac{c-2a}{b}$ pro Q*o*, tertius 237 autem terminus $\dfrac{oo}{b}$ pro R*oo*. quarti coefficiens S evanescere,...

268 $\sqrt{1 - \frac{mm}{nn}}$ (this expression in the first long bracket is a misprint.)
XY ad YG ... XY ad YG
Pro DN, BD, NX scribantur ... (misprint)
269 capiatur VY aequalis $n \times$ VG, est reciproce ut XY.

Resistentia autem in eodem loco G sit ad Gravitatem ut S in $\frac{XY}{A}$ ad 2RR, id est XY ad $\frac{3nn + 3n}{n + 2}$ VG.

269 Scholium. Quoniam motus non sit in Parabola...

Compleatur parallelogrammum XYGT, & ex natura harum Hyperbolarum facile colligitur quod recta
270 Gt tangit Hyperbolam...
resistentia autem ad vim gravitatis ut GT ad $\frac{3nn + 3n}{n + 2}$ VG.
occurrat Asymptoto NX in H, actaque AI occurrat alteri...
ac resistentia ibidem ad Gravitatem ut AH ad $\frac{3nn + 3n}{n + 2}$ in AI...
Si servetur Medii densitas in A & mutetur...

271 Hyperbolae minor est quam in loco A, ut servetur densitas...
densitas in A, per Regulam tertiam, diminui in ratione paulo minore quam semisummae Tangentium ad Tangentem AH.
& minus accuratae in ejus descensu ad G; & contra. (misprint)
272 invenienda sunt plura puncta N: & tum demum si per omnia agatur Curva linea regularis NNXN, haec abscindet SX quaesitae... determi-

$\sqrt{1 + \frac{mm}{nn}}$ 238
3XY ad 2 YG ... 3XY ad 2YG
Pro BN, BD, NX scribantur...* 239
capiatur VY aequalis $n \times$ VG, densitas illa est reciproce ut XY.*
sit ad gravitatem ut 3S in $\frac{XY}{A}$ ad
4RR, id est, XY ad $\frac{2nn + 2n}{n + 2}$ VG.
(Note 9)

Scholium. Eadem ratione qua prodiit densitas Medii ut (down to)... 240
Sed redeamus ad Curvas simpliciores. (Note 10)
Quoniam motus non sit in Parabola...

Compleatur parallelogrammum XYGT, & recta GT tanget Hyperbolam...
resistentia autem ad vim gravitatis ut GT ad $\frac{2nn + 2n}{n + 2}$ GV.
occurrat Asymptoto MX in H, actaque AI eidem parallela occurrat alteri (MX is a misprint)...
AH ad $\frac{2nn + 2n}{n + 2}$ in AI... (Note 9)
Si servetur tum Medii densitas in 241
A, tum velocitas quacum corpus projicitur, & mutetur... (a)
in loco A, ut habeatur densitas... 242
densitas in A augeri in ratione paulo majore quam semisummae harum tangentium ad minimam tangentium GT. (Note 11)
ad K...
puncta N: & per omnia agenda Curva linea regularis NNXN, secans rectam SMMMM in X. Assumatur demum AH... Augenda est

(a) Cf. Cotes to Newton, 15 April 1710, Edleston pp. 8-12.

CORRECTING THE PRINCIPIA

273	Agatur CH, occurens ipsis AK & KF, illi in C,... *(misprint)*	
274	$\sqrt{\dfrac{2\mathrm{TG}q}{nn - n\mathrm{XVG}}}$	
	De motu corporum quae resistuntur partim in ratione...	
	Si corpus resistitur... & sola vi... proportionales, quadam quantitate...	
276	capiendo GD ad GR ut est velocitas... spatium quodvis ABED descriptum.	
278	summa virium gravitatis DBq ... *(misprint)* est ut summa resistentiae APq + 2ABP... (also on p. 279)	
279	angulo DAB recto... *(misprint)*	
280	Prop. XIV. Prob. IV. *Iisdem positis, dico quod spatium ascensu vel descensu descriptum, est ut summa vel differentia areae per quam tempus exponitur...*	
281	*Corol. Igitur si longitudo aliqua V sumatur in ea ratione ad arcum ET, quam habet linea... (down to) ... adeoque,*	
282	ubi V & AP quam minimae sunt, in ratione aequalitas. Aequalis igitur est area quam minima...	
283	*rectanguli TQ × PS ad PQ quad. erit ratio aequalitas.* TS vel PS ad PE, seu PO ad PS. ut PQ ad PO... PQ ad PS... aequalis PQ × PS.Q.E.D. *(misprint)*	
284	Prop. XV. Theor. XI. Temporibus aequalibus describat corpus arcus quam minimos PQ & QR, sintque areae PSQ, QSr aequales. Et quoniam... PQq × SP ... in dimidiata ratione... in dimidiata ratione... in dimidiata ratione...	
285	In Medio non resistente areae	

	autem densitas Medii per Reg. 4; & resistentia modo inventa, si in eadem ratione augeatur, fiet accuratior. *(Note 12)* illi in E,...*	243
	$\sqrt{\dfrac{2\mathrm{GT}q}{nn - n\mathrm{XVG}}}$ *(Note 13)*	244
	*De Motu Corporum quibus resistitur partim in ratione...**	245
	*Si corpori resistitur... & idem sola vi... proportionales, data quadam quantitate auctae,...**	
	capiendo GR ad GD, ut est velocitas... spatium quodvis RSED descriptum. *(Note 14)**	247
	summa virium gravitatis DAq..* resistentiae APq + 2BAP...* (also on p. 279)	248
	angulo DBA recto...*	249
	Propositio XIV. Theorema XI. *Iisdem positis, dico quod spatium ascensu vel descensu descriptum, est ut differentia areae per quam tempus exponitur... (Note 15)*	250
	Corol. Igitur si longitudo aliqua V sumatur in ea ratione ad duplum longitudinis M, quae oritur... (down to)... adeoque	251
	ubi areae DET & DAP quam minimae sunt, in ratione aequalitas. Aequalis igitur est area... *(Note 16)* (b)	252
	*rectanguli TQ × 2PS ad PQ quad...** seu 2PO ad 2PS.* ut PQ ad 2PO... PQ ad 2PS... aequale TQ × 2PS *(Note 17)**	253
	Propositio XV. Theorema XII. Tempore quovis, in Medio resistente, describat corpus arcum quam minimum... *(down to)... quas simul generant. Quoniam...* $\tfrac{1}{2}$PQq × SP... in subduplicata ratione... in subduplicata ratione... in subduplicata ratione...*	254
	Quoniam decrementum arcus PQ,	255

(b) Cf. EDLESTON, p. 10.

aequales PSQ, QSr (per Theor. I. Lib. I.) temporibus aequalibus describi... *(down to)...* Est igitur resistentia ut...
coeuntibus, SP & SQ coincidunt; & ob similia triangula...

286 Nam vires illae sunt ut lineae Rr × TQ seu ut $\frac{\frac{1}{4}VQ \times PQ}{SQ}$, & $\frac{PQq}{SP}$ quas simul generant, hoc est ut $\frac{1}{4}$VQ & PQ, seu $\frac{1}{2}$OS & OP. corpus descendet ad centrum, dimidia semper cum velocitate qua probavimus in superioribus... fieri. Unde tempora descensus hic erunt dupla majora temporibus illis atque adeo dantur.

Si centro S intervallis duobus datis describantur duo circuli; numerus revolutionum quas corpus... circumferentias complere potest... sive ut Tangens anguli quem... earundem ut $\frac{OP}{OS}$, id est reciproce ut...

287 in dimidiata ratione... (id est, ut BS ad mediam proportionalem inter AS & CS) corpus illud...

& quam proxime ut $\frac{2}{3}$ AS ad AB.

288 & statue numerum revolutionum... esse ad numerum revolutionum... esse Tangentem anguli... ad tangentem anguli quo... angulorum secantes ita esse tempora revolutionum... revolutiones eisdem ab invicem...
Prop. XVI. Theor. XII
Si Medii densitas in locis singulis sit reciproce ut dignitas aliqua distantiae locorum a centro, sitque...

ex resistentia oriundum... *(down to)...* quadratum temporis conjunctim; erit resistentia ut... *(Note 18)*
coeuntibus, SP & SQ coincidunt, & angulus PVQ sit rectus; & ob similia triangula...
Nam vires illae sunt ad invicem ut 256 $\frac{1}{2}$Rr × TQ sive ut $\frac{\frac{1}{4}VQ \times PQ}{SQ}$ & $\frac{\frac{1}{2}PQq}{SP}$, hoc est, ut $\frac{1}{4}$VQ & PQ, seu $\frac{1}{2}$OS & OP. *(Note 19)*
corpus descendet ad centrum, ea cum velocitate quae sit ad velocitatem qua probavimus in superioribus... fieri, in subduplicata ratione unitatis ad numerum binarium. Et tempora descensus hic erunt reciproce ut velocitates, atque adeo dantur. *(Note 20)*
Si centro S intervallis duobus quibuscunque datis... Circuli; & manentibus hisce Circulis, mutetur utcunque angulus quem Spiralis continet cum radio PS: numerus revolutionum... circumferentias, pergendo in Spirali a circumferentia ad circumferentiam, complere potest... sive ut Tangens anguli illius quem... earundem ut $\frac{OP}{OS}$, id est, ut Secans anguli ejusdem, vel etiam reciproce ut...
in subduplicata ratione... (id est, ut AS ad mediam proportionalem inter AS & BS) corpus illud... *(Note 21)*

sive ut $\frac{2}{3}$AS ad AB quam proxime. 257
& statue tempus revolutionum... esse ad tempus revolutionum... esse Secantem anguli... ad Secantem anguli quo... angulorum tangentes ita esse nu- 258 meros revolutionum... revolutiones iisdem ab invicem...
Propositio XVI. Theorema XIII.
sit reciproce ut distantia locorum a centro immobili, sitque... ut dignitas quaelibet ejusdem distantiae: dico...

CORRECTING THE PRINCIPIA

289 *ut distantia in dignitatem illam ducta: dico...*

sive ut $\dfrac{\frac{1}{2}n\text{VQ}}{\text{PQ} \times \text{SP}^n \times \text{SQ}}$ adeoque ut $\dfrac{\frac{1}{2}n\text{OS}}{\text{OP} \times \text{SP}n^{n+1}}$. Et propterea densitas in P est reciproce ut SP^n.

sive ut $\dfrac{(1 - \frac{1}{2}n) \times \text{VQ}}{\text{PQ} \times \text{SP}^n \times \text{SQ}}$, adeoque ut $\dfrac{(1 - \frac{1}{2}n) \times \text{OS}}{\text{OP} \times \text{SP}^{n+1}}$, hoc est, ob datum $\dfrac{(1 - \frac{1}{2}n) \times \text{OS}}{\text{OP}}$, reciproce ut SP^{n+1}. Et propterea, cum velocitas sit reciproce ut $\text{SP}^{\frac{1}{2}n}$, densitas in P erit reciproce ut SP. *(Note 22)*

NOTES

The following notes relate chiefly to the major differences between the first and the second editions of the *Principia*, in the sections of the second book here discussed. Variations which require no explanation receive no comment. I have in general translated the reading of the first edition, while that of the second is available (with few modifications) in the published Motte-Cajori translation; this should not be relied on in detail, however, without careful comparison with the original Latin text.

The headings given below are those of the first edition. The relevant page numbers of both editions are quoted for convenience.

Note 1. [pp. 240/214. Prop. III. Prob. I. Corol. I. 'Therefore the greatest velocity that the body can acquire in falling, is to the velocity acquired in any given time, as the given force of gravity perpetually acting upon it, to the excess of this force over the force of resistance at the end of that time'].

The version given in II and III is sufficiently explained by considering the second paragraph of the proposition. For (in Newton's figure) the greatest velocity of descent (V_T) is BACH, which also represents the force of gravity; and the velocities (V_I) after equal times of descent are represented by the rectangles ABkK, ABlL etc., to which by supposition the resistances are proportional. That is, generally,

$$\text{BACH} : \text{AB}x\text{X} = \text{BACH} : \text{AB}x\text{X}, \text{ or } V_I = \frac{R}{g} V_T.$$

Thus when $R = g$, $V_I = V_T$, for no further acceleration is possible. In I, however, Newton effectively put

$$\text{BACH} : \text{AB}x\text{X} = \text{BACH} : (\text{BACH} - \text{AB}x\text{X}), \text{ or } V_I = \frac{g-R}{g} V_T,$$

which is impossible since as R increases $(g - R) \to 0$

Note 2. [pp. 250/223. Prop. VII. Theor. V. Corol 2. 'For the time is increased in the ratio of the reduced resistances, and the distance is increased in the ratio of the time.'] (1)

Doubtless this sentence was omitted because it is virtually repeated lower on the same page, in Corol. 5.

Note 3. [pp. 251/224. Lemma II. 'Be cautious, however, in your understanding of finite particles. Moments, as soon as they are of finite magnitude, cease to be moments. To be finite is in some measure contrary to their continual increase or decrease. They are to be understood as the just nascent principles of finite magnitudes.']

As is well known, Newton had great difficulty in expressing accurately his conception of moments, and in justifying their use in terms of mathematical theory. In I he asserts that moments are infinitely small. In II he reverses the statement, so as to say that finite 'particles' are not moments, and says further that they are quantities generated by the moments. This leaves the status of the 'moment' itself very obscure. Cf. MOTTE-CAJORI, pp. 653-4. Mathematically, of course, the 'moment of A^n' is equivalent to $\delta(A^n) = n\delta A . A^{n-1}$.

Note 4. [pp. 253/226; 254/227; 256/228].

The variants on these pages result from the correction of fairly obvious mathematical or typographical errors. Thus $\frac{a}{2A^{\frac{1}{2}}}$ is clearly $\frac{1}{2}aA^{-\frac{1}{2}}$, not $2aA^{-\frac{1}{2}}$.

Note 5. [pp. 265/228. Prop. VIII. Theor. VI. Corols 4 and 5. 'But the instant of time in which the least distance NKLO is described in descent, is as the rectangle KN × PQ. For since the distance NKLO is as the velocity multiplied by the time, the instant of time is as that distance divided by the velocity, that is, as the least rectangle KN × KL divided by AP. Above, KL was as AP × PQ. Therefore the instant of time is KN × PQ or, which is the same thing, as $\frac{PQ}{CK}$. Q.E.D.

(*Corol.* 5). By the same argument, the interval of time in which the least space *nklo* is described in ascending is as $\frac{pq}{ck}$.']

Presumably in revising the *Principia* Newton thought these relations of insufficient general interest to stand as corollaries. They are, however,

---

(1) A proposed alteration in NEWTON's interleaved copy of I reads 'Nam tempus quo corpus datam motus partem amittit augetur in . . .'

CORRECTING THE PRINCIPIA 311

required in Prop. IX. Theor. VII. (pp. 257/229, 258/230); since these relations were omitted as corollaries from II, it was necessary to expand the text of this proposition somewhat in the revised edition.

In I, p. 258, last line, 'Corol. 5' is a mistake for 'Corol. 4.'

Note 6. [pp. 259/231. Prop. IX. Theor. VII. Corol. 1. 'Hence if AB is equal to a quarter of AC, the space ABRP which the body describes in falling during any time ATD, will be to the space which the body could describe in the same time by moving uniformly at half its maximum velocity AC, as the area ABRP (which expresses the distance fallen) to ATD (which expresses the time). For as AC to AP is as AP to AK, 2AP.PQ equals AC.KL (by Corol. 1, Lemma II of this [Book]), and likewise $\frac{KL}{PQ} = \frac{2AP}{AC}$.

Thus
$$\frac{LK.KN}{\frac{1}{2}PQ.AD} = \frac{LK.KN}{DPQ} = \frac{2AP.KN}{\frac{1}{2}AC.AD}.$$

But $\frac{DPQ}{DTV} = \frac{CK}{AC}$. Equally, therefore, $\frac{LK.KN}{DTV} = \frac{2AP.KN.CK}{\frac{1}{2}AC^3}$

that is, because $CK.KN = \frac{1}{4}AC^2$, as $\frac{AP}{AC}$; that is, as the velocity of the falling body to the maximum velocity that it can attain. Since therefore the moments LKNO and DTV of the areas ABKN and AVD are as the velocities, all the parts of these areas generated in the same times will be as the spaces described in the same times; and similarly the whole areas ABKN and AVD, generated from the beginning, [are] as the whole spaces described from the beginning of the descent. Q.E.D.].

This corollary was thoroughly revised in the second edition. (2)

There is indeed something odd about the Q.E.D. of I. Whereas Newton asserts at the commencement
$$\frac{S}{S_1} = \frac{ABRP}{t} \quad (t = ADT; S_1 = \frac{1}{2}AC.t);$$
he concludes
$$\frac{S}{S_1} = \frac{ABNK}{t + \delta t} \quad (t + \delta t = ADT + DTV = ADV).$$

---

(2) For translation of the new version, see MOTTE-CAJORI, p. 256. Note here, line 10, a misprint; read instead KN : AC or AD = AB : CK.

The interleaved copy of I contains a partial correction of this corollary.

While $t + \delta t > t$, ABNK < ABRP. Wisely, therefore, in II he omits all mention of the area ABRP (which does not figure in the proof of the Corollary in I), and writes in the first sentence that ABNK expresses the (lesser) distance, agreeably with the conclusion. This substitution appears to rectify a simple mistake in notation. But the error of writing AVD $(t + \delta t)$ in the conclusion of the argument, in place of ADT (t), also corrected in II, is more complex. It appears to arise from the curious construction with which Cas. 2 begins ('Draw DQV cutting off the least intervals TDV and PDQ of the sector DAV and of the triangle DAQ...'), for that is what this line DQV does *not* do; rather it *adds* the moments DTV, DFQ to the already existing areas ADT, ADP. Until DQV is drawn ADV and DPQ do not exist. Since the body is falling, AD$t = t$, and DTV $= \delta t$, while AP $= v$ and PQ $= \delta v$. Newton's instructions for the construction (not amended in either II or III) would make ADV $= t$, and DTV $= -\delta t$. Confused by his own misleading expression, in the conclusion of the corollary in I he makes DTV the (negative) moment of ADV instead of the (positive) moment of ADT, which it properly is. Hence the conclusion of II:

$$\frac{S}{S_1} = \frac{ABNK}{t} \quad (t = ADT)$$

is correct.

It will be observed that though the geometrical argument of II has been recomposed, it is identical with that of I and arrives at the same result in the penultimate sentence, i.e. that $\frac{LKNO}{DTV} = \frac{AP}{AC}$. Hence the word *semisse* (I, p. 259, line 8) is a third mistake, for AC represents the terminal velocity, not its half (Prop. VIII, Corol. 2). This again is duly corrected in II.

Note 7. [pp. 260/232. *ibid.*, Corol. 6. 'Hence from the given time there is given the space described in ascent or descent. For the maximum velocity of the body in an infinite fall is given (by Corol. 2, and 3. Theor. VI. BK. II.), whence *both the space that can be described at half that velocity in the given time, and* the time in which the body would acquire that velocity by falling in a non-resisting space, is [sic] given...'] (3).

The omission of the italicised words is necessitated by the correction just discussed. The other modifications of the text of the corollary simply serve to make the matter more clear.

---

(3) The interleaved copy reads '. . . & spatium quod velocitate illo dato tempore . . .'

CORRECTING THE PRINCIPIA

Perhaps it may be remarked that the argument of Prop. IX (in both versions) is very closely dependent on that of Prop. VIII. It is impossible to comprehend the former without constantly bearing in mind what has been said in the earlier argument.

Note 8. [pp. 260/232 *et seq.* Prop. X. Prob. III. '*Suppose the uniform force of gravity to tend directly to the plane of the horizon, and the resistance to be as the product of the density of the medium and the square of the velocity. it is required to find the density of the medium at every point, which shall make a body move in any given curved line, and the velocity of the body at those points.* Let AK be a plane perpendicular to the plane of the figure; ACK a curved line; C a body moved along it; and FC*f* a straight line touching it at C. The body C is supposed first to progress from A to K by the line ACK, then to regress by the same line; and in its progress it is imagined to be impeded by the medium, while in its return it is equally assisted by the medium. Thus in the same points the advancing and returning velocities of the body will be always the same. In equal times the body will describe during its advance the least arc CG, and in its return the arc C*g*; and CH, C*h* are equal straight lengths which the body, in its motion from the point C, would describe in these times were the effects of the medium and of gravity abstracted. From the points C, G, *g* the perpendiculars CB, GD, *gd* are dropped to the horizontal plane AK, of which GD and *gd* meet the tangent [at C] in F and *f*. Because of the resistance of the medium against the advance of the body, instead of the length CH it describes only the distance CF; and because of the force of gravity the body is brought from F to G; thus the little lines HF, FG [representing] the force of resistance and the force of gravity are generated together. In the same way (by Lem. X Bk. I) the little line FG is as the force of gravity and the square of the time conjointly, and thus (since the gravity is given) as the square of the time. And the little line HF is as the resistance and the square of the time, that is, as the resistance and the little line FG. And hence the resistance is as HF directly and FG inversely, or as $\frac{HF}{FG}$. These relations hold when the little lines are nascent. For when they are of finite magnitude these ratios are not accurate (4).

And by a similar argument *fg* is as the square of the time, and so, because the times are equal, is equal to FG; and the impulse by which the returning body is urged forward is as $\frac{hf}{fg}$. But the impulse on the

---

(4) Cf. Note 3 above.

returning body and the resistance to its advance at the beginning of the motion are equal, and thus the two proportionals $\dfrac{fh}{fg}$ and $\dfrac{HF}{FG}$ are equal, and because $fg = FG$, hf and HF are also equal. Thus CF, CH (or Ch) and Cf are in arithmetical progression, and hence HF is half the difference between Cf and CF; and the resistance which was stated above as $\dfrac{HF}{FG}$ is as $\dfrac{Cf - CF}{FG}$. (5)

However, the resistance is as the density of the medium and the square of the velocity. But the velocity is as the length traversed CF directly, and the time $\sqrt{FG}$ inversely, which is as $\dfrac{CF}{\sqrt{FG}}$, and thus the square of the velocity is as $\dfrac{CF^2}{FG}$. For which reason the resistance, proportional to $\dfrac{Cf - CF}{FG}$, is as the density of the medium and $\dfrac{CF^2}{FG}$ conjointly, and hence the density of the medium is as $\dfrac{Cf - CF}{FG}$ directly and $\dfrac{CF^2}{FG}$ inversely. That is, as $\dfrac{Cf - CF}{CF^2}$. Q.E.D. (6)

Corol. 1. And thus it is found, that if Ck is taken in Cf equal to CF, and the perpendicular ki is dropped to the horizontal plane AK cutting the curve ACK in l, the density of the medium is as $\dfrac{FG - kl}{CF(FG + kl)}$.

For fC will be to kC as $\sqrt{FG}$ or $\sqrt{fg}$ to kl, and by division,

$$\dfrac{fk}{kC} = \dfrac{Cf - CF}{CF} = \dfrac{\sqrt{FG} - \sqrt{kl}}{\sqrt{kl}},$$ which is (if both terms are multiplied by $(\sqrt{FG} + \sqrt{kl})$:

$$\dfrac{Cf - CF}{CF} = \dfrac{FG - kl}{kl + \sqrt{FG \cdot kl}} = \dfrac{FG - kl}{FG + kl},$$ for the initial ratio of the nascent [quantities] $(kl + \sqrt{FG \cdot kl})$ and $(FG + kl)$ is equal. Therefore

---

(5) I.e., from the argument and the figure, $Cf = Ch + fh$, $CF = CH - FH$, hence $Cf - CF = fh + FH = 2\,FH$. The relation given above should be $\dfrac{\frac{1}{2}(Cf - CF)}{FG}$.

(6) Read $\dfrac{Cf - CF}{2CF^2}$, and below, $\dfrac{FG - kl}{2CF(FG + kl)}$.

CORRECTING THE PRINCIPIA   315

$\frac{FG - kl}{FG + kl}$ is written for $\frac{Cf - CF}{CF}$, and the density of the medium, which was $\frac{Cf - CF}{CF^2}$, becomes $\frac{FG - kl}{CF(FG + kl)}$.

Corol. 2. Whence since 2HF and $Cf - CF$ are equal (7), and since the sum of FG and kl (because of their ratio of equality) (8) is 2FG, 2HF will be to CF as FG — kl to 2FG; and hence HF to FG, that is the resistance to the gravity, is as the rectangle CF(FG — kl) to 4FG².

Corol. 3. And so if the curved line [ACK] is defined by the relation between the base or abscissa AB, and the applied ordinate BC (as is usual) and the value of the applied ordinate be resolved into a converging series, the problem may be expeditiously solved by the first terms of the series, as in the following examples.']

With the third corollary, and the discussion of converging series, the text of II substantially follows for a time that of I, and the translation appears *mutatis mutandis*, in Motte-Cajori, p. 260, line 6, through to p. 261, line 17. From this point, however, II develops very differently, and I continue with the translation of I.

[pp. 264/236. 'Whence, by the way, appears the not despicable usefulness of these series in the solution of problems which depend upon tangents and the curvature of curves. Moreover CF is equal to $\sqrt{CI^2 + IF^2}$, that is, $\sqrt{BD^2 + \frac{a^2o^2}{l^2}}$. (9) And FG + kl is equal to twice the third term, and FG — kl equal to double the fourth. For the value of DG is converted into the value of il, and the value of FG into the value of kl, by writing Bi for BD, or —o for +o. Hence as FG is $\frac{-n^2o^2}{2e^3} - \frac{an^2o^3}{2e^5}$ etc., kl will be $\frac{-n^2o^2}{2e^3} + \frac{an^2o^3}{2e^5}$ etc. And of these the sum is $-\frac{n^2o^2}{e^3}$, the difference $-\frac{an^2o^3}{e^5}$. The fifth and following terms I neglect here, as they are infinitely too small to be considered in this

---

(7) See preceding note and compare page 314.
(8) It seems curious to argue that FG + kl = 2 FG, while FG — kl ≠ 0.
(9) Note that NEWTON here identifies the successive *geometric* elements of the line IG in his figure with the successive terms of his algebraic series, excluding the first term. But there is no formal proof that the elements and the terms do, in fact, correspond exactly. This procedure is also followed in the revised version of II, but somewhat more cautiously.

problem. Therefore if we designate the series universally by these terms: $\pm Qo - Ro^2 - So^3 \ldots$ etc., CF will be equal to $\sqrt{o^2 + Q^2o^2}$, $FG + kl$, equal to $2Ro^2$, and $FG - kl$ equal to $2So^3$. For CF, $FG + kl$, and $FG - kl$ these values are written, and the density of the medium which was $\dfrac{FG - kl}{CF(FG + kl)}$ becomes $\dfrac{S}{R\sqrt{1 + Q^2}}$. Therefore by reducing the problem to an infinite series, and here writing the terms of the series corresponding, then taking the resistance of the medium in any point G to be to the gravity as $S\sqrt{1 + Q^2}$ to $2R^2$, and the velocity to be that with which the body C, issuing along the line CF, would [*in vacuo*] move along a parabola having the diameter CB and latus rectum $\dfrac{1 + Q^2}{R}$, the problem is solved (10).

Thus in the problem already solved, if $\sqrt{1 + \dfrac{a^2}{e^2}}$ or $\dfrac{n}{e}$ is written for $\sqrt{1 + Q^2}$, $\dfrac{n^2}{2e^3}$ for R, and $\dfrac{an^2}{2e^5}$ for S, the density of the medium will work out as $\dfrac{a}{ne}$, that is, since n is given, as $\dfrac{a}{e}$ or $\dfrac{OB}{BC}$, that is, as the length of the tangent CT which terminates at the semidiameter OL erected perpendicular to AK; and the resistance will be to the gravity as a to n, that is as OB to the radius of the circle OK, but the velocity will be as $\sqrt{2BC}$. Therefore if the body C, with a certain velocity, leaves L moving parallel to the line OK, and the density of the medium is in every place C as the length of the tangent CT, and the resistance also in every place C is to the gravity as OB to OK, the body will describe the quadrant of a circle LCK. Q.E.I.

But if the same body were to issue forth from A along the line perpendicular to AK, OB or a must be taken on the opposite side of the centre O, and therefore its sign must be changed by writing $-a$ for $+a$. But Nature does not admit of a negative density (that is, one which would accelerate the motion of the body), and therefore it cannot naturally happen that a body describe the quadrant of circle AL by

---

(10) These expressions are, of course, approximations neglecting minor terms. Thus $2(R + So)^2$ has been silently approximated to $2R^2$.

ascending from A. To produce such an effect the body would have to be accelerated by an impelling medium, not impeded by a resisting one.'] (11)

It will be observed, from a comparison of the texts of I and II, that while a similar algebraic argument is adopted in both versions, the geometrical parameters fed into it from the discussions of the physical situation (as represented by the figures) are different. The result is, that while the expressions for the density of the medium $\left(\frac{a}{e}\right)$ and the velocity of the body ($\sqrt{2e}$) are the same in both texts, the ratio of the resistance to the gravity is modified by a factor of $\frac{3}{2}$. Thus, taking Example 1 (the circle) this ratio appears in I as $\frac{a}{n}$, in II as $\frac{3a}{2n}$. Thus in his second edition Newton accepted the corrected expressions printed by Johann Bernoulli in the *Mémoires* of 1711 and the *Acta Eruditorum* of 1713 (12).

In Theorem VI of his paper Bernoulli demonstrates the following proposition: 'In order that a body moving in a resisting medium may describe a circle LCK, on the supposition that a uniform gravity tends directly towards the horizontal, I say that the resistance in each point C will be to the gravity as 3OG to 2OK.' This hypothesis for the resistance is the same as Newton's, and his results differ only by this factor of 3/2.

In a scholium following his theorem Bernoulli criticises Newton's proposition in the *Principia* (I), translated above.

'The ratio of 3OG to 2OK assigned by us between the resistance and the gravity certainly departs from the Newtonian, in as much he gives it as OG to OK, that is in the proportion of 2 to 3 less than ours. Lest any one who is unable to examine these matters more deeply should

---

(11) This last rather ridiculous paragraph—for (ignoring the rotation of the Earth) a body projected vertically from its surface can never move other than in a straight line—is repeated also in II.

This erroneous proposition stands uncorrected in the interleaved copy of I, which therefore must have been prepared before NEWTON knew of BERNOULLI's paper of 1713. There are drafts of revisions in C.U.L. MS Add. 3965 (12), fols. 190-199. A version almost exactly agreeing with that printed in II is found on fols. 192-3.

(12) The former seems not to have been noticed by NEWTON. Cf. his letter to COTES (14 October 1712): 'There is an error in the tenth Proposition of the second Book, Prob. III, w[ch] will require the reprinting of about a sheet & a half. I was told of it since I write to you, & am correcting it.' NEWTON and COTES had already passed these pages as correct. EDLESTON, *op. cit.*, p. 142.

wonder whether perhaps we were mistaken in confuting what has been disclosed with so much labour by this most acute man, I will demonstrate here that this Newtonian ratio leads to a contradiction. For if the resistance be to the gravity as OG to OK as Newton has it, then since the gravity itself is to the tangentical force as OC or OK to OG, equally the resistance would be to the tangential or motive force as OG to OG; therefore the resistance will be equal to the motive force, and the velocity at any point C uniform, whereas we previously showed it to be $\sqrt{CG}$, and consequently non-uniform, as Newton himself agrees.' (13)

Bernoulli continues with an analysis of the source of Newton's error:

'The mistake into which he fell does not lie in his own solution, which may be taken as just and free from vitiating paralogisms (though it is not a little tortuous and difficult to comprehend) but is to be sought in its method of application. . . . In the series which expresses DG he takes every term for some differential of the indeterminate DG, or as he calls it, a fluxion of so many degrees as there are powers of o in that term, which may be true of the first and second but for the rest not at all. For example, let DG be as some simple power of OB or a, so that DG may be taken as $(a + o)^p$ which expressed in a series in the Newtonian manner yields:

$$DG = a^p + pa^{p-1}o + p\frac{(p-1)}{2!}a^{(p-2)}o^2 + p\frac{(p-1)(p-2)}{3!}a^{p-3}o^3 + \text{etc.}$$

The terms [of this series] should, in Newton's opinion, successively express the differentials of DG of all degrees, in the same order. However, excepting the first and second terms, that all the rest differ from the true differentials is indicated by the ordinary rules for differentiation. For, taking a as indeterminate, of which the differential δa is supposed constant, if the power a^p is successively differentiated it is found that the first differential is $pa^{p-1}\delta a$, the second $p(p-1)a^{p-2}\delta^2 a$, the third $p(p-1)(p-2)a^{p-3}\delta^3 a$, the fourth $p(p-1)(p-2)(p-3)a^{p-4}\delta^4 a$ &c. Whence, substituting the letter o for δa, and taking a^p (inasmuch as it is the differential of the lowest or zero degree) for the first term, there arises the series: $a^p + pa^{p-1}o + p(p-1)a^{p-2}o^2 + p(p-1)(p-2)a^{p-3}o^3 +$ etc. The sum of these differentials, it is obvious, is different from that of the other [Newton's] series . . . for although the first two terms agree in both, the others differ in being multiplied by numerical coefficients.'

In fact if the terms of the series to which geometrical elements are made equivalent are modified to $Qo - 2Ro^2 - 6So^3$ . . ., in order to

---

(13) I.e., in NEWTON's notation, $\dfrac{R}{g} = \dfrac{a}{n}$; but $\dfrac{g}{f} = \dfrac{n}{a}$; thus $f = R$.

cancel the binomial coefficients, the ratio of the resistance to the gravity can be made correct. But the new series does not give the density accurately. Thus Bernoulli's suggestion fails to work, because he had not noticed Newton's simple numerical error, already pointed out, in which the expression $\dfrac{Cf - CF}{FG}$ and everything derived from it is too great by a factor of 2. No doubt Bernoulli was assisted in jumping to his mistaken exposure of the paralogism by Newton's treatment of second and third fluxions in the *Tractatus de Quadratura Curvarum*, though he does not mention this work (14). Here, in the introduction (§ 10), the fluxion of $(x)^n$ is taken from the binomial expansion of $(x + o)^n$ in such a way as might suggest that the second fluxion would be the second term of the expansion, that is, $\dfrac{n(n-1)x^{n-2}x}{2}$. (15) And in the final scholium of the *Tractatus* Newton wrote:

'We said formerly that there were first, second, third, fourth &c. Fluxions of flowing Quantities. These Fluxions are as the Terms of infinite converging Series.

Thus if z^n be the flowing Quantity, and by flowing become $(z + o)^n$, and afterwards be resolved into the converging Series

$$z^n + noz^{n-1} + \frac{n^2 - n}{2} o^2 z^{n-2} + \frac{n^3 - 3n^2 + 2n}{6} o^3 z^{n-3} \ldots \&c.$$

The first Term of this series will be that flowing Quantity; the second will be the first Increment or Difference, to which consider'd as nascent, it's first Fluxion is proportional; the third $\dfrac{n^2 - n}{2} o^2 z^{n-2}$ will be it's second Increment or Difference, to which consider'd as nascent the second Fluxion is proportional . . .' (16).

---

(14) NEWTON claimed that this treatise was written in 1676; it was published as an addition to the first edition of *Opticks* in 1704.

(15) SAMUEL HORSLEY, 'Isaaci Newtoni Opera quae exstant omnia,' London, 1779, I, 336-7. JOHN STEWART, 'Sir Isaac Newton's two Treatises of the Quadrature of Curves,' London, 1745, 4.

(16) HORSLEY, *op. cit.*, I, 384; STEWART, *op. cit.*, 30. STEWART (275) was right in supposing, and HORSLEY (384, note) mistaken in denying, that it was KEILL who suggested that the word 'ut' had been thrice omitted, so amending the text to read, 'the second [third, fourth . . . term] will be *as* the first [second, third . . .] increment or difference . . .' It appears in KEILL's letter to NEWTON, Apr. 20 1714, Add. 3985, fol. 5, cf. *Journal Littéraire*, 2nd edn., IV, 348. In any case NEWTON did not state that the fluxions would be given by omitting the numerical coefficients, which would have been correct.

This plainly says that the second fluxion is $\frac{n(n-1)}{2} z^{n-2}\dot{z}$, etc. Who could blame Bernoulli for supposing that Newton's ideas about second and third fluxions were confused? (17)

Edleston states the source of Newton's error correctly (18). He had, from page 262 onwards, taken FG ($= \text{R}o^2 + \text{S}o^3$) in place of fg ($= \text{R}o^2 + 2\text{S}o^3$). Thus the ratio of the resistance to the gravity should be

$$\frac{\text{CF}(fg-kl)}{4\text{FG}^2} = \frac{3\text{S}\sqrt{1+\text{Q}^2}}{4\text{R}^2}$$

and the density of the medium should be (see p. 316 above).

$$\frac{fg-kl}{2\text{CF}(fg+kl)} = \frac{3\text{S}}{4\text{R}\sqrt{1+\text{Q}^2}}. \quad (19)$$

Forced by Bernoulli's report to revise the whole of this proposition, Newton was nevertheless able to adhere to his belief in the utility of series for the solution of such problems, of which Bernoulli had ventured to be sceptical. Thus the new version of Prop. X follows the same mathematical lines as the old, though the geometry is very different. Thus Newton had his revenge, by proving that the problem could be solved by the method he had chosen for his demonstration in the first instance, and without the detested Leibnizian differentials!

Note 9. [Prop. X, *continued*]. It is unnecessary to discuss these various minor changes in formulation in detail, since they are all consequential on the revision already described, and in the proportion already enunciated by Bernoulli.

A separate figure for the parabolic trajectory (*Exempl. 2*) appears for the first time in III.

Note 10. [pp. 269/240. *Scholium*.] The first paragraph in II, presenting the most general function relating the density and resistance, is a straightforward addition to the text.

---

(17) KEILL, while seeking to vindicate NEWTON, really accuses him of the same fault. For he—unwisely ignoring NEWTON's careful declaration that he had avoided fluxions altogether in Prop. X—makes NEWTON assign the correct quantity to a line representing the second fluxion: which line for NEWTON himself represented a term in a series! KEILL thus does not at all account for the error.

(18) *Op. cit.*, 171, note.

(19) These are the results of II, although NEWTON with typical casualness forgets the numerical coefficients.

CORRECTING THE PRINCIPIA 321

Note 11. [pp. 271/242. *Reg.* 4. 'Since the density of the medium is less near the vertex of the hyperbola than it is at the point A, in order to preserve a mean density, the ratio of the least of the tangents GT to the tangent AH should be found, and then the density at A ought to be diminished, by Rule 3, in a proportion a little less than that of half the sum of the tangents to the tangent AH.'] (20)

The problem here is to describe the trajectory of a projectile, assuming that (in the resisting medium) this approximates to an hyperbola. But for the projectile to move *exactly* in a hyperbola, the density of the medium would have to be greater about the vertex, than towards the ends of the curve. That the version of II is correct on this point may be easily seen by inspecting the lengths of $\frac{1}{XY}$ on the figure, Examples 3 and 4.

But in fact the density of the air is nearly constant, and certainly does not increase with height above the Earth's surface; hence it is necessary to introduce the correction of Rule 4, which is reversed in II because the position was wrongly stated in I.

Note 12. [pp. 272/242. *Reg.* 7. 'By the like method, several points N may be found from assumed lengths AH. Then, lastly, if the regular curve NNXN is drawn through all of them, it cuts off SX equal to the required length AH. For mechanical [i.e. practical] purposes it is enough to make the lengths AH, AI, the same for all angles HAK. If, however, the figure is to be used for determining the resistance of the medium more accurately, these lengths should always be corrected in accordance with the fourth Rule'.]

This is incorrect. In the first step, AI and AH were assumed lengths which have the effect of determining (with the given angles HAK, *h*AK) the shape of the conic hyperbolae taken to represent the trajectories, and hence the location of their asymptotes. But if AH was ill chosen with respect to AI in the first place, and a fresh value AH′ = SX be established by following the procedure of the second step, it is still necessary to make the new value AK′ (found from AI, AH′, and ‹ HAK) correspond with the value of AK obtained in the experiment. The second step of I, by itself, gives only the correct *ratio* of AK to A*k*, and hence of AI to AH′. The final correction is made by a third step, added in II, which adjusts AI and AH′ to their proper values, without altering the ratio between them, so that all the elements of the figure are upon the same scale.

---

(20) There is a partial revision in the interleaved copy.

Note 13. [pp. 274/244. *Reg.* 8]. The root sign in I, p. 274 line 2, appears to be a straightforward mistake or misprint. The function two lines further down contains the 'Bernoulli error' (see above), which an inadvertence escaped correction in II. It was altered to the correct value $\left(\frac{2n(n-1)}{n-2}\text{ VG}\right)$ in III.

Note 14. [pp. 276/247. Prop. XII. Theor. IX. *Corol.* 2.]
In the figure annexed to Prop. XII (in I and II the same figure as for Prop. XI, but differing slightly in III), the hyperbolic area ABED represents the time of the motion, and DESR the space traversed during that time. If the velocities at the beginning and end of these time and space intervals are V_o and V_1 ($V_o > V_1$, clearly), then by Prop. XI $\frac{V_o}{V_1} = \frac{GD}{GA}$. Prop. XII establishes that $\frac{V_o}{V_1} = \frac{GR}{GD}$ also.

Therefore, in considering Corol. 2 of this proposition, it appears that ABED (I) is a mistake for DESR (as in II), since it is a space of which D and R are the limits. Further, by confusion probably with Prop. XI (where reciprocals were involved), Newton appears to have been thinking of $\frac{V_o}{V_1} = \frac{1/GR}{1/GD}$, instead of the direct relation $\frac{V_o}{V_1} = \frac{GR}{GD}$.

Note 15. [pp. 280/250. Prop. XIV. Prob. IV. 'The same things being supposed, I say that the space described in the ascent or descent is as the sum or difference of the area by which the time is expressed, and of some other area which is augmented or diminished in an arithmetical progression: if the forces compounded of the resistance and the gravity be taken in a geometrical progression.]
The words 'summa vel' are a mistake, arising perhaps from some first draft of the argument. There is no question in the proposition of the summation of areas, but only of their subtraction.

Note 16. [pp. 281/251-282/262. *Ibid., Corol.* 'Therefore if any length V is taken in the ratio to the arc ET, of the time DA to the line DE, the space that the body will dsecribe in the resisting medium in its total ascent or descent, will be to the space that could be described in the same time in a non-resisting medium as the difference of these areas to $\frac{\text{BD} \times \text{V}^2}{4\text{AB}}$, and thus is given from the time. For the space in a

CORRECTING THE PRINCIPIA

non-resisting medium is as the square of the time, that is as V^2, and since BD and AB are given, as $\dfrac{BD \times V^2}{4AB}$. However, the time is as DET, or $\tfrac{1}{2}BD \times ET$, and the moments of these areas are as $\dfrac{BD \times V}{2AB}$ mult.plied by the moments of V, and $\tfrac{1}{2}BD$ multiplied by the moment of ET, that is, as $\dfrac{BD \times V}{2AB} \times \dfrac{DA^2 \times 2m}{DE^2}$ and $\tfrac{1}{2}BD \times 2m$, or as $\dfrac{BD \times V \times DA^2 \times m}{AB \cdot DE^2}$ and $BD \cdot m$. And moreover the moment of the area V^2 is to the moment of the difference of the areas DET and AKNb as $\dfrac{BD \times V \times DA \times m}{AB \times DE}$ to $\dfrac{AP \times BD \times m}{AB}$, or as $\dfrac{V \times DA}{DE}$ to AP. Therefore, when V and AP are least, [they are] equal. Thus the least area $\dfrac{BD \times V^2}{4AB}$ is equal to the least difference of the areas DET and AKNb, whence since the spaces described in both mediums [the resisting and the non-resisting] approach equality alike at the beginning of the descent and the end of the ascent, they are respectively as the area $\dfrac{BD \times V^2}{4AB}$ and the difference of the areas DET and AKNb. From their analogous increase it follows that in any equal times they are respectively as that area $\dfrac{BD \times V^2}{4AB}$ and the difference of the areas DET and AKNb Q.E.D.

The translation of the corollary in II is as follows:

'Therefore if any length V is taken in the ratio to a length 2M, M being equal to the area DET divided by the length BD, of the line DA to the line DE, the space that the body will describe in the resisting medium in its total ascent or descent, will be to the space that could be described in the same time in a non-resisting medium as the difference of these areas to $\dfrac{BD \times V^2}{4AB}$, and thus is given from the time. For the space in a non-resisting medium is as the square of the time, or as V^2, and since BD and AB are given, as $\dfrac{BD \times V^2}{4AB}$. The moment of this area, or of the equal area $\dfrac{DA^2 \times BD \times M^2}{DE^2 \times AB}$, is to the moment of the

324

difference of the areas DET and AbNK, as $\dfrac{DA^2 \times BD \times 2M \times m}{DE^2\ AB}$ [m being the moment of M] to $\dfrac{AP \times BD \times m}{AB}$, that is, as $\dfrac{DA^2 \times BD \times M}{DE^2}$ to $\tfrac{1}{2}BD \times AP$, that is, as $\dfrac{DA^2}{DE^2} \times DET$ to DAP. Thus when the areas DET and DAP are least, [these] are equal. Therefore the least area $\dfrac{BD \times V^2}{4AB}$ is equal to the least difference of the areas DET and AbNK.'].

The heart of this corollary is obviously the proof that 'the least area $\dfrac{BD \times V^2}{4AB}$ is equal to the least difference of the areas DET and AKNb', from which the general conclusion follows. There are two mistakes in the process by which this equality is demonstrated in I. (i) It is written that the moment of $\dfrac{BD\,.\,V^2}{4AB}$ is $\dfrac{BD\,.\,V\,.\,DA^2\,.\,m}{AB\,.\,DE^2}$, whereas it is in fact $\dfrac{BD\,.\,V\,.\,DA\,.\,m}{AB\,.\,DE}$: (ii) in the next sentence, 'the moment of the area V^2' is written for 'the moment of the area $\dfrac{BD\,.\,V^2}{4AB}$,' the moment of this latter quantity being now correctly stated. The rest presents no unusual difficulty, save that it might have been better to write 'when ET and AP are equal . . .' The moment of the arc ET is, of course, $2m$.

Instead of correcting these rather trivial slips, Newton rewrote the central part of the argument, introducing a new symbol M = $\tfrac{1}{2}$ET. Therefore V = $\dfrac{DA}{DE}$. ET (as in I), and m is the moment of M. With this modification the rest of the argument is unchanged; it is rendered shorter, but hardly more lucid. The errors of I are corrected in II.

Finally, in III, the corollary was again rewritten with some simplification of expression, the length V being now made equal to $\dfrac{DA}{DE}$. M (instead of 2$\dfrac{DA}{DE}$. M. Consequently the arbitrary constant $\tfrac{1}{4}$ is omitted from the expression $\dfrac{BD\,.\,V^2}{4AB}$.

Note 17. [pp. 283/253. Sectio IV. Lemma III.]
The ratio PQ : PO in I becomes PQ : 2PO in II (and III), with con-

CORRECTING THE PRINCIPIA

sequential changes in the rest of the lemma. It can be shown that $\frac{PD}{PQ}$ approximates to $\tan \frac{\angle POQ}{2}$, and that $\frac{PQ}{2PO}$ approximates to $\frac{1}{2} \sin \angle POQ$. When the angle POQ is infinitely small these two functions become equal. The mistake in I may have been due to the misapprehension that $\frac{PD}{PQ}$ tends to $\sin \angle PQD = \sin \angle POQ$—i.e. twice its proper value.

Note 18. [pp. 284/254-285/255. Prop. XV. Theor. XI.]
The revisions here are fairly trivial. An insignificant numerical constant is altered to agree with the new form of Lemma III. However, the sentences in I :
'In a non-resisting medium the equal areas PSQ, QSr, (by Theor. I, Bk. I.) ought to be described in equal times. The difference in these areas, RSr, arises from the resistance; and moreover the resistance is as the decrement Rr of the little line Qr, multiplied by the square of the time in which it is generated. For the little line Rr (by Lem. X, Bk. I) is as the square of the time.'
were not well expressed, and are therefore replaced in II by a fuller argument at the opening of the proposition. In fact Newton meant, not R α R$r \times t^2$, but R$\alpha \frac{Rr}{t^2}$ (i.e. *subduplicato* for *quadrato*), as is clear from the next expression. And if PR = $2 vt - 4 kt^2$, R$r = 2kt^2$ (as in II), not $3kt^2$ which is the decrement of QR.

Note 19. [pp. 286/256. *Ibid, Corol.* 3].
A double error in I produces the correct function ($\frac{1}{2}$ OS : OP). For in I the value of the resistance is mistakenly doubled (R$r = 2kt$), and also the expression for the centripetal force (employing Lemma III) is too large by a factor of 2. It will be noticed that Newton's method of argument by ratios leads to some uncertainty (and indeed arbitrariness) in the use of numerical constants. Cotes had great difficulty here: cf. EDELESTON, pp. 11, 12-19.

Note 20. [pp. 286/256. *Ibid. Corol.* 4. 'Therefore the body cannot revolve in this spiral, unless the force of resistance is less than half the centripetal force. Let the resistance be equal to half the centripetal force, and the spiral will coincide with the right line PS, and in that right line the body will descend to the centre, always with half that velocity with which (as we proved above, Theor. X. Bk. I) the descent would be made in a non-resisting medium in the case of the parabola.

Whence the times of descent here will be twice as great as the times in that case, and are therefore given.']

When the resistance is half the centripetal or moving force, the acceleration is halved and therefore the velocity is divided by 2, as in II. The error of I may have arisen from taking the velocities as proportional to the centripetal forces directly, rather than to their square roots.

Note 21. [pp. 287/256. '. . . and that with a velocity which shall be to its first velocity at A reciprocally as the square root of the distances from the centre (that is, as BS to the mean proportional between AS and CS . . .)]. It is difficult to see why the line CS was brought into the proportion at all, since (as II states correctly):

$$\sqrt{AS} : \sqrt{BS} = AS : \sqrt{AS \cdot BS}.$$

Note 22. [pp. 288-9/258. Prop. XVI. Theor. XII]

The phrase *ut dignitas aliqua distantiae locorum a centro* seems to involve a redundancy, prompted perhaps by the condition that the centripetal force be inversely as any power of the distance; for the density-relation in this theorem is unchanged from that of the preceding proposition. Thus it appears in the proof that the density is inversely as the distance. Otherwise the reference to the preceding proposition would be invalid. The whole argument is bad. It is that of Prop. XV, *mutatis mutandis* (the velocity being $\frac{1}{SP^{\frac{1}{2}n}}$ instead of $\frac{1}{\sqrt{SP}}$ etc.), but the algebra is bodged so that $\frac{1}{2}n \cdot OS$ is obtained in place of $(1 - \frac{1}{2}n)OS$. Since this is a constant the error is unimportant, but then in deriving the density $\left(d = \frac{KR}{V^2} = \frac{KSP^n}{SP^{n+1}}\right)$ NEWTON obtained $\frac{K}{SP^n}$ instead of $\frac{K}{SP}$! Even this does not justify the theorem, for the power chosen for the argument was $(n + 1)$.

One would guess that the drafting of the 'proof' preceded the formulation of the theorem, that in examining the general case $\left(F \propto \frac{1}{SP^{+1}}\right)$, by errors in calculation, Newton arrived at a false law for the density (that he had never proved!) and so wrote this law into the theorem. Certainly revision was very needful here.

The reader may profitably consult my book *Philosophers at War* (Cambridge, 1982) and D.T. Whiteside, *Mathematical Papers of Isaac Newton*, vol. VIII, Cambridge, 1981.

VI

NEWTON'S 'MECHANICAL PRINCIPLES'

By Marie Boas and Rupert Hall

Although the hypothetical discussion of the fundamental properties of matter characteristic of the *Quaeries* to the *Opticks* and of other lesser fragments would seem totally alien to the mathematical rigor of the *Principia,* nevertheless a particulate theory of matter does underly the whole structure of Newton's greatest work.[1] Whereas in other instances Newton's use of the mechanical philosophy is comparable to that of Boyle, it is precisely in the *Principia* that the difference between the general and qualitative explanations of physical phenomena offered by the latter or by Newton himself in the *Quaeries,* and exact mathematical theorems becomes obvious. The particles of the *Principia* are those of mathematical physics; this is never the case with Boyle, or indeed with any other exponent of the mechanical philosophy. From the time of Galileo, the most important property of material particles, other than their impenetrability, had been their capacity for motion. Thus, in the later stages of the mechanical philosophy, the variety of phenomena was ascribed to the variety of corpuscular motions. Despite the mathematization of motion effected by Galileo, however, no progress had been made before the time of Newton in treating the motion of *particles* in a mathematical way, and there was thus no true particulate dynamics. Descartes had seen something of the necessity for this—in recognizing the importance of the laws of impact, for example—but failed to implement it, and so left his particulate theory in a wholly non-mathematical form, a weakness to which Roberval had drawn attention.[2] The concepts of particulate dynamics were widely entertained, and were commonly applied to account for the phenomena of heat, chemical reaction, and so on, but in such physical hypotheses the dynamics of the particulate motions remained as vague and indeterminate as those of the projectile or falling stone in pre-Galilean physics.

This in itself is a curious situation. If the basic premise of the mechanical philosophy be accepted, then dynamics is the fundamental science, the science of the motions of bodies including those of the elementary particles of matter. Indeed, at the macroscopic level, dynamics was the most advanced of seventeenth-century sciences. Yet before the *Principia* no attempt had been made to see whether the broad effects attributed to corpuscular motions were consonant with the principles of the mathematical science of motion that the

---

[1] Cf. Marie Boas, " The Establishment of the Mechanical Philosophy," *Osiris,* X (1952), 506.

[2] R. Lenoble, " Roberval ' éditeur ' de Mersenne et du P. Nicéron," *Revue d'Histoire des Sciences,* X(1957), 241.

VI

century had formulated. For while, on the one hand, the science of motion had become increasingly, in the hands of Galileo's successors —Roberval, Pascal, Wallis, Huygens—a branch of applied mathematics; on the other, the evolution of corpuscularian physics was the product of an essentially non-mathematical tradition—that of Gassendi, Descartes, Boyle, and Hooke. Thus, even though many of the mechanical philosophers were themselves notable mathematicians, there was no interpenetration of the notions of mathematics and natural philosophy in this case.

To the corpuscularian philosophers, a mechanical explanation in terms of matter and motion seemed the very antithesis of a peripatetic explanation in terms of forms and qualities: the one was rational, modern, and reasonable; the other occult, outmoded, and mystical; the former employed real entities, the latter semantic images. Indeed, the mechanical accounts of heat, light, magnetism, and so forth, incline one to immediate agreement, at least when these are compared with the older manner of explanation. Yet consideration suggests that "mechanical explanations" were nearly, if not quite, as occult as the forms and qualities they were designed to replace. For were not the corpuscles as imaginary as the qualities? The philosophers themselves did not and could not agree on their attributes, which were simply postulated as required for the explanation of various phenomena. Despite the sophisticated structure of the mechanical philosophy, it included such primitive elements as Descartes' invention of screwed particles to account for magnetism, or Boyle's occasional association of acidity with the sharpness of the corpuscles, and sweetness with their sphericity.

Moreover, it was intrinsically impossible for any experiment whatever to demonstrate the existence of corpuscles as conceived by seventeenth-century philosophers, much less the correctness of their detailed explanations. Even Boyle could only claim to illustrate the mechanical philosophy by experiments; he did not assert that he could prove his favorite hypothesis. Clearly the great weakness of the mechanical explanation of any phenomenon was its *post hoc* character. For, as formulated before the time of Newton, the corpuscular philosophy permitted neither prediction nor confirmation, being neither mathematical nor truly experimental. Like the ancient philosophies of nature, the seventeenth-century mechanical philosophy provided, for those who accepted its basic premises, a satisfying picture of the world around them, but this picture could no more be derived inevitably from the phenomena than could that of earlier philosophies.

In an age which emphatically demanded that its philosophies be either truly experimental or truly mathematical, this was clearly an anomalous situation, which cried aloud for redress. Newton, steeped as he was in the mechanical philosophies of Descartes and of Boyle, could not avoid accepting the corpuscular philosophy; but equally he could not avoid being acutely aware of its inherent defects. The earliest records of Newton's scientific thought indicate his attachment to corpuscular mechanisms as clearly as do the oft-quoted statements from the *Opticks;* combined with this he understood in a more decided way than most of his contemporaries the rigor and empirical confirmation required for the enunciation of any firm theoretical propositions in science. Since he recognized throughout the veritably hypothetical character of any explanation of phenomena that rested upon the corpuscular structure of matter (the notion of such a structure not being a necessary and unavoidable inference from any experiment), Newton was reluctant to set forward any theoretical proposition (what he sometimes calls his " doctrine ") in such a manner that its authenticity could be judged to stand or fall upon the authenticity of the corpuscular philosophy, in his terms an hypothesis. He might privately hold the tenets of this philosophy, but it was not to be said that his discoveries were founded on his private hypothesis. Hence his careful avoidance of a corpuscular theory of light in 1672, though he favored such a theory; hence his retorts to his critics in subsequent years, and his eagerness to show that his " doctrine " of colors was consistent with both a corpuscular and a pulse theory of light. Hence also the fact that his clearest published utterances concerning the corpuscular philosophy are cast in the conjectural form—except when he is concerned to treat the dynamics of a particle, which *could* be handled in a rigorous, that is, in a mathematical manner. It may be significant that after he had succeeded in this enterprise, in the *Principia,* he allowed himself to discuss the nature and properties of corpuscles with a freedom he had previously denied himself.[3]

Obviously, if a natural philosopher denies himself the use of Aristotelian forms and qualities, and equally that of hooked atoms and other such devices, he is left with nothing but hard particles of matter,[4] possessing only the properties of mass and the capacity to move in accordance with the universal laws of motion, and the forces —whatever they may be—acting between the particles and so conferring motion upon them or perhaps, in a given situation preventing them from moving. If it be assumed that matter does in fact

---

[3] An exception may be made for the " Letter to Boyle " of 1678, but this was a private communication, not for publication, and was in any case highly suppositious.

[4] To assume, at any stage, the existence of other than hard particles is merely to postpone the arrival at smaller constituent particles which must, at least, be taken to be hard.

VI

consist of such particles, then the scientist has only two further problems: what are the natures and properties of the various forces that set the particles in motion (or retain them in a state of rest)? What is the way in which a particle, subjected to the influence of such forces, will move (including in this query the effects of collision between similar or dissimilar particles)? If such questions could be resolved, the theory of matter would be complete. It seems to have been Newton's principal contribution to corpuscular mechanism to have recognized the beautiful, but deceptive, simplicity of this situation. For this is the significance of that celebrated sentence in the *Principia,* from the Preface:

> I wish we could derive the rest of the phenomena of Nature by the same kind of reasoning from mechanical principles, for I am induced by many reasons to suspect that they may all depend upon certain forces by which the particles of bodies, by some causes hitherto unknown, are either mutually impelled towards one another, and cohere in regular figures, or are repelled and recede from one another.

By " the rest of the phenomena " Newton means all of physics apart from the celestial motions and those of the tides, whose theory he had in fact succeeded in deducing from " mechanical principles "—the principles of the mechanical philosophy—by mathematical reasoning. The one universal force in nature, however, to which he could apply both mechanical principles and mathematical reasoning was the force of gravity. And mathematical analysis—" the same kind of reasoning "—could be applied to any other force only if its characteristics were known.

Thus it appeared that *one* of the two fundamental problems of physics was in principle at least capable of solution: the problem of treating the motions of the particles mathematically. This is a purely intellectual problem: the very fact that it is a mathematical problem renders it a question of formal science, not physical science. As he put it,

> In mathematics we are to investigate the quantities of forces with their proportions consequent upon any conditions supposed; then, when we enter upon physics, we compare those proportions with the phenomena of Nature that we may know what conditions of those forces answer to the several kinds of attractive bodies. And this preparation being made, we argue more safely concerning the physical species, causes, and proportions of the forces.[5]

The determination of the forces that do move the particles remains as a problem of a different order altogether. This is a purely physical problem, one that can only be settled by attention to the phenomena, by observation and experiment. And the examination of the forces,

---

[5] Book II, Section XI, Scholium.

Newton suggests, is itself a double task: from the crude, experimental phenomena of Nature the corresponding corpuscular motions must be discovered, and then in turn the related forces investigated once these microscopic motions are known. Such investigation is the ultimate desideratum of physics: the intracorpuscular "forces being unknown, philosophers have hitherto attempted the search of Nature in vain."[6]

In the *Principia* little more is said of these other forces, which are not the gravitational force. But the *Quaeries* are more informative. The forces most cognate to that of gravity are obviously those of magnetism and electricity (*Quaeries* 8, 21, 22, 31): "these Instances shew the Tenor and Course of Nature, and make it not improbable that there may be more attractive powers than these. For Nature is very consonant and conformable to her self."[7] Other such forces suggested are that by which bodies and light act upon each other (*Quaeries* 1–5, 31); forces conveyed through the aether, or by which the aether acts on bodies (*Quaeries* 17–24, previously discussed in the "Letter to Boyle"); and the forces which variously cause bodies to cohere together, to dissolve and recombine in chemical reactions, and to ferment and burn, discussed at length in *Quaery* 31. Thus a relatively small number of forces would be adequate to account for the chief phenomena of Nature: indeed, it is not even necessary to suppose that Newton intended to indicate that each of them was a *distinct* force. They are simply traced by him from the effects, for the "force" exists as a cause, or the "principle responsible for . . ." the phenomena. Thus both gravity and the "cause of Fermentation" are "active Principles," as is the cause of cohesion.[8] Or, to put it more plainly, the magnetic force would be the active principle which causes iron to be drawn towards the magnet. Since Newton's criterion for distinguishing such forces lies in the superficial characteristic differences of the effects, it was impossible for him to determine whether any two different types of phenomena might require the action of two active principles, or a single one.[9] In all this discussion, Newton is content to include gravity along with all the other, less well understood causes:[10]

[6] Preface to the First Edition.   [7] *Quaery* 31.   [8] *Ibid.*
[9] However, there were exceptions, again arising from his understanding of gravity. He had indicated in the *Principia* (Bk. II, Prop. VI, cor. V) that magnetism and gravity must be distinct sorts of forces. For "the power of gravity is of a different nature from the power of magnetism; for the magnetic attraction is not as the matter attracted. . . . The power of magnetism in one and the same body may be increased and diminished; and is sometimes far stronger, for the quantity of matter, than the power of gravity; and in receding from the magnet decreases not as the square but almost as the cube of the distance, as nearly as I could judge from some rude observations."   [10] *Quaery* 31.

VI

It seems to me farther, that these [solid, massy, hard, impenetrable, movable] Particles have not only a *Vis inertiae*, accompanied with such passive Laws of Motion as naturally result from that Force, but also that they are moved by certain active Principles, such as is that of Gravity, and that which causes Fermentation, and the Cohesion of Bodies.

All these exert what Newton calls in a shorthand way "attractive Powers," which since he is a corpuscularian belong not to bodies as such, but to their fundamental particles.[11] Gravity, however, is singular in that it alone of these forces seems to lack a repulsive, though possessed of an attractive component. The more general model of the intracorpuscular force—derived from magnetism, electricity, and probably chemical effects—would have to allow for repulsion as well as attraction, as Newton hints in the Preface to the *Principia* (quoted above), and declares more firmly in the *Quaeries:*

as in algebra, where affirmative Quantities vanish and cease, there negative ones begin; so in Mechanicks, where Attraction ceases, there a repulsive Virtue ought to succeed. And that there is such a Virtue seems to follow from the Reflexions and Inflexions of the Rays of Light.[12]

And in chemistry, the particles of a dissolved substance spread through the body of a solvent, and "does not this Endeavour imply that they have a repulsive Force by which they fly from one another . . . ?"

This duality of forces would appear to present a physical complication of some magnitude, though, as Franklin was to demonstrate in the eighteenth century, it was not so severe as might appear at first sight, since he reduced the duality of electrical repulsion and attraction to a unitary theory.[13] It does not in this case involve a fresh mathematical problem, since repulsion is simply the inverse of attraction. Yet the singularity of gravity does have an important implication for the development of Newton's own theories, in that he gave no extensive treatment of problems involving both attractive and repulsive forces,[14] his only mathematical analysis being of gravitational attraction. The obvious exception to this statement is in Book II of

---

[11] "What I call Attraction may be perform'd by impulse, or by some other means unknown to me. I use that Word here to signify only in general any Force by which Bodies tend towards one another, whatsoever be the Cause" (*Quaery* 31). Cf. "I here use the word *attraction* in general for any endeavour whatever, made by bodies to approach each other . . . " (*Principia*, Bk. I, Section XI, Scholium).

[12] *Quaery* 31.

[13] However, Franklin could not account for the repulsion of two negative charges.

[14] The mechanical rotation of bodies does, of course, occasion a centrifugal acceleration from the center which implies a form of repulsive force. Such a force—like all mechanical forces—is not, however, a natural intracorpuscular force, nor does it have any function in theories involving the basic properties of matter.

the *Principia* (Section V, Prop. XXII), for here Newton evaluates the repulsive force between the particles of a fluid, when the density of the fluid varies always as some determinate power of the compressive force applied to it. This permits him to present a demonstration of Boyle's Law from the "mechanical principles" of the corpuscular philosophy: if the repulsive force between the particles of a fluid is reciprocally as the distance between them, the density varies directly with the pressure.[15] And, further, Newton writes, "as to our own air, this is certain from experiment, that its density is either accurately, or very nearly at least, as the compressive force." Yet the demonstration is inadequate to assert the *truth* of the mechanical principles, for:

> whether elastic fluids do really consist of particles so repelling each other is a physical question. We have here demonstrated mathematically the property of fluids consisting of this kind, that hence philosophers may take occasion to discuss that question.[16]

As indeed, Newton might have added, they had been doing ever since pneumatics had developed as a serious branch of science in the early seventeenth century. And as they were to continue to do, for many years to come.

In this instance of the application of mathematical reasoning to mechanical principles in order to elucidate the behavior of elastic fluids, Newton might well hesitate to adopt a more than tentative position. The mode of application of his hypothesis is, physically, not very plausible; and there were obvious difficulties in attributing both a gravitational attraction and a special repulsive force to the particles of an elastic fluid at one and the same time. He was far from possessing the complete physical theory of intracorpuscular forces needed to account for the behavior of the particles of a substance, like water, which is observed to exist in the solid and liquid as well as the gaseous state (through it is doubtful how far Newton was aware of the essentially gaseous properties of steam). Clearly a satisfactory theory of the gaseous state could be only a portion of such a complete theory: such a repulsive force as Newton supposed in this proposition could not be inferred really to exist, so long as there was but a single instance of the utility of the inference. Generally in the *Principia* Newton referred to his mathematical deductions from assumed intracorpuscular forces in a similar offhand manner, except in relation to gravitation. A clear example is his reference to the propositions on

---

[15] Newton's proof assumes (cf. *Scholium*) that the repulsive force exerted by each particle terminates at each adjacent particle; "if the force of any particle diffuse itself every way *in infinitum,* there will be required a greater force to produce an equal condensation of a greater quantity of the fluid." [16] *Prop.* XXIII, *Scholium.*

the motion of light (Book I, Section XIV). Here he deduces, from assumptions about the motion of a particle through the interface between the two different media, towards one of which it is attracted, the laws of reflection and refraction. Of these propositions he writes:

> These attractions bear a great resemblance to the reflections and refractions of light made in a given ratio of the secants, as was discovered by *Snell;* and consequently in a given ratio of the sines, as was exhibited by *Descartes.* ... Therefore because of the analogy there is between the propagation of the rays of light and the motion of bodies, I thought it not amiss to add the following Propositions for optical uses, not at all considering the nature of the rays of light, or inquiring whether they are bodies or not; but only determining the curves of bodies which are extremely like the curves of the rays.[17]

Even more offhand are the references to the possibility of the mathematical presentation of other forces, like those involved in the transmission of sound (Book II, Section VIII), which Newton here derives from a consideration of the mode of propagation of motion in an elastic medium. One of the complications in this instance is that allowance must be made for "the crassitude of the solid particles of the air," which, however, Newton thought himself able to estimate with sufficient accuracy, at least for his own satisfaction, though the desired agreement between theory and observation was by no means exact. Indeed, Newton was defeated by a problem to which he frequently recurred, in both the *Principia* and in the *Quaeries:* that it was essential to a detailed presentation of the corpuscular mechanism to know with some accuracy the distance between the particles, which, though ultimately ascertainable through a study of specific gravity or density (properties dependent on the number of particles in a given volume), yet was still rather something to be found out, than something immediately knowable. Gravity alone was dependent upon the quantity of matter, a directly measurable property, rather than upon the structure of matter, a property still to be measured. Gravity alone therefore provided the experimental basis which was essential to further mathematical reasoning. This being the case, Newton was left in a quandary. He could offer nothing but conjectures and sup-

---

[17] Prop. XCVI, Scholium. Cf. *Opticks,* Prop. VI (3rd ed., 1721), 68. Here Newton demonstrates Snell's Law "upon this Supposition. *That Bodies refract light by acting upon its Rays in Lines perpendicular to their Surfaces."* And, he says, "This Demonstration being general, without determining what Light is, or by what kind of Force it is refracted, or assuming any thing farther than that the refracting Body acts upon the Rays in Lines perpendicular to its Surface; I take it to be a very convincing Argument to the full truth of this Proposition." But in fact the Proposition, whose proof Newton says "Mathematicians will easily find out, and therefore I shall not trouble the Reader with it," involves the propositions of the *Principia,* which are themselves demonstrated for the motions of corpuscles.

positions, dangerously close to hypotheses, not subject to rigorous mathematical presentation. He had the grand design clear in his mind; but mathematical analysis, observation, and even theoretical ingenuity did not suffice to permit his dealing competently and rigorously with any force except gravity. No wonder that he felt so keenly the necessity to defend himself against what he could not but know to be a deserved attack; he could only protest, somewhat disingenuously, that

> to derive two or three general Principles of Motion from Phaenomena, and afterwards to tell us how the Properties and Actions of all corporeal Things follow from those manifest Principles, would be a very great step in Philosophy, though the Causes of those Principles were not yet discover'd: And therefore I scruple not to propose the Principles of Motion above mention'd, they being of very great Extent, and leave their Causes to be found out.[18]

This is a confession of faith rather than a triumphant justification of what he had once set out to do, and which after the success of the *Principia* in dealing with gravity must have seemed fairly easily attainable.

Perhaps if we endeavor to interpret both Newton's writings on physics other than the *Principia*—the *Opticks,* the letters to Boyle and to Bentley, the oddly tantalizing fragments of the early notebooks—and the *Principia* itself in the light of the mechanical philosophy, some of the sense of discontinuity that has troubled historians from time to time may be dissipated. Some confusion has undoubtedly been caused by treating the *Principia* as though its full title were *Mechanicae Coelestis Principia Mathematica,* instead of *Philosophiae Naturalis Principia Mathematica.* Historians discussing the origins of the *Principia* and the Newtonian synthesis are therefore apt to commit the venial sin of fitting that great work into a purely astronomical tradition. Yet Newton meant what he said, what he would still have meant had the general title been *De Motu Corporum.* He was writing for Euler as well as for Laplace, and in fact of the origins of Book II—which has been described as more original than the rest of the work (a singular opinion perhaps) [19]— almost nothing is known. That Book II is seventeenth-century mechanical philosophy given a superb (though in the first edition frequently erroneous) mathematical garb is too obvious to require illustration. In Book I, it is true, the first eleven sections are purely mathematical, being concerned either with problems in geometry, or with a kinematic treatment of moving bodies; here, therefore, Newton insists:

[18] *Quaery* 31.
[19] C. Truesdell in *Isis* 47(1956), 450, col. 2.

I ... use the words attraction, impulse or propensity of any sort towards a centre, promiscuously and indifferently, one for another; considering those forces *not physically but mathematically;* wherefore the reader is not to imagine that by those words I anywhere take upon me to define the kind or the manner of any action, the cause or other physical reason thereof, or that *I attribute forces, in a true and physical sense,* to certain centres (which are only mathematical points); when at any time I happen to speak of centres attracting, or as endowed with attractive powers.[20]

And again at the opening of Section XI the idea of attraction towards an immovable center that has been adopted for mathematical purposes is excluded as a physical possibility: Newton announces " these propositions are to be considered as purely mathematical," he is " laying aside all physical considerations." Clearly, if a set of propositions is denied any physical status, it can have no relevance to the corpuscular or any other physical hypothesis, for in that case they are not propositions in dynamics. However, as soon as Newton comes to write dynamically (Sections XII–XIV) he then explicitly avows the mechanical philosophy. Thus he writes, " We are to compute the attractions of the bodies by assigning to each of their particles its proper force, and then finding the sum of them all. . . . Let us see, then, with what forces spherical bodies consisting of particles endowed with attractive powers in the manner spoken of must act upon one another; and what kinds of motion will follow from them." [21]

In the following proposition LXX Newton postulates equal centripetal forces tending to every *point* of a spherical surface; here it is clear that we do not add an additional hypothesis, or misconstrue Newton's outlook, if we read " particle " for " point." There is no sense in which an attractive capacity could be an attribute of a geometrical point; the attribution of a physical property—attraction—to the point implies that a punctiform mass exists there. The corpuscle to the mathematical physicist is the analogue of the infinitesimal or differential to the mathematician; it is strictly impossible for one who denies the corpuscular hypothesis to use such tools of mathematics to effect the summation of unit forces belonging to units of matter that Newton proposes to exploit. Explicitly, then, it is for Newton impossible, *even in the case of gravitational attractions,* to step from the mathematical kind of reasoning to a physical kind of reasoning without introducing the corpuscular hypothesis.

Even the astronomical sections of the *Principia* are by no means independent of the corpuscular conception. There are in the Third Book numerous allusions to Newton's belief in the corpuscular

[20] Definition VIII (italics added).
[21] Proposition LXIX, Scholium.

structure of matter.²² The argument of Proposition X—that the planets revolve without losing motion, since the medium in which they move is sensibly without density—is derived from the corpuscular studies of Book II, while the demonstration in that Book (Section IX) of the fallacy of the Cartesian vortex theory is founded upon the specific hypothesis that fluids have parts. Again, in the third of the "Rules of Reasoning in Philosophy" of Book III, Newton presents the mechanical or corpuscular conception as a commonplace that requires no justification:

> The extension, hardness, impenetrability, mobility, and inertia of the whole [body], result from the extension, hardness, mobility and inertia of the parts; and hence we conclude the least particles of all bodies to be also all extended, and hard, and impenetrable, and movable, and endowed with their proper inertia. And this is the foundation of all philosophy.

He continues with the usual reservation regarding atomism:

> that the divided but contiguous particles of bodies may be separated from one another is a matter of observation; and in the particles that remain undivided, our minds are able to distinguish yet lesser parts, as is mathematically demonstrated. But whether the parts so distinguished, and yet not divided, may, by the powers of Nature, be actually divided and separated from one another, we cannot certainly determine. . . .

Yet clearly he had no real physical doubts.

Newton never supposed that a competent picture of the universe could be obtained by unwrapping the consequences of a mathematical equation; he was well aware that it was possible in mathematics to work out the detailed features of what might look like a physical system, but had in fact no relation to the actual world. And that was the kind of *a priori*, nonempirical system he did not intend to develop. The establishment of a mathematical theory of a physical kind demanded hypotheses of particulate structure, an inverse square law of attraction, and so on; by nature, this theory demanded that the hypotheses be capable of verification by experiment or observation.²³ The distinction between the physical hypotheses of the *Principia*, and those of the *Quaeries* in the *Opticks* is merely that the former are given an exact mathematical expression and then checked by reference to Nature, whereas the latter even Newton could only illustrate from experiments, much as Boyle had, still more elaborately, illustrated the applications of his corpuscular philosophy by experiments.

Alexandre Koyré has drawn attention to Newton's use of hypo-

---

²² Prop. VI, Corol. IV; Prop. VII, Corol. II; Prop. VIII. Cf. also *System of the World*, [18].

²³ Cf. Book I, Section XI, Scholium, quoted above, note 11.

thesis in the structure of even the *Principia*,[24] and I. Bernard Cohen has emphasized the contrast between mathematical Newtonian science and speculative, experimental Newtonian science.[25] One can hardly doubt that Newton was both a speculative and an exact theorist, both an experimenter and a mathematician; but the very fact that the *Principia* does not exclude hypotheses reveals the absence of any sharp distinction between the two levels of his activity. Only part of his work was expounded on the higher, mathematical level; the rest remained in the state in which the theory of fluids had been before the second book of the *Principia* was written. But Newton clearly believed that *all* of natural philosophy could gradually be transferred to the higher level, that this mathematization of the whole of physics would be effected on the foundation of the mechanical philosophy, and that probably this could be done by developing the various hints he offered. He did not imagine that the theories of light, of chemical reaction, and so forth would remain indefinitely non-mechanical and non-mathematical, nor that the development of such theories would be totally unlike the evolution of mechanics. He might have been astonished to discover that history was to disrupt the unity of his scientific conception, admiring it, indeed, where he had given it mathematical expression, yet regarding the rest as a series of conjectures that had yielded little in the way of fertile progeny, and that were even unworthy of their own progenitor. For the link between the two levels of Newtonian science—the speculative and the mathematical—existed in the mechanical philosophy, in those ideas of the structure of matter and the nature of phenomena which to Newton were of universal validity. At one level the universal principles were completely, because mathematically, demonstrated; at the other they were not. But that they would be so demonstrated one day Newton firmly believed. Thus the " speculative " science of Newton is merely Newtonian science incomplete; it is not of a different kind from the mathematical science of the *Principia*. The *Quaeries* are, as it were, points of departure for further revelations of the mathematical principles of natural philosophy; Newton's failures, perhaps, but for him sources of hope rather than of despair. They prepared the way for those companion volumes to the *Principia* that he could not write, and that therefore never were written.

---

[24] *Revue d'Histoire des Sciences*, VIII (1955), 19–37; *Bulletin de la Société Française de Philosophie* (Avril–Juin 1956), 59–79.

[25] *Franklin and Newton* (Philadelphia, 1956), esp. ch. 5.

VII

Newton's Theory of Matter

By A. Rupert Hall and Marie Boas Hall *

A CLEAR understanding of Newton's real thoughts about the nature of matter and of the forces associated with material particles has always been (to borrow his own phrase) "pressed with difficulties." That a corpuscular or particulate theory was unreservedly adopted by him has long been abundantly evident from many passages in the *Principia,* and from the *Quaeries* in *Opticks,* to mention only discussions fully approved for publication by Newton himself. So far, then, Newton was undoubtedly a "mechanical philosopher" in the spirit of his age, the spirit otherwise expressed, for example, by Boyle and Locke. But of the exact content and form of his mechanical philosophy it is less easy to be certain. In the *Principia* it is set in a strictly mathematical mould, and Newton for the most part restricts his statements to what is necessary for the development of a mathematical theory of gravitational force: only phenomena of motion are considered. In the *Quaeries,* on the other hand, Newton treats the mechanical philosophy qualitatively, and, having deliberately given to his thoughts a speculative dress, in order not to seem utterly committed to them, he roams widely over the phenomena of optics, heat, surface tension, chemistry, and so on, rarely being definite and on occasion being inconsistent. As Newton intended, the *Quaeries* tantalize: we are never sure whether he really means what he says or not.

Interpretations of the *Quaeries,* and of certain passages in the *Principia,* have been further complicated by overemphasis of the positivist element in Newton's scientific method. When the philosopher who declared "Hypotheses non fingo" is found to be framing hypotheses and formulating conjectures, should these be taken seriously or not? Even if we recognize that Newton did not—for he could not—avoid or mercilessly condemn any entertainment of a hypothesis, it is often tempting to distinguish between Newton the mathematical theorist, and Newton the author of philosophical speculations.

Similar doubts obscure other discussions, especially the *Hypothesis of Light*[1] and the *Letter to Boyle:*[2] again, when touching on fundamental explanations, Newton seems to don a cloak of elusiveness. Of the former he wrote almost in terms of impatience. Considering, he said, that a hypothesis would illustrate his optical papers, or at least that they were felt to need such an explanation by some great virtuosos in the Royal Society whose heads ran much upon

---

* University of California, Los Angeles. This paper was read at the annual meeting of the History of Science Society in Chicago, 28 December 1959. A longer version accompanied by transcriptions and translations of the manuscripts referred to below will be incorporated in a forthcoming book, *Unpublished Scientific Papers of Sir Isaac Newton.*

[1] Published in T. Birch, *History of the Royal Society* (London, 1756-7), III, 247-269, 296-305. (Reprinted in I. B. Cohen, ed., *Isaac Newton's Papers and Letters on Natural Philosophy* [Cambridge, Mass., 1958], pp. 178-235).

[2] First published in Birch, *The Life and Works of the Honourable Robert Boyle* (London, 1744), I, 74 (1772, cxvii-cxviii and *Papers and Letters,* 254).

© 1960 The University of Chicago Press. Reprinted from *Isis* 51, 1960 pp. 131-144. Used by permission.

hypotheses: "I have not scrupled to describe one, as I could on a sudden recollect my thoughts about it; not concerning myself whether it shall be thought probable or improbable, so it do but render the papers I send you, and others I sent formerly, more intelligible." And he made it clear that he was not to be supposed to accept this hypothesis himself, or to be seeking adherents for it. This is as much as to say: if the virtuosos must amuse themselves with hypotheses, I will supply one, as good as any other.[3] As for the *Letter to Boyle*, it begins with an apology for reproducing notions so ill digested "that I am not well satisfied my self in them; and what I am not satisfied in, I can scarce esteem fit to be communicated to others; especially in natural philosophy, where there is no end of fancying." And the letter ends yet more discouragingly: "For my own part, I have so little fancy to things of this nature, that, had not your encouragement moved me to it, I should never, I think, have thus far set pen to paper about them."[4]

These pieces, together with *De natura acidorum*,[5] are so brief and so *ad hoc* in their composition, and so little related to the main stream of Newton's mathematical and experimental enquiry, that they have defied accurate assessment. Historians have been inclined to take Newton at his word and dismiss them as occasional pieces not truly representative of his permanent convictions. Although Newton was thirty-three in 1675 and had by this time performed original work of outstanding quality—indeed, no truly creative thought entered his mind after this date—it has been tempting to suppose that these papers were juvenilia, products of a state of mind which the author of the *Principia* has outgrown. That Newton only renounced almost total public silence in 1717 with the final group of *Quaeries* seemed to indicate that his thoughts were uncertain until that time. Even after going into print (with all the safeguards of the *Quaery* form) Newton was still undecided, apt to plan further discussion and then draw back. For he informed Roger Cotes, editor of the second edition of the *Principia*, that "I intended to have said much more about the attraction of the small particles of bodies, but upon second thoughts I have chose rather to add but one short Paragraph about that part of Philosophy."[6] This was with reference to the final passage of the *General Scholium*, which Newton ultimately re-wrote so mysteriously that its meaning has escaped commentators ever since.[7] Once more Newton could not speak his mind openly and plainly; once more his compulsion to utter only unchallengeable truths or perplexing generalities prevailed over his sense of the importance of explaining his theory of matter.

We can extend our understanding of Newton's intention by consideration of unpublished manuscript sources, papers which Newton wrote at various periods of his life, which cover a wide variety of subjects. These include the following, given here in the order of their composition, as far as that can be determined:

(1) Notes on Hooke's *Micrographia* (ca. 1665).[8]

[3] T. Birch, *History of the Royal Society*, III, 248-249.
[4] Birch, *Boyle*, 1744, I, 70, 73.
[5] John Harris, *Lexicon Technicum*, II, 1710, introduction (*Papers and Letters*, 256-258).
[6] 2nd March 1712/13. Letter LXXV in Joseph Edleston, *Correspondence of Sir Isaac Newton and Professor Cotes* (London, 1850), p. 147.
[7] See below p. 142.
[8] Cambridge University Library, MS. Add. 3958, fols. 1–2.

(2) *De Gravitatione et aequipondio fluidorum*[9] (before 1670); an elaborately written though unfinished work, violently anti-Cartesian, and hence containing a long disquisition on the nature of matter.

(3) *De Aere et Aethere*,[10] an unfinished and much corrected work, in two short chapters (about 1674).

(4) *Conclusio*,[11] the original ending to the *Principia*.

(5) Draft of the Preface to the *Principia*, much longer than the printed version.[12]

(6) Drafts of the *General Scholium*[13] (for the second edition of 1713). These documents clearly prove that it was not lack of continuity in his ideas, nor want of an impulse to publish them that caused Newton to hover between silence and oracular utterance. Newton planned and drafted more versions of his theory of matter both before writing the *Principia* and in conjunction with it than have been known hitherto. The various versions with their similar phrases and identical examples form a continuous chain over the years 1675-1713 to show that the basic fabric of Newton's theory of matter remained always the same. Moreover, despite all his overt professions, Newton was genuinely anxious to discuss his theory of matter in detail and publicly. Three times he tried to find a place for it in the *Principia*: in the *Conclusio*, in the *Preface* and in the *General Scholium*; and three times he rejected it. Somewhere, he seems to have felt, some notice should be given of the microscopic architecture of nature side by side with the majestic system of celestial motions unfolded by mathematical analysis. But all that at length emerged after painful reflection was a cautious hint in the printed version of the Preface to the first edition, to be followed years later by the oracular but confusing conclusion to the *General Scholium* in the second edition. No one can be sure of knowing the reasons for the ultimate suppression of his cherished ideas. The most plausible is Newton's persistent fear of committing himself to some position which might be made to seem foolish. It may also have struck him that the juxtaposition of the mathematical positivism of the *Principia* (where he was so careful to deny that when he spoke of gravitational *attraction* he meant attraction at all) and speculations about half-a-dozen other attractive forces (even less well known than gravity) would be particularly strange. Especially since the *Principia* was the work which Newton was the most anxious to make immune from attack. His second thoughts were no doubt tactically wise, and helped avoid bitter controversy; yet, as we shall try to show, the annexing of an essay in the mechanical philosophy to the *Principia mathematica* would have been by no means so paradoxical as it might seem.

Newton's adherence to the mechanical philosophy was a very early development. In his student days he had read with care the *Principia Philosophiae* of Descartes, the *Origin of Forms and Qualities* among many works of Boyle, and the writings of Henry More and Robert Hooke, with others of the generation somewhat senior to his own.[14] His annotations portray him as thoroughly im-

---

[9] C.U.L. MS Add. 4003.
[10] C.U.L. MS Add. 3970, fols. 652–653.
[11] C.U.L. MS Add. 4005, fols. 25–28, 30–32.
[12] C.U.L. MS Add. 3965, fol. 620.
[13] C.U.L. MS Add. 3965, fols. 357–365.
[14] A. R. Hall, "Sir Isaac Newton's Note-Book, 1661-1665," *Cambridge Historical Journal*, 1948, 9: 239-250. [See now study I in this volume]

bued with the mechanical philosophy, and among his earliest original notes there occur, for example, speculations "Of Attomes." A very little later—perhaps about 1665—there is a sketch of an attempt to trace colour to the reflection and absorption of light in the pores of solid bodies.[15] Probably to this same period—it can hardly be very much later—belongs *De gravitatione et aequipondio fluidorum* which also indicates the mechanical outlook, and which contains some traces of the later Newtonian theory of matter. The first surviving document fully devoted to this theory we believe to be *De aere et aethere*, in which it emerges in a tolerably complete form. The existence of this document, in fact, belies Newton's own statement to Boyle that his ideas would never have been committed to paper but for the latter's persuasion, or the earlier claim to Oldenburg, that it was only to gratify the virtuosos that he had written a hypothesis of light. The well-organized though summary treatment in two chapters suggests that it was intended as a synopsis of a more ambitious work. From internal evidence it seems to have been written between 1673, when Boyle's calcination experiments which it mentions were described in his *New Experiments to Make Fire and Flame Stable and Ponderable*,[16] and 1675 when Newton wrote the *Hypothesis on Light*. Comparison of *De aere et aethere* with parallel passages in the *Hypothesis* and in the *Letter to Boyle* indicates that while the same observations and examples were used in all three, as they were to be used many times more until Newton's ideas crystallized in print in the *Quaeries*, the explanations offered of the observed phenomena represents a less mature stage of development than those of the *Hypothesis*.

The feature of *De aere et aethere* that immediately distinguishes it from Newton's other discussions of phenomena of attraction and repulsion (the examples here are capillary attraction, the lack of cohesion in a dry powder, the difficulty of pressing two surfaces together, the walking of flies on water— all to be used repeatedly again) is that he here finds the cause of the effect in the repulsive force of air particles. In later works (the *Hypothesis of Light* and the *Letter to Boyle*) these forces were transferred to an aether. Thus, in *De aere et aethere* the particles of air are, so to speak, active agents in phenomena by virtue of their intrinsic repulsive force. In the *Letter to Boyle* this is no longer the case: particles of air or of other matter, even light-rays, are passively subjected to the force exerted by aether particles, to which the intrinsic repulsive force has now been transferred. Some economy of explanation is gained by the change. For instead of supposing that material particles are endowed with a variety of forces, gravitational, chemical, electrical and so forth, it may be possible to reduce all these to one force in the aether—but unfortunately for economy, Newton did not succeed in this. On the other hand, there has necessarily been a multiplication of entities in a fashion to invite the slash of Ockham's razor. Besides, the aether cannot be inferred from the phenomena; it can only be imagined.

This was a perpetual problem in Newton's philosophy of matter. He could adopt either of two kinds of language. He could speak of forces between the material particles (of whose existence he was confident) as being the cause of phenomena; or he could speak of the forces between the aetherial particles,

[15] *Ibid.*, pp. 243, 248.   [16] Birch, *Boyle*, 1772, III, 706 ff.

VII

NEWTON'S THEORY OF MATTER

which in turn acted on the material particles, as being the true causes of phenomena. Sometimes, but not always, he could translate from one language to the other. It would be tempting, perhaps, to consider that when Newton attributed forces to material particles, he always meant that these forces were produced by an aether. But this, as we shall show, was not the case; and in any event the aether-version of the particulate theory of matter as Newton developed it cannot be considered as a profounder theory underlying the force-version, for it takes a totally different view of the ultimate properties of material particles.

Using this criterion, Newton's writings on the theory of matter fall into two groups. He used aether-language in the *Hypothesis* of 1675, the *Letter to Boyle*, and certain of the *Quaeries*. He attributed forces directly to material particles, without the interposition of an aether, in *De aere et aethere*, the whole text and printed preface of the *Principia*, the suppressed *Conclusio* and draft preface, and certain other *Quaeries*. It is significant that when dealing with some of the most obscure—because not directly observable—phenomena of attraction and repulsion, in chemical reaction, Newton never introduced the aether at all, but always spoke of forces between the reactive particles.[17] On the other hand, Newton was particularly careful not to commit himself to the aetherial hypotheses of 1675 and 1678; the aether-language is always qualified by a cautionary note, whereas when he spoke of forces exerted by material particles he felt no such disclaimer to be necessary.

One should hesitate, therefore, before thinking that Newton's theory of matter consisted of nothing but a series of hypotheses about the aether and its importance in phenomena. Rather, the solid part of this theory consisted of the view that phenomena result from the motions of material particles, and that these motions are the result of the interplay of forces between the particles. This he suggests again and again, both in print and in previously unpublished drafts. Nothing could be more emphatic than the statement of *Quaery 31*, free from conjectural disguises and disclaimers about hypotheses:

> It seems probable to me that God in the beginning formed matter in solid, massy, hard, impenetrable, moveable particles. . . . it seems to me farther that these particles have not only a *vis inertiae*, accompanied with such passive laws of motion as naturally result from that force, but also that they are moved by certain active principles, such as is that of gravity, and that which causes fermentation, and the cohesion of bodies.

Nothing that Newton wrote furnishes authority for going beyond this, nor for fathering upon him the opinion that aether was the ultimate cause of everything, as was mistakenly and ridiculously done by Bryan Robinson in the eighteenth century.[18] It is true that Newton, going beyond the bounds of his theory, would speculate on the hypothesis that all the forces of Nature might originate in the properties of an aether, but this speculation is no more essential to the theory proper (as described in so many passages where there is no men-

---

[17] There would appear to be an exception in the discussion of solution in the *Letter to Boyle;* but in the hypothetical explanation offered there, any reference to the role of the aether is quite superfluous.

[18] *A Dissertation on the Aether of Sir Isaac Newton,* 1743; *Sir Isaac Newton's Account of the Aether, with some additions by way of an appendix,* 1745. The latter was occasioned by the first appearance in print of the *Letter to Boyle.*

VII

tion of an aether) than Darwin's hypothesis of pangenesis is to the theory of evolution, or (for that matter) Maxwell's aether is to Maxwell's equations.

Without seeking to cramp Newton's thought into a Procrustean bed of positivism, to which indeed his theory of matter is ill adapted, it seems unnecessary to run to the opposite extreme and (with Lord Keynes) make Newton a *magus* whose scientific thinking was at the mercy of inexplicable whims and mediaeval fancies. Nor can we agree with Professor Cohen, who has suggested that, although "Newton presented his thoughts on the aether with some degree of tentativeness, he did so over so long a period of time that the conclusion is inescapable that a belief in an aetherial medium, penetrating all bodies and filling empty space, was a central pillar of his system of nature."[19] For, since Newton always presented his aetherial hypotheses tentatively, even at the height of his scientific prestige, there is no reason to suppose that he regarded them as other than tentative; he was certainly not equally coy about his theory of particulate motions and forces, which in a far more real and effective sense he looked upon as offering a key to the understanding of the inner mysteries of nature. It may be that in a sense Newton pointed the way up a blind alley. The very fact that he speculated at all on the aether as a mechanism to account for the forces attributed to material particles gratified the prejudice of an age that, lacking any concept of field-theory, loathed the notion of action at a distance and saw in the push-and-pull mechanism of an aether the only escape from it. Faced with a choice between a universe of Cartesian, billiard-ball mechanism rewritten in Newtonian terms and a universe requiring the inconceivable concept of action at a distance, the seventeenth, eighteenth and nineteenth centuries preferred the former. But, because this was so, and Newton himself shared the general contempt for the notion of action at a distance, we should not suppose that Newton was unaware of the distinction between a hypothesis and a theory; nor should we conclude that his speculations on the aether were the foundation of his theory of matter, when in fact they were at most no more than hypothetical ancillaries to it.

If, then, the existence of forces is an ultimate fact of nature, one that despite Newton's own aetherial hypotheses cannot in the last resort be explained away by a simple Cartesian type of mechanism, what does the word "force," or, as he otherwise termed it, power, virtue, or active principle mean for Newton? Unfortunately, he gives no specific answer. The forces between particles are certainly of the same nature as those between macroscopic bodies;[20] they can be qualified as gravitational, magnetic, electric, "and there may be more attractive powers than these;" they are identifiable from experimental phenomena. But precisely what their nature is Newton never did declare, because he could not discover it. Confronting this difficulty, Professor Alexandre Koyré takes the view that, as Newton knew that forces could not be explained in terms of aetherial mechanisms, he held "them to be non-mechanical, immaterial and even 'spiritual' energy extraneous to matter."[21] As Newton wrote to Bentley, "It is inconceivable, that inanimate brute Matter should, without the Medi-

---

[19] *Papers & Letters,* General Introduction, p. 7.
[20] *Quaery* 31, *Opticks,* 5th edition (London, 1931), p. 376.
[21] *From the Closed World to the Infinite Universe* (Baltimore, 1957), p. 209.

ation of something else, *which is not material,* operate upon, and affect other Matter, without mutual contact. . . ."[22] Forces would thus require, for Newton, "in the last analysis, the constant action in the world of the Omnipresent and All-powerful God."[23] Professor Koyré's position appears to be this: Newton was much too intelligent not to perceive that the mechanical hypotheses of forces lead to infinite regress, therefore he must on the contrary have believed that forces are non-mechanical, quasi-spiritual.

Undoubtedly Newton was a teleologist for whom the celestial system was the product of divine design, who believed that God had created particles with such properties, and moved by such forces, as were necessary to create the phenomena intended in the divine plan. Just as Newton rejected Descartes' contention that God could not create extension without matter, so he would have denied that God could not create matter without forces. Therefore forces were certainly not innate in matter. If asked why the planetary orbits have certain parameters and not others, or why particles have certain forces and not others, Newton would reply: Because God made them so. God could have made our world differently if he wished.[24] So, to discourse of God "from the appearances of things, does certainly belong to Natural Philosophy" for natural philosophy teaches "what is the first Cause, what power he has over us, and what benefits we receive from him."[25] Moreover, Newton seemed to require God's activity not in the first creation alone, but continually. Why should not the matter in the universe congregate together, unless a divine power prevented it?[26] How could the action of comets and planets upon each other avoid a disturbance of the celestial harmony, unless the same power preserved it?[27] And how could the quantity of motion in the universe be hindered from decreasing?[28]

For attributing such a ceaseless activity to God Newton was criticized by Leibniz and in turn defended by Samuel Clarke who, nevertheless, did not challenge the accuracy of Leibniz's understanding of Newton's views.[29] Professor Koyré believes that the metaphysical opinions of Newton's champion accurately represent those of Newton himself, as seems indeed probable.[30] Clarke maintains that there is no true distinction between "natural" and "miraculous" things, both being the work of God; the former are regular and common, the latter irregular and rare.[31] Nothing, even a miracle, (allowed by both Clarke and Leibniz) is more the result of divine intervention than anything else, since everything that is depends always on God's actual government of the world.[32]

As Clarke wrote,

[22] *Four Letters from Sir Isaac Newton to Doctor Bentley* (London, 1756), p. 25; *Papers & Letters,* 302. Italics added.
[23] Koyré, *op. cit.,* p. 217.
[24] *Quaery* 31, pp. 403-404.
[25] *General Scholium,* F. Cajori, *Sir Isaac Newton's Mathematical Principles of Natural Philosophy* (Berkeley, 1946), p. 546; *Quaery* 31, p. 405.
[26] *Quaery* 28, p. 369. *Four Letters,* p. 29; *Papers & Letters,* p. 306. However, in a draft of the *Scholium Generale* Newton supposes that the stars are too remote from each other to experience a centripetal tendency.
[27] *Quaery* 31, p. 402.
[28] *Quaery* 31, p. 397-399.
[29] H. G. Alexander, *The Leibniz-Clarke Correspondence* (Manchester, 1956).
[30] Koyré, *op. cit.,* p. 301.
[31] Alexander, *op. cit.,* pp. 23-24, 35.
[32] Alexander, p. 117.

VII

138

> The notion of the world's being a great machine, going on without the interposition of God, as a clock continues to go without the assistance of a clockmaker; is the notion of materialism and fate; and tends, (under pretence of making God a *supra-mundane* intelligence) to exclude providence and God's government in reality out of the world.[33]

Clarke here argues that the Newtonian conception of forces involves nothing extraordinary when God's relation to the world is properly understood; forces are divinely produced because the whole of nature is divinely maintained; they are not mechanically produced because the universe is not a machine.

There is no more spiritual quality to forces, than to matter itself; and matter, Newton had long believed, depends immediately on God for its very existence. This had, in fact, long been his prime argument against the Cartesian notion of matter as extension; he had written in the early *De gravitatione et aequipondio fluidorum:* "If we say with Descartes that extension is body, do we not offer a path to Atheism, both because extension is not created but has existed eternally, and because we have an absolute idea of it without any relationship to God?" Extension only became matter when endowed by God with attributes; and that there was a moment of creation by divine will does not mean that matter is now independent of God. On the contrary, matter exists by a continued act of God's will; equally the properties of matter—the result of particles acting on one another through forces defined by God—must exist because of a continued exertion of God's will. Natural forces are certainly immaterial, equally they are physical, subject to law and open to experimental investigation in a way that miracles and spiritual powers are not.

This is a difficult, perhaps an impossible, metaphysic. Clarke, accepting it, was nevertheless forced by Leibniz into seeking for a middle position where there seemed to be none. Neither he nor his mentor Newton (who said nothing about the question openly) was able to give a clear idea of forces that, although within the natural order of things, were at the same time neither material and mechanical, nor miraculous and spiritual. Leibniz presented the nature of forces as a metaphysical problem, in which Clarke (and Newton) were invited to say that they were *either* spiritual *or* mechanical, one or the other. Clarke wanted a *tertium quid,* which he could not define, because Newton could not solve the problem of force in physical terms. Leibniz was right: Newton's conception of force could not be justified by his metaphysic; it could only be justified by its empirical usefulness in physics.

The content of this theory, discernible in published work such as the *Quaeries,* is made still clearer in the suppressed *Conclusio* to the *Principia.* Here the motions of the particles in hot, fermenting and growing bodies (such, in other words, as exhibit the principal phenomena of change) are said to be strictly analogous to "the greater motions that can easily be detected," and these motions offer the chief clue to "the whole nature of bodies as far as the mechanical causes of things are concerned." The same reasoning applies to the lesser motions as to the greater one, and just as the latter "depend upon the greater attractive forces of larger bodies," so do the former upon "the lesser forces, as yet unobserved, of insensible particles." In chemical phenomena the

---

[33] Alexander, p. 14.

VII

rapid motion of particles is made especially evident, but Newton suggests that the attractive force actively involved in chemical reaction is the same as that responsible for the static cohesion of particles; and the interplay of cohesive force with particulate shape yields the varying characteristics of fluidity, hardness, elasticity, and so on, that different bodies exhibit. Particles both repel and attract: the repulsive force acts more strongly at greater distances while the attractive force, diminishing more rapidly with distance, preponderates when particles are in close proximity. For this reason contiguous particles in a solid cohere; but as soon as the particles are separated, whatever the means, they fly further apart, forming an air or vapour whose particles are mutually repellent. If the particles were sufficiently heavy and dense, as Newton had explained in *De aere et aethere,* they would constitute permanent air, and in fact he expressly stated that metals were the most apt to do this.

Many other phenomena are discussed, and then Newton pauses a moment to consider his purpose in entering into so much detail:

> I have briefly set these matters out, not in order to make a rash assertion that there are attractive and repulsive forces in bodies, but so that I can give an opportunity to imagine further experiments by which it can be ascertained more certainly whether they exist or not. For if it shall be settled that they are true [forces] it will remain for us to investigate their causes and properties diligently, as being the true principles from which, according to geometrical reasoning, all the more secret motions of the least particles are no less brought into being than are the motions of greater bodies which as we saw in the foregoing [books] derived from the laws of gravity.

After this he turns to a problem that often excites his interest, that of order and pattern in the arrangement of particles. They are not, he says, thrown together like a heap of stones, for "they coalesce into the form of highly regular structures almost like those made by art, as happens in the formation of snow and salts." This occurs, he suggests, because the individual particles join up into long elastic rods, the rods in turn forming retiform corpuscles, and so on until visible bodies take shape. Bodies assembled in this regular way will transmit light and the vibrations of heat, and permit variation of density through chemical change. "Thus," writes Newton, "almost all the phenomena of nature will depend upon the forces of particles if only it be possible to prove that forces of this kind do exist."

The theory of matter in the *Conclusio* could, indeed, almost be reconstructed from scattered passages in the published writings. It is presented in compressed form in the well-known sentence of the printed Preface:

> I wish we could derive the rest of the phenomena of Nature by the same kind of reasoning from mechanical principles, for I am induced by many reasons to suspect that they may all depend upon certain forces by which the particles of bodies, by some causes hitherto unknown, are either mutually impelled towards one another, and cohere in regular figures, or are repelled and recede from one another,

which is a perfect summary of Newton's thinking on the subject. And a fuller account of this theory as a part of the *Principia* itself would hardly have been inappropriate. The *Principia* is, for the most part, a treatise on the one force of nature, the gravitating force which ultimately resides in the particles of matter and whose laws Newton was able to determine. Having determined these laws, and believing that real theoretical physics was mathematical physics and not a parlour game of hypotheses, Newton went on to work out mathematically the consequences of the laws of gravity and to show that these correspond with observable phenomena.[34] This was Newton's second great advance in the mechanical philosophy, arising from his conception of particulate forces—that which rendered it mathematical. None of his predecessors had succeeded in this, or even attempted it, though many had seen its desirability. But the "mechanical principles" of the *Principia* require that the forces acting on particles and the motions produced by them be exactly calculated. In the *Principia* dynamics and the mechanical philosophy are united—but only with respect to the force of gravity. This, as Newton conceived it, was to be the general pattern of theoretical physics; if only it were possible to extend this union of dynamics and the mechanical philosophy until it embraced the operation of other forces, such as those of electricity or chemical reaction, and thereby effected a precise correspondence between theory and phenomena such as he had achieved for the force of gravity, then indeed these phenomena of nature would be rationally understood.[35] This extension of a philosophy that was at once mathematical and mechanical Newton did not expect to accomplish himself, and the suggestions he made in *Opticks* and elsewhere were intended for the guidance of others. Yet perhaps the best guide he could have provided, in some such explanation of his widest conception of matter and its forces as he drafted in the *Conclusio*, he denied them. This remains inexplicable. The sentence in the Preface already quoted survived as an indication of his hopes; was he afraid of influencing posterity too much by offering more explicit directions?

Before the final version of the Preface went to the printer, Newton again contemplated a more open statement. In this draft he proposed

> the inquiry whether or not there be many forces of this kind never yet perceived, by which the particles of bodies agitate one another and coalesce into various structures. For if Nature be simple and pretty conformable to herself, causes will operate in the same kind of way in all phenomena, so that the motions of smaller bodies depend upon certain smaller forces just as the motions of larger bodies are ruled by the greater force of gravity.

As before, particles are said to exhibit both repulsive and attractive forces, the former having a longer range, and in general the discussion is much like that of the *Conclusio*, with the same examples, though of course on a smaller scale. Once more, however, Newton changed his mind and omitted all but the simple statement of his hopes already quoted.

There the matter rested until Newton composed the *Quaeries* in *Opticks*, nearly twenty years later, demonstrating both the continuity of his thought by the essential similarity between the *Quaeries* and the earlier drafts, and

---

[34] This is, of course, a summary of the intellectual architecture of the book; how Newton formed his ideas and developed his theory of gravitation would be a very different story.

[35] We have discussed this view of the *Principia* more amply in our article on "Newton's Mechanical Principles," *Journal of the History of Ideas*, 1959, 20: 167-178.

the liveliness of his interest in these oft-considered problems by the vigour of this fresh attempt to express his mind.

The *Quaeries* show, however, that Newton's theory of matter had made no progress since 1687, or even earlier, for its roots are visible in the chapter *De aere* written before 1675. His conception of the production of natural phenomena from the motion of material corpuscles caused by action of a variety of forces, illustrated by many observations and experiments, had not been given greater definition. He was not even sure whether there was one basic force, or a pair of repulsive and attractive forces, or as many forces as there were classes of phenomena—gravitational, magnetic, electrical, optical, chemical and physiological—involving such forces. For the further development of this theory three requirements had to be met. It was necessary to be able to analyse the motions of particles mathematically; some of the methods of doing this had been established in the *Principia*. Secondly, it was necessary to know more, from experiments, of the nature of the force or forces; in comparison, the discovery of the laws of gravitation and of the way in which these explained the phenomena of astronomy and tidal motion had been a relatively straightforward task. Newton recognized that the experimental insight available to him was far too shallow to carry a theoretical superstructure. "I have least of all undertaken the improvement of this part of philosophy," he wrote in the *Conclusio*. Too much, indeed, was founded on his reiterated assumption (found in the Third Rule of Reasoning in the *Principia*) that "Nature is always simple and conformable to herself." That this principle could be relied on in the study of particulate forces had never been experimentally (or mathematically) proved, though it seemed to be confirmed in the case of gravity. And thirdly, it was necessary to resolve the philosophic doubt concerning action at a distance, always lurking in the attribution of forces to material particles. In the *Principia,* when speaking of gravity as an attractive force, Newton several times asserted that he used such terms as attraction only in a loose or popular sense, not considering how the motion so described was produced. "Attraction" at this level was a description of an observable effect, seen when an apple falls or iron is drawn to a magnet, without causative implications. By extension Newton applied the same word "attraction" to, for example, chemical phenomena where the motions of invisible particles could not, like those of the iron or the apple, be actually seen but were inferred. It now described an unobservable effect and in such cases again, when revealing his theory of matter, Newton was careful to assert that his language was not to have implications fastened upon it; he was not considering the cause of the particle's motion, though he could call this cause a force because forces are the causes of motions.[36]

This last presented him with a supreme conceptual difficulty. In the *Principia* Newton had penetrated as deeply into the nature of the gravitational force as science seemed to permit; he had a far more complete understanding of this force and its effects than he could hope to attain of any other. Yet he had failed to discover the cause of gravity or any approach to such a discovery; he could

---

[36] *Conclusio:* "The force of whatever kind by which distant particles rush towards one another is usually, in popular speech, called an attraction. For with common folk I call every force by which distant particles are impelled mutually towards one another, or come together by any means and cohere, an attraction.

say only that it existed, in proportion to the quantity of matter. Far less, therefore, could he hope to elucidate the cause or origins of the forces that seemed to operate in optics and chemistry, whose laws and phenomena were quite unknown. When pressed—or soliciting himself—to declare the cause of gravity and the manner of its action between material bodies (to avoid the charge of countenancing action at a distance) Newton could only fall back on speculative hypotheses, as Descartes and Huygens had done before him. Yet such hypotheses are far from central to Newton's theory of gravitation; indeed he always maintained that this theory had no need of them. He did, indeed, frame aetherial hypotheses of light and gravity; he never even attempted to do this for magnetism and electricity, or cohesion, or chemical combination. Whatever mechanism he describes, it is quite clear that Newton thought of his aether neither in Cartesian terms nor in terms of a "field," for it was invariably particulate and mechanical.

Without doubt the most puzzling of Newton's declarations of his aetherial hypothesis is that concluding the *Scholium Generale* of the second edition of the *Principia*. We have described in *Isis* a fuller version of the *Scholium Generale*, which permits explanation of the words in the printed version.[37] This unpublished version contains Newton's last private thoughts upon the origin of the natural forces by which particles are moved and visible phenomena occasioned, and they are very hard to interpret. The electric spirit there spoken of is the cause of cohesion, for it causes a strong attraction between contiguous particles; at the same time it causes repulsion at greater distances. It permeates all bodies, emits and bends light, and when vibrating rapidly causes the sensation of heat. Physiologically, it is the vehicle by which sensation is transmitted to the brain, and by which that organ commands the muscles; it also effects nutrition. This is virtually to allege that the electric spirit effects all the phenomena of nature; yet Newton's propositions do not say what it really is, nor how it operates. The statement that the electric spirit emits light reminds one of the experiment with the frictional machine described in *Quaery* 8, where the glass globe becomes luminous when rubbed, and it suggests that Newton understands "electric" in the normal sense. Seemingly, the electric spirit was the "fluid" (as the eighteenth century would have said) collected by friction on glass and sulphureous materials. Newton appears to suggest that whereas in experiments in electricity large forces give rise to conspicuous effects of attraction, repulsion and luminous discharge, in the minute world of material particles electric forces might exist normally without excitation, though such "attraction without friction extends only to small distances."[38] This undetectable electric force might cause the invisible motions of the particles that are sensed as heat, light or chemical change. But it is hard to understand how Newton could imagine that the electric force between particles which is a force of attraction at microscopic distances could become a force of repulsion between bodies at macroscopic distances, if that is what he means. And although it is easy to see how electrification could be associated with attraction and repulsion, and light and hence heat, its connection with animal physiology seems obscure.

[37] *Isis*, 1959, *50*: 473-476.
[38] Cf. *Quaery* 31: " . . . and perhaps electrical attraction may reach to such small distances, even without being excited by friction."

Nor does this hypothesis really solve his difficulties in giving a true explanation of natural forces, for to convert the aether or earlier writings into an electric spirit may avoid the implications of the word "aether," so inevitably associated with Cartesian and plenist speculations, and it may offer an analogy. But it leaves the cause of these forces no less mysterious than before, and no less removed from any experimental verification.

However hard he struggled, Newton could not devise a theory which would overcome the supreme deficiency which he always recognized: lack of experimental information. His aetherial hypotheses, early or late, could do nothing to remedy this. As a mechanical philosopher Newton knew that no theory of matter could be firmly established until the forces effecting phenomena were thoroughly understood from experimental investigation of the phenomena themselves, while as a mathematical physicist, he required such a theory to have mathematical rigour. When Newton wrote adversely of hypotheses he was (though condemning himself) methodologically correct in the sense he meant, for the theory of matter could not be advanced by framing hypotheses that were neither verifiable nor falsifiable, especially at a time when even an elementary theory of the transmission of light, the strength of bodies, and the formation of chemical compounds was still totally lacking. He was aware that his own theory of interparticulate forces was defective and incomplete, except perhaps in the case of gravity. It could not even explain adequately how water was variously a solid, a liquid and a vapour, yet this was apparently a relatively easy problem for the mechanical philosophy to solve. As for fundamental mechanical causes—the true cause of the forces of gravity, cohesion, optical refraction, chemical attachment and so on—insight into these was almost impossibly remote. Hence Newton's remark:

> To tell us that every species of things is endow'd with an occult specifick quality by which it acts and produces manifest effects, is to tell us nothing; But to derive two or three general principles of motion from phaenomena, and afterward to tell us how the properties and actions of all corporeal things follow from those manifest principles, would be a very great step in philosophy, though the causes of those principles were not yet discover'd. And therefore I scruple not to propose the principles of motion above mention'd, they being of very great Extent, and leave their causes to be found out.[39]

This is primarily Newton's justification for using the words "attraction" and "repulsion": they were not occult qualities to him. One may translate his statement: if a few more phenomena could be verifiably accounted for in terms of attractive and repulsive forces, as I have accounted for gravity, that would be a great deal; let the elucidation of the causes of those forces come afterward, when it may. Hypotheses about the causes—which could only be finally discovered *after* the first objective was attained—were of merit in the meantime only insofar as they suggested new experimental enquiries; otherwise they were as useless as Hooke's hypothesis of colour or Descartes' of gravity, which were formulated before the basic theories of colour and gravity were known.

And yet—after all this, and after allowing Clarke to underline his metaphysical opinions, Newton still continued to face both ways. The *Quaeries* of

---

[39] *Quaery* 31, p. 401-402.

1717 confuse his role as the mechanical philosopher who wrote the *Principia* with his role as a maker of mechanical hypotheses. One is left with an enigma. Newton appears to have been in some part of his mind a Cartesian *malgré lui:* conscious of the folly of aetherial speculations (which, for him, had neither physical basis nor metaphysical justification) he could not wholly resist playing that beguiling game, even if it meant inventing an aether 49×10^{10} times more elastic than air in proportion to its density.[40] Leibniz seemed to show that the heads of the virtuosos still ran upon mechanical explanations, as they had forty years before. In response Newton could devise plausible mechanical explanations, though he knew that they could not contain the ultimate cause of natural forces. One remembers his *cri de coeur* to Bentley: "You sometimes speak of Gravity as essential and inherent to Matter. Pray do not ascribe that Notion to me. . . ." From this peril the aetherial hypothesis, the concept of force as mass multiplied by acceleration, a shock-wave in a line of billiard-balls, offered an escape—or at least a reprieve.

"I have not yet disclosed the cause of gravity, nor have I undertaken to explain it, since I could not understand it from the phenomena," he said in one draft of the *General Scholium*. In one obvious sense this is true, and that sense knocks the bottom out of aetherial hypotheses In another sense it is false: Newton knew that God was the cause of gravity, as he was the cause of all natural forces, of everything that exists and happens. That his statement could be both true and false was Newton's dilemma; in spite of his confident expectations, physics and metaphysics (or rather theology) did not smoothly combine. In the end, mechanism and Newton's conception of God could not be reconciled. The *tertium quid* demanded by Clarke's arguments was not really available. Newton's mind must make the enormous leap from particles and forces (the proximate causes of phenomena) to the First Cause—as though leaping a chasm were a proof of its non-existence. Forced to choose, Newton preferred God to Leibniz.

[40] *Quaeries* 21 and 22.

VIII

Newton and his editors

On 14 September 1669 the Secretary of the Royal Society, Henry Oldenburg, wrote to his correspondent in Liège, René François de Sluse, a brief note on the analytical method of a young Cambridge mathematician, Isaac Newton by name.[1] This note marks Newton's first appearance before the learned world at large, where in a few years' time he was to become far better known in the field of optics, and it is interesting that the treatise upon which Oldenburg's note was ultimately based, the *De analysi*, was only to be printed forty-two years later when much of its freshness was, inevitably, dimmed; and then not by Newton himself but by his protégé William Jones. As I think is generally known, such a delay in publication of his work was by no means unusual with Newton; *Opticks*, of which a large part had been communicated to the Royal Society by 1675, was published only in 1704, while the Cambridge optical lectures on which that book was in part based only saw print some sixty years after their delivery, when Newton himself was dead. Only one of Newton's books, the one with which I am chiefly concerned this afternoon, was written in the actual heat of intellectual discovery. We know that in the summer of 1684 Newton possessed but the barest outline of the future *Philosophiae Naturalis Principia Mathematica*, if so much; yet by June 1687, less than three years later, the book was in print after the last section of it had been written twice over.

Let me review – it will not take long – the story of Newton's major publications. The Cambridge Varenius of 1672 need not detain us; but for the title-page there is almost nothing of Newton in it. Next a long interval during which, however, Newton's name appeared frequently in the *Philosophical Transactions*, until the *Principia* in 1687; and another even longer gap before *Opticks* in 1704. Then, indeed, in Newton's seventh decade, partly under pressure from the claims and criticisms of Leibniz and his supporters, Newton's work came frequently before the public; *Opticks* was reprinted several times in both Latin and English, his early mathematical writings were published by Whiston (in 1707) and Jones (in 1711), and selections from his mathematical correspondence of long before appeared in the *Commercium epistolicum* of 1712. However, as I have said, *Lectiones opticae* like

[1] Numbered notes appear on pages 415–417.

the *Chronology of Ancient Kingdoms* and the *Prophecies of Daniel and John* appeared only after Newton's death.²

A number of points may be made about this division of Newton's life into a great creative phase, during which he published only one book, the *Principia*, and its last twenty-five years during which Newton published or republished much. First, just as the *Principia* was brought out by Halley, who was quite as much as Shakespeare's W. H. its only begetter, so in these sere years Newton was aided by a host of men, Samuel Clarke, Richard Bentley, Roger Cotes, John Machin, Henry Pemberton, Abraham de Moivre, William Whiston, William Jones, the Abbé Conti, John Harris, who with or without Newton's own active cooperation saw his writings into print. To the best of my knowledge *Opticks* was the only one of Newton's books produced by himself alone and even this book has the mildly curious feature that it was produced under the transparent anonymity of the initials 'I.N.'. According to Brewster, the Latin translation of *Opticks* was made by De Moivre but the publication was directed by Samuel Clarke, who was richly rewarded by Newton for his pains.³ Newton aided Jones in the preparation of his *Analysis per Quantitatum Series, Fluxiones, ac Differentias*, whereas he quite reasonably deplored and indeed obstructed so far as he could Whiston's printing, without prior agreement, of the algebraic lectures he had read at Cambridge long before.⁴ The *Arithmetica Universalis* was also anonymous; equally its true authorship was everywhere recognized. To make the best of a bad job some years later Newton had John Machin produce a revised edition under his own control. Somewhat similarly it is said that the writings of George Cheyne impelled Newton to increase the then very thin body of Newtonian mathematics in print by adding two treatises (one being *De quadratura*) to his *Opticks* in 1704.

From all this one derives the impression that though a man whose pen was always in his hand, an indefatigable transcriber and draughtsman who has left many thousands of manuscript pages behind him, Newton scarcely ever finished a manuscript to his satisfaction. Omitting the *Principia* for the present, we note that though Newton seems to have been satisfied with the text of *Opticks* as we have it, nevertheless it was an incomplete work, and the *Queries* filling out the unwritten Book III underwent several additions. Otherwise only two or three mathematical essays were deliberately prepared for the press by Newton himself; the rest of his work was snatched or suppressed and a great deal has only become known in our own time.

That Newton was temperamentally reticent there can be no doubt; his was no facile pen embarking on a career by a smooth appeal to patron or public. He seems not to have shared his thoughts freely or frequently with Isaac Barrow, though the readiness to impart his work from which Collins benefited continued until 1676 at least, the year in which he also prepared the long *Epistola posterior* for Leibniz. By this time, however, the opportunity for a major early publication on either optics or mathematics had passed by. There can be no doubt that Newton seriously contemplated, in the early 1670's, publishing books reflecting either his

The Wilkins Lecture, 1973

mathematical or his optical discoveries or both, and proof-sheets possibly connected with one or other of these projects have been found.[5] Not to enter into needless detail, initial moves were made towards the printing of Newton's early mathematical essay, of his Cambridge optical lectures, of his improved version of a Dutch algebra, and of his *Philosophical Transactions* communications. That all these moves ended in nothing should by no means be attributed solely to Newton's reluctance to commit himself to print, for the refusal of the stationers in both Cambridge and London to risk certain of these undertakings was decisive. Yet one can discern in the various negotiations Newton's strong and justified feeling that none of his own writings was sufficiently mature for publication *in extenso*. We may recognize here a genuine and rational hesitancy on Newton's part – the evidence for so describing it can be found in Dr Whiteside's volumes – one which reappears, for instance, in Newton's letter to Oldenburg of 25 January 1676 when he declined to allow the printing of his 'Discourse of Observations' in optics recently read to the Royal Society.[6] We must distinguish this from the perhaps too-well-known, almost hysterical cries that were wrung from Newton at intervals all through his life:

'I have long since determined to concern myself no further about the promotion of philosophy' (5 December 1674).[7]

'I see I have made myself a slave to Philosophy, but if I get free of Mr Linus' business I will resolutely bid adieu to it eternally, except what I do for my private satisfaction or leave to come out after me. For I see a man must either resolve to put out nothing new or to become a slave to defend it' (18 November 1676).[8]

'I am grown of all men the most shy of setting pen to paper about anything that may lead into disputes' (12 September 1682).[9]

(To Flamsteed) 'I do not love to be printed upon every occasion much less to be dunned and teased by foreigners about mathematical things or to be thought by our own people to be trifling away my time about them when I should be about the King's business' (6 January 1699).[10]

Every good Macaulay schoolboy knows that Newton's first public appearance on the scientific scene was greeted not with applause alone – there was plenty of that – but with strong continuing criticism also. For three years and more after his optical discoveries were first made public in 1672 Newton was constantly defending the originality and value of his reflecting telescope, the accuracy of his prismatic experiments, and the necessity for his new theory of light and colours. This critical reception was not wholly unjustified, and Newton's critics were not all fools; many problems in the development of the new telescope on a practical scale were to be encountered; Newton had been neither complete nor clear in his initial description of his prism researches; his theoretical position was not completely candid nor perhaps so transparently logical as he himself supposed.[11] Because he was patient and modest, because he was young and naïve, or because he was proud and confident, or because of a combination of all such reasons, Newton answered his critics elaborately though rather by argument than by disclosing fresh experimental evidence. So laborious was this defence that Newton came to feel (as he wrote to Oldenburg in 1676) that the 'frequent interruptions' arising from 'the letters of various persons (full of objections and other matters) quite deterred me from the design' of publishing further on optics and mathematics 'and caused me to accuse myself of imprudence because in snatching at a shadow I had sacrificed my peace, a matter of real substance'.[12]

Throughout his life Newton tended to feel that the 1670s had warned him that printers were breakers of his private peace. Recollection of this drove him in certain circumstances but by no means invariably when publication of his work was urged upon him – as the appearance of Jones' *Analysis*, not to say *Principia* and *Opticks* reminds us – into utterances of paranoiac stridency. It did not happen when his writings were being handled by men whom he trusted, from whom he could tolerate a good deal of criticism and dissent. Even in his relations with Hooke – which are fortunately not within my province this afternoon – until the final breach over the *Principia*, Newton made repeated attempts to establish the point that fair criticism as to facts or their interpretation was welcomed by him. I do not wish to seem overkind to Newton, who was certainly a 'nice man to deal with', but it would be a mistake not to recognize that what angered him in the conduct of Hooke, or Leibniz, or Johann Bernoulli, or Flamsteed was not intellectual weakness but moral weakness, nor (despite his obvious self-involvement) can one easily deny that Newton was just in his discernment of their moral weaknesses. Let me at once admit that Newton's own moral position was on certain issues far from impregnable also, and perhaps we may see an instance of this later; but this is no reason for exaggerating his sensitivity to polite technical criticism, which is a different matter altogether.

In what follows I shall consider some aspects of Newton's relationships with three men: Edmond Halley, Roger Cotes and Henry Pemberton, all of them editors of the *Principia*. I do this not so much for any bibliographical reason – for the changes made in the various editions of the *Principia* and to some extent even the participation of the latter two editors in them have been revealed by Professor I. Bernard Cohen in his recent monumental edition of that book. I hope rather to throw some light on Newton's intellectual character as a scientific author, and also on his moral character as a human being. There is no question but these three editors of the *Principia* were men whom Newton liked personally, and whose intellectual qualities he admired; particularly is this true of Halley and Cotes. The execution of their editorial responsibilities for Newton placed no permanent strain on their personal relations with him; in the case of Halley and Pemberton, at any rate, there was no dissension at any time, and we have every reason to believe that Newton was highly satisfied with their work. Thus there can be no question but that we are seeing Newton at his best.

The immediate origins of the *Principia* have often been described.[13] I will begin at the point where Edmond Halley recollects a conversation between Sir Christopher Wren, Robert Hooke and himself about the inverse square law of

Edmond Halley (1656–1742). The Royal Society's portrait by Thomas Murray.

Bust of Roger Cotes (1682–1716) in the possession of Trinity College, Cambridge.

Sr   Cambridge March 31st 1711

I have received your Letter with the inclosed Paper & am very well satisfied with yr solution of the difficulty which I formerly proposed to You concerning the velocity of the effluent water. I find that 25 & 21 express the proportion of $\sqrt{2}$ to 1 as nearly as it is possible for so small numbers to do it, whence it is probable yt the exact proportion of the diameter of the hole to ye diameter of ye stream is that of $\sqrt{2}$ to 1, & then ye proportion of 44 to 37 will be much nearer the truth than yt of 25 to 21. I am sensible of the undeserved honour you do me in one of yr additions & I return you my thanks for yr kindness. After I had read your paper I was extremely pleased to see the whole Theory (as I thought) so well settled: however I was resolved to read over the Propositions once more, with all the care I could, before I delivered them to the Printer.

It seems to me that, in transcribing the Copy, you have omitted something in the first Section of ye 36th Proposition. For, as I have it, I cannot be certain yt I do fully & precisely understand your sense & design. I think Your Idea is this: You imagine that as the water descends freely from AB by the force of its own gravity so by some other force, whatever that be, it is moved at the same time with an Horizontal motion towards ye Axis of ye Stream which Horizontall motion is supposed so to be adapted to the motion of Descent that it may not anywise accelerate or retard it, but only just suffice to keep the Stream intire and uninterrupted; & by this meanes ye Space ABNFEM is always full of water, but ye Space around this (viz:t AMEC, BNFD) is alwayes void of water. If this be Your Idea, you have not express'd it in Your Copy. I am perswaded it is Your Idea, for otherwise I cannot see any argument in this section, or understand the sense of Your words [uti prius] in ye 2d section. But yr words [defluere in vas, & ipsum perpetuo implere] & a little lower [& vas perpetuo plenum manebit] lead the Reader to think this is not Your Idea since you seem by these words to suppose the whole Cylinder to be perpetually full. I cannot think you intend in this place to represent the whole Cylinder as perpetually full; for if so You are got no further in the 3d Section than you was in the first. I will transcribe the first section from Yr Copy that I may supply what is wanting. Cas. 1. Sit ACDB vas cylindricum, AB ejus orificium, CD fundum horizonti parallelum, EF foramen circulare in medio fundi, G centrum foraminis, & GH axis cylindri horizonti perpendicularis. Et producatur axis GH ad J ut sit JH ad JG in duplicata ratione areæ foraminis EF ad aream circuli AB, et per punctum J ducatur linea horizontalis KL vasi hinc inde occurrens in K & L. Concipe cylindrum glaciei APQB ejusdem esse latitudinis cum cavitate vasis, et uniformi cum motu perpetuo descendere, et partes ejus quamprimum attingunt Superficiem AB liquescere et in aquam conversas gravitate sua defluere in vas & ipsum perpetuo implere ut constans & uniformis sit aquæ defluxus per foramen EF. Sit autem ea glaciei descendentis velocitas quam aqua cadendo & casu suo describendo altitudinem JH acquirere potest; & vas perpetuo plenum manebit, et velocitas aquæ per foramen EF effluentis ea erit quam aqua cadendo, & casu suo describendo altitudinem JG, acquirere potest, ideoq per Theoremata Galilæi, erit ad velocitatem aquæ in circulo AB in subduplicata ratione JG ad JH, id est (per constructionem) in simplici ratione circuli AB ad aream foraminis EF, et propterea transibit per foramen EF & transeundo implebit foramen illud accurate. Nam circulus horizonti parallelus per quem aqua cadens adæquate transit, est reciproce ut velocitas aquæ. De velocitate aquæ horizontem versus hic agitur. Et motus horizonti parallelus ~~quem aquæ cadens adæquate transit quo partes aquæ cadentis ad invicem acce~~dunt, cum non oriatur à gravitate, nec motum horizonti perpendicularem a gravitate oriundum mutat, hic non consideratur.

In the 2d Section of the 36th Proposition you have these words [& pondus totius columnæ aquæ ABNFEM impenditur in defluxum ejus generandum.] It may possibly appear to some Readers that you have committed a mistake in these words

VIII

Sr

What is contained in pag. 509. l. 12, 13, 14. in the sheet, which comes to you with this note is ~~an will find~~ an expression, which I think is inconsistent with what you have said at the end of your Opticks; viz. in Qu. 11. Here in this sheet you declare it as your opinion, that ~~the~~ the time which globes retain heat increases in a less proportion than their diameters increase; whereas the sentiment expressed in your Opticks implies the contrary, viz. that the time which globes will retain their heat must increase faster than their diameters; because you suppose that if a globe ~~amounts~~ to a certain magnitude like that of the sun or fixed stars it shall for ever retain its heat. Therefore the time, which the sun or a fixed star will retain its heat will bear a greater proportion to the time that a lesser globe will continue hot, than the diameter the sun or star bears, to the diameter of the lesser globe; for the time, which the sun or star will naturally retain its heat, is supposed by you to be infinite.

The blank space left in pag. 506 is for a copper cuts of the comet. I am
Your humble
and most obedt. Servt.
H. Pemberton

Jul. 17. 1725.

Part of a letter from Pemberton to Newton of 17 July 1725
(University Library, Cambridge: MS Add 3986 (23)).

The Wilkins Lecture, 1973

centripetal force in the solar system, from which law, Hooke declared, 'all the laws of the celestial motions were to be demonstrated and that he himself had done it... however' – I continue with Halley's own narrative of the incident – 'I remember Sir Christopher was little satisfied that he could do it, and though Mr Hooke then promised to show it to him, I do not yet find that in that particular he has been as good as his word. The August following [that is, August 1684] when I did myself the honour to visit you, I then learnt the good news that you had brought this demonstration to perfection, and you were pleased to promise me a copy thereof, which the November following I received with a great deal of satisfaction.'[14] Now what Halley then received was almost certainly the whole or a part of a little treatise that we might call 'Newton's *De motu*', so impressive to Halley that he hurried off to Cambridge again in order to persuade Newton to let his 'demonstration' be made public by communicating it to the Royal Society, in which mission he was successful. Whether or not Halley first laid before Newton the idea of working up his rapidly developing ideas in mechanics into a much more thorough and ample treatment than *De motu* I do not know, and I imagine that on the contrary the impulse to do so was internal to Newton himself; for there can be no doubt that after the stimulus of Halley's August visit Newton had gone rapidly and deeply into mechanics, and that in the autumn of 1684, before Halley's second visit of November, Newton had formulated a number of new propositions, unknown to him *before* August, not all of which are to be found in *De motu*. Thus Newton's great work of discovery was already begun, and though he was doubtless encouraged by Halley's second appeal it can have had little immediate effect upon the course which Newton was already taking before it.

Edmond Halley (1656–1742), half a generation younger than Newton, does not figure even by allusion in Newton's correspondence until after 1680. He was elected F.R.S. on 30 November 1678 after his return from his astronomical expedition to St Helena. Before his close association with Newton began he had already published (in 1679) his resultant catalogue of the southern stars besides seven scientific papers, mostly in the *Philosophical Transactions*, from which Newton could have gathered that Halley had some skill in mathematical as well as observational astronomy. Moreover, in the 1680s Halley is mentioned very frequently in the correspondence of Newton and Flamsteed as a student of comets. It does not appear likely that Halley and Newton can have had a close personal acquaintance before 1684, since most of Newton's absences from Cambridge were spent in Lincolnshire where he had inherited the family estate after the death of his mother in the summer of 1679.[15] We may guess – but no more – that Halley before he made his epoch-making journey to Cambridge in August 1684 would have learned from Collins and others that Newton had made extraordinary advances in pure mathematics, and from Flamsteed of Newton's interest in astronomy; of Newton's early studies in mechanics he probably was quite unaware, unless in so far as he had heard Hooke's reports to the Royal Society of his correspondence with Newton in 1679–80.

Having appeared so dramatically on the scene, Halley almost disappears from it again for nearly two years. Almost, but not quite. Thanks to detective work by modern scholars,[16] we now know that Halley saw a draft of Book I of the *Principia*, which then included a large part of Book II as the work was finally printed, presumably reading that (now incomplete) manuscript which passed into the Lucasian Papers at Cambridge and Professor Cohen has denoted as LL_α. A still extant paper of comments, anonymous but in Halley's hand, clearly relates to this manuscript and may well have been written by mid-1685, possibly even at Cambridge. It is true we have no direct evidence of such a visit, nor indeed of any correspondence either, but it is really against all probability that Newton and Halley should have been completely out of touch from November 1684 to May 1686, and the paper of comments now assures us that they were not. Of course, the fact that the Royal Society so readily committed the editorial responsibility to Halley, and even the tone of Halley's first extant letter to Newton, also suggest a continuing intercourse between them.

It is more regrettable that we have no details of it because the explicit record of Newton's progress in writing the *Principia* is virtually blank. In February 1684/5 he told Aston that an unspecified 'it' was fairly soon to be completed, perhaps a draft of Book I of the *Principia* as it then was; and in Newton's correspondence with Flamsteed we see him in September and October 1685 engaged on the theories of the tides and comets.[17] It was about this time (Newton later told Halley) that he got stuck in the theory of comets, spending 'two months in calculations to no purpose for want of a good method, which made me afterwards return to the first Book and enlarge it with divers Propositions some relating to Comets other to things found out last Winter'.[18] This passage informs us, then, that the shorter version of Book I in LL_α, which Halley had previously seen, was replaced by a longer version, denoted LL_β, the extra length chiefly coming from a new Section V which is concerned with the sort of geometrical problems which had to be solved if the orbits of comets were to be traced and proved parabolical; the enlargement occurred in the winter of 1685–6.

Now I must explain that at this time Newton's plan was for the *Principia* to consist of two Books only. The first Book, of which Halley had seen the early, shorter version already, contained material extending at least up to our present Book II, Proposition XXIII, as Dr Whiteside has established[19] – not, of course, *all* the material up to that point as it was ultimately to be printed. Thus Book I gave the general theory, including rational fluid mechanics, just as in the outline of Newton's *De motu* of 1684. This he followed by the application of the principles to actual phenomena in Book II, which Newton at that time called simply *De motu corporum liber secundus*. The manuscript of this is still extant and it forms a natural continuation of the (incomplete) LL_β. It was to be printed in an English translation, in the year after Newton's death, as *The System of the World*.

When, as I have just explained, Newton added the present Section V to his existing Book I, and possibly expanded the number of propositions on fluid mechanics also, he separated the latter out as a separate Book II and – very likely about the same time – decided to rewrite the former *De motu corporum liber secundus* in a more rigorous fashion. He told his readers about this in the *Principia*:[20] 'It remains for me to expound, upon these same principles [that is, the laws of motion and force] the disposition of the system of the World. I had composed a third Book dealing with this subject on a popular plan, so that it might be read by the multitude; but since those who have not sufficiently grasped the principles laid down can scarcely perceive the force of their consequences nor lay aside the prejudices familiar to them over many years, and furthermore in order not to involve the business in arguments, I transmuted the gist of that Book into propositions, in the mathematical way, so that it might be read only by those who had first examined the principles'.

We cannot be sure when Newton got Book III into more or less its final shape, but it must have been by the summer of 1686, because he then writes to Halley as if it were so, as we shall see.

But to return now to the relations between Newton and Halley, it seems that though, about mid-1685, Newton allowed Halley to read the first version of Book I, presumably to whet his appetite, and although Newton adopted various verbal revisions suggested by Halley, he permitted him to know nothing of the enlarged Book I, or the subsequent development of the *Principia*, until after he had sent the manuscript of the new Book I only to London in April 1686. However, I think we may well surmise from an expression of Halley's which I shall quote in a moment, that Halley had been earlier apprised of Newton's intention of writing a subsequent book containing applications to the System of the World, that is, long before the printed manuscript of Book I reached him.

The surviving correspondence between Newton and Halley begins with the latter's letter of 22 May 1686, telling Newton that the manuscript of Book I, dedicated to the Royal Society, had been presented to that body on 28 April (a fact of which surely Newton must have been informed earlier) and that he himself had been 'instructed to look after the printing it [on behalf of the Society, that is]; and I will take care [Halley continues] that it shall be performed as well as possible, only I would first have your directions in what you shall think necessary for the embellishing thereof... what you signifie as your desire shall be punctually observed'.[21]

Now although the Society had boldly agreed to print Newton's book it was in fact at this time exceedingly impoverished, its chief asset being, apparently, the unsold stock of Francis Willughby's *Historia piscium* or 'Book of Fishes'.[22] Accordingly an offer from Halley – who was no Croesus – not only to produce the *Principia* but to pay for it was received with alacrity by the Society on 2 June. He must already have settled on a printer, Joseph Streater, and the typesetting must have started, for on the seventh Halley was able to send Newton a proof of the first gathering for his approval of the type and paper. The great work was begun; printing it was to take about a year – for Newton was eager to proceed slowly – what were Halley's contributions towards its appearance during the next twelve months?

One of the most important is presaged in a letter of 7 June where Halley writes: 'I hope you will bestow the second part, or what remains of this, upon us as soon as you shall have finished it; for the application of this Mathematical part, to the System of the World, is what will render it acceptable to all Naturalists, as well as Mathematicians; and much advance the sale of the book.'[23]

Halley's thought is transparent. A formal exposition of theoretical mechanics, however original and brilliant, would have neither the interest nor the conviction of a work that applied the theory to the actual phenomena of sun, moon and planets; moreover, the power of Newton's theory in accounting for the phenonena of tides or the shape of the Earth, for example, could hardly be made manifest at all without such developed applications. Nor could the superiority of Newton's new mathematical physics over the qualitative physics of Descartes be cogently demonstrated save by the exact analysis of actual examples; it was, of course, a distinctive difference *in kind* between the two physics that the former could generate from theory and the injection of known parameters precise numerical values capable of comparison with observed values.

Now the passage I have just quoted makes it clear that, having studied Book I (already so entitled in the manuscript, of course), Halley knew that Newton intended a Book II; but he did not know where this would begin, or what it would contain, or anything of the further development of the book. Subsequent letters from both Halley and Newton completely confirm this interpretation. On 20 June, however, Halley learned from Newton that he 'designed the whole to consist of three books, the second was finished last summer being short and only wants transcribing and drawing the cuts fairly. Some new Proportions I have thought of [Newton adds] but these I can as well let alone. The third wants the theory of comets.'[24]

In these words Newton announces to Halley his *second* plan for the *Principia* which corresponded to that finally printed. For various reasons, including the fact that Newton did not modify his manuscript of *De motu corporum Liber secundus* to make it the third Book of the *Principia*, we may imagine that our present Book III was by now well advanced, apart from the treatment of comets, where (as we have seen) Newton stuck fast in the autumn of 1685.[25] Note, by the way, that Newton's letter (probably inadvertently) fails to inform Halley that the new second book was devoted to fluid mechanics, so that Halley remained for the next half year in ignorance of Newton's intentions with regard to this topic.

However, having described his second or three-book plan to Halley, Newton continued immediately: 'The third [Book] I now design to suppress. Philosophy is such an impertinently litigious Lady that a man had as good be engaged in Lawsuits as to have to do with her. I found it so formerly and now I no sooner come near her again but she gives me warning.'[26]

Newton had indeed thought of reverting to the simpler title of *De motu corporum libri duo* for the work thus curtailed, for the sake of leaving the purely theoretical treatment more obscure and thus avoiding philosophical wrangles. Just the reasons that led Halley to hope that Newton would include a fairly accessible phenomenalistic section in the *Principia* now induced Newton to exclude it, even in mathematical form. The reason for Newton's adoption of Plan Three was, of course, Robert Hooke's angry charge of plagiary against Newton, which Halley himself had been compelled to report.

Newton was so far serious in this plan (as Dr Whiteside has discovered) that he wrote a draft paragraph for the preface of the curtailed *Principia* explaining the omission of what we know as Book III. After the sentence in the present preface which reads:

'For the whole difficulty of philosophy seems to turn upon this, that we should investigate the forces of Nature from the phenomena of motions, and then from these forces demonstrate other phenomena.'

he proposed to add:

'The System of the World which we have written is an example of this approach, if we can possibly be persuaded to lay that book before the public some day. For there we demonstrate from certain phenomena that gravity does exist in all bodies universally and that it is proportional to the [quantity of] matter in individual bodies; further, we derive from the gravity of the Earth, the Sun and the Planets the motions, densities, and elliptical shapes of these bodies, as also the precession of the equinoxes, the motions of the Moon and of Comets, and the ebb and flow of the sea.'[27]

Clearly (as Halley may have guessed) Book III of the *Principia*, heavily indebted to the earlier *De motu corporum liber secundus*, was now in virtually its final form.[28] Well aware of its value to the whole design of the *Principia*, Halley at once begged Newton 'not to let his resentment run so high as to deprive us of your third book wherein the application of your mathematical doctrine to the theory of comets, and several curious experiments which, as I guess by what you write, ought to compose it, will undoubtedly render it acceptable to those that will call themselves philosophers without mathematics, which are by much the great number.'[29]

Again, it is evident that Halley did not know precisely what to expect, nor did he learn more for many months while the slow work of printing Book I continued. In his next letters, while acknowledging 'the great kindness of the Gentlemen of your Society, far beyond what I could ever expect or deserve', Newton made no reference to the restoration of Book III to the *Principia*.[30]

Here I must pause a moment to deal with the puzzling fact, to which no strict chronological interpretation can be given, that in the summer of 1686 or perhaps earlier, but certainly before October 1686,[31] Halley did read a manuscript of the *Principia* divided into three books and make comments upon it. What happened is mysterious. The comments, neither bulky nor important, survive but the manuscript is lost. It was neither of the Lucasian Lectures manuscript, obviously, nor was it the Royal Society manuscript, yet it was already very like the latter. If Halley read Books II and III in draft before 20 June 1686, why did Newton have to explain so much as he did in the letter to Halley of 20 June?

And if Halley read it between June and October why had he forgotten, by the end of the year, that Book II opened with a discussion of the motions of bodies in resisting mediums? In the absence of complete documentation, all the problems of the relations between Newton and Halley cannot be resolved, for they were clearly closer than the extant correspondence shows. I can only offer the following hypotheses: (1) in the manuscript seen by Halley, Books II and III were both shorter than the printed versions, as is the extent of Halley's comment upon them; and (2) Newton impressed upon Halley that his work was incomplete, and the manuscript he saw far from ready for the printer; hence Halley might feel considerable doubt about Newton's final intentions, especially after his June decision to remove Book III.

As evidence of such doubt – to come back now to firmer ground – we have Newton's letter to Halley of 13 February 1687,[32] in which Newton dealt with a query which had reached him from the Royal Society via Paget, whether or not he intended to deal with resisted motion in the *Principia*. It must surprise us to find that Halley (who was present at the meeting when the question was raised) neither knew the answer to it, nor transmitted the question to Newton; and to learn that Halley had not only failed to secure from Newton the finished copy of Book II after Newton had told him it was to be ready but failed also to communicate in any way with Newton for some three or four months![33] I am going to guess at the reason for this; my hypothesis is that in a letter now lost, of 20 August 1686, Newton again refused to allow our Book III to be printed, but told Halley that the second and as then proposed final Book would be ready for him when he needed it. I imagine Halley was rather miffed and the printing temporarily stopped.[34] At any rate, by February 1687 Newton had only received the first 88 pages of the book in proof.

The jolt from Newton seems to have aroused Halley from his bad temper or indifference, for he wrote back promising to do nothing else till the *Principia* was finished, and offering to engage a second printer to work upon Book II, which he received at last from Newton in the first days of March 1687. At the same time he made it clear to Newton that the Royal Society would hardly be satisfied without some spectacular exemplification of the usefulness of the theory of gravitation to astronomy; particularly the Society desired Newton to determine the solar parallax from the parallactic inequality of the Moon's motion: 'it being the best means of determining the dimensions of the planetary system...they intreat you not to desist, when you are come so near the solution of so noble a problem.'[35]

Moreover, as he read the manuscript of Book II, Halley perceived that Newton had been so far neglectful of his resolution to expunge Book III, 'On the System of the World,' that he had left references to it in the manuscript; accordingly, being assured that its inclusion would afford 'universal satisfaction', he now offered to start another printer on this also, if Newton would send it, 'being resolved to engage myself upon no other business till such time as all is done, desiring hereby to clear myself from all imputations of negligence in a business wherein I am much rejoiced to be any ways concerned in handing to the world that that all future ages will admire'.[36] Book III reached him on 5 April.

It is just possible, though not highly probable, that but for Halley's friendly persistence and reassurance Newton's pique would have led him to suppress the crowning exposition of the *Principia*. However, I think it more than likely that Newton had taken his decision to include Book III 'in mathematical form' in the autumn of 1686, when he was out of touch with Halley, for it was then that he prepared the final version of Book II with its references to Book III that Halley found. It is my interpretation of events that although Newton was perfectly ready to conciliate Halley on minor points, and would address him as 'your affectionate friend and humble servant', he was far too tough a character to give way on a point of substance, against his own better judgement, or against his own interests. I believe that had Newton felt his own interests to be opposed to those of Halley in this matter, he would have preferred them. For our understanding of the relations between the two men, it is a grave pity that the existing record is so defective;[37] but for a few scrappy pages at Cambridge, we should know nothing of Halley's preliminary suggestions for the rewording of the text, which the extant letters seem almost perversely to conceal. One has the impression from the letters that Newton, the author, kept himself aloof from and above his editor though always highly friendly; but the fact that Newton was so far informal with Halley as to show him drafts of the *Principia* belies that 'official' impression. One might almost imagine that the documents had been deliberately purged. Why?

I think it would be far-fetched to imagine that Newton wished to eliminate from his file of correspondence all evidence of Halley's connexion with the text of the *Principia*, for the sum of his intervention is really so slight. Halley proposed a number of verbal and expository changes in the manuscripts first submitted to him, some of which were adopted by Newton for the printer's copy while others he rejected. Then again Halley silently modified the printer's copy in trivial ways. The details may be found in Professor Cohen's work. It was Halley, too, who decided to print the diagrams as woodcuts inset on the page, rather than use separate plate-pages at the end of the book. But there is very little evidence to show that Halley examined Newton's arguments in the *Principia* very attentively – as regards the second and third Books he had no time to do so – and certainly in the next few years Newton (and others also) found that this first edition did contain, besides many misprints, numerous fairly trivial errors and a few subtle and serious ones. I have the impression that Halley contributed (by his criticism) nothing of either philosophical or scientific importance to the improvement of Newton's text, and that his work was rather that of a sub-editor. One may perhaps wonder whether Halley was quite capable of catching Newton's errors, and certainly this rather easy-going character stood in awe of Newton. But perhaps the picture would look a little different if we possessed the whole Halley–Newton correspondence.

In what survives there is only one instance of Halley's drawing attention to a substantial fault in the text (in the scholium to Proposition 31), where a factor of one-half had been omitted.[38] Newton rewrote a few lines and thanked Halley for pointing out the fault.

Halley once told John Wallis that having been very intent upon the publication of Mr Newton's book, he had forgotten his obligations to the Royal Society's correspondents, but he hoped the book when published would excuse his neglect.[39] Certainly posterity has never forgotten Halley's role in the publication of the *Principia*, nor the service to the Newtonian theory done by Halley's work on comets. Neither did Newton ever forget or underrate Halley. He paid him a deserved if not effusive tribute in the Preface to the *Principia* and remained always his friend and supporter, promoting Halley's career at every opportunity even when (according to Flamsteed) this nautical astronomer 'now talks, swears and drinks brandy like a sea-captain'.[40] Halley, of whose deep and lasting admiration for Newton there can be no doubt, was in turn one of Newton's most loyal partisans in his wars with Flamsteed and Leibniz. Whether he would have had the *Principia* without Halley is idle speculation, but one can be confident that without Newton Halley's chequered career would have been even more difficult.

We now come to another of those curious problems in Newton's behaviour that must always torment his biographers. Given that the *Principia* rapidly became an unobtainable book, that Newton began the revision of it energetically, that he was not lacking in eager would-be Halleys, why did Newton delay the second edition of the *Principia* for over a quarter of a century?[41] Let us in the first place be a little cautious about defining Newton's real intentions. A great deal of the working-over of the text he did in his annotated copies is rather trivial, though it did include the correction of a number of howlers such as that in Book II, Proposition 37, where Newton had originally argued that a vertical jet of water could attain only half the height of the pressure-head. A good many tricky issues remained on which it was not easy for him to pronounce in public; philosophical issues, like the status of gravitation, or God's role in the universe, or atomism; and personal issues – what form of words was he to use about Hooke, Leibniz, Flamsteed? I doubt whether Newton had ever quite made up his mind. Then he knew well that he was far from having succeeded in bringing such problems as the calculation of the precession of the equinoxes, of the axial shortening of the Earth's diameter, and above all, the motions of the Moon, to a complete satisfactory resolution. Then again I believe we should take with a pinch of salt the assurance of David Gregory or Fatio de Duillier that the *Principia* was practically within their grasp.

We must suppose that Newton's sexagenarian success – as Master of the Mint, as President of the Royal Society, as a Knight, and perhaps especially as author of *Opticks* and survivor of Robert Hooke – inspired him to take the long-meditated action; this and the urging of the eager Richard Bentley who, by the way, did

VIII

The Wilkins Lecture, 1973

very nicely out of the whole adventure, as Newton intended. Bentley knew a good deal about both printing and Latin, but he could not have examined Newton's mathematical arguments; it was therefore a kind of accident that he introduced as a substitute for himself in performing the editorial chores a man who could. When this happened, in 1709, Roger Cotes had been for three years the first Plumian professor of astronomy at Cambridge. He was forty year's Newton's junior and felt a strong sense of obligation to the great man, but we have no information concerning their earlier relationship. Newton had left Cambridge before Cotes went up to Trinity (1699) but we know that Cotes was one of the few students of his (unpublished) Lucasian lectures.

Like Halley, Cotes received an incomplete quantity of copy from Newton – partly, one supposes, printed sheets of the first edition – which he was to see through the press 'correcting only such faults as occur in reading over the [proof] sheets to correct them as they are printed' as Newton put it.[42] But – as appears from his first surviving letter to Newton[43] – Cotes was eager to do far more. He examined the copy with great care for logic, factual accuracy, and consistency, not hesitating to call Newton's attention firmly to any failing. Like Halley again, Cotes trusted himself (with a proper apology) to make trivial and sometimes more than trivial alterations to the text without consulting Newton 'it not being possible for me without great inconvenience to the work and uneasiness to yourself to have your approbation in every particular';[44] but unlike Halley, Cotes also played the part of a keen and tireless critic of Newton's text over the three and a half years of their collaboration. In consequence, a correspondence developed between author and editor amounting to 84 (extant) letters, often of bulk, sometimes accompanied by long enclosures. About half the *Principia* was reset in its new form without difficulty – that is, all Book I and the first part of Book II – but after that the text was debated almost line by line.

Let me emphasize at once that Cotes's efforts were highly productive of that accurate and consistent text which was to be, in all essentials, the lasting edition of the *Principia*. He insisted that Newton should be clear, he pointed out cases where Newton's text confused quantities or terms, he showed him where a correction had only been partially carried through.[45] In Book III particularly Cotes saved Newton from countless errors of computation and all kinds of minor inconsistencies, errors and omissions; for here many numbers were to be worked out by theory and compared, rather too precisely, with the results of observations. Cotes was, if anything, even more eager than Newton to render the 'fit' in every instance exact and consistent, and even more ready to juggle with numbers to attain this end.[46] A great deal of Newton's printer's copy was worked over two and three times before Cotes was at last satisfied.

Now it is obvious that all this caused Newton a good deal of extra labour and delayed the printing. Nor was the end result always very significant. For example, with relation to the troublesome Book II, Proposition 37 (renumbered 36), in the new copy Newton had correctly revised the demonstration to make the height of a vertical jet equal to that of the pressure-head. Cotes objected against this (also with reason) that the new velocity-relation was not confirmed by experiments on the *volume* of water extruded by jets in a given time.[47] He left it to Newton to clear up the discrepancy by discovery of the 'vena contracta' effect, while progress was halted for six months.[48] Again, Cotes raised some rather obscure difficulties about Newton's treatment of the vibration of air-particles in developing the mathematical theory of wave-motion;[49] he renewed his criticism against Newton's first reply, but in the end conceded that 'as to the business of sounds I do entirely agree with you upon considering that matter over again'.[50] In this discussion seven and a half months slipped by, for Newton refrained from answering Cotes's letter of 30 July 1711 until 2 February 1712, and then wrote with no apology for this long silence, beginning his letter abruptly

'Sir,

I have at length got some leisure to remove the difficulties which have stopped the press for some time and I hope it will stop no more.'[51]

It was now almost two years since the project first began. Similarly, although Cotes's care in reviewing Newton's lunar theory is beyond praise, it must be said also that he worried Newton with many possibly insignificant details, and raised a number of points of criticism that proved unfounded on further examination. Cotes in no way modified the substance of Newton's theory of the moon as he had developed it for the second edition, and his careful review may have made Newton even more painfully aware of its shortcomings.

I make these points so that we should not exaggerate Cotes's role in the second edition as compared with Newton's, partly to explain the (fortunately temporary) want of kindness Newton displayed towards Cotes. On his side Newton – occupied not only with Mint and pressing family concerns, but with the various aspects of the Leibniz quarrel – found the grind of pushing on with the Cambridge printing increasingly tedious; and perhaps it might be hazarded that for his part Cotes excelled at the tactics of mathematical science rather than the strategy, brilliant though he was. Certainly we find in Newton's early letters many cordial and grateful remarks: 'Many thanks for your trouble in correcting this edition'; 'I beg your pardon for so long a delay'; 'The corrections you have made are very well and I thank you for them.'[52] But such phrases cease in the summer of 1712, and henceforward the final phase of the Newton–Cotes correspondence about the *Principia* reveals frigid feelings on Newton's side, hurt feelings on Cotes's side. In a letter of 31 March 1711 Cotes thanked Newton for a compliment to himself inserted into the text, surely acknowledging Cotes's acuity in improving it; no such compliment can be found now. Again, we know that in a draft preface to this second edition – probably prepared in the summer of 1712 – Newton expressed proper appreciation of Cotes's services; in the second preface as published he ignored Cotes completely. Further, Newton refused to take any interest in Cotes's *Logometria* or in his editor's preface to the new edition of which, surprisingly, he washed his hands. And finally, when the book was distributed, Newton overwhelmed Cotes by sending by way of thanks, without any letter, a long list of printer's errors and other *corrigenda*, plus some afterthoughts which he had failed to convey to Cotes.

Why did Newton behave thus badly to his young editor? There was, of course, a particular failing which Newton laid (most unfairly) upon Cotes's shoulders besides the resentment against his excessive zeal, reflected in such an ominous warning as 'ever since I received yours of June 23 I have been so taken up with other affairs that I have had no time to think of mathematics'; we know that if Newton was too busy for mathematics it was because he wished to be so. The particular fault was this. For all his care, Cotes could not examine *ab origine* every proposition in the *Principia*; and he had passed as correct Book II, Proposition 10, dealing with the motion of a projectile in a medium resisting as the square of the velocity. The proposition was in fact erroneous; the error had become known to the Swiss mathematicians Johann and Nicholas Bernoulli, though neither could spot the fault in Newton's demonstration as printed; and Nicholas was able to convince Newton of the fault in October 1712, when Newton himself discovered his own geometrical slip and how to correct it.[53] What Newton feared was that (*a*) he ought in decency to thank the Bernoullis for detecting the error; and that (*b*) the fact of his making a rather serious mistake would be invoked against his mathematical competence in the calculus dispute; this actually happened.[54] Newton resolved to give away as little as possible to his opponents by silently correcting Proposition 10, without reference to the Bernoullis, and making only the most general allusion in his Preface to the correction of errors found in the first edition. Cotes's tribute and acknowledgement were sacrificed into the bargain; Newton could not quite stomach thanking Cotes for his acuity while ignoring the more subtle amendment for which he was indebted to the Bernoullis. I do not really know whether Newton imagined that Cotes ought to have detected the error found by Johann Bernoulli, which had escaped his own vigilance over so many years; but certainly in order to protect his pride he made Cotes pay the penalty as though the fault were his. Further, if he had wished to pay a posthumous tribute to Roger Cotes he could have done so when the *Principia* was published a third time, long after Leibniz was dead. He did not.

However, one distinction at least cannot be stripped from Cotes – of the three editors of the *Principia* he alone contributed a preface to the work – in effect an essay on Newtonianism which is certainly more significant than Halley's summaries and possibly than Pemberton's whole book.[55] This preface is not concerned with the technical content of the *Principia*; it defends the book against the Cartesian version of the mechanical philosophy, and more especially against Leibniz. It is perhaps unfortunate that because we now know a great deal more about Newton's own reflexions on atomism, God, the vacuum, determinism and so forth than the men of Cotes's or several succeeding generations could do, Cotes's statements (appearing, as they did, in a context enforcing attention) seem less interesting than they should; for in 1713 little exegesis of the Newtonian concept of the universe was readily accessible. How many readers at this time, for example, were cognisant of Newton's direct moulding of Richard Bentley's *Confutation of Atheism* (1693)?[56]

Of course, one is inclined to ask of Cotes (as of all the Newtonians) whether his expressions are really in accord with Newton's own thoughts. We have the letter in which Cotes sent a preliminary sketch of his Preface to Newton and to which neither Newton nor Bentley objected.[57] There is surely much in Cotes's defence of experimental and mathematical natural philosophy of which Newton approved; nor I think can Newton have taken amiss Cotes's spelling out of the deficiencies of the theory of cosmic vortices, though he himself had not cared to undertake the task. But at one point Cotes approached, if he did not actually encounter, real danger; I mean in his attempt to demonstrate that Newtonian gravitation is no occult quality. For here he risked compromising the new mechanistic science which Newton, like Boyle and Cudworth, was ever concerned to cleanse of Epicurean atheism. Newton himself had denied that gravity was an inherent, necessary attribute of matter, believing rather that it was a contingent feature of the Universe as God had decided to create and uphold it. Critics like Leibniz objected that this was to make gravity a perpetual miracle.[58] To refute this charge Cotes now embraced the alternative that Newton had renounced in his letters to Richard Bentley and elsewhere: 'either,' he wrote, 'gravity will have a place among the primitive qualities of all bodies universally, or extension, mobility and impenetrability will not'.[59] We know too that Cotes's sentence was no casual utterance, for the dangers of such a line had already been pointed out to him by Newton's metaphysician, Samuel Clarke.[60] To Cotes's younger and more matter-of-fact generation the subtleties of metaphysics as applied to mathematical physics perhaps seemed less tremendous than they had in the days of Descartes and Henry More; at any rate, Cotes's successors seem to have been content to abandon them.

I have traversed this last incident to show – as more technical examples would equally well do – that Cotes was far from being Newton's ape or drudge. The third editor of the *Principia*, Henry Pemberton, can be dealt with more briefly. He was a physician by profession, a mathematician by avocation. He seems to have been introduced into Newton's circle by John Keill, about 1722, when he was twenty-eight years of age and Newton eighty. Why, in the following year, Newton engaged this young and undistinguished mathematician as his editor, rather than say John Machin or Keill himself, no one knows; one may guess at Newton's fear lest these better-known mathematicians might look askance at the routine duties and make nuisances of themselves over larger issues. Pemberton remains obscure, but for this edition and his popular review of Newtonian science,[55] which is said to have inspired Newton to remark of his former editor that Pemberton evidently had 'more in him than he imagined'.[61] Nevertheless, he was 'a very poor third to Halley and Cotes', unqualified 'to do any editing in a real creative sense'.[62] We are able to judge his performance by 24 extant letters to Newton, to which no replies survive if they were written. These show that Pemberton was diligent but stupid. He proposed many trivial alterations and some more ambitious ones that Newton rightly ignored; for example, Pemberton's wish to revise Book II, Propositions 36 and 37.[63] Pemberton was guilty of the only really silly misunderstanding of Newton's text in his editors that I recall. Newton had added to the copy for the printer the words 'a clock with a spring that oscillated four times in each second', and Pemberton, objecting that the spring of a clock is not the part that oscillates, wished to read instead 'a clock with a *pendulum* that oscillated four times in a second', oblivious of the fact that in the experiment a balance-spring watch had been used.[64] Pemberton's would-be amendments to the copy were not all so foolish, and some were approved by Newton, but the end-results of Pembertons' labours were trivial.

The fact is that Newton had begun preparations for a new edition of the *Principia* virtually before the second issued from the press.[65] We cannot tell whether at age eighty-one or two Newton was still perfecting his book, but certainly he added fresh material after 1719.[66] He meant to get it out if he could with these improvements, but not to be bothered by examining someone else's ideas for further emendations. Pemberton simply was not strong enough to convince Newton of his own rectitude, as Cotes had done; probably Newton simply deleted or ignored Pemberton's proposed 'amendments'. Consider this instance; on 17 July 1725 Pemberton wrote particularly to Newton reminding him that in Book III, Proposition 41, as in the previous edition, he gave it as his opinion that the cooling of hot bodies varies in a ratio rather less than the ratio of their diameters; and Pemberton thought that this view was inconsistent with what Newton had said about the cooling of the Sun and stars in *Opticks*, Query 11. Newton simply took no notice. It is easy to see why, for Query 11 deals with a special high temperature reaction between matter and light whereby the intense radiation of these celestial bodies keeps them intensely hot. Of course this had nothing to do with the heat of comets in Proposition 41, but Newton probably never explained the issue to Pemberton.

Clearly, we cannot learn much of Newton from Pemberton; even if we possessed his lost commentary on the *Principia* – supposing it were ever completed – it would tell us very little. How much rather one would have Halley's or Cotes's picture of Newton! For both knew his weaknesses as well as his strength, yet admired him and served him loyally none the less. In studying their relationships with Newton, I am first of all impressed anew by the ascendancy of the man over two colleagues who were both of the first rank; and there is absolutely no question but that Halley and Cotes freely admitted his ascendancy. Secondly, one learns that all three editions of the *Principia* were really Newton's editions; Newton was prepared to examine verbal improvements or major scientific corrections with equal care, if they were seriously offered, but right through to his eighties the forms of redrafting or revision were very largely *his* forms, and every sentence bore Newton's personal mark. He would – sometimes – thank others for help but he would resign to no one the slightest share of responsibility and ultimate credit. He did not claim infallibility, but he certainly claimed proprietorship.

One cannot escape also in these records the evidence of those darker seams in Newton's character on which Augustus de Morgan first insisted more than a century ago. Far be it from me to claim to disclose the secret springs of Newton's mind and personality. But certain aspects of his behaviour, actually affecting his conduct as a scientist, are too obvious to pass over; those who justly or unjustly became Newton's enemies felt their full force. Flamsteed, for example, complained bitterly of Newton's unrelenting ruthless egoism, his deviousness, and of his pride. I do not think we can declare Newton wholly guiltless of these characteristics even in his dealings with his friends. To preserve his pride he would have made Halley suffer, and he did make Cotes suffer. Newton was generous with money and with an empty word of praise for Pemberton, but could not utter even a private word of thanks to Roger Cotes. In truth, Newton was no more successful than most of us in following Burns's advice to see ourselves as others see us. He did not see, for example, that it really was a grave moral failing not to make an acknowledgement to the Bernoullis in the *Principia*, not merely because this was a lapse from his own standards of integrity but because it necessitated a grave wrong to Cotes. And because he lost his moral touch Newton committed a grave tactical error: his attempt to conceal his obligation to Leibniz's friends gave them a fresh handle against him; in their eyes it proved Newton's true character as a cheat.[67]

But let me end on a pleasanter note, recollecting Newton's extraordinary vigour in perfecting the *Principia* over forty years, a feat almost as great as that of first writing the book in a period of 17 or 18 months. Few works can ever have received such concentrated intellectual attention from their authors over so long a period of time. And to this I must add a special last tribute to the young Cambridge mathematician, Roger Cotes, who certainly wrote more of the *Principia* than any other editor, and who alone challenged Newton staunchly, if not always successfully, on points of scientific logic and philosophical sense. So far as it was possible for an editor to do so, it was Cotes who took in hand the transformation of the *Principia* from being the apex of seventeenth-century science, to being the essential groundwork of classical physics.

PLANS FOR THE *PRINCIPIA*

plan I   *De motu corporum liber primus + Liber secundus*
            (= LL_α)   (= 'System of the World')
plan II   *Philosophiae naturalis principia mathematica*
{end 1685   Libri I + II + III
{early 1686   (LL_β + extra matter) + (no MS)
plan III   *De motu corporum libri duo*
 June 1686   Libri I + II (as above)
    (However, Newton decides to retain the *Principia* title for the curtailed book.)
plan IV   *Philosophiae naturalis principia mathematica*

NOTES

1 See A. R. and M. B. Hall, *The Correspondence of Henry Oldenburg*, VI (University of Wisconsin Press, 1969), p. 233. This letter of Oldenburg was based on a 'model' provided for him by the mathematical amateur John Collins, also printed *ibid.*, pp. 226–229. Collins had a copy of *De Analysi* in his possession.
2 Conti first printed an *Abrégé* of the *Chronology* (without Newton's consent) in 1725. Other writings of Newton's not without interest including *De natura acidorum* (1704) and his currency papers (1717) should also be recorded for this period.
3 Sir David Brewster, *Memoirs...of Sir Isaac Newton* (Edinburgh, 1855) I, 248. Nothing about this survives in Newton's known correspondence.
4 See D. T. Whiteside, *Mathematical Papers of Isaac Newton*, V (Cambridge, 1972), 8–14.
5 A. R. Hall in *Archives internationales d'histore des sciences*, XIII (1960), 39–61; I. Bernard Cohen, *ibid.* XI (1958), 357–375; D. T. Whiteside, *op. cit.* II, 281–294, and III, 3–10.
6 *Correspondence*, I, 414.
7 *Ibid.* I, 328.
8 *Ibid.* II, 182–183.
9 *Ibid.* III, 381.
10 *Ibid.* IV, 296.
11 Indeed, the reflector did not become an effective instrument in Newton's lifetime. The full account of his experiments on the spectrum only appeared in *Opticks* (1704). For a modern analysis of the difficulties inherent in inferring Newton's theory from his experiments see A. I. Sabra, *Theories of light from Descartes to Newton* (London, 1967).
12 *Correspondence*, II, 114.
13 Briefly, from S. P. Rigaud, *Historical essay on the first publication of Sir Isaac Newton's Principia* (Oxford, 1838), through W. W. Rouse Ball, *An essay on Newton's 'Principia'* (London and New York, 1893), and A. R. and M. B. Hall, *Unpublished scientific papers of Isaac Newton* (Cambridge, 1962), to John Herivel, *The background to Newton's Principia* (Oxford, 1965), I. Bernard Cohen *Introduction to Newton's Principia* (Cambridge, 1971) and R. S. Westfall, *Force in Newton's Physics* (London and New York, 1971). Also to be mentioned are the contributions of Alexandre Koyré collected in his posthumous *Newtonian Studies* (Cambridge, Mass., 1965).
14 *Correspondence*, I, 442.
15 Newton's absences from Cambridge are recorded in Joseph Edleston, *Correspondence of Sir Isaac Newton and Professor Cotes* (London, 1850), lxxxv. During the composition of the *Principia* Newton went out of residence for only three weeks in the three years 1684–6 (*ibid.* lxxxii), while in the three preceding years his total absence amounted to only $14\frac{1}{2}$ weeks. The longer absences of 1679 and 1680 were doubtless consequent on his mother's death (for which see *Correspondence*, II, 300, and 303, note 2). Newton's private life during the period 1680–4 is totally concealed.
16 I. Bernard Cohen, *Introduction*, pp. 122–124, 336–344; I am also greatly indebted to Dr Whiteside for his prior communication of material to be published in the sixth volume of his *Mathematical Papers* and unfailing generosity.
17 *Correspondence*, II, 415, 419–430.
18 *Ibid.* II, 437; Newton to Halley, 20 June 1686.
19 Private communication.
20 *Principia*, 1687, 401.
21 *Correspondence*, II, 431.
22 Sir Henry Lyons, *The Royal Society, 1660–1940* (Cambridge, 1944), 81.
23 *Correspondence*, II, 435. Halley's words imply, possibly, previous knowledge of Newton's design. Note that Halley could not tell from the MS he had in his hands that Book I (now)

ns on fluid mechanics included in the original version of Book I.
24 *Ibid.* II, 437.
25 My wife and I gave an earlier account of the composition of Books II and III of the *Principia* in the work noted above, note 13, pp. 232–6. While that account is by and large correct, and its identification (following Rouse Ball) of *De motu corporum liber secundus* with *The System of the World* is accepted in Cohen, *Introduction*, ch. IV, it needs modification in detail. We do not now suppose that Newton's abandonment of the popular plan for the *Liber Secundus* was provoked by Hooke's reaction to the *Principia*, and therefore now assign the completion, rather than the commencement, of the ultimate Book III to the summer or autumn of 1686. The *Liber secundus* was never intended by Newton to be part of a three-book *Principia*.
26 *Correspondence*, II, 437.
27 Translated from U.L.C. Add. 3965, f. 183 r, of which Dr Whiteside kindly supplied a transcript.
28 Had Halley already seen the *Liber secundus* ('System of the World'), cf. note 23 above? The absence of his comments upon it does not prove that he did not, while the tone of the correspondence does not deny it either.
29 *Ibid*, II, 443. The mention of 'curious experiments' suggests Halley's possible knowledge of those made by Newton on the descent of bodies in fluids.
30 *Ibid.* II, 443 and ff.
31 On 14 October 1686 Halley wrote to Newton about a defect in Book I, Problem 23 (ibid. II, 452); Newton made calculations relating to Halley's difficulty on the reverse of the sheet (U.L.C. MS Add. 3965, f. 96; see Cohen, *Introduction*, 124).
32 *Ibid.* II, 464. It is a reply to a vanished letter from Halley, asking Newton to replace a part of the copy of Book I, lost by the printer. Clearly Book I was moving at a snail's pace at this time.
33 In December 1686, as Clerk to the Royal Society, Halley asked Wallis to send up his ideas about the motion of projectiles in a resisting medium, supplying him with a copy of Newton's two propositions on the subject in *De motu*, without any hint that Newton had done more since – nor, indeed, did Newton imagine that Halley would know more (*Corr.* II, 464), which is curious since Halley, seemingly, had read Book II, Proposition 10 in draft already. However that may be, Wallis sent up a paper on resisted projectile motion to the Royal Society (later printed) and when this was read the Society wished to know what Newton proposed to do in the same field. See E. F. MacPike, *Correspondence and Papers of Edmond Halley* (London, 1937), 74; Thomas Birch, *History of the Royal Society* (London, 1756–7), IV, 521; *Correspondence*, II, 456 ff.).
34 *Ibid.* II, 445, note (5) and 464.
35 Halley to Newton, 24 February 1686/7, *Ibid.* II, 469–70; see also *ante*, pp. 465–466, notes (8) and (9). The problem was not to be dealt with in the first edition of the *Principia*.
36 *Correspondence*, II, 472.
37 Another defect is lack of information about Halley's private affairs; there is a hint that he had some personal difficulty in the autumn of 1686 (MacPike, *op. cit.* note 33, p. 74).
38 *Correspondence*, II, 452.
39 MacPike, *op. cit.* note 33, p. 80.
40 Francis Baily, *Account of Flamsteed* (London, 1835; repr. 1966), 215.
41 Surely Newton's delay inhibited continental reprints – Cotes's edition was pirated soon enough at Amsterdam.
42 To Cotes, 11 October 1709. The whole of the Newton–Cotes correspondence will be printed in *The correspondence of Isaac Newton*, vol. V; I give simply date references here.
43 18 August 1709.
44 To Newton, 15 April 1710.
45 To Newton, 1 June 1710, 11 June 1710, 7 May 1710.
46 For a more detailed examination see R. S. Westfall in *Science*, **179**, 751–758.
47 To Newton, 21 September 1710.
48 Newton to Cotes, 24 March 1711.

The Wilkins Lecture, 1973

49 To Newton, 23 June 1711.
50 To Newton 7 February 1712.
51 To Cotes, 2 February 1711/12.
52 To Cotes, 1 July 1710, 30 September 1710, 24 March 1711, 18 June 1711.
53 For all this, see the forthcoming vol. VI of *The correspondence of Isaac Newton* and the references there cited.
54 Johann Bernoulli had known of the faultiness of Proposition 10 for more than two years; he had communicated the fact to Leibniz, and prepared a paper in which it was announced to appear in the *Mémories* of the Académie Royale des Sciences at Paris. Although corresponding with Abraham de Moivre in London, there is no evidence of his intention to impart the fault in Proposition 10 privately to Newton before his nephew Nicholas's visit to London in October 1712. Nicholas's kind reception in London stimulated him to share the secret with Newton himself.
55 Henry Pemberton, *A View of Sir Isaac Newton's Philosophy*, (London, 1728).
56 See, conveniently, I. Bernard Cohen (ed.), *Isaac Newton's papers and letters on natural philosophy* (Cambridge, Mass., 1958), 271–394; and Henry Guerlac and M. C. Jacob in *Journal of the History of Ideas*, **30**, 1969, 307–318.
57 To Newton, 18 March 1713.
58 Newton to the *Memoirs of Literature*, May 1712.
59 *Principia* (1713), c1 verso.
60 Cotes to Clarke, 25 June 1713.
61 I. Bernard Cohen, 'Pemberton's Translation of Newton's *Principia*...', *Isis* **54** (1963), 334; the same author has also considered Pemberton in his *Introduction to Newton's 'Principia'*, 65–79 and in his variorum *Principia*, II, 827–847.
62 Cohen, *Introduction*, 275.
63 Cohen, *Principia*, II, 845–847.
64 *Ibid*. I, 506, II, 837; *Introduction*, 278.
65 Edleston, *Correspondence*, 160–165, a paper of addenda and corrigenda to the second edition of the *Principia* sent to Cotes in November/December 1713. It is evident that to a large extent this consists not of corrections for Cotes's oversights but of Newton's afterthoughts – which he began to collect for the next edition. Compare *Newton Correspondence*, *volume* VI (forthcoming), Letter 1088, A. de Moivre to Johann Bernoulli, 28 June 1714.
66 *Principia*, 1726, 353.
67 See Johann Bernoulli to Leibniz, 6 February 1715 NS in C. J. Gerhardt, *Leibnizens Mathematische schriften*, vol. III/2, 936–937.

IX

BEYOND THE FRINGE: DIFFRACTION AS SEEN BY GRIMALDI, FABRI, HOOKE AND NEWTON

Beginning his third 'Account of a Book' in no. 79 of his *Philosophical Transactions* (22 January 1671/2) Henry Oldenburg wrote: 'This learned Treatise was not to be altogether omitted in these *Philosophical Transactions* though an Account of it hath been deferr'd (too long), it being but lately fallen into the *Publisher's* hands.' (1) The work in question was Francesco Maria Grimaldi's *Physico–Mathesis de Lumine* (Bologna, 1665); Oldenburg accorded it a moderately long review of almost three pages. He noted that Grimaldi had introduced a fourth manner of propagation of light, that is, 'not only directly, and by *refraction*, and *reflexion*, but also by *diffraction*' thus coining a new technical word for the English language. But alas! the account leaves the new phenomenon very obscure, for Oldenburg continues: 'which last, according to him, is done, when the parts of Light, separated by a manifold dissection, do *in the same medium*, proceed in different ways.' The essence of a typical 17th century diffraction experiment – a narrow beam of light partially obstructed by a sharp edge – is not mentioned.

We may provisionally assume that Grimaldi's book was not widely read in England within a generation of its publication. Newton did not own a copy. But Grimaldi's experiments and ideas were disseminated by others, not least by the Lyons Jesuit Honoré Fabri (1607–88), a man whose writings, especially those on pure mathematics, were well known. Isaac Newton, by his own affirmation, learnt of the diffraction effect from the first dialogue in Fabri's *Dialogi physici* [*sex*] (1669).

In his 'Hypothesis explaining the Properties of Light discoursed of in my severall Papers' (7 December 1675) Newton recollected Robert Hooke' 'speaking of an odd straying of light caused in its passage neare the edge of a Rasor, Knife, or other opake body in a dark room; the rays wch pass very neare the edge being thereby made to stray at all angles into the shadow of the knife.' (Note here, at the beginning, the 'straying *into* the shadow of the knife.) We may presume, as Newton did, that Hooke had seen the diffraction fringes. A 'pertinent' intervention by Sir William Petty (2)

> made me [Newton], having heard Mr Hook some dayes before compare it to the straying of Sound into the quiescent Medium, say, that I took it to be onely a new kind of refraction, caused perhaps by the externall aethers (3) beginning to grow rarer a little before it come (3) at the Opake body, then it was in free space;

Newton's aether-theory could indeed easily accommodate the bending of the beam round the edge; less easily, perhaps, account for the fringe effect. Hooke did not like this belittling of his discovery and in consequence he was then 'pleased to answer, that though it should be but a new kind of refraction, yet it was a *new one*.' Now Newton could not resist a further twist: Hooke's remark

> made me afterwards, I know not upon what occasion [!], happen to say among some that were present to what past before, that I thought I had seen the Experiment before in some Italian Author. And the author is *Honoratus Faber* in his Dialogue *de Lumine*, who had it from *Grimaldo*.(4)

If we ask how Newton came to be so happily familiar with the Italian mathematician's book, John Harrison gives us the answer (5): it was already in Newton's library, where it still remains. John Collins, that indefatigable collector of mathematical books from overseas, sent '2 small tracts' by Fabri to Newton on 30 April 1672, with the derogatory comment that 'though of no use to your selfe, you may bestow [them] on some of your Pupills' (6). We may agree with Harrison that the *Dialogi* was one of them, the other being *Synopsis geometrica*, also 1669, for Newton owned no more books by Fabri.

Can we date the little confrontation of Hooke and Newton more accurately? We can. Strangely enough in our view, Newton presented himself for admission as a Fellow of the Royal Society only on 18 February 1675, more than three years after his election (7). He can have been present on no occasion before this day, when the time was largely filled by Nathaniel Henshaw's large discourse of his travels in Denmark and a letter from Christiaan Huygens about his new pocket-watch. The next two meetings were no more productive of optical business, but on 11 March 1675, when the appointed speaker failed, an old discourse of Boyle's about shining flesh was read and this 'gave occasion to some hints for A General Hypothesis for explaining the Nature of Light; concerning which Mr. Hooke gave his thoughts as follows: That light was a vibrating or tremulous motion in the Medium... (etc)' (8). Later, and perhaps in compliment to Newton's presence, Hooke 'was desired to have ready, for the usual day, the Apparatus necessary for the making Mr Newton's Experiments formerly alledged by him for evincing the truth of his New theory of light and colours...'

On 18 March Hooke did not, in fact, touch directly on Newton's experiments. Instead, he read a discourse of his own, possibly prepared some time previously, in which he detailed 'severall new Properties of Light, not observed, that he knew of, by Optick Writers'(9). The lecture, to which Newton may have listened with less than perfect patience, as is evident from what has gone before, has long been taken to be that published in Hooke's *Posthumous Works* (1705, pp.186–90) (10). Yet this text (if we may judge it to be as complete as it appears) does not accurately correspond to the summary of Hooke's lecture given in the Journal Book, perhaps with Hooke's approval. It can hardly be said that the published lecture deals with *several* new properties of light, and items five to eight in the summary are not at all represented in it (11). However, the printed lecture is certainly a review of experiments upon diffraction.

As such, we may in the first instance take it as representing what Newton and others heard about this phenomenon from Hooke in March 1675. The first point to note is that nowhere does Hooke speak of *colour*. The 'new' phenomenon here first found was a shadowy ring inside the bright circle of the Sun's image projected through a small hole; in other words, the sunlit circle did not terminate in a sharp boundary as Hooke expected it should do. There was 'a Penumbra or darker Ring encompassing the lighter Circle'. He also speaks of an enlightening of the shadow. Measuring the breadth of this penumbra, Hooke found it 'sometimes five or six times as broad' as the hole through which the beam of light was admitted and so (he reasoned) 'it could not proceed from a *Penumbra* caused by the bigness of the Hole upon the common Principles, that is, from the Supposition of the Rays from every point of the Sun proceeding in strait Lines:...' The inference was that some light had been bent outwards, beyond the circular boundary of the hole's projected image according to geometry, and conversely Hooke suggests (though he does not explicitly state) that the bright solar image within the penumbra is smaller than it ought to be. So that, as he says, 'the Rays of the Sun which cross each other in the Hole of the Shutter *HO*, do not proceed on in straight lines, but deflect, some this way, some that way...' He also noted that reducing the size of the hole increased that of the penumbra and vice-versa, 'contrary to the common Principles of Opticks'. In all this there is no word of colour nor indeed of fringes.

When Hooke used a razor to divide the cone of light, so that half the area of the cone fell on the side of the blade and was obstructed by it, he found that (instead of deep shadow) in the obstructed region beyond the razor light, or as he now calls it Radiation, extended far down, even to the line of a half right angle to the direction of the beam, from the razor. The greater the angle of its deflection the weaker the Radiation became.

The second point to note is that Hooke was chiefly impressed by the size of the shadowy penumbra extending beyond the bright solar image. It is quite clear that he was most of all struck by light's extending into geometric shadow, albeit faintly.

We may now compare this with what Fabri had to say about 'Grimaldo's experiment', without casting any doubts upon Hooke's independent observation of diffraction. Fabri's *Dialogi physici* is a verbose little book in which he tediously expresses his dissent from (with hindsight be it said) greater men than himself: besides Grimaldi, Giovanni Alfonso Borelli and Geminiano Montanari (12). In the first dialogue he reports Grimaldi's experiment only in order to explain it by his own qualitative theory of light, rejecting Grimaldi's fluid or quasi-undulatory theory. He suggests that the experiment itself is doubtful (pp.6–7). As figure 1

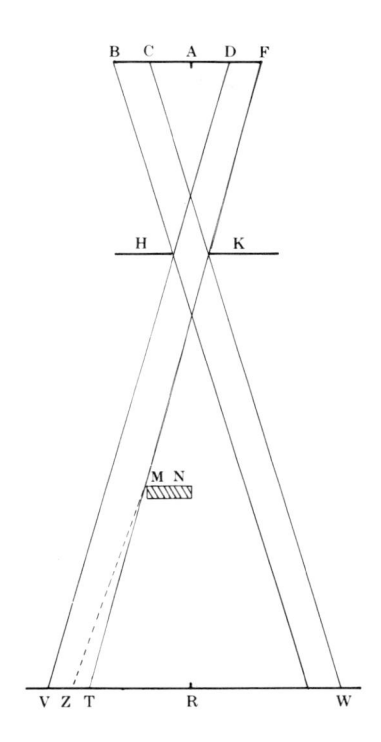

FIGURE 1. Fabri's figure, after Grimaldi. *BF* is the solar disk, centre *A*. *HK* is a very small hole admitting light to an otherwise dark chamber. *VW* is the image of the solar disk formed on a distant screen. *MN* is an opaque body inserted in the beam (of which the *RH* side appears to be omitted!). *TR* is the breadth of the geometric shadow cast by *MN*. *Z* marks the actual limit of 'shadow'. In reality *CW*, *DV* are almost parallel.

shows, Grimaldi discovered that the shadow of an object placed in the narrow beam is larger than geometry dictates. Fabri expresses Grimaldi's own interpretation of this result as follows:

> [The incident light] as it does not fall upon a reflecting body cannot be reflected; nor can it be refracted, because it is extended through the same medium; therefore the experiment cannot stand nor be accounted for in any way unless we say that light is a tenuous fluid body that is scattered when it runs up against the obstruction *MN*, and hence strikes and bends the adjacent rays (p.5).

He draws the analogy with wave-motion in water. After discussing this strange deflection of light to an ageometrical position, Fabri reports the rest of Grimaldi's observation, that 'in the bright region *VT* (for I exclude the deflection of the rays) three bands appear of which the exterior ones are coloured blue and red; the former being at *T*, the latter at *V*' (p.11). (There is thus, it seems, though Fabri does not make the comparison, a kind of rainbow or double halo surrounding the enlarged shadow of the obstruction.) However, it may also be the case that three more bands of colour can be seen in the shadowy region *TR*: these are very difficult to account for (p.14).

Fabri's own interpretation of these phenomena is not without interest. Like Newton later, he dissented from Grimaldi in believing that the deflection of the rays was caused by a peculiar kind of refraction in the adjacent air. So far as I can make out, his notion of refraction (for example, in a prism) was that white rays incident at slightly different angles (because of the breadth of the Sun) form the various coloured bands of the spectrum. Light passing close to the edge of the obstruction *MN* and reflected from its corner *N* heats the adjacent air; this air of less density forms a refractive prism which can (by analogy) produce two sets of coloured bands, as in Fabri's figure (figure 2). *Perfectam autem huius effectus analogiam in dicto trigonis habes.* ('Thus you have a perfect analogy with the prism', p.3). As for the extreme colours, Fabri says that blue arises from the more diffuse rays, red from those that are more compacted: '*ex radiis distractioribus... ex radiis magis unitis*' (p.14),

To return to Newton, my understanding of his exchange with Hooke on (?) 18 March 1675 is different from that of Richard S. Westfall, who has written that 'Newton owed his very knowledge of diffraction to Hooke's discourse at a meeting of the Royal Society early in 1675' (13), because his allusion to 'some Italian Author' (14) makes it plain that Newton recollected having read of the same enlargement of the shadow before hearing Hooke's lecture. Newton may not have picked up

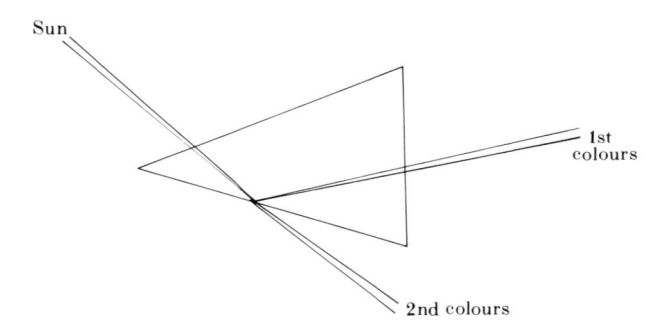

FIGURE 2. Fabri's diagram showing how two sets of coloured bands may be formed by a single prism.

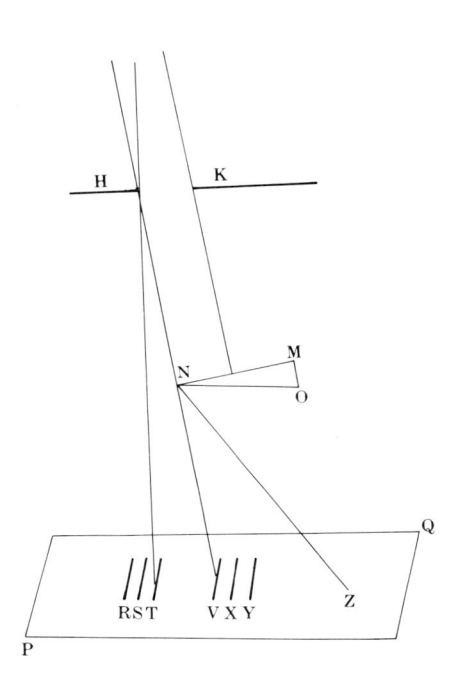

FIGURE 3. Newton's version of Fabri's figure, 1675. In printing the letter *R* on the screen was misprinted as *K*.

Grimaldi's term *diffractio*, but Hooke did not use this word either, while Fabri mostly speaks of *deflectio*.

Newton's 1675 summary of Fabri's account of 'Grimaldo's experiment' indicates an imperfect apprehension, and I agree with Stuewer that Newton had not yet himself seen diffraction effects (15). Nor does he claim to have done so. Newton merely represents himself as reporting from Fabri's book, introducing his own version of Fabri's diagram with the words: 'I am to describe [i.e. write down] something further out of him, wch you will apprehend by this figure...' Newton adds: 'The author describes it [diffraction] more largely in divers schemes. I have time only to hint the sum of what he sayes'. (16)

However, Newton's version of Fabri's diagram departs far from the original and is very strange indeed. It shows one ray of light without any deflection or even close passage to the edge *N* producing three rows of colours, and another three produced by an equally rectilinear ray which just touches the edge. Here is Newton's description:

> Suppose the Sun shine through the little hole *HK* into a dark roome upon the paper *PQ*, & with a wedge *MN0* intercept all but a little of that beam, & you will see upon the paper

six rows of colours *R, S, T, V, X, Y,* & beyond them a very faint light spreading either way, such as rays broaken like *HNZ* must make.

At least Fabri's lettering is faithfully reproduced, but Fabri had printed no diagram showing the positions of 'rows of colours'. Moreover, each of Fabri's three or more *fascia* is of a single colour only, while Newton has taken each *fascia* to be a little spectrum of many colours. And if Newton can have had no experimental authority for placing such a 'row of colours' within the geometrical shadow of the wedge, as Stuewer insists (17), neither had he any documentary authority for attributing such a phenomenon to Fabri's account.

Supposing Newton to have been, in December 1675, entirely dependent upon Fabri's *Dialogo primo* for his relation of the diffraction effect, albeit he treated Fabri in cavalier fashion, it may be less surprising that Newton's theoretical ideas at this date also seem similar to Fabri's. Like his source, Newton thought diffraction could be treated as a mode of refraction. Like his source, Newton supposed the medium (aether for him, air for Fabri) to be altered in density near the edge N so that a ray passing close to it was refracted. Like his source again, Newton had long supposed that there is some physical differentiation between the various coloured rays causing them to possess their respective refrangibilities. If Newton recalled Fabri when he wrote at the opening of the Third Book of *Opticks* (p.317). 'These broad Shadows and Fringes have been reckon'd by some to proceed from the ordinary refraction of the Air, but without due examination of the Matter' he omitted to confess that he had himself, formerly, to all intents and purposes held the same view (18).

If we consider Newton's knowledge of diffraction at the end of the year 1675, based on Fabri and Hooke (for he had read nothing of Grimaldi), we can only judge it to have been vague and confused. The experiments he had come across were few and imprecisely stated; the phenomena of diffraction were indeed resistant to exploration, yielding paradoxical and sometimes, apparently, contradictory results. The accounts of Fabri and Hooke have little in common apart from the enlargement of the shadow and the formation of a 'penumbra' of confused light instead of the expected sharp boundary between light and darkness. Hooke spoke of a faint light extending deep into the geometric shadow, but I do not find that Fabri had done so. Hooke said nothing of colours and Fabri is hardly clear about their position. Every writer on diffraction (including Grimaldi) seemed preoccupied with his concern to make the new phenomena fit in with some preconceived theory of light: Newton long followed the same pattern. The notion that light is bent round sharp edges suited his 1675 aether-theory very well and he set out the vague data at hand in the way that best supported his theory.

When did Newton perform his own experiments on diffraction, described in the Third Book of *Opticks*? So far as I am aware, they appear in none of the MS notebooks written before about 1670. The 'Hypotheses' make no claim that Newton himself has yet observed the phenomena, and his comment at the close of the passage on diffraction (and of the whole paper) that he expresses himself with diffidence on this topic 'haveing not made sufficient observations' need not imply that he had made any observations at all specifically upon diffraction. But on these questions (as much else) we shall learn more from A.E. Shapiro's edition of Newton's *Optical papers*, when this reaches the stage at which unpublished manuscripts on diffraction may be expected to appear.

Newton's knowledge of diffraction like his knowledge of double refraction came far too late to have any effect during 'the prime of his age for invention'; indeed, it is widely agreed that Newton's principal period of experimentation in optics was over by the end of 1671. Newton's latest biographer throws no light on this question beyond the remark that he did 'extend his investigation of diffraction' during the early 1690s, when he was composing *Opticks* (19). Steuwer has pointed out that Newton's aetherial explanation of the diffraction effect in his long letter to Robert Boyle (28 February 1679) departs little from that which he had given three years before and his account of 'Grimaldo's experiment' is just as second-hand:

> ...why light,... passing by the edge of a knife, or other opake body, is turned aside, and *as it were refracted*, and by that refraction makes several colours [my italics](20).

As before, Newton in the annexed diagram shows light-rays bending inwards round the edge into the geometric shadow to form a kind of spectrum on the screen.

In the *Principia*, however, less than 10 years later, Newton made the positive assertion that he had himself tried Grimaldi's experiment with success, confirming that

> rays of light... in their passage near the angles of bodies, whether transparent or opaque... are bent and inflected round the bodies, as if they were attracted towards them. And those of these rays which in their passage approach closer to the bodies are the more curved, as though more strongly attracted, as I myself have carefully observed. In the diagram, let s denote the edge of a knife-blade or wedge of any kind AsB, and *gowog, fnvnf, emtme, dlsld* are rays of light, curving inwards towards the blade, with a curvature more or less, as their distance from the blade is less or more. However, as this curvature of the rays takes place in the air beyond the blade, so the rays which impinge on the blade ought to be bent inwards towards it in the air before they reach the blade. And the same thing happens with rays impinging upon glass. For refraction occurs not at the point of incidence but gradually through a continuous bending of the rays, taking place partly in the air before they reach the glass, partly (if I mistake not) within the glass (21).

We must bear in mind that these words are taken from a mathematical rather than an experimental treatise. As Newton had formerly used the diffraction effect to support an aetherial theory of the interaction of light and matter, so he now uses it to support a dynamical theory of that interaction. And, as before, diffraction (like reflection) is treated as a special case of refraction: another mode of that curvature of light in the neighbourhood of matter which is always brought about by the same physical mechanism. In fact we can see by comparing the 1675 'Hypothesis' with Section XIV, Book I of the *Principia* that it was really quite easy for Newton to translate his aether-ideas into force-ideas, light itself being always considered a stream of particles and matter inherently inert. The translation is so good that the later force-theory seems to me the strict equivalent of the former aether-theory and the observational base (such as it is) is the same. There is nothing to suggest that Newton's understanding of the phenomena of diffraction was in 1685 any different from what it had been 10 years before. The fundamental effect is still the bending of light round the obstacle into the geometric shadow, rather than an extension of the shadow. In the 1687 *Principia* there is no word of colour in diffracted light and Newton's figure shows all rays inwardly bent round the obstacle. I therefore find it impossible to believe that in 1685 Newton had already made the exact diffraction experiments described in *Opticks*, Book III.

Most of the lines of scientific work pursued by Newton in his mature years were prepared by his youthful interest. The two obvious exceptions were his investigations and speculations about electricity and diffraction. Both caused him immense difficulties, for neither could easily be made to fit dynamical theories. It has been plausibly suggested that the electric phenomena revealed by Francis Hauksbee induced Newton to revive the aether-theory in the extended versions of the optical *Queries* (22). Diffraction forced Newton to abandon *Opticks* unfinished. Its Book II had ended on a successful note, after Newton had demonstrated to his own satisfaction the homogeneity of reflection and refraction, and of prismatic, reflected and refracted colours. In the third book, no doubt, he planned to bring the phenomena of diffraction into the same picture. Nothing that he understood of it before he began his own experiments gave him reason to fear that his own simple model of 'exterior refraction' might prove inadequate or that diffraction colours would prove more recalcitrant than those in thin plates.

When he at last came to the diffraction experiments described in *Opticks*, perhaps about the year 1692, experiments whose extreme accuracy has been praised recently by Stuewer like others before him, he must have been appalled to realize how much more perplexing the phenomena were, than he had supposed them to be. None of his former notions were appropriate. Not that Newton completely renounced the refraction model, as Observation 2 in Book III of *Opticks* makes plain. However, the single optical force of refraction and reflection in the *Principia* could no longer suffice, and Newton was compelled to postulate a *repulsive* force by which

> the Hair [diffracting a narrow beam] acts upon the Rays of Light at a good distance in their passing by it. But the Action is strongest on the Rays which pass by at least distances, and grows weaker and weaker accordingly as the Rays pass by at distances greater and greater...(23)

Accordingly, in the final edition of the *Principia* (1726) Newton remembered to revise his former model by adding a new sentence to the end of Section XIV 'And those [rays]which pass at greater distances are less bent, and those at still greater distances are a little bent the contrary way and form three fringes of colours' (24).

These relatively distant rays, now *repelled* from the edge of the knife (thus illustrating Newton's general principle that when a positive force declines to zero it is succeeded by a negative force and vice-versa) form coloured fringes lying not in the geometric shadow but in the sunlight beyond the blade (compare *Opticks*, Book III, Observation 7).

Such late patching could hardly conceal the fact that experiments on diffraction had taught Newton that neither the analogy with refraction nor the dynamical model were adequate to provide a theory of its phenomena, nor able to account for his own carefully measured results. Grimaldi's discovery of the extension of the shadow beyond the geometric limit was confirmed. So was Hooke's observation of light penetrating far *into* the geometric shadow. The 'three Parallel Fringes or Bands of Colour'd Light' were not at all as he had formerly imagined them. Because diffraction effects proved so resistant to analysis in terms of the ideas of light and of the interaction between light and matter that Newton had hitherto formed, he cast the remainder of his ideas into the form of enigmatic Queries.

NOTES

(1) *Philosophical Transactions*, no, 79, pp. 3068–70. It may not be wholly fanciful to think that Newton may have had a recollection of Oldenburg's account in mind when preparing the latter part of his own 'New Theory', to be published in the next issue of this same journal. Newton's affirmations about the nature of colour are almost exact negatives of Grimaldi's (as reported).
(2) Sir William Petty, a Vice-President, was at this time very active in the Society's affairs and frequently presided at meetings.
(3) Read: 'aether's'; 'came'.
(4) H.W. Turnbull (ed.), *The correspondence of Isaac Newton*, vol. I, Cambridge 1959, pp.383–84.
(5) J. Harrison, *The library of Isaac Newton*, Cambridge 1978, no. 599, p. 142.
(6) Turnbull, loc. cit., pp. 147, 161.
(7) Thomas Birch (ed.), *History of the Royal Society*, vol. III, London 1757, 181.
(8) Ibid., p. 193; Royal Society Journal Book (Copy), IV, pp. 163–64.
(9) Birch, ibid., p. 194; Journal Book. p. 165. Hooke in his *Diary* recorded Newton's attendance at the Society's meetings on 18 and 25 February, but not later. This is not strong evidence against Newton's presence in March. Hooke noted that he spoke about optical matters on 11 March ('I propounded my hypothesis of Light and Colours by the Length of the pulse') and 18 March ('read my paper of new propertyes of light'.) *Diary*,(ed.) H.W. Robinson & W. Adams, London 1935, pp. 145, 152, 153.
(10) Richard Waller (ed.), *Posthumous Works of Robert Hooke,* London 1705, *pp. 186-90*. Waller suggests that this was the lecture delivered on 18 March 1675; he also found a

(11) summary [in Hooke's hand] identical with that in the Journal Book for this day.
Item no. 5 'That colours may be made without Refraction' is especially interesting, since diffraction colours are not mentioned in the printed lecture.
(12) Honoratus Fabri, *Dialogi physici /sex/ quorum primum est de Lumine*, Lyons, 1669; a very small octavo. The first Dialogue bears the heading: 'In quo nova quaedam de lumine Grimaldi Experimenta discutiuntur, & ad veram luminis Hypothesin reducuntur'. It extends to 96 pages.
(13) R.S. Westfall, *Never at rest: a biography* (Cambridge, 1980) p. 272.
(14) Improperly named 'Faber' by Newton (and Westfall).
(15) However, he is clearly mistaken in asserting that Newton reported his (inaccurate) description of diffraction to be true, and therefore the logic of his argument is defective. See R.H. Stuewer, 'A critical analysis of Newton's work on Diffraction', *Isis*, **61**(2) 188–205, 1970.
(16) Turnbull, loc. cit., p. 384.
(17) Steuwer, loc. cit., p. 193.
(18) Isaac Newton, *Opticks*, (Dover reprint, New York 1952), p.317. In *De Aere et Aethere* Newton seems to consider the consequences of substituting aether for air as the medium effecting physical phenomena (A. Rupert Hall and Marie Boas Hall, *Unpublished Papers of Isaac Newton*, Cambridge 1962, pp. 214–228). Diffraction is mentioned in this text as a form of refraction in air, p. 215.
(19) Westfall, loc. cit. (note 13), p. 520.
(20) Turnbull, op. cit. (note 4), II, Cambridge 1960, p. 289.
(21) Isaac Newton, *Philosophiae naturalis Principia mathematica*, London 1687, pp. 231–32. Note that Newton was careless in writing 'magis vel minus pro distantia eorum a cultro' since the bending effect is *'inverse* pro distantia a cultro.'
(22) H. Guerlac, *Essays and papers in the history of science* (Baltimore & London 1977) 107–30
(23) *Opticks*, ed. cit.(note 18), p. 319.
(24) Ibid., third edition (London 1726) p. 226

X

Two Unpublished Lectures of Robert Hooke

IT is not the purpose of the present paper to widen the discussion of the merits of Hooke's contributions to the development of the theory of universal gravitation or to enter into the even more delicate question of the justice of historical opinion. The older Newtonian scholars — Edleston, Brewster and Rouse Ball — were not so partisan as to overlook Hooke's claims to the prior statement of some of the nodal ideas of the theory, though in general, under the influence first of Oldenburg's reporting of events, and then of the uncritical devotion to Newton which the Royal Society showed in its conduct during the early years of the eighteenth century, they were apt to portray Hooke as the framer of brilliant but unsubstantiated and uncoordinated hypotheses.[1] In 1913 Philip E. B. Jourdain thoroughly re-examined the work that Hooke had done on the theory of gravity before 1684, and concluded that while he showed himself the equal of Newton in scientific imagination, as a mathematician he was vastly inferior at a time when the solid progress of celestial mechanics could be achieved only through the physico-mathematical method.[2] Recently in these pages Miss Patterson has joined the late R. T. Gunther and Professor E. N. da C. Andrade in the task of rescuing the intellect and character of the indefatigable curator of experiments from oblivion and misrepresentation. Over the last thirty years more attention has been directed to Hooke than to any of his English contemporaries with the exception of Boyle and Newton himself; no one will now dispute that he was one of the most thoughtful and energetic of the early Fellows of the Royal Society, but he remains something of an enigma. For while opinion has changed, the publication of his private diaries has been the only notable addition to the material. Invaluable as these are, works printed two centuries ago remain the principal source of an insight into Hooke's scientific mind, especially the collections of Waller and Birch. In fact a number of his papers do still exist unpublished, and his extant correspondence is probably considerably larger than the few printed letters would indicate. Until all this material has been investigated our knowledge of Hooke must be held incomplete, and any judgements based upon it, tentative.

No one's posthumous testimony is perfect in its entirety, though it may be that Hooke was singularly unfortunate. Some scholar may hit upon the sheet "writ [as Newton declared] some time before I had any correspondence with Mr. Oldenburg, and that's above fifteen years ago, [in which] the proportion of the forces of the planets from the sun, reciprocally duplicate of their distance from him, is expressed," and thus substantiate the account of his early discoveries.[3] In part, however, the

---

[1] "The *speculations* of our distinguished countryman, Dr. Hooke, respecting the cause of the planetary motions exceeded greatly in originality and value the crude views of Borelli, and form a decided step in physical astronomy. . . . In this remarkable passage, the doctrine of universal gravitation, and the general law of the planetary motions are clearly laid down." Sir David Brewster: *Memoirs . . . of Sir Isaac Newton* (Edinburgh 1855), 1, 283, 287.

[2] "What made it impossible for them [i.e. Wren, Hooke and Halley], and possible for Newton, to unlock the door which guarded one of the secrets of the heavens was simply due to the happy circumstances that Newton was a great and far-seeing mathematician, and the time was ripe for the reduction of infinitesimal ideas into a powerful method." Robert Hooke as a Precursor of Newton, *The Monist*, 23 (Chicago 1913), 359.

[3] W. W. Rouse Ball: *An Essay on Newton's Principia* (London 1893), 157. [See now study III in this volume]

evolution of his ideas can be dimly traced in surviving notes and papers, so that, with this partial confirmation, it seems misleading to dismiss Newton's recollections at the time of Hooke's accusation of plagiarism (put down, moreover, as rough notes and unpublished for over a century) as valueless evidence. That the relations between Newton and Hooke are a matter to be discussed is patent, but little fresh light can be gained from the materials at present in print.

However this may be, there follow the most significant passages, omitting only introductory and purely descriptive remarks, from two of Hooke's later lectures in which he defended his two great contributions to the scientific thought of the later seventeenth century. In the spring of 1690, in the course of his regular addresses to the Royal Society, Hooke gave an account of Huygens' *Traité de la lumière*, the first copies of which were distributed by the author early in February of that year.[4] At this time, as Waller relates, Hooke was very weak and ill, "being often troubl'd with Head-achs, Giddiness and Fainting, and with a general decay all over, which hinder'd his Philosophical Studies, yet still he read some lectures when ever he was able."[5] The manuscript of these two, from a period when little is known of Hooke's activities, has not been noticed by Waller, Derham or Gunther, though the earlier editors may be assumed to have known of it, since it is now preserved along with other papers of Hooke's initialled by them in the Library of Trinity College, Cambridge.[6] It is precisely dated by Hooke's note after the draft of the first lecture: "Read at a meeting of y^e R. Society Febr: 19:16 $\frac{89}{90}$ present S^r. R. Southwell Sr J. Hoskins Mr Hill Mr Waller Mr Pitfield Mr Lodwick Houghton Hally Wallis Dr Slone, Slare, Dr Harewood & divers others."[7] The hand is on the whole firm and clear, but towards the end of the second lecture Hooke's control of the pen seems to become more shaky and the final passages are legible only with difficulty.

It would not be surprising if Waller and Derham were reluctant to print criticisms of their president, Newton. Hooke could still declare, speaking of the hypothesis of light that he had put forward in *Micrographia* (1665): "I confesse I have not yet found any phenomenon or hypothesis propounded by any writer since that time that has given me cause to alter my sentiments concerning it." The complete omission of Newton's name from the discussion of the recent progress of optical theory is very striking, though it is only fair to add that in this disregard for Newton's experimental work Hooke was following his author, Huygens, for whose own studies, however, it was less relevant than it was for Hooke's theory of colours. And it would have been tactless at least to revive Hooke's charges of plagiarism when the *Commercium Epistolicum* affair was at its height. Whatever the reason, these papers were not printed in the collections, though there is a heading attached that they are to follow "y^t of Light or in the Miscellany" — which indicates that publication was considered at some time.

Hooke begins by taking up the reference to his own undulatory theory on page 18 of the *Traité de la lumière*, where it is criticised by Huygens as lacking the fundamental concept of the wave-front. He points out that though Huygens still entertained some Cartesian notions of the cause of light in celestial bodies, they were agreed in regarding it as an extremely rapid and short vibrative motion. There follows a calcula-

---

[4] *Traité de la lumière, où sont expliquées les causes de ce qui arrive dans la reflexion, & dans la refraction* etc. Par C.H.D.Z. (Leyden 1690).
— Huygens sent copies to eight Fellows (Newton, Boyle, Wallis, Wren, Halley, Locke, Flamstead, Fatio de Duillier). Hooke's name was put in one list, then crossed out. Christiaan Huygens, *Oeuvres Complètes*, 9, 358, 380.

[5] Richard Waller: *Posthumous Works of Robert Hooke* (London 1705), xxiv.
[6] MS O 10a 1^{14}, which the Council of the College have kindly permitted me to examine.
[7] Thomas, Earl of Pembroke was President, Southwell succeeding him on 30 November 1690. Only a J. Houghton is recorded in the *Record of the Royal Society*.

Two Unpublished Lectures of Robert Hooke

tion, based on Roemer's observations of the periods of the moons of Jupiter, that the velocity of propagation of light is 133,333 miles per second, a higher value than had been guessed in *Micrographia*.[8] The defence of his own hypothesis fills the remainder of the lecture and is quoted here with paragraph divisions added for convenience.

The Principall issue of his treatise seems to have been designed for explication of the former of these two Subjects to witt the Double Refraction made in the body of the *Chrystallum Islandicum Disdiathlasticum* [sic] as Era. Bartholinus[9] calls it, and in order to the Explaining of y^t I suppose he thought upon or Contrived this propriety in the Propagation of Light: Namely that Every point of the propagated Ray doth also propagate a hemisphericall undulation: of which hemisphere notwithstanding, he makes noe more use than of only one line or Ray all the Rest he supposing to be insignificant and producing noe sensible effect, nor does that single ray any more than the Rest according to his supposition but as it is coincident or contemporary with other single Rays of other parts of the same Ray which together serve to form or Compose the wave or undulation which he makes always to move at Right angles with the progressive motion of that Ray. this is that characteristick of the Ray of Light upon which he builds all his Consequences wch he hath made to be coincident with the Invention of *Monsieur Fermatt*,[10] concerning Refraction wherein he supposeth quite contrary to the principle of *Monsieur Des Cartes*, namely that the *medium* that Refracteth the Ray of light trajected through it neerer to the perpendicular is soe much the more Dense and propagates the puls soe much the more slow than the other *medium* out of which the Ray commeth as the signe of the Angle of Incidence is greater than the signe of the Angule of Refraction.

This Proposition of *Monsieur Fermat* I some years since Explained in this Society in this Place & shewed a Demonstration thereof which I had then made and applyed to the same Purpose, but with this Supposition Differing both from what M^r. *Fermat* hath Printed and from what *Monsieur Huygens* here maketh use of it for, and that was to shew that the Refracted Ray from a point in one *medium* to a point in another *medium* moved the least quantity of matter that could be moved by any Ray passing through those two *mediums* soe qualifyed and situated; and therefore that that must be the only Ray that could be moved being more easy to be moved then any other. whereas they both lay the stresse of their argument upon the velocity or swiftnesse of its passage from point to point as being the swiftest of all other rayes whatever. This thought of Mon^r. Fermat I confesse was very Ingenious & serves very well to Explaine a Reason of the Proportion of the Signes of the angles of Refraction to the signes of the angules of Incidence, if that were the only phenomenon to be taken notice of in the Refracted Ray; which both Mo^r. Fermat and $Mons^r$. Huygens seem to Regard, both of them at the same time neglecting another effect altogether as Remarkable and Significant which is the Coloration or tingeing of the sayd Refracted Ray with Colours, which neither M^r. Fermat nor $Mo\underline{r}$ Huygens nor Pere Pardy[11] nor Pere Angot[12] have at all taken notice of. Nor has Mon^r. Descartes (though he hath taken notice of it) sufficiently provided by his hypothesis to Explain it (as I have els where in two or three Discourses proved at large[13] nor has any other person that I have yet mett wth produced a better Solution than that which I have published in my micrography, which I conceive sufficient to explaine the Reasons of all the phenomena of light and Colours of which I have yet heard or seen, though I should be very gladd to meet with a Better from some other hand.

But this shibolet alone is a sufficient conviction that this hypothesis of M^r. Fermat, $Mo\underline{r}$ Huygens, Pere Pardies, Pere Angot and Emanuel Maignan[14] and Divers others who have gone upon the Same grounds is insufficient to make

---

[8] In a lecture on light in 1680 he argues for instantaneous propagation and doubts Roemer's deduction of a finite velocity. (Waller, op. cit. 77.)

[9] *Erasmi Bartholini Experimenta Crystalli Islandici Disdiaclastici quibus mira & insolita Refractio detegitur* (Hafniae 1669).

[10] Cf. *Synthesis ad Refractiones* printed in P. Tannery et Ch. Henry, *Oeuvres de Fermat, 1* (Paris 1891), 173; written in 1662; this paper was first published in the *Lettres de Mr Descartes* (Paris 1667), 3, 258 et seq.

[11] Père Pardies' attempt to reinterpret Newton's optical experiments was published in the *Philosophical Transactions*, No. 84; for his unfinished treatise see Huygens' *Traité*, p. 18.

[12] *L'Optique divisée en trois livres on l'on demontre d'une manière aisée tout ce qui regarde 1° la propagation & les proprietez de la lumière 2° la Vision 3° la figure & la disposition des verres qui servent a la perfectionner. Par le P. Pierre Angot, de la Compagnie de Jésus.* (Paris 1682). Angot was at once an admirer of Aristotle's and Descartes' physics; and admitted to borrowing his ideas largely from Pardies.

[13] The only discussion by Hooke on these lines in his printed works that I have come across (after *Micrographia*) is in *Lampas* (1677); cf. R. T. Gunther: *Early Science in Oxford*, 8 (Oxford 1931), 189 seq.

[14] Emmanuel Maignan (1601–76) published (1) *Perspective Horaria, sive de horologiographia, tum theorica, tum pratica, libri iv* (Romae 1648) — the work referred to here; (2) *Cursus Philosophicus* (Tolosae 1653), and theological works.

out the phenomena of Refraction and soe ought to be Rejected. For it necessaryly follows from their Principles that Refracted Rayes differ not at all in their effects from Reflected Rayes, and Consequently they Exclude one of the Greatest beautyes of the Creation, namely the Glorious and Ravishing variety of Curious Colours which adorne and Distinguish the Clothings of the creatures or products of the Creation, and reduce all things to a *Mezzo Tinto* hue Differing only in the variety of the mixtures of Blacks & whites or in the Compositions of Greys. This Phenomenon therefore of the variety of Colours produced by Refraction though purposely omitted by Mo^r. *Huygens*, and I suppose, upon this very account, that he found himself unable to Explain the phenomena thereof by the suppositions he hath made choice of, as he seems to intimate in his preface saying. *I hope also there will be such as prosecuting these beginnings will penetrate much farther into this matter than I have been able Since there are matters enough yet behind wch have not been hitherto brought to light. This appears by the places which I have marked, where I leave the difficultys without Resolving them, and yet 'tis more evident by the things which I have not touched at all. Such as are the Diverse kinds of Shining bodys, and all what has Relation to Colours, in which noe one hitherto can boast of his having adjusted it. In fine there remaines much more to be inquired into concerning the Nature of light, than I pretend to have Discovered, and I shall owe much obligation to him that shall supply what knowledge is wanting to me concerning it.*

This *Phenomenon* therefore (I say) of the Coloration of the Rayes by Refraction becomes a watch word, Lapis Lydius or touch-stone by which the various hypotheses of Authours ought to be tryed. for if they doe not answer to this they must necessarily be fals and Sophisticate: it followes therefore that either this Supposition (*of Fermat, Maignan, Pardies, Angot* and M^r. *Huygens*) that the undulations of Refracted Rayes as well as of Reflected Continue to move at Right angles with the Ray, is fals or at least insufficient to make the Distinction between them that Nature maketh, or els that there is some other propriety of these Rayes or undulations omitted, which must be found out and added to what is already sayd of it before it ought to be admitted. Since nothing is more evident to one that sees, then that Nature doth make y^t Difference. This is in brief what I thought necessary to be considered before what I have formerly Deliverd concerning Light be rejected and before what is here Deliverd be Received, for though I doe readily assent that Mo^r. Huygens & others much more Able than myself may penetrate farther into the true causes of the *Phenomena* of Light, than I had done at that time; yet I confesse I have not yet found any *phenomenon* or *hypothesis* propounded by any writer since that time that has given me cause to alter my sentiments concerning it. However I should be very gladd to meet with any such and shall be as Ready to Relinquish this Upon the meeting with a better as I was in the making choice of it for the best at the time of the publication.

And though *Pere Angot* in his Optiques has Asserted it unsufficient to explaine the proportion of Refractions according to the Sines, Yet he had Done well if he had Demonstrated that his assertion: since if it were as he affirmes a very few lines would have served to have overturned all the superstructure I had built upon it, which seems to bee that which he principally aimed at, in the making mention of my Discourse, And the preceding compliment, pag. 89, was only to intitle him to the greater power to overthrow it. The scope of his Discourse in french is to this effect after he hath confuted Mo^r. *Descartes, Pere Maignan* and some others he says pag. 89. "The Demonstration which "Father Grimaldi [15] pretends to make is not at "all [16] more Regular [than the others he has "confuted]. And for y^t which *Mr. Hooke* has "given in his *micrography*, where there are soe "many things soe curious, I find that one cannot "at all soe advantageously serve himself of his "thoughts for the explaining of the Refractions "by the motion of the undulation, as I have "served myself by that of *P. Pardies*. for first he "wills that ,the rayes doe break themselves and "approach nearer to the perpendicular after they "have entred into a Medium [17] where the undula-"tions goe more Swift, and by consequence he "wills that they goe more swift in the water "than in the air which is conformable to what "we have found of *Descartes*.[18] Secondly he has "moreover [19] other Difficultys *particular in his* "*hypothesis which appear unsurmountable*, be-"cause if the Rayes are soe broken as he would "have them by approaching the perpendicular "when the undulations goe more swift, the "Rayes must cutt the undulations obliquely as "he has proved himself. But 'tis proved (as I "conceive) [mark the strength of his argument "against me] that the Rayes by which the com-"munication of the motion is made are perpetu-"ally perpendicular to the undulations and that "it is by their perpendicular motion that one "measures their effort in regard of the sensation "(that is to say) that it is by the perpendicular

---

[15] Francesco Maria Grimaldi (1618–1663): *Physico — Mathesis de Lumine, coloribus et iride aliisque adnexis libri duo* (Bologna 1665).

[16] The words "at all" are not in the original French.

[17] Angot's phrase is: "les rayes se rompent en s'approchant de la perpendiculaire lors qu'ils entrent dans un milieu . . ." (*L'Optique*, 90).

[18] "Ce qui est conforme à ce que l'on a trouvé à redire dans Mr. Descartes . . ."

[19] "Secondement il y a encore dans son hypothèse . . ."

X

Two Unpublished Lectures of Robert Hooke

"to the tangent of the place of the undulation,
"which striketh the Organ. Soe that when the
"ray shall be oblique, it shall notwithstanding
"be sensated as if it had come perpendicular,
"to which Mr. H. has not at all taken regard."
this is indeed to me unintelligible, and I thinke
nothing to the Purpose there is more in the
same treatise as little significant to overthrow
my Hypothesis, which I omitt.
"But for to make the Inconveniences of his
"hypothesis to be seen more cleerly.[20] Let us
"figure that the ray, ab, is oblique (if it May
"be done) to the undulation, bcd, and y^t
"surface of another medium is found disposed
"soe as to touch y^e undulation just at y^e point,
"b, one may take a part of the undulation soe

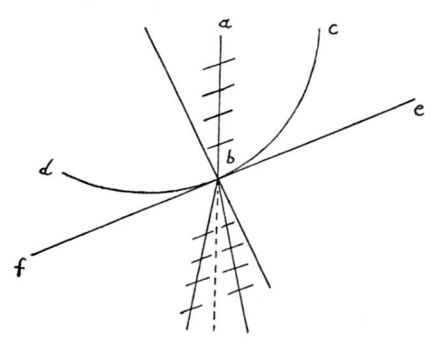

"small at the point, b, that we may consider
"it as a Little straight line applyed to the line,
"ef, upon which it shall fall as if it had come
"parallel from a. then this line plunging into
"this other medium which we have named
"continues to goe parallel in departing from the
"point b. and if its motion be broken or
"fracted, whether it be towards the perpendicu-
"lar, or from the perpendicular, it must remain
"always parallel to the surface, ef, having
"nothing which causes it to change its situation.
"Now this entirely Destroys the hypothesis of
"Mr. Hook as tis easy to conceive, for the
"sensation of the effort of the undulation is
"not made at all according to the oblique ray,
"ab, but only according to another Ray which
"one conceives to be perpendicular to it. He
"gives this which I have sayd I have Remarked
"that in this Hypothesis of Mr. Hooke,[21] there
"is not demonstrated at all the proprietys of
"Refractions which respect always the analogy
"of the Sine. This was notwithstanding a thing
"which he ought to have taken the paines to

"prove, and which in my opinion cannot pos-
"sibly be proved in this hypothesis." — *Parturi-
unt montes nascitur ridiculus mus.* he that
can find a syllable of argument against my
hypothesis in all this understands more than
my head is yet capable of. for who has demonstrated that the bredth of the undulation must
always proceed at Right angles with the Ray.
none that I know of but some that have taken
such an hypothesis, but an hypothesis is but
an hypotheticall argument, and needs to be
proved to be it self true, before it can be produced in Evidence against another hypothesis.
if indeed he had proved that my hypothesis had
destroyed itself he had done his work. but that
he has not nor could not doe. However he does
Last of all indeavour his . . .[22] effort, but alasse
the poor man is short. he says in his opinion
It could not be proved by my hypothesis that
the Refracted Rayes must observe the analogy
between the Signes of the Angles of Incidence
and those of Refraction. I conceive he speaks of
his own abilitys to make the Demonstration.
And soe I can readily consent with him, that
he could not doe it but anyone that understands
but a little geometry May as easily doe it as
Demonstrate the first proposition of Euclid. he
hath therefore upon the whole demonstrated his
own ignorance and Ill invention but for all the
Dirt he hath thrown, there is nothing sticks
faster than that the least breath will blow it
off and spread it upon his own face.

But Mo^r. Huygens is much more civill and
only says that the propriety which he himself
had found out to be in every point of the
propagated Ray had not at all been thought
of by those who before himself had begun to
consider the undulations of light amongst whom
are Mr. Hooke in his micrography, and P.
Pardies in a treatise of which he had done him
the favor to let him see a part, but had not
lived to finish it. Now whether I had any
Notion of such a propriety I will appeale to a
Discourse & Experiment which I many years
since shewed the Society in a Dark room of
the spreading of the ray from a point of the
propagated Ray almost to a quadrant, which
yet I looked upon and doe still conceive to
have another concurring cause also, it would not
els have Diverged only in a line but in a
hemisphere, and were Mo^r. *Huygens* Supposition true many other very Differing phaenomena
from what Nature now produces must become
visible.

There is one other physicall Observation
concerning Light and that is concerning the
Refraction of the Light by the air. In all which
he doth perfectly agree with the Doctrine I

---

[20] The figure to which the letters refer is not found with the MS, but taken from *L'Optique*, 92. The whole of this paragraph has been struck out by two strokes of the pen.

[21] Hooke seems to have had difficulty with the French idiom: "Outre ce que je viens de dire, j'ay remarqué dans cette hypothèse de Mr. Hooc . . ."

[22] Illegible: "closest"(?)

have Delivered in my Micrography and Calld Inflection as may be seen in the 58 Observation of that Booke from pag: 218 to pag: 240 nor is there any difference save in the aforementioned Notion of Density & Rarity as to Refraction or Inflection.

Easily the most curious feature of this account is the fact that Hooke pays no tribute to Huygens' inventiveness in the field of mathematical optics, especially in the study of the difficult problem of double refraction. He considers Huygens' wave-front superfluous: he does not even notice that Huygens' construction gives a mathematical proof of Descartes' (or Snel's) law of sines, the truth of which is assumed in *Micrographia*. As in his other essays on optics, Hooke's chief interest lies in the investigation of the physical nature of light and of the various media through which it is propagated. The view that makes him predominantly an empiricist and experimenter is very one-sided, for the devising of hypotheses was very attractive to him, perhaps dangerously so; and the assertion that the study of the mathematical optics of refraction is fruitless unless the theory of physical optics has been settled first — by the adoption of his own hypothesis — is dogmatic rather than reasoned. To defend his own ideas against the passing reflections of Huygens is legitimate; to suppose that another's line of research is useless because it is incompatible with his own indicates a limited outlook. Hooke wants to make the theory of colours the touchstone of all thought on the phenomena of refraction; but this overlooks (for instance) the fact that the phenomena could be studied experimentally — as Newton had done — with monochromatic light. Even if this last point be ignored, since the importance of this method was not very apparent in Newton's experiments, whose force as it happened Hooke never succeeded in appreciating, it remains true that his incomprehension of the significance of a remarkable research springs from a difference between himself and Huygens as to what is an important question in science. Hooke's hypothesis of colour was brilliant, but Huygens was right in treating it as irrelevant to his own task. Though Hooke and Huygens are usually linked as the two great exponents of the wave or pulse theory of light in the seventeenth century, the lecture shows how little the former liked the adaptation of his ideas by the latter.

In the second lecture, after a few more words on the subject of light, including quotations from *Micrographia* and a criticism of "the Industrious Morianus," [23] Hooke passes on to an analysis of the *Discours sur la cause de la pesanteur*. It is unnecessary to quote here Hooke's summary of Huygens' hypothesis that the cause of gravity is to be found in the revolution of a vortex of aethereal matter about the earth at a velocity of 25930 feet per second (Hooke's computation). After mentioning his own dissatisfaction with this Cartesian notion, Hooke thinking "that there is somewhat else wanting to make out the phenomena of Gravity," the manuscript continues:

And indeed he [Huygens] seemes, in the sequell [24] to be somew^t of that opinion himself at the present though when he compiled & communicated this Discourse to the Royall accademy of Paris in 1678 he were better satisfyed with it. For what follows afterwards is additionall to that Discourse as he himself Declares in his preface, which is concerning those prioritys of Gravity which I myself first Discovered and shewed to this Society many years since, which of late M^r. Newton has done me the favour to print and Publish as his own Inventions. And Particularly that of the Ovall figure of the earth was Read by me to this Society about 27 years since upon the occasion of the Carrying the Pendulum Clocks to Sea And at two other times since, though I have had the Ill fortune not to be heard, And I conceive there are some present that may very well Remember and Doe know that M^r. Newton did not send up that addition to his book till some weeks after I had read & shewn the experiments & Demonstration thereof in this place and had answered the Reproachfull Letter of D^r. Wallis from Oxford. However I am well pleasd to find that truth will at length prevaile when men have Layd aside their prepossessions & prejudices. And as that hath found approvers in the world And those thinking men too, Soe I doubt not but that Divers other Discoverys

---

[23] *Sic*, and in *Micrographia*, 100. Perhaps a misnomer for Mersennus.

[24] I.e., the *Addition* to the *Discours*, written after the publication of the *Principia*.

which I have here first made will (when they come to be well considered and Examined) be found not soe unreasonable or Extravagante as some would willingly make them.

And though there have been Diverse who have Indeavoured to Represent me to the world as one that hath done nothing towards the Advancement of Naturall knowledge and that the same passes under the Name of the Declaration of this Society in the transactions[25] yet I hope In time I may obtain a Declaration of it to the Contrary, which is a peice of Justice which I am confident they will not Deny to any other person whatsoever. For though I had done nothing Els yet I conceive that Discovery of the Cause of the Celestiall motions to which neither M^r. Newton nor any other has any right to Lay Clayme might have been argument sufficient to have hindred such Expressions. Since I conceive it to be one of the greatest Discoverys yet made in Naturall Philosophy. And Mo^r. Huygens is soe ingenuous as both to admire the Discovery of it and expressly to acknowledge that he had noe thoughts of it, till he had met with it in M^r. Newtons booke though he had in his Horologium Oscillatorium considerd the gravitation of pendulous motions in order to demonstrate the Isochrone motion of a circular pendulum, which I had also Discoverd, made and shewn to the Society above 7 years before as will appear by their Journalls & Registers thereof.[26]

The Discovery of the Degree of Planetary Gravitation I first Communicated to S^r. Christopher Wren about 15 or 16 years Since Sometime before I published my attempt to prove the motion of the Earth, in which I have set down my hypothesis in Generall as may be there seen, and through [sic] he could never be of opinion which was all Demonstrable yet he can bear me witnesse that I Discovered it to him. The other person that I communicated it to was M^r. Newton of Cambridge in the year. 1679 — when after he had Declared his not knowing anything of it and his first attempts to make a Demonstration of gravitation in Circular motion upon a wrong supposition which was the Imagining Gravitation at all Distances to be the same which M^r. Huygens does also in expresse termes declare he till now believes I did in expresse termes tell him what the gravitation was and the effects that were produced in Circular motion by that gravitation which was all the celestiall motions & the reason of them i.e. that the motion of the body soe acted upon was in an ellipse about the focus thereof as likewise the Reason why the plaine of that motion did always passe through the center of the gravitating body &c which Letters both of my communication and his answers thereupon were shewn to and Read at the publique meetings of the Society the truth of which may be attested by severall of this Society and Divers of the Letters which I have hitherto preserved will put it out of Doubt. and he has since a good part of his book was printed acknowledged as much in a Letter written to one of his Correspondents wherein also he promised to doe me that Justice as to acknowledge it though all he has done is as much as Just nothing unless it be to assert that he himself was the Inventor of it, he setts up for the positive asserting thereof as will in time be made appear more at large and makes a pretence of falling out and being much offended with me who should Dare to chalenge what was my owne. But to Lett alone that Dispute for the present.

M^r. Huygens is now convinced of the Ovall figure of the Earth and particularly as he alledges by the Observations that have been made by some of the french at Cayen neer y^e equator in America he thereby computes what diminution of the gravity of a Body must be caused by the Diurnall motion of the Earth which he thereby finds to be as 1 to the square of 17 that is $\frac{1}{289}$ part of its terrestiall Gravity. and consequently that a Pendulum under the equator now the earth is moved round once in 24 hours ought to be $\frac{1}{289}$ part shorter then it should be if the earth were not moved with any Diurnall motion at all but kept the same Gravitating power it now hath. hence he deduceth the same Conclusions which I did in my Lectures about 3 or 4 years since namely that the figure of the Earth is a prolated Spheroid that is an ovall moved upon its shortest Diameter; that the surface of the water is of this figure: that the perpendicular doth not Respect the center of the earth in any parts of it but under the equator and under the Poles. All which particulars I did Demonstrate in my aforesaid Lectures against which Dr. Wallis writt his objections. which I doubt not but that many present may well Remember. Mo^r. Huygens by his computation makes the aequinoctiall Radius longer than the Polar by $\frac{1}{578}$ part, and concludes M^r. Newton's calculations to proceed upon a wrong hypothesis which he can by noe meanes Grant,[27] the 578th part amounts to 36200 feet, or $6\frac{7}{8}$ miles.

As an addition to this Discourse he gives an

---

[25] This refers to the Council Minute of 20th November 1676, published in the *Philosophical Transactions*, No. 129, in which Oldenburg's "management of the Intelligence of the Royal Society" was vindicated against Hooke's aspersions.

[26] The circular pendulum was demonstrated by Hooke, 23 May 1666 (Gunther 6, 267–8, 269, 276).

[27] Cf. Huygens, *op. cit.* 154 et seq. A detailed comparison of Huygens' and Newton's methods of calculation is given in Isaac Todhunter: *Theories of Attraction and Figure of the Earth* (London 1873), which regrettably omits Hooke's contribution.

account of the tryalls Lately made at Sea for the Discovery of the Longitude by means of the Pendulum Clocks. by which tryalls hee has found (as he alledges) that the account kept from the Cape of Good Hope till the Ships arrivall in the Texell did nott vary from the truth above 5. or 6. Leagues, taking the Longitude of the Cape to be 18 degrees more east then Paris, of which he takes himself to be ascertained by the Jesuits that went to Siam from France in the year 1685, and by other ways also. of which he hath made a Relation at Large to the Directors of the East India Company who have given order for a further tryall thereof. of which in time we may have an account together with which will be an account also of the differing motion of the Pendulum in Differing Latitudes which is the same thing which I have Engaged Cap^n Knox to make in his voyages to & from the Indies and in severall parts there. I only fear that the Directors there will furnish these observers with a much better apparatus than 40.^{lbs} will procure for Cap Knox here however I doubt not but that he will be as carefull in the use of what he shall have as they can be with theres nor shall he want Directions how to make them pertinently for the Purpose destined.

But to proceed: Mo^r. Huygens hath nothing to object against the Vis Centripeta which M^r. Newton is . . .^{28} (what I cald Gravity) that it doth make the planet gravitate towards the Sun and the moon towards the earth, because there is such a thing as gravity observed here upon the earth which causeth bodys to fall. And though he had been hence of the opinion that the . . .^{28} of the Sun proceeded from such a gravity he Ingenuously confesseth he had noe thought of extending that power soe far as to reach the planets, nor from the earth to the moon because he was prepossessed with the opinion of Mo^r. Descartes Vortices. Nor did he (as he expressly sayes) think of the Regular Diminution of that Gravity in Reciprocall proportion of the Squares of the Distances from the Center. which is a new & very remarkable propriety of gravity. of which he sayes M^r. Newton would doe well to shew a Reason. However seing it doth produce ye effect he doth not Doubt of the hypothesis. And soe much the rather because it solves all those Difficultys which the Vortices of Descartes are uncapable of performing. by it also ye Reason is plaine why the plains of all the orbs passe through the Sun. and how the Comets can soe variously traverse our Systeme and that sometimes with motions contrary to that of the Planets, and those also not Elliptical. But for that M^r. Newton would have all the space of the cartesian vortices to contain nothing but a very rare or thin body, he cannot easily agree with him. — for that he cannot conceive how the Action of Light & gravitation can be performed. to explaine this therefore he rejects the thin dispartion of particles with great interspersed vacuitys & admittes the small interspersed vacuitys where ye solids doe touch. Which Solids he supposeth perfectly hard & unalterable. but exceedingly small & exceeding Rapidly moved which proprietys he conceives sufficient to make it sufficiently fluid not to hinder the motion of ye planets. this he explains by the falling of a down feather in the Experiment of Vacuum which I have Diverse times shewn here, wherein yet he conceives there is a plenitude of aether. He agrees with M^r. Newton that bodys weigh according to the quantity of matter they contain yet thinks that weight is given them by the flying off of the aetheriall matter from the center. As in the progresse of Sound he is not of M^r. Newtons mind that it spreads laterally after it has passed through a hole as he has observed the waves on water, but from the phenomena of Echos he supposeth it only passeth forwards in streight lines, and is returned only by Reflection. He then proceedeth further to give his reasons for those his sentiments.

There are two other things in this hypothesis or Systeme which he much admires. And the first is the exact agreement of the motion of the moon about the Earth to the proportion of the gravity of the Earth at that Distance of 60 semidiameters, whence according to the aforesd proportion reciprocall as y^e square of y^e Distance the gravitating power of y^e earth at the moon is but $\frac{1}{3600}$ part of y^e gravitation here upon the earth. whence y^e Indeavour of Recesse arising from its velocity which he calls the Centrifuge motion must but just counter poise it which in effect it is found to doe if we consider that the Levitation or Centrifuge motion under the aequator is but $\frac{1}{289}$ part of the Reall gravity of a body upon the Earth.

Hence he thinks there may arise Doubt whether this greater Elongation from the center under the aequator may not introduce a Second inequality in the motion of the pendulums, but upon the whole thinks it will not be sensible, especially because he has found noe reason to make any allowances for it in the accounts that the Pilots have given him. and besides according to his hypothesis that Reciprocall proportion is not soe exactly observed neer the surface of the earth as at greater Distances. but yet he cannot be of M^r. Newtons mind that the gravity doth Diminish to nothing in the center because he thinks M^r. Newtons theory of the Reason of Gravity, not at all to be allowed.

The 2nd thing he is pleased with is that M^r. Newton hath by this hypothesis found a way to compare ye severall Gravitys of the Sun & the Planets with this of our Earth. But he thinks them but conjecturall because they depend upon Supposed Distances which he supposeth to be much otherwise. for whereas M^r. Newton puts the Sun at 5000 Diameters of the Earth distance.

---

^{28} The manuscript is here imperfect and illegible.

Cassini put it at 10000 and himself at 12000 and whereas M^r. Newton puts ye Suns gravity to be 12 times greater then it is on Earth, he puts it to be 26 times. wherefore the aether about the Sun must move 49 times quicker than the aether about the earth, which yet is 17 times quicker than the motion of ye Earth under ye Aequator. Now he conjectures that this exceeding quick motion of the aether about the Sun doth produce that vivid . . . . . which enlightens the world. This is the summe of what his Ingenious discourses of Light and Gravity . . . . knowledge, the other parts are for the most part Geometricall, in which . . . .[29]

There is one passage in this lecture that seems to demand more elucidation than a footnote can contain. It is that in which Hooke claims to have expounded the hypothesis that the earth's figure is oblate, apparently as a deduction from the properties of central forces, and in connection with the determination of the seconds' pendulum, as early as 1663.

At the end of the previous year Lord Kincardine returned to London with two pendulum clocks which had been adapted by Huygens and himself for marine use with the object of ascertaining longitude at sea. These clocks were tested on a voyage to the Downs in March 1663, and on a longer cruise to Lisbon in the summer.[30] It was doubtless in the first of these trials that Hooke played some part. If experiments with the pendulum had led him to think that the shape of the earth must be determined by the difference in centrifugal force at the equator and towards the poles, then he had indeed made a remarkable advance in physics. For he must not only have been capable of imagining a centrifugal *force* set up by rotation which could be opposed to the force of gravity, but have had some idea of calculating its magnitude. Huygens — to whom the priority in this investigation is universally granted — had calculated the diminution of gravity at the equator caused by the earth's diurnal revolution as 1/265th part as early as 1659; his researches were first described in *Horologium Oscillatorium* (1673), and there seems to be no other evidence beyond this statement for Hooke's claim to an independent discovery.[31] Moreover Richer's expedition to Cayenne, in the course of which the necessity for shortening the pendulum to beat seconds was discovered, only took place in 1672. Both Birch and Gunther are silent on this point, and at best it seems that Hooke could only have made a fortunate guess without adequate data to support it.

It is well known that he expounded his theory of the earth's shape to the Royal Society on several occasions after 1673. In *A Discourse of Comets & Gravity* (read, according to Birch, in October 1682) he speaks of the earth's rotation as the cause of a "Renitency" against the uniform power of gravity which is greater at the equator than at the parts of the earth towards the poles, and deduces a probability that the earth itself is oval, or "Turnep-form, the longest diameter being in the Equinoctial"; and in *A Discourse of Earthquakes* (1686/7) he not only refers to Richer's observations and those of Halley at St Helena on the pendulum but illustrates geometrically the displacement of the plumb-line at points intermediate between the equator and the poles owing to the action of two forces upon it which he analyses vectorially — a sound piece of work.[32] In spite of this introduction of mathematics Hooke's theory lacked a quantitative form; he did not calculate, as Huygens had done, the magnitude of the centrifugal force, nor, as Newton was to do, the ratio of the axes. As a comparison of Proposition XIX, Problems III and IV of the *Principia* with Hooke's lectures will show, Newton's demonstrations and calculations relative to this property of the earth which Hooke had first stated indicate an independent conception, and are given with a precise rigour which Hooke did not attain.

---

[29] The last sheet of the manuscript is imperfect.

[30] Huygens: *Oeuvres complètes*, 4, 284–5, 290–1, 318, 446.

[31] *Ibid.*, *16*, 304. Galileo had sought to prove that the force was not sufficient to project bodies from the earth's surface.

[32] Thomas Birch: *History of the Royal Society* (London 1754), *4*, 162, 523; Waller, *op. cit.*, 181, 349 seq.

On the point of chronology, however, Hooke's remarks in 1690 were perfectly just. The lectures in which he "had the Ill fortune not to be heard" were read long before the third book of the *Principia* was written. The full "discourse concerning the probability of the hypothesis that the earth is of the figure of a prolate spheroid, whose shortest diameter is the axis" (Birch's summary) was pronounced on 2 February 1686/7, whereas the complete manuscript of Newton's work only reached Halley during March. But Hooke's implied claim that the relevant section had been put together in this "some weeks" interval is obviously absurd, especially as the hypothesis had been public knowledge for several years. In this, as in other instances, Hooke's own eagerness made his defence illogical, so that by provoking his colleagues in the Royal Society, he prevented the just appreciation that he desired and deserved.

Perhaps, unfortunately, Hooke's fertile imagination did not stop at this point. He speculated further upon geological history in such a way as to incur the criticism of another whom he was to count among his enemies, John Wallis of Oxford. If, Hooke said in a lecture on 26 January 1686/7, the poles of the earth are not immutably fixed, but have shifted their positions even in the historical past (as the discrepancies between ancient observations of latitude and those now obtained seemed to show), different parts of the earth would at different times have been sunk beneath or raised above the level of the sea, which would always tend to be deeper in the equatorial regions. In this way the formation of sea-bed deposits now found high above sea-level might be accounted for.[33] Seeking for evidence in support of this suggestion, and of the movement of the earth's axis which it assumed, on 7 February and subsequently Hooke described a variety of methods whereby the meridian of any place might be exactly determined and its variations with time discovered. One at least of these methods, however, does not distinguish between ascertaining a change in the earth's axis of rotation (the point in question) and a shift among the stars of the imaginary celestial pole such as, indeed, the Chinese astronomers had long ago observed by somewhat similar procedures.

Although the astronomical evidence in favour of the hypothesis was doubtful, Hooke was forward in its defence. In the course of correspondence, summaries of his lectures were transmitted by Edmond Halley (who had been appointed Clerk to the Royal Society) to the companion Philosophical Society at Oxford. Halley, the friend of Newton who was most active in bringing forth the *Principia*, openly recognised Hooke's priority on the theory of the earth's shape, writing in an account of affairs in the capital: "I have now lately received the last Book of that [i.e. Newton's] treatise, wch is entituled de Systemato Mundi. . . . How [Here?] he falls in with Mr Hook, and makes the Earth of the shape of a compressed spheroid, whose shortest diameter is the axis. . . ."

Hooke's ideas were discussed at Oxford on 22 February and 1 March, the sense of the discussion, as represented by Wallis in his replies to Halley's bulletins, being by no means favourable to Hooke.[34] The Oxford philosophers "seemed not forward, to turn ye world upside down, without some cogent reason for it; not onely, that possibly it might be so; but that indeed it hath been so." Variations in the poles there might have been, though the latitudes of places seemed to have remained for many ages nearly the same, but "we cannot think that there ever was, or perhaps ever will be, such great variation as is pretended; as that thereby the whole surface of the Earth hath been *many times* all covered with sea, & uncovered again." As for the earth's shape, its appearance during an eclipse of the moon, and the perpendicular descent of falling bodies, argued that it was approximately if not mathematically spherical; indeed the opinion at Oxford was that the earth's axial diameter was probably the longer

---

[33] Gunther: *Early Science in Oxford*, 7, 700 seq.; Waller, *op. cit.*, 343 seq.
[34] Dated at Oxford, 4 March 1686/7 and 26 April 1687. Bodleian Library, MS Ashmole 1813 f. 327–330. They were read to the Royal Society on 9 March and 11 May.

"that being better fitt for motion, & more likely to preserve ye Axe in its proper place" — a rather curious notion. However, Wallis protested that he intended no disrespect for Mr Hooke, but only declared himself with "the liberty we use to take (& do allow to others) to express our thoughts freely in matters of Philosophy."

The avowal of philosophic candour did not soften Hooke's rejoinders.[35] Wallis's letters, he complained, were made up "partly of misrepresentation, partly of designed satyr" arising out of prejudice conceived against him on account of former discourses. Naturally it was not difficult for him to retort that Wallis's objections were too crude to carry weight; that the theory was supported by mathematical demonstrations and mechanical observations; and that in any case it was "propounded as an hypothesis to be examined by Experiments, and not as a positive assertion." So far Hooke justifies himself. But of the more tenuous hypothesis of the submersion of the earth's surface, even to the summit of the Alps (in which posterity was to prove Hooke correct for the wrong reasons), which Wallis had attacked more hotly with references to the known geography of the world since Adam, it can only be said that it confused the issue and endangered a sound application of the principles of dynamics. Contemporaries saw Hooke's theory of the earth as a whole; they could not easily distinguish his plausible hypothesizing from the other notions which rested on speculation. If Wallis misunderstood Hooke in part, the fault was by no means entirely Wallis's. Scientific ideas are necessarily frail, though their correctness may be vindicated, if they are neither rigourously nor clearly expressed. It was because his presentation was so much more lucid, rigourous and demonstrative that Newton, rather than Hooke, induced men to consider the earth as a dynamical body. In this instance, at least, it was not so much that they preferred to be instructed by Newton than by Hooke, as that the propositions of the former were logically linked by mathematical processes to the principles and phenomena of mechanics, whereas Hooke's theories were qualitative, disconnected, and apparently enmeshed in a mere conjecture about the past.

This was not an age in which criticism was accepted calmly, and Hooke reacted more violently than most. For those who could not follow his often inspired hypotheses, the accusation of dullness was not enough; increasingly he saw his critics as wilful and persistent enemies, eagerly using every opportunity to detract from his reputation. It seems that by 1687 he could no longer allow that he was receiving his deserts from the Royal Society, either intellectually or financially. The bitterness and scorn already shown for some of his colleagues in the earlier diary (and not only those who had taken the parts of Oldenburg or Newton) caused him to become increasingly reserved. He consoled himself in May 1687 with a thought that was to recur, "I have some encouragement to hope that the Society will in time see that what things I have proposed are such as are before well considered, and not things taken up wthout good ground, or such as I cannot with good Reasons defend if there be need thereof." And, indeed, Waller and Derham did what they could to preserve his works and memory.

At about this time the active part of Hooke's scientific life came to an end. The Royal Society itself was lethargic, and Hooke had no longer the energy or the ambition to invigorate its meetings. Though Newton's position in the scientific movement remained for some time one of academic rather than national eminence, the rise of elaborate mathematical methods in mechanical science gave less scope for the particular genius of Hooke. Perhaps after a career during which he had received many disappointments and rebuffs that had not failed to arouse resentment, the applause which greeted the *Principia* — the triumph of the "mathematical drudge" over the experimental philosopher — came as the crowning injustice. Hooke paraded his belief that Newton had stolen the secret of the heavens, and he never forgave the Society its

---

[35] *An Answer to Dr. Wallis's way to find ye Meridian* (26 April 1687) and *An Answer to Dr. Wallis's Letter of Apr 26 1687* (11 May 1687). Royal Society, *Classified Papers*, 20, Nos. 73, 75.

refusal to take his claim seriously. It is a pathetic incident, for clearly Pepys was in this (as in other questions of character and ability) a shrewd judge: Hooke did much more than he promised. He was a genius whose ideas were often remarkable for their quality of vision; but in admitting this it is not necessary to suppose that they were always emphatic in guiding the scientific thought of the age, or that his work was always the inspiration of those who, working in the same intellectual environment and at the same problems, were more strategically effective than he in defining their contributions to knowledge.

XI

Newton's First Book (I)

The first book (or publication of any sort) to bear the mark of Newton's hand was Isaac Barrow's *Lectiones XVIII Cantabrigiæ in Scholis Publicis habitæ : in quibus Opticorum Phænomenon Genuinæ Rationes Investigantur, ac exponuntur* (London, 1669) (1). In his *Epistle to the Reader* Newton's assistance was acknowledged by Barrow in laudatory terms :

> Like a delicate mother, I committed this new-born infant to the foster-care of complaisant friends, to deal with as they thought fit, either to bring it up or to expose it. One of them (for I acknowledge them by name, to do them honour), Mr. Isaac Newton, our colleague and a truly outstanding man of genius and remarkable knowledge, revised one copy, advising us of some points to be corrected and, with no little pains, suggesting some things which you may here and there discover annexed, with commendations, to our own (2).

In fact Newton was the author of a « singularly elegant and expeditious method » (Brewster) of tracing the image formed by a lens, printed at the end of lecture XIV. It has often been pointed out that Barrow's would have been a better book had it also incorporated the new theory of colours that Newton had already formed. But there is no evidence to indicate whether Newton had described his work to Barrow or not (3). In any case Newton's share in the book is a very slight one.

Newton's name next appeared in print as the writer of the famous letter to Henry Oldenburg on light and colours, dated 6 February 1671/2 and printed in the *Philosophical Transactions*, number 80, 19 February 1671/2. The first book to have Newton's name on the titlepage was *Bernhardi Vareni Med. D. Geographia Generalis in qua Affectiones Generales Telluris explicantur summa cura quam plurimis in locis Emendata, & XXXIII Schematibus Novis. Aere Incisis, una cum Tabb. aliquot quae desidera-*

---

(1) *Eighteen Lectures given in the public schools of Cambridge, in which the genuine reasons for the phenomena of optics are investigated and explained.* The imprimatur is dated March 1668/9.
(2) The original Latin is quoted by Sir David BREWSTER, *Memoirs of Sir Isaac Newton* (Edinburgh, 1855), I, 27, note 3 and copied by L. T. MORE, *Isaac Newton* (New-York, 1934), 80, note.
(3) The question is discussed by I. Bernard COHEN in *Franklin and Newton* (Philadelphia, 1956), 49-53.

bantur Aucta & Illustrata. Ab Isaaco Newton Math. Prof. Lucasiano apud Cantabrigienses (Cambridge, 1672) (4). The first edition had been published at Amsterdam in 1650 (5). Newton's attention to this work has always been something of an enigma. His only personal claim to have contributed anything to the Cambridge edition was that he had « described Schemes » (6). The statement of the translator of the English version of 1736, that Newton intended Varenius « to be read by the audience while he was delivering lectures upon the same subject from the Lucasian chair » lacks all probability. For in these years Newton was lecturing on optics, nor (so far as is known) did he ever lecture on geography, though he did reckon geography among the mathematical sciences. Professor Turnbull suggests less precisely that the edition was prepared « for the benefit of his pupils » (7); it may be that Newton was expected to teach private pupils (if he had any) some geography, or that those who consulted him in his « office hours » needed guidance in this subject. I know of no evidence for such suppositions. It is more likely that Varenius's *Geography* had been commended to the University Press as a book suitable for republication in England, especially for student use, and that Newton was engaged to improve it. He seems to have found little interest in the task. Nevertheless, the fact that Newton (technically) had this edition of Varenius « in the press » is of some historical interest, if only for the reason that it confuses the record of Newton's intentions as a writer at this time.

The first volume of his own authorship to appear under Newton's name was the *Principia* in 1687.

But Newton certainly had other publishing adventures in mind during these early years, quite apart from the series of papers

---

(4) *A General Geography, by Bernard Varenius M. D., in which the General Properties of the Earth are explained. Corrected in many places with great care, and enlarged and illustrated with 33 new figures engraved on copper together with certain Tables that were lacking. By Isaac Newton, Lucasian Professor of Mathematics at Cambridge.* A second edition « larger and more correct » was printed in 1681. I have used this, as the first is very rare.

(5) And again at Amsterdam in 1671.

(6) Newton to Collins, 25 May 1672. H. W. Turnbull (ed.), *The Correspondence of Isaac Newton,* vol. I (Cambridge, 1959; hereafter cited as *Corr. 1*).

(7) *Ibid.,* 148, note 3.

XI

NEWTON'S FIRST BOOK ☆

he contributed to the *Philosophical Transactions*. There are clear signs that he intended to print some of his papers on light and colours, and on mathematics. It will be simplest to deal with these seriatim.

1) *Kinckhuysen's Algebra* (8). — This work had been known to the London mathematical clerk John Collins for some time before he sent a Latin translation of it to Newton (probably through Isaac Barrow — the letter is lost), at some time between August 1669 and January 1670, when Newton wrote to Collins that he was making notes upon it (9). Collins wished Newton to « review » (that is, prepare a comment upon) Kinckhuysen's book; but Newton decided « it was not worth the paines of a formall comment, There being nothing new or notable in it wch is not to bee found in other Authors of better esteeme » (10). Nevertheless, he despatched his notes together with the translation to Collins in July 1670, leaving to him the decision whether or not the notes should be included in the publication of the translated algebra that Collins contemplated, adding that since it would be « esteemed unhandsom & injurious to Kinckhuysen to father a book wholly upon him wch is soe much altered » the words « et ab alio Authore locupleta » should appear on the titlepage (11).

Collins next wanted advice on the improvement of Kinckhuysen's treatment of surds, whereupon Newton asked him to return the package of papers so that he might rewrite this part himself, and make some further additions (12). The task was completed by September, when Newton reported that he had toyed with the idea of composing a new introduction to algebra himself because Kinckhuysen's methods of forming equations were not general, but had given it up (13). Near the end of the year 1670 Collins could write to his friend, the Scottish mathematician James Gregory, that « Kinckhuysen's Introduction to Algebra with notes thereon and additions thereto made by the learned Mr. Isaac Newton of Cambridge (at the request of Dr. Barrow),

---

(8) Gerard KINCKHUYSEN, *Algebra, ofre stel-konst* (Haarlem, 1661).
(9) *Corr.* I, 20. It is possible that Newton's first letter to Collins acknowledged receipt of the translation, which is only casually mentioned at the end of this one. If so, it is lost.
(10) *Ibid.*, 24.
(11) *Ibid.*, 30-31.
(12) *Ibid.*, 34-35.
(13) *Ibid.*, 42-44.

is ready for the Presse » (14). But « the Bookseller Pitts » (Moses Pitt, who was apparently the proprietor of the translation) was not anxious to promote a speedy publication, though Collins suggested that the book should now pass under Newton's name on account of the many improvements he had made in it, « and thereby find the better entertainment and more Speedy Sale ». One reason why the edition of Kinckhuysen never appeared was certainly the reluctance of the booksellers and printers to undertake any advanced mathematical treatise, of limited appeal, without a considerable « dowry ». Those who had been concerned with Barrow's *Optical and Geometrical Lectures* had gone bankrupt, which scared the rest. Nor was Newton himself in a hurry : it was now July 1671, and he had made some fresh additions to the *Algebra* in the preceding winter, but « partly upon Dr. Barrow's instigation » he had begun to « new methodiz[e] ye discourse of infinite series », intending to add this work to the *Algebra* to justify the appearance of his name on its titlepage. His progress had been delayed by illness, and he did not expect to continue with it for some months, when he hoped to « get into ye humour of completing them before ye impression of the » *Algebra*. Both Collins and Newton were now viewing the book in a more ambitious light. For Collins it was becoming a new work, not just a translation from the Low Dutch. For Newton it offered an opportunity to publish « something wch I may call my owne, & wch may bee acceptable to Artists [in mathematics] as well as ye other to Tyros » (15).

The next news of the enterprise is nearly a year later. In spite of his engagement with optics, Newton had not entirely neglected mathematics. By May 1672 the additions to Kinckhuysen were « long since » completed, particularly a « discourse concerning invention or the way of bringing Problems to an Aequation » (this was later incorporated in *Arithmetica Universalis*). « Those », he wrote Collins, « are at your command ». If Collins was not resolved to print the *Algebra*, however, he would possibly print what he had written « with the discourse con-

---

(14) *Ibid.*, 56. Presumably Collins meant that Barrow had been an intermediary between himself and Newton, for certainly the enterprise was Collin's and not Barrow's.

(15) *Ibid.*, 66, 68.

cerning Infinite Series » (16). But the « bookseller Pitts » was now more anxious to dispose of the awkward manuscript translation, than to risk printing it with or without Newton's improvements and discourses. Newton persuaded a Cambridge bookseller to offer £3 for it (sight unseen), and it seemed that a bargain might be struck, even at Collins's expense (17). Finally the translation was bought by Newton himself, about the end of 1672 or early in 1673, for £4 (18). Possibly it was Newton's intention to have it published as his edition by the University Press, like the Varenius, accompanied by his own discourses. The Press refused his offer, and the last we hear of it (in September 1676) is that it was « in the hands of a bookseller here [Cambridge] to get it printed », but Newton had now decided not to add his own papers to it (19). I do not know the fate of this manuscript; there are, however, « Observations on the Algebra of Kinckhuysen » (unpublished) in the Cambridge University Library, Portsmouth Collection, Ms. Add. 3959, no. 1.

The sad story of the Kinckhuysen translation is not important in itself, so much as for the delay that befell the publication of Newton's mathematical papers. It is very probable that had Collins been able to find an enterprising publisher in London some of Newton's own mathematical discoveries would have seen the light in 1671 or 1672, at a time when he was allowing his results to be communicated freely by Barrow, Collins and others, and when he himself revealed no paranoiac reluctance to go into print. Encouragement was certainly not lacking from the best mathematicians. Of Collins own enthusiasm there could be no doubt, though his means did not allow him to subsidize a book for Newton (who was far from impoverished himself). Richard Towneley wrote to Collins (4 January 1672) :

[I] long to see Kinckhuysen's *Introduction to Algebra,* with those wonderful additions of Mr. Newton (20).

Wallis regarded Newton as so far superior to Kinckhuysen that it was much preferable, in his view, for the former to pre-

---

(16) *Ibid.,* 161.
(17) *Ibid.,* 215, 222, 226.
(18) *Ibid.,* 271.
(19) S. P. RIGAUD, *Correspondence of Scientific Men of the Seven-* [Dr C.J. Scriba discovered the MS. translation in the Bodleian Library: see D.T. Whiteside, *Mathematical Papers of Isaac Newton,* vol. II, Cambridge 1968, p. 294, note 1.]
(20) *Ibid.,* I, 184.

pare his own *Algebra* (21). Oldenburg reported the forthcoming new edition to Huygens on 6 May 1672 (22). And James Gregory, who attended with high interest to all he could learn of Newton's discoveries, was willing to defer publication of his own methods so that Newton should enjoy priority. There is no trace of a critical or hostile voice. When two or three more years had gone by, however, Newton's distaste for publication had markedly increased, so that he had cut his own contributions from Kinckhuysen's book by 1676. Even if a publisher had been available it was now too late.

2) *The Dioptrick Lectures, with or without mathematical papers.* — Newton inaugurated his professorship at Cambridge with a series of lectures on optics in the Lent Term 1670, beginning probably in January (during subsequent years he always lectured in the Michaelmas Term). The course was continued in Michaelmas 1670, 1671, and 1672 (23). By the statutes of his chair, Newton was required to deposit copies of all his lectures in the University Library, and accordingly a volume containing the optical lectures was deposited in 1674. Hence they had to be fully worked up for public reading and were necessarily (in a limited sense) « published ». There was no great further labour involved in having the lectures printed, as Barrow had done.

(21) *Ibid.,* II, 529.
(22) *Corr.,* I, 156.
(23) I follow the statement of W. W. ROUSE BALL, *An Essay on Newton's Principia* (London, 1893), 27-28 and note. The printed title of *Lectiones Opticæ* (1729), however, states that the lectures were delivered in 1669 [i. e. 1670 N. S.], 1670 and 1671. The manuscript in the Cambridge University Library (MS.Dd, 9-67) bears this note by the University Librarian :

These lectures of Mr. Isaac Newton ye Mathematick Professor were delivered by him into ye hands of Dr. Spencer ye Vice-Chancellor of the University & by Mr. Vice-Chancellor delivered unto mee for to place in ye University Library according to ye order of ye founder of that Lecture.
October 21th 1674.

Robert PEACHEY.

(John Spencer, 1630-1693, Master of Corpus Christi College, was Vice-Chancelllor 1673-1674). Part I, 39 folios written on both sides, is divided into 15 lectures and has the date « Jan. 1669 » at the commencement. Part II, 52 folios, is divided into 16 lectures. The figures are neatly drawn on separate folios at the end of each Part. The MS is neatly written by an amanuensis. On a hasty check the printed text seemed to depart very little from the MS.

The earliest suggestion that Newton intended to publish his optical lectures in the wider sense appears in a letter from Collins to James Gregory (23 February 1672) :

> Mr. Newton (as Dr. Barrow informs me) intends to send up all the lectures he hath read since he was Professor to be printed here, which he sayth will be 20 Dioptrick Lectures, and some about infinite series, with his additions to Kinckhuysen's Introduction (24).

His next letter returns to the subject, mentioning Newton's dioptrics as the book next to be urged for publication and as « exceedingly commended by Dr. Barrow » (25). Then Collins wrote to Newton himself offering assistance (30 April 1672) :

> A little before Christmas the Reverend Doctor Barrow informed me you were buisy in enlarging your generall method of Infinite Series's or quadratures, and in preparing 20 Dioptrick Lectures for the Presse, and lately meeting with Mr. Jonas Moore he informed me that he heard you had something at ye Presse in Cambridge possibly about ye same Argumt, if so I am very glad... now Sr as soone as this Booke (26) is done if yours be not undertaken at Cambridge I shall most willingly affoard my endeavour to have it well done here, and if so, what you have written might be sent up the sooner in order to the Preparing of Schemes (27).

Newton, deeply immersed in the controversial correspondence over his optical discoveries that reached him through Oldenburg, now gave first signs of reluctance to have any further business with printers (25 May 1672) :

> Your kindness to me also in profering to promote the edition of my Lectures wch Dr. Barrow told you of, I reccon amongst the greatest, considering the multitude of buisinesse in wch you are involved. But I have now determined otherwise of them; finding already by that little use I have made of the Presse, that I shall not enjoy my former serene liberty till I have done with it; wch I hope will be so soon as I have

---

(24) H. W. TURNBULL (ed.), *James Gregory Tercentenary Memorial Volume* (London, 1939), 218. The implication that Newton had already lectured on mathematics is incorrect, since Newton gave 31 lectures on optics, not 20 as Collins evidently thought. If Rouse Ball's statement that the lectures of Michaelmas Term 1672 were also on optics is correct, it may be that Newton had some notion of beginning his mathematical lectures in that term but postponed them to the following year.

(25) 14 March 1672. *Ibid.*, 225. *Corr.*, I, 119.

(26) Collins refers to the edition of Jeremiah HORROX's *Opera Posthuma* on which, with John Wallis, he was then engaged.

(27) *Corr.*, I, 146-7.

made good what is already extant on my account. Yet I may possibly complete the discourse of resolving Problemes by infinite series of wch I wrote the better half ye last christmas with intension that it should accompany my Lectures but it proves larger than I expected & is not yet finished.

The Book here in Presse is Varenius his *Geography,* for wch I have described Schemes; & I suppose it will be finished about six weeks hence (28).

Another letter, six weeks later, confirms this decision though stating that Newton was uncertain whether he would publish his work on infinite series, still incomplete. Later Oldenburg had the same story; Newton intended « nothing further for the publick », though he was prepared to satisfy any of Oldenburg's « private acquaintance » by sending further experimental particulars (29). At the same time he gave Oldenburg permission to print in the *Transactions* his reply to Hooke's critique of his original paper on light.

That seems to be the end of the story, so far as the *Lectiones Opticae* are concerned, for over fifty years. A few manuscript copies were made of the manuscript lying in the Cambridge University Library, otherwise Newton's optical researches were known to his contemporaries until 1704 only from his contributions to the *Philosophical Transactions.* The abrupt change of mind concerning publication that took place in the spring of 1672 seems to be largely attributable to the criticism his first paper on light encountered. But not entirely. If, as seems likely, Newton originally intended to print mathematical papers with his lectures (as indeed he did with *Opticks*) then he could scarcely have gone to press in 1672, for he was still hard at work developing his mathematical methods in due form. At a later time,

---

(28) *Ibid.,* 161. In the following paragraph, after a complimentary phrase on the Royal Society, Newton wrote that the freedom of communication he had hoped to enjoy was cut short, because he could not enjoy it « without giving offence to some persons whome I have ever respected ». Was the giving of offence a figment of Newton's imagination or real, and if the latter, to whom? There is no evidence that Newton's writing's had offended Barrow (who was later to encourage the publication of Newton's *Lectiones*) or anyone else in the Royal Society. Newton may have thought he had made Hooke his enemy — if he did, he was in error — yet it seems strange that he should describe Hooke (whom he had read, but scarcely knew), as a « person I ever respected ».

(29) *Corr.,* I, 238. 21 September 1672.

when the mathematical papers were ready, the optical lectures themselves had become somewhat out of date — because of the discussion between Newton and his critics in the *Philosophical Transactions*. In fact, Newton soon began to show interest in issuing a work on optics which was not the twenty dioptric lectures, and perhaps not the *Lectiones Opticæ* at all.

3) *Another work on optics, with or without mathematical appendices*. — In the spring of 1672, when he gave up the idea of printing the dioptric lectures, Newton appears still not to have completed his course on optics, and possibly the last few lectures were not yet written. By July Newton had already composed his answers to Auzout, Pardies, Moray, Bercé and Hooke on the theory of light and the reflecting telescope, and all except the answer to Hooke had been printed in the *Philosophical Transactions*. On 13 July 1672 he assented to Oldenburg's publication of Pardies's second letter, together with his own reply, adding,

I intended to suspend it for a while thinking it would be more convenient to print together what shall be said of this subject, especially since there are some other papers at Cambridg to be added to them. But if what hath passed be inserted into the *Transactions* to entertain them at present that are in expectation of further information about these matters, they may be hereafter reprinted by themselves if it shall be thought fit (30).

Actually Oldenburg must have anticipated Newton's permission since the two documents were published on the 15th, the day that Newton's letter reached him in London. One may guess that Newton would also have published his answer to Hooke in the collection he mentioned; what the « other papers at Cambridg » were may be inferred from other letters. As early as 10 February 1672 Newton had offered Oldenburg « such remarques & experiments as might be collected by considering the assigned laws of refractions; some of wch I believe wth the generality of men would yet be almost as taking as any of those I have described » (in the famous first paper) (31). On 19 March he advised Oldenburg he was holding back his answer to Hooke's critical observations in order to complete some further explanation of the theory of colours, that he designed to accompany it. On 21 May, however, Newton wrote :

(30) *Ibid.*, 217.
(31) *Ibid.*, 109.

But yet upon the receipt of your letter I deferred the sending those things which I intended, and have determined to send you alone a part of what I prepared, as I told you, to accompany my Answer, for the sake of wch I have hitherto suspended it. The subject of this discourse is the Phenomena of Plated Bodies, concerning which I shall by experiments first show how according to their several thicknesses they reflect or transmit the rays indued with severall colours, and then consider the relation which these thin transparent Plates have to the parts of their naturall Bodies, in order to a fuller understanding of the causes of their colours also (32).

Thus Newton's study of interference phenomena was certainly prepared in the spring of 1672, though it was not to be submitted to the Royal Society until 7 December 1675 (33). The exact meaning of the first sentence of this passage is hard to disentangle. The « Answer to Hooke » was to be separated from other writings prepared to accompany it, of which only a part, apparently, was the discourse on the colours of thin plates. In fact — as the 13 July letter makes plain — Newton had now abandoned the idea of a separate publication, and correspondingly for a time set aside the papers that he had been preparing for it.

To recapitulate : it was in May, 1672, that Newton decided against publishing either his optical lectures, or the other separate work on the theory of light which was to incorporate his answer to Hooke. The motives behind this double decision are obscure. Newton can hardly have been influenced solely by the criticisms of Pardies, Hooke, and others, for he had known of these some months before he changed his mind about publication, and he had himself qualified all of them as slight and easily answered. Moreover, two and a half years later he did send both the *Hypothesis of Light* and the *Discourse of Observations* on the colours of thin plates to the Royal Society, where they were just as open to the critical appraisal of Hooke and others as if they had been printed. It seems not unlikely that Newton was moved by a professional and quite impersonal consideration. He may well have thought that what he had already prepared was not in the most suitable form for publication. The optical lectures did not really meet the new situation, in which Newton had to main-

(32) *Ibid.*, 122, 160.
(33) This investigation had been begun years before. See A. R. Hall, « Further Optical Experiments of Isaac Newton », *Annals of Science*, XI, 1955, 27-43.

tain his theory of light and colour against critical objections; nor did they include his additional material on thin plates. The other materials he had were disjointed and incompletely prepared. They were not sufficient either to state his theories with complete clarity and full experimental support, nor were they either so set out as to meet possible objections and misunderstandings. No one will doubt that Newton regarded the role of the writer on scientific topics with extreme gravity. He was never inclined to popularize, except in private communications, and (so long as he was a University professor) he seems to have regarded Latin as a more fitting language for scientific communication than English. He even looked on his scientific letters to Oldenburg as rather lightweight, and apologized (not quite sincerely perhaps) for their taking up so much of the Royal Society's time. It would not have been out of character for him to feel — after some months of controversy — that the only book really worth publishing was one that would deal with light, colour, refraction, diffraction, interference phenomena and so on thoroughly and finally. He had the materials for such a book at hand, and a partial but imperfect exposition in the *Lectiones Opticæ*, but he had not yet written it. That book was to be *Opticks*, which of course incorporates both the work described in the first paper of February 1672, most of Part II of the *Lectiones*, and the *Discourse of Observations* read to the Royal Society in January 1676 (34).

Some further information on these matters can be gained from letters written after this last event. Even before the reading of the *Discourse on Observations* was complete the Society had instructed Oldenburg to request Newton for permission to print them. On 25 January 1676 Newton replied to Oldenburg:

As to ye Paper of Observations wch you move in ye name of ye Society to have printed, I cannot but return them my hearty thanks for ye kind acceptance they meet wth there; & know not how to deny any

---

(34) The most obvious proof of Newton's dissatisfaction with *Lectiones Opticæ* is that in writing *Opticks* he discarded almost the whole of Part I of the older work, and completely reconstructed Part II. Probably Newton refers to the MS copies of the *Lectiones* that were circulating when he writes in the Preface to Opticks « If any other Papers writ on this Subject are got out of my Hands they are imperfect... » But of course this does not prove that his dissatisfaction developed so early as I have suggested.

thing wch they desire should be done. Only I think it will be best to suspend ye printing of them for a while because I have thoughts of writing such another set of Observations for determining ye manner of ye production of colours by ye Prism, wch, if done at all, ought to precede yt now in your hands, & will do best to be joyned with it. But this I cannot do presently by reason of some incumbrances lately put upon me by some friends, & some other buisines of my own wch at present almost take up my time and thoughts (35).

The additions that I intended, I think I must after putting you to so long expectations disappoint you in; for it puzzels me how to connect them with what I sent you; & if I had those papers yet I doubt ye things I intended will not come in so freely as I thought they might have done... I have therefore at present only sent you two or three alterations... (36).

Newton was evidently aware that his writings hitherto, published or unpublished, and anything more he could rapidly add to them piecemeal, were not coherent and failed to do full justice to his investigations and his conceptions. His refusal to print the *Discourse on Observations* in the *Transactions* clearly sprang from reluctance to add to the number of his disparate writings on light, and from a perhaps rather vaguer intention to produce a work that should be complete and unified.

Was Newton at work on *Opticks* in 1676? Rumours certainly continued to circulate. On 5 September of that year Newton denied a report that had reached Collins through a certain Dr. Lloyd of his having a book in the press (37). Still more circumstantial is Collins's letter to Newton of 5 March 1677 :

Mr. Loggan informs me he hath drawn your effigies in order to a sculpture thereof to be prefixed to a book of Light, Colours, [&] Dioptricks which you intend to publish, of which we whould be glad to have more certain notice (38).

Newton's reply appears to be lost. No print of an engraving from Loggan's plate seems to be recorded, but it is certainly

(35) Presumably this refers to his chemical studies.
(36) *Corr.*, I, 414. The « additions » mentioned in the second paragraph may also be referred to in an earlier letter (13 November 1675, *Corr.* I, 358) where Newton complains that it goes « against ye grain to put pen to paper any more on yt Subject ». This may have been an expression of merely temporary low spirits.
(37) RIGAUD, *op. cit.*, II, 398. Newton thought the reference was to KINCKHUYSEN's *Algebra*.
(38) NEWTON, *Correspondence*, II, 200-201.

true that David Loggan, the engraver, was in Cambridge in 1676, making studies for his book *Cantabrigia Illustrata* (1690). The plate of Great St Mary's Church, Cambridge, in that volume is dedicated in flattering terms to Newton, which implies that he subscribed generously to the enterprise (as did Trinity College). It is likely, therefore, that Loggan had met Newton, but the rest remains a mystery. It is just possible that Collins completely misunderstood some information from Loggan about his « engraving for Mr. Newton ».

4) *The Waste Sheets.* — Professor I. Bernard Cohen has already described in the *Archives* these two copies of pages 9 to 16 of an otherwise unknown early printed version of Newton's first optical paper (6 February 1672) (39). Some further notes on them have since appeared in the first volume of the *Correspondence of Isaac Newton* (40).

At whose instigation were these sheets struck off? It is at least certain that Newton revised the text as printed in them, altered the diagram, and added long explanatory notes. The sheets are plainly not a simple copy from the *Philosophical Transactions* and it seems plausible to suppose that they were printed in the years not far distant from 1672. If so, then the person who arranged the printing must in all probability have been either Oldenburg or Newton himself. Who else would have added the final sentence from Sir Robert Moray's paper of proposed experiments that was omitted from the printed version in the *Transactions?* On the other hand, the sheets cannot have been printed before the controversy on the original paper was fairly extended, since in note (d) (p. 12) Newton refers to « letters » in the plural.

One might well suppose that Henry Oldenburg was responsible for the abortive publication, even though there is no reference to it in his letters to Newton (some of which are lost, however). He had many dealings with the booksellers as a translator, and as agent for Robert Boyle, and on at least one occasion he published

(39) *Archives internationales d'Histoire des Sciences,* XI, 1958, 357-375.
(40) *Corr.,* I, 105-107. The most important variants are in the diagram, a new sentence added in explanation of it, and the added notes.

in a pamphlet a series of letters addressed to himself (41). Oldenburg would have been in a position to secure Newton's consent to a reprint. Moreover Oldenburg and Oldenburg alone — besides Newton — knew that Newton had unpublished optical letters and papers on hand. It is possible, for instance, that a reprint of the early optical papers could have been made by him in 1676, when he was expecting Newton to return the *Discourse of Observations*, possibly accompanied by other papers, with a view to their publication (42). And indeed, there is clear evidence that a publication of fresh papers (together, presumably, with a reprint of the old), *was* intended, and that Newton had consented to it.

But first, consider the likelihood that Newton himself was responsible. The preceding discussion suggests only two periods when that is at all likely. The earlier time is about March-April 1672, when (as has been shown) Newton had thoughts of publishing his answer to Hooke and other papers independently. Professor Turnbull favours this suggestion (43). But the few remarks Newton made about this proposal seem rather to presage a new discussion — starting from Hooke's criticisms — than a reprint of what had already come out, followed by the answer to Hooke and other new materials. If Newton now wished to make a fresh and effective statement, to seek to do so by adding notes to an unchanged text seems a little strange. Why should he not have started afresh? The later period is about 1676-77, as recorded by Collins. Now, as already stated, it seems more reasonable to believe that Newton was intent (if that is not too strong a word) on a separate and ample publication. What seems to have changed Newton's mind was the continuation (much against his wish) of the correspondence with Lucas, and the death of Henry Oldenburg — in whom Newton seems to have vested

---

(41) Indexed in the British Museum Catalogue under Lawrence, Anthony : *Nurseries, Orchards, profitable Gardens and Vineyards encouraged... in several letters to H. Oldenburg Esqr. The first from A. Lawrence, all the rest from J. Beale D. D.* (London, H. Brome, 1677). Licensed 22 November 1676 (*Term Catalogues*, I, 257). Many of Beale's letters were printed in the *Philosophical Transactions*, but as I have not seen this book I do not know whether these had been.

(42) The *Discourse* was returned to Newton after it had been transcribed (with the *Hypothesis of Light*) into the Register-Book of the Royal Society. Newton promised to send it back to Oldenburg for printing (RIGAUD, *op. cit.*, II, 394-5).

(43) *Corr. I,* 107, note 40.

some trust and perhaps affection — in September 1677. A few months later (18 December 1677) he wrote to Hooke — of all people! :

Mr. Oldenburg being dead I intend God willing to take care y^t they [the letters to and from Lucas] be printed according to his mind, amongst some other things w$_{ch}$ are going into y^e Press (44).

There are, I believe, two possibilities. Either the sheets represent the remains of a publication begun (with Newton's consent) by Oldenburg, which Newton told Hooke he intended to continue, or else they represent the beginning of such a publication by Newton as a kind of memorial to Oldenburg. For this is the only point in the history of Newton's early ventures into print to which they can conceivably be attached. And like the rest, this scheme too came to nothing.

In conclusion, it is clear that Newton several times came near to issuing a major publication in the years 1671-1677, in addition to what was published in the *Transactions*. It might have included either his optical or his mathematical work, or both. We have evidence that one such publication with which he was concerned reached the proof stage at least. The legend that an insuperable objection to publication was immediately aroused in Newton by the criticism his work received in the late winter of 1672 has been shown to be a gross exaggeration — one must not take Newton's expressions of peevishness as though they were fixed principles of conduct (45). Other factors were at work — notably the tepidity of the booksellers towards scientific books, of which there is such frequent evidence in Collins's letters. Had Moses Pitt printed the translation of Kinckhuysen he would in all likelihood have printed Newton as well. And as regards Newton's optical writings, his own consciousness that his ideas and experiments deserved a full-scale exposition (which he had not prepared for them by the end of 1675) seems to have

(44) NEWTON, *Correspondence*, II, 239.

(45) To my mind the worst effect of the long critical discussion was that it made Newton thoroughly bored with optics. He had prepared one long account in the *Lectiones*. The long-drawn controversy prevented him getting on with the important task of rewriting that account to make a better book. When his feeling of boredom had passed off that is just what he did.

XI

limited his willingness to publish either the *Lectiones Opticæ* or any of the shorter pieces he wrote. This suggests, finally, that it may have been about 1676-77 that Newton's thoughts turned towards the preparation of the book that became *Opticks*.

Newton's First Book (II) [1]

Varenius's *General Geography*, which Isaac Newton edited and corrected for the Cambridge press in 1672, was a book of much wider scientific scope than its title might suggest (2). For Varenius treated many topics that were debated by the natural philosophers of the later seventeenth century, and while his book has little in common with any modern handbook on world geography, it contains on the other hand many geometrical demonstrations that render Newton's connection with it explicable. When republished in England it remained for many years a successful textbook, despite advances in geographical knowledge. Newton revised it again in 1681. It was re-issued in 1712 after a fresh revision by James Jurin, and the translation of this version into English by Dugdale and Shaw in turn ran through several editions (3).

The *General Geography* is composed of three books, the first of which (*Pars Absoluta*) is as long as the other two (*Pars Respectiva; Pars Comparativa*) put together. The author (who originally published his work at Amsterdam in 1650) plunges swiftly into scientific matters with a discussion of the shape, size, and astronomical situation of the Earth. After describing the ancient geodetic measurements he cites that of Snel, which gave the length of the degree as 342.000 Rhineland feet (4). He gives firm support to the Copernican hypothesis, reciting eight reasons for so doing, only one of them unusual enough to mention. For, Varenius says : « It is much easier to sail from the West eastwards, than from the East westwards », the journey from Europe to India taking four months, and the return trip six. This is

---

(1) This is the continuation of the previous article.
(2) Except where otherwise stated, I refer to the second edition by Newton (1681). The differences between this and the earlier Newton edition (1672) are discussed later.
(3) This translation incorporates many footnotes correcting or amplifying the text in the light of the recent discoveries of Newton and others. I have used the third edition (1736).
(4) 107.388 m., or about 97 % of the true value. Newton was thus in possession of a fairly correct estimate of the size of the Earth from at least 1672.

XI

because « sailing in the former direction one goes the same way as the Earth, whereas in the latter direction one opposes the motion of the Earth » (5). The Copernican arguments do not indeed prove the double revolution of the Earth, but they render it probable. Varenius refers to Kepler (though not to his Laws), Lansberg, and Galileo (whose evidence from observation with the telescope he uses) as the chief proponents of the heliostatic system; and like the last of these he tacitly ignores the system of Tycho Brahe. In a rather strange table he gives the mean distances in terms of the radius of the Earth from the Earth to the other celestial bodies as: moon (60), Mercury (110), Venus (700), Sun (1.150), Mars (5.000), Jupiter (11.000), and Saturn (18.000) (6).

The bulk of Book I is concerned with « Earth-science » in the broadest sense. The substance of the globe Varenius takes to be composed of Water, Oil (or Sulphur), Salt, Earth and a « certain Spirit which some call Acid, which may be the Mercury of the Chemists » (7). (He seems by implication to reject the revived Epicurean theory of Descartes as well as the Aristotelian elements and the *tria prima*.) Salt is particularly important because it is the cement that sticks solid bodies together. Later Varenius returns to chemical considerations in discussing the composition and origin of mineral springs; he also deals with hot springs, petrifying waters, petroleum seepages, and has a good deal to say on the occurrence of metals and of the minerals commonly mined for use. Needless to say he does not omit wonders of nature, such as lakes that appear and disappear, rivers that hide themselves under the ground, others that emit strange sounds or run coloured, and the like.

At a more serious level Varenius discusses the distribution of land-masses and oceans, the action of the sea in changing the configuration of the shore, the origins of mountains and the cause of volcanoes. He describes in some detail the mathematical procedures for measuring the height of mountains, estimating that the Pic de Teneriffe is probably not more than 3-4 miles high and is as lofty as any mountain in the world. He has a

---

(5) (Edn. 1681), 35. The reasoning is false, of course.
(6) *Ib.*, 39.
(7) *Ib.*, 42.

good deal of material on oceanography and hydrography; he believes that a Suez Canal would be practicable (because there is probably no serious difference in level between the Mediterranean and Red Seas) and that only the indolence and commercial jealousy of the Sultans of Egypt have hindered its construction (8). Tidal movements of the sea are discussed in a section apart (9). Varenius supposes that they are manifestations of a general east — west flow of the oceans, associated with the passage of the moon, and accounts for them in the manner of Descartes while proposing some necessary modifications to the Cartesian theory. He rejects any occult influence of the moon upon the sea. At the same time he describes (with mathematical detail) how the time of high tide at any place may be computed from tables of the moon's altitude. Meteorology also is encountered in several contexts, but especially in the section devoted to winds : Varenius thinks that they are caused by the sun's heating and dilating the air, the hotter, lighter region accompanying the sun in its daily journey from east to west. The thermoscope is described, but not the barometer. The atmosphere, in Varenius's opinion, is nothing but « a texture of many little bodies, adhering to the Earth like the down on a peach » (10); it contains many different exhalations, watery, spirituous and saline, and sulphureous ones giving rise to fiery meteors. The atmospheric refraction of light is treated at some length in geometrical propositions with the aid of Snel's Law. From the quantity of refraction Varenius estimates the height of the atmosphere as between 10.000 and 20.000 feet (11).

Inevitably in all this mass of information and explanation of matters that were not at all well understood in the seventeenth century there are times when the author seems absurdly credulous. In general Varenius was rational enough; for instance, he did not believe that there are bottomless places in the sea (for the oceans merely fill depressions in the earthy globe), nor that only a continual miracle prevents the sea from flooding over the land. He regarded the Caspian sea as a true lake, denying

---

(8) *Ib.*, 99.
(9) *Ib.*, 117-137.
(10) *Ib.*, 222.
(11) *Ib.*, 239. It will appear again from this figure that Varenius paid no heed to the experiments of Torricelli, still less of Pascal.

that underground passages connect it with the Black Sea and Mediterranean. He denied also that the oceans contain fresh water at the bottom, but he did not know why they are salt. But the treatment of rivers was full of mythical snares. In the first place, Varenius believed that all river-beds not actually carved out at the creation of the world were man-made, refusing to admit that the surface flow of water could cut new channels. And so he seriously argues that there are no *salt* rivers because men have not dug channels for the useless salt water! (12) Moreover he believes — as so many believed then — that the water flowing from springs and rivers in hilly country down to the ocean is drawn underground from the ocean itself, losing its salt on the way. For (he says, among many other reasons) we find lakes deep underground which could not possibly be filled by rainfall (13).

The last two books of the *General Geography* are so mathematical that a very brief account will serve to characterize them. *Pars Respectiva* begins with an explanation of some further astronomical terms and continues with a discussion of latitude; it contains a long discussion of the seasons, the divisions of time, and the motions of the sun and moon, together with notes on the construction of sun-dials. Longitude is dealt with in *Pars Comparativa :* six methods of determining longitude are described (including the method of lunar distances and the use of clocks), as well as the procedures for computing longitude from measures of distance. Tables of the co-ordinates of notable places, of the sun's right ascension and of the principle fixed stars are given. Next follow the construction of globes and maps, and some propositions in spherical trigonometry; finally, the third book ends with six chapters on shipping, navigation and the use of the compass.

It is easy to see that there is much in all this that only a skilled mathematician could critically review. Like the Renaissance scholars, Varenius conceived of geography as a mathematical science, closely allied to astronomy; and indeed in his

---

(12) *Ib.*, 165-6.
(13) *Ib.*, 157-8. I cannot resist quoting from the note of the translators of 1736 when, commenting on the superiority of natural water over distilled for drinking, they eulogise « the Richness and Spirituousness of the *Thames Water* at Sea, which no doubt it receives from it's Impregnations by the Soil, and Filth, of the *London* Kennels » (I, 217).

day the description of countries with their natural features, cities, industries, and agriculture was generally assigned to writers on topography — travellers, not mathematicians. Besides this training in applied mathematics (which we know Newton regarded as necessary for students), the reader of Varenius would gain much instruction in matters then included in « natural history ». All in all, from this one compact book of over 500 pages in the Newton editions, the student could learn enough to equip him to understand perhaps half the papers in the *Philosophical Transactions*. Varenius nowhere touched upon the highest levels or the most profound issues of seventeenth century science, but his book could furnish no insignificant part of the background for following what was going on. Whether it was important enough to justify *Newton's* expenditure of time on it is a matter of opinion : probably not. But it was a perfectly respectable task for the Lucasian Professor of Mathematics in the University of Cambridge to undertake on behalf of mathematical and scientific studies.

Yet it is probable that Newton did not spend much time on it. The typography and layout of Newton's small octavo are very different from that of Varenius's thick duodecimo of 786 pages; Newton took the figures that Varenius had printed on the page and printed them on folding plates, re-drawing and correcting several of them (e. g. those on p. 91, 180, 354, and 379 of the edition of 1650). He made some minor verbal changes — probably more than I noticed, as I did not attempt a complete collation of the two editions. German words used occasionally by Varenius stand untouched in the Newton edition. An error in the numbering of the propositions of Book I, Chapter XVII (1650, p. 300; 1672, p. 196) was corrected by Newton. On the other hand both Newton editions err in the numbering of the propositions of Book I, Chapter XVI, where the 1650 edition is correct; for some reason a row of asterisks on page 150 (in both) appears to indicate an omission between Propositions VIII and XI, where the numbering of the original is continuous and there is, in fact, no omission. In both Newton editions the words indicated in brackets below are left out of the demonstration of Proposition XXV (1650, p. 359; 1672, p. 234) :

3 4 L major quam 9 4 L, hoc est quam [nfT refractio : sinum T 4 L

est major quam excessus sinus TfN supra sinum TfL. Quare angulus 3 4 L est major quam angulus] nfL & ideo... (14).

This may have been deliberate. A few pages farther on (1650, p. 364; 1672, p. 237) there is a more substantial change, for Newton omits three lines after the table and completely re-works the algebra of the demonstration. So again, pages 682-445, he corrected Varenius's arithmetic. But he seems to have found only few mathematical mistakes in the edition of 1650.

It seems, then, that the re-printing of Varenius cost Newton little more trouble than a careful review of the original text and reading the proofs of the new. The book left his hands almost exactly as it came to them. In his second edition of 1681 Newton introduced a few further changes. One can judge from the differences in printing that the volume was entirely reset, though the signatures, pagination and print of nearly all the pages are identical. Newton re-wrote page 368 (dealing with the movement of shadows in the Tropics) fairly thoroughly; altered figure 23; and added Cambridge, Dublin and Toledo to the list of latitudes and longitudes (p. 429-430).

With very minor exceptions, then, Newton did not add to or subtract from Varenius's book. He introduced no word of comment, explanation, or reservation of his own. Yet we must presume that he was content to have students read it; although it contained much that he could have improved and some things of which (we may be sure) he was already more than doubtful. For it would be too much to infer that because Newton had a share in the English reprinting of Varenius, he endorsed every one of Varenius's opinions. After all, the book was Varenius's, not his, and without further evidence it would be unreasonable to make Newton as editor responsible for everything in it. On the other hand he would hardly have associated his name with a book that he regarded as full of errors or scientifically pernicious; at almost exactly the time when he was working on Varenius Newton's tepidity towards Kinckhuysen's *Algebra* and his strong feeling that that book should be re-written (a task he began) was, at least in part, the reason why the English edition of Kinckhuysen never appeared. Negatively, it seems reasonable to suppose that there was nothing in Varenius's book to which Newton was

(14) The same words are omitted by the English translators.

strongly opposed in 1672 or 1681; or anything objectionable enough to outweigh the merits of the book as a whole. His name on its titlepage could certainly be considered a recommendation, and to that extent we are entitled to suppose that even in 1681 Newton considered Varenius's views scientifically reputable enough for presentation to students (*).

(*) I wish to thank Mr. Jacob Zeitlin for lending me a copy of the 1672 Varenius to compare with the edition of 1681.

XII

HOROLOGY AND CRITICISM: ROBERT HOOKE

Despite the counter-example of Lytton Strachey, the line between hagiography and biography is often slender. Those who have devoted most study to that strange, many-sided, uneven genius of seventeenth century science, Robert Hooke, have not sought to diminish his fame; rather they have lamented with one voice the unjust neglect of his true merits. Even the personal reputation and the scientific achievement of Isaac Newton himself have not emerged unscathed from the researches of Hooke's historians[1]. The object of this paper is not to attempt an assessment of Hooke's contribution to the success of the early Royal Society (which, all would agree, was very great), still less to measure his stature in seventeenth century science as a whole (where the judgement is both more difficult and more doubtful), but rather to examine his work in one controversial area, that of time-measurement, and the claims of Hooke scholars that this work was — like so much else of Hooke's — badly rewarded.

I. WHAT HOOKE ACCOMPLISHED

To summarize the state of horology in the mid-seventeenth century very briefly: the verge escapement with plain balance or foliot bar, long used for both clocks and watches, was a very imperfect mechanism. Various improvements had been proposed, with some success, but all were superseded by Christiaan Huygens' application of the

---

[1] Among the more important assessments of Hooke's achievements in science are: E. N. da C. Andrade (Wilkins Lecture, 15 December 1949; *Proc. Roy. Soc.*, A, 201, 1950, pp. 439—73); M. Espinasse, *Robert Hooke* (London, 1956); R. T. Gunther, *Early Science in Oxford* (especially Vols. VI, VII, VIII; Oxford, 1930, 1931); Mary Hesse, "Hooke's Philosophical Algebra", *Isis*, 57, 1966, pp. 67—83; *eadem*, "Hooke's Vibration Theory and the Isochrony of Springs", *ibid.*, pp. 433—41; Alexandre Koyré, "An Unpublished Letter of Robert Hooke to Isaac Newton" (in his *Newtonian Studies*, Cambridge, 1965, pp. 221—60); Johs. Lohne, "Hooke versus Newton," *Centaurus*, 7, 1960—61, pp. 6—52; L. D. Patterson, "Hooke's Gravitation's Theory and its Influence on Newton", *Isis*, 40, 1949, pp. 327—41; 41, 1950, pp. 32—45; "Pendulums of Wren and Hooke", *Osiris*, X, 1952, pp. 277—321.

pendulum to clocks (1656). Huygens employed the old mechanism of escape-wheel and pallets, controlling the oscillation of the verge carrying the pallets by means of the pendulum. It was now possible to construct a clock that was more than adequate for ordinary social purposes and could even be employed in astronomy. Would it also suffice for a far more lucrative purpose, the determination of longitude at sea? Resolutely ignoring the difficulty of reconciling the smooth oscillation of pendulum and pallets with the irregular pitching and heaving of a ship at sea, Huygens steadfastly believed that it could; he staked many years, much treasure, and his own reputation on the futile endeavour to stabilize an instrument in an irregularly moving environment. He was right in supposing the broad principle to be correct.

Whether or not it could become a marine chronometer, the pendulum clock could certainly never be miniaturized into a pocket-watch. About 1675 there appeared from various quarters, but most obviously with the prestige of Huygens, an analogous yet distinct conception. The merit of the pendulum for horology is obviously that it observes a regular harmonic motion; so may the vibration of an elastic body, such as a spring. If the spring is thin and highly flexible, if the inertia of the system is increased by connecting it to an oscillating mass, a harmonic motion with a period of some fraction of a second may be produced and applied through an escapement to control the wheelwork of a clock or watch. In fact the quite simple addition of a spiral spring to an existing verge-watch could greatly improve its timekeeping. Here was a new promise for the longitude: even the spring-controlled balance was not immune to shock, but it had a far more plausible look than the swinging pendulum.

The essential activity of Robert Hooke in horology falls between these two dates, 1656 and 1675. It is symbolised in the inscription said to have been borne by a watch that Hooke presented to Charles II: "Robert Hooke inv[enit] 1658 T. Tompion fecit 1675"[2]. An autobiographical fragment of unknown date, quoted by Waller, makes Hooke "in the Year 1656 or 1657" contrive "a way to continue the motion of the *Pendulum*" but Hooke seems to have recognized Huygens as the inventor of the true pendulum clock and it is well known that John and Ahasuerus Fromanteel brought Huygens' new construction to London in 1658 from Holland, where they had learned it from Huygens' licensee[3]. In fact among all Hooke's multifarious experi-

---

[2] For the presentation of this watch to the King see *The Diary of Robert Hooke, 1672—80* (London, 1935), H. W. Robinson and W. Adams [eds.], 7 April 1675 (p. 157: "With the King and shewd him my new spring watch, Sir J. More and Tompion there. The King most graciously pleased with it and commended it far beyond Zulichems [Huygens']. He promised me a patent and commanded me to prosecute the degree [longitude]"). 17 May 1675 (p. 161: "With Sir J. More to the King who received the watch very kindly, it was locked up in his closet"). 18 May (p. 161: "Met the King in the Park, he shewd watch, affirmed it very good"). 19 May (p. 161: "With the King ... received the watch back, proposed longitude by time"). Etc.

[3] Richard Waller, *Posthumous Works of Dr Robert Hooke* (London, 1705), iv.; reprinted in Gunther, VI, 10. John Aubrey affirms (in his *Life* of Hooke): "'Twas Mr [sic] Robert Hooke that invented the Pendulum-Watches, so much more usefull than the other Watches". The statement

ments before the Royal Society there is no record of his concern for horology until March 1665 when, a propos of Sir Robert Holmes' shipboard trials of Huygens' marine clocks, Hooke asserted his conviction that pendulum clocks would never do for the longitude, and promised to put his own secret method into the President's hands[4]. In succeeding years, however, Hooke's fertile brain suggested several modes of improving pendulum clocks for land use. In January 1668 he offered to make them "so as to prevent all checks [stoppages]", and in October 1669 produced

> a new kind of pendulum-clock, designed to keep time more exactly than others, for astronomical observations, and so contrived, that the swing being in this clock fourteen feet long, and having a weight of three pounds hanging to it, was moved by a very small force, as that of a pocket-watch, the swing making its whole vibration not above a degree, and going seventy weeks[5].

This description has been claimed by writers on Hooke as evidence for his invention of the anchor escapement, somewhat tendentiously described as essential to the full exploitation of the pendulum[6]. Of course it is obvious that a small excursion of the pendulum may be obtained in several ways; and indeed it would be difficult to make the excursion so small as one degree with the anchor. In fact the record of an earlier meeting of the Royal Society shows that Hooke did, actually, employ other ways than the anchor:

> [6 May 1669] Mr. Hooke produced a new kind of pendulum of his own invention, having a great weight appendant to it, and moved with a very small force; viz. by such a contrivance, that a pendulum of about fourteen feet long ... with an excursion of half an inch or less, having a weight of three pounds hanging on it, and moved by the sole force of a pocket-watch, with four wheels, shall go fourteen months, and cause very equal vibrations.

Since half an inch subtends much less than a degree at fourteen feet, and seventy weeks equals sixteen months, only a very strained imagination would deny that the two reports refer to the same mechanism, described as follows:

> [Hooke] shewed two several contrivances for it; one was with a pin upon the balance of a pocket-watch, making a bifurcated needle to vibrate on one end, on the other end the pendulum: another was with a thread fastened on one end to the balance of the watch, and on the other end to the pendulum, and so moving it to and fro[7].

---

seems a result of Aubrey's confused zeal for his friend. See E. G. R. Taylor, *Mathematical Practitioners of Tudor and Stuart England* (Cambridge, 1954), pp. 249—50.

[4] Thomas Birch, *History of the Royal Society* (London, 1756), II, p. 24.

[5] *Ibid.*, pp. 240, 398.

[6] See R. W. Symonds, *Thomas Tompion, his Life and Work* (London, 1951), 113, followed by Mrs. 'Espinasse in *Hooke*, pp. 62—3. The latter adds the argument that "the greatest mechanical scientist of the age" was more likely to have invented the anchor escapement than an "obscure clockmaker". By the same logic one may credit the invention of the synthetic soda process to Lavoisier. No surviving document of Hooke's own claims that he had invented this escapement, but it was claimed for him by William Derham, *The Artificial Clockmaker* (London, 1696), by R. T. Gunther, *Early Science in* Oxford, VI, pp. 68—9, and by Miss Patterson in *Osiris*, 10, 1952, 279; the claim is not made in the *Lives* by Richard Waller (*Posthumous Works*) and John Ward (*Lives of the Gresham Professors*) nor by Andrade (p. 456).

[7] Birch, *History*, II, 361; quoted in 'Espinasse, *Hooke*, p. 62.

We may confidently suppose that Hooke's watch employed a verge escapement since no other was yet in existence. Clearly Hooke did *not* propose the anchor, or any other new escapement, in this case but merely a coupling between the long pendulum and a conventional watch. This is confirmed by Stephenson, writing in 1674, "thus as the Ingenious Master Hook first proposed, I have hang'd a swing [pendulum] by my Clock to regulate it upon a Pin, that it may freely vibrate" the pin being on the "Ballance towards the back side". Stephenson's words exactly agree with the Royal Society record, and absolutely fail to fit the anchor escapement (which was in use from at least 1671)[8].

At about this time Hooke began to employ Thomas Tompion, the clockmaker, then almost unknown; Hooke certainly assisted him to fame. In Hooke's *Diary* there are many entries relating to his instruction of Tompion[9]; whether this instruction was so concretely valuable to the young clockmaker as is often supposed, it is hard to tell; it seems certain that Tompion derived from Towneley rather than Hooke the idea of using long pendulums for the Greenwich Observatory clocks, and Hooke had nothing to do with their construction. The escapements employed were devised by Tompion himself and by Richard Towneley[10]. There seems to be no evidence relating any *particular* feature of the evolving pendulum clock to Robert Hooke, and his experiments with pins, string, bits of wire and magnets produced no known lasting results.

If (as seems likely from the context) Hooke's longitude invention, whose secret he promised to impart to Viscount Brouncker in March 1665, had to do with a clock of some kind, but not a pendulum clock, what kind of a clock was it? Fortunately

---

[8] For Stephenson see Mrs. 'Espinasse, p. 63; this writer did not realise that the descriptions faithfully quoted by her are completely irreconcileable with even an "embryonic stage of the anchor escapement", whatever that might be. A reconstruction of the 'pin and slot' device by Mr. M. C. Aimer may be seen in the Science Museum, London; the "bifurcated needle" is placed below the long-pendulum bob, and engages the pin mounted normally to the balance of the (unmodified) contemporary watch. In a letter of 26 June 1669 [*New Style*] Christiaan Huygens reports seeing a drawing of this device sent to Carcavy: "Il paroit qu'il [Hooke] prend la pendule par en bas, comme je me l'estois imaginè dont je crains tousjours qu'il n'arrive quelque inegalitè..."; this supports the reconstruction above. However, in his reply (5 July 1669) Oldenburg told him Hooke's view that the pendulum bob was to heavy to permit any irregularity, and that the movement was eighteen inches above the bob. Overlooking the minor difference between say, 14 feet and 12' 6" from the point of suspension, Huygens' report may still be correct if Hooke's reply related not to the "bifurcated needle" but to the "string" method, which could be conveniently applied anywhere (Christiaan Huygens, *Oeuvres Complètes*, VI, pp. 460, 474; A. Rupert Hall and Marie Boas Hall, *The Correspondence of Henry Oldenburg*, VI, (Madison, 1969), pp. 43, 45, 91, 93; Charles K. Aked in *Antiquarian Horology*, 6 (1968—70), p. 417—20).

[9] *Diary*, 2 May 1674: "To Thomkin in Water Lane. Much discourse with him about watches. Told him the way of making an engine for finishing wheels, and a way how to make a dividing plate... about another way of wheel-work; about pocket watches and many other things".

[10] See Derek Howse, "The Tompion Clocks at Greenwich and the Deadbeat Escapement", *Antiquarian Horology*, 7 (1970—71), pp. 18—34, 114—127.

one of the Hooke manuscripts in Trinity College, Cambridge, makes this pretty clear, and it was certainly a most original mechanism[11]. The date of this manuscript may be fixed fairly definitely by Hooke's reference to the pendulum clock "lately invented by Mr. Zulichem" and by the concluding paragraph which addresses Charles II, declaring that the invention was known to none but Hooke himself and "two friends to whom I very lately revealed it; which I have had perfect as it is now, by me several years". These words suggest that Hooke was writing after the Restoration, yet that the pendulum clock was relatively new. Now according to Hooke's own narrative[12], "in the year 1660 ... I was in treaty with several Persons of Honour ... for the discovery of [the longitude invention], upon proposed Articles of encouragement", but due to Hooke's dissatisfaction with the terms proposed "our Treaty was broken off, and I concealed the farther discovery of any of the other more considerable parts of my Inventions, for the regulating of Time-Keepers..." This story is confirmed by Sir Robert Moray (writing to Christiaan Huygens on 30 September 1665)[13]:

> Il y a bien 3. ans que Monsieur Hook m'a parlé d'une invention qu'il avoit pour mesurer le temps en mer mieux que peuvent faire les pendules mesme aussi bien qu'ils le font a Terre. Mais ayant pour lors esté persuadé qu'il en pourroit tirer beaucoup de profit il a esté si sage que de ne reveler point en quoy son invention consistoit.

This dates the Treaty as no later than 1662. However, Moray's letter then continues:

> Depuis, il y a environ un an ou comme cela, il a revelé son secret a Monsieur nostre president et moy avec obligation de nen parler point, et a mesme donné une espreuve de son invention a nostre president sur une Montre que je luy prestay.

Hence the "two friends" of the Trinity College MS must be Brouncker and Moray, and the date of the revelation (and so of the manuscript) must be 1664. Bearing in mind that (in fact) Hooke made only a *partial* revelation of his invention to his friends, and that he also claimed to have disclosed its nature to the world (but again only partially) in 1664[14], it seems reasonable to suppose that the former, private revelation occured in the spring of that year, while the public disclosure was made in Hooke's autumn lectures at Gresham College. Obviously Hooke must have

---

[11] MS 10 11a. 1[15A]. I discussed this MS in *Notes and Records of the Royal Society*, 8, 1951, p. 170—5, whence the figure reproduced here is taken; see also Mary Hesse in *Isis*, 57, 1966, 438—41.

[12] Im the *Postscript* to *A Description of Helioscopes*, 1676; see Gunther, VIII, p. 146—7. Waller (*Posthumous Works*, iv—vi; Gunther, VI, p. 11—13; Ward, *Lives*, p. 171—2) in telling this story names the persons concerned as Viscount Brouncker, Sir Robert Moray, and Robert Boyle. In some of the documents in the negotiation seen by Waller Hooke was referred to as M. A.; hence they were written after 1663. Moreover, Hooke's awareness in the MS. of the failure of the shipboard trial of Huygens' marine clocks suggests a date later than 1662.

[13] *Oeuvres Complètes de Christiaan Huygens*, V, p. 503—4. For consistency I use Old Style dates throughout this paper.

[14] Also in the *Postscript*; Gunther, VIII, p. 149.

written this manuscript in the interval between the private and the public disclosures (or *partial* disclosures)[15].

In the manuscript Hooke first analyses the various known methods of determining longitude at sea, concluding that mechanical timekeeping is the most promising. The desideratum was a mechanism resistant to all shocks and irregularities of motion, in which the beat of the balance would be perfectly regular. Only the last point was secured by Huygens' invention, which failed in every other respect as trial had shown. Continuing the analysis further, Hooke decided that the main causes of trouble were (1) "the Irregular or uneven force of the crown wheel against the ballance" and (2) "the swing or sweep of the Ballance it self which by the moving of the whole frame might easily be alter'd"[16].

To cope with the first difficulty, Hooke proposed a type of constant-force escapement (Fig. 1) such as was used by later inventors also, in which the spring C (or an equivalent weight) gives a uniform impulse to the balance-wheel once in each

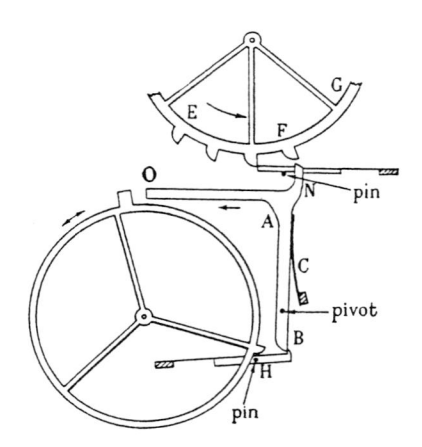

Fig. 1. This is only a very crude attempt to give some meaning to Hoke's description. When the projection on the balance strikes the pin on H, it is depressed, C presses AB forward, so that O impels the balance on the swing in the opposite direction. When AO advances far enough, N strikes the pin releasing the 'trigger', so that the 'saw-wheel' revolves, a tooth engages on N and re-cocks AB on the trigger H ready for the next cycle. The balance-wheel is free to oscillate through almost 360°, receiving a single impulse each cycle, and time is measured by the revolutions of the saw-wheel, realesed at regular intervals.

of its revolutions; the spring in turn is re-cocked or re-set by a wheel EFG which is part of the going train of the clock. All this is highly ingenious and practical, but Hooke seems thus far to imagine that the simple balance will now move with perfect regularity; he ignores the fundamental significance of the pendulum's motion (known to Huygens and even Galileo) that it is harmonic, and so isochronous.

To cope with the second difficulty, Hooke states that the balance must be perfectly centered and he envisages using (like Harrison in his early chronometers)

---

[15] For the reasons stated I have changed the proposed date of the MS from 1660 to 1664. Of course it may well be based on an earlier document. My views on the content of the MS are unchanged from my paper of twenty years ago.

[16] Hall (*loc. cit.* note 11), p. 172.

two counter-rotating geared balances, so that the effect of any acceleration is neutralized. He now adds the curious comment that "because naturall gravity could take noe hold of it [the balance-wheel] as to its motion about its center; I contriv'd an artificiall one which should perform the same effect" — curious because, of course, gravity had no effect on the balance of the common clock in use since the fourteenth century.

> And that was done by applying of two Springs soe contriv'd that the motion they imprest on the ballance should not receive any irregularity from the shog of ye Instrument. These springs which may be applayed to the Ballance very many ways as *ABC* soe determin'd the circular motion of ye wheel that such and such particular parts of ye wheel had a tendency (or artificial gravity as I may soe call it) not towards the center of ye earth but towards such or such determinate points of the frame that contain'd it soe that if the wheel were remov'd out of yt situs or position, it would after many vibrations returne to it. And there stay. To this I apply'd my former Expedient of the Cocke [described above] which compounded an Instrument in all points such as was Desir'd...

The sketches *ABC* are missing from the MS.

Hooke still makes no mention of harmonic motion or isochrony: "There is nothing in all to imply that the vibrations of the springs are or need to be isochronous, since the equal arcs of the balance['s motion] are regulated not by the springs but by the constant-force escapement"[17]. In fact at this time Hooke had no theory of springiness at all, and (as is evident from the above) the springs were only added to the balance as a result of a mistaken intuitive analogy[18]. It was to be a fortunate addition, of course, but we shall see how even ten or fifteen years later Hooke was quite undecided about the best role of springs as applied to oscillating bodies.

No evidence survives from the early 1660s to indicate what kind of springs Hooke intended to apply to his balance, or how he would apply them, or whether he made any mechanism to exemplify his ideas. His employment by the Royal Society probably diverted his attention to other inquiries; in 1663 and 1664, for example, he was engaged in pneumatic experiments and microscopic observation, later published in *Micrographia*. He seems at all times to have kept the master-secret of his longitude invention, the "cock" or constant-force escapement, to himself but in 1664 and 1665 he began to discuss his spring controlled balance and explain it in terms of a broader theory;[19] thus he recalled in his *Postscript* to *A Description of Helioscopes* (1676):

---

[17] Mary Hesse, *Isis*, 57, p. 439.

[18] One might imagine Hooke reasoning somewhat as follows: the pendulum keeps good time because gravity pulls it down equally during each half-swing, and resists equally during the other half. A vertical, unbalanced wheel would behave similarly — so indeed would any unbalanced wheel whose axle is inclined to the perpendicular (hence Hooke introduced the inclined pendulum). A balanced wheel escapes this action of gravity; an unbalanced wheel is sensitive to shocks. But a balanced wheel constrained by springs will behave like an unbalanced wheel, and so like a pendulum.

[19] I do not here consider either Hooke's vibration theory or his mechanical algebra, both already treated by Dr Hesse in *Isis*, 57, 1966.

> At the earnest importunity of a Dear Friend of mine, since deceased, I did, in the year 1664, read several of my first *Cutlerian Lectures* upon that Subject [time-measurement] in the open Hall at *Gresham* Colledge... I there shewed the ground and reason of that application of *Springs* to the *Ballance* of a Watch, for regulating its motion...[20].

It would be naive, perhaps, to suppose that in 1676 (after the publication of the *Horologium oscillatorium*) Hooke knew no more mechanics than in 1664, or *a fortiori* 1658. But there is independent evidence relating to Hooke's Gresham Lectures. Again it comes from Sir Robert Moray, writing to Huygens on 22 July 1665[21]:

> Jusqu'icy Je ne vous ay iamais parlé d'une autre chose qu'il a avancé dans ses lectures sur la Mechanique (dont il fait une tous les Mercredis hors du Terme). C'est une invention toute nouvelle ou plutost une vintaine pour mesurer le temps aussi exactement que font vos horloges a pendule, tant sur mer que sur Terre... C'est en un mot, en appliquant au Ballancier, au lieu de pendule, un Ressort, ce qui se peut faire en cent diverses facons, et mesme il nous a entretenu dun discours dans lequel il a entrepris de prouver qu'il y a moyen dadiuster les excursions en sorte que les petites et les grands seront Isochrones. Il seroit long de vous les decrire en detail et il pretend publier le tout dans quelque temps, et cependant vous y comprendrez sans doubte une bonne party de ce qu'il y a à considerer.

In the *Postscript* to *Helioscopes* already cited Hooke used almost identical phrases: "I explained above twenty several ways by which *Springs* might be applied... and how the *Vibrations* might be so regulated, as to make their Durations either all equal, or the greater slower or quicker than the less, and that in any proportion assigned ... the models of which I there produced..."[22]. However, comparison of the passages suggests that Hooke, though recognizing in his lectures the possible isochrony of springs which he had not in the earlier manuscript, attached less importance to this than Moray did in writing to Huygens. One may doubt whether even now Hooke recognised the importance of isochrony in the balance, no doubt because he relied rather on his still secret invention, the constant-force escapement. As for the mechanical details, they are still unknown to us since Hooke never composed the promised printed explanation.

The first printed hint of Hooke's activities in horology — other than the optimistic boast in the Preface to *Micrographia* (no doubt written about this same time)[23] — ap-

---

[20] Gunther, VIII, p. 149; Mary Hesse, *Isis*, 57, p. 440. Mrs. 'Episnasse (*Hooke*, p. 67) writes of these lectures that "in the minutes of the [Royal] Society's meetings [Henry] Oldenburg [Secretary of the Royal Society] omitted to record the demonstrations" omitting herself to notice that — as is plain from Hooke's and Moray's words — these were Culterian lectures given by Hooke at Gresham College (also the meeting-place of the Royal Society, of course) and not part of the Royal Society's meetings.

[21] *Oeuvres Completes de Christiaan Huygens*, V, p. 427; Mary Hesse, *Isis*, 57, p. 439—40.

[22] Gunther, VIII, p. 149.

[23] "The *Invention* of a way to find the *Longitude* of places is easily perform'd... to as great an *accurateness* as the *Latitude* of places can be found at Sea; and perhaps yet also to a greater certainty then that has been hitherto found, as I shall very speedily freely manifest to the world". For Huygens' somewhat caustic comment on this typical Hookism see *Oeuvres Complètes*, V, p. 486.

peared in Thomas Sprat's *History of the Royal Society* (1667) where, without mention of the name of Hooke or any other inventor, a list of timekeeping devices is given,[24] among them

> Several new kinds of *Pendulum Watches* for the Pocket, wherein the motion is regulated, by Springs, or Weights, or Loadstones, or Flies moving very exactly regular.

Here one observes a division of aim that becomes more manifest later. Hooke seems to be trying to provide for every contingency and already envisages, as an alternative to the isochronous spring, a mechanism more like a centrifugal governor whereby, as the balance-wheel rotates more rapidly, weights fly outward against restraining springs (and vice-versa) so creating an analogy with the circular pendulum. While the reason for the springs is obvious, such a device seems little suited to rapid reciprocating motion. Further evidence of Hooke's modified watches comes from Lorenzo Magalotti's record of a visit to the Royal Society's assembly (with Paolo Falconieri) on 20 February 1667/8[25]; Magalotti saw:

> a pocket-watch with a new pendulum invention. You might call it a bridle, the time being regulated by a little spring of tempered wire which at one end is attached to the balance-wheel, and at the other to the body of the watch.

While this sounds very like a description of the modern hair-spring, one cannot be sure that the description is incapable of any other interpretation. Presumably this watch did not include the "cock" either[26].

There is, possibly, no further allusion to the watch untill 18 February 1674/5, when Henry Oldenburg communicated to the Royal Society Christiaan Huygens'

---

[24] The full quotation is: "A great many ways of making *Instruments*, for keeping time very exactly, both with *Pendulums*, and without them; whereby the intervals of time may be measur'd both on the *Land* and Sea ... [Hooke].

A new kind of *Pendulum Clock*, wherein the *Pendulum* moves circularly, going with the most simple, and natural motion, moving very equally, and making no kind of noise. [Hooke]

A *Pendulum Clock* shewing the aequation of Time. [Huygens]

Three new ways of *Pendulum* for *Clocks*, and several ways of applying the motion of the Watchwork to them". Thomas Sprat, *History of the Royal Society*, 3rd edition (London 1722), p. 247.

[25] See H. W. Robinson in *Notes and Records of the Royal Society*, 1, 1938, pp. 93–4, referring to R. D. Waller, "Lorenzo Magalotti in England, 1668–9", *Italian Studies*, 1, 1937, 54. Magalotti attended the meeting on the 20th, although Birch, *History*, II, p. 252 (from the Journal-Book) records his presence only at the following meeting. At the former, Mr. Hooke was ordered "to give an account of [an experiment] in writing; as also to bring in the description of the new cyder-engine, the astronomical instruments, and the new pendulum moving strait without any check". Oldenburg clearly expected Hooke to deposit his own description of the watch perhaps hesitated to record his own without Hooke's authority; but as Hooke failed to leave the description the remaining minute appears incomplete.

[26] The passage can be found at greater length in 'Espinasse, *Hooke*, p. 67. Her comment that Oldenburg (i. e. Birch, *History*, II, p. 251) "has ... no reference to a watch" is not strictly accurate. One must remember that the Society had seen a good deal of the watch over the years, though it came fresh to Magalotti.

letter describing his application of a hair-spring to the balance of a verge escapement; Hooke protested his priority, appealing to the Journal-Books, Sprat's *History*, and the memory of Fellows[27]. In fact Boyle had privately advised Hooke of Huygens' invention the day before, and on the nineteenth he showed "Sir Ch[arles] Scarborough my spring watch. He and Dr Whistler desired the like"[28]. On 20 February Hooke noted "Zulichem's spring not worth a farthing". Early next month, before any detailed knowledge of Huygens' mechanism had reached London, irritated by the news that an English patent might be granted for it (a *Privilège* had already been issued in Paris), Hooke applied himself to the perfection of his own ideas. On 8 March he showed Tompion his "way of fixing Double Springs to the inside of the Ballance Wheel, thus" (Fig. 2). A modified watch, perhaps incorporating this

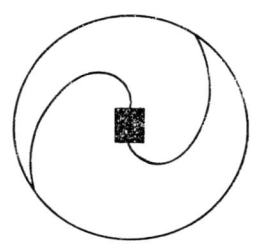

Fig. 2. After Hooke, *Diary*, 8 March 1674/5.

idea, was made by Tompion at a cost of five shillings and shown to the King on 7 April, who approved it highly[29]. A little later Sir Jonas Moore liked (unspecified) "way with Springs", a "perpendicular Spiral Spring" was tried at Tompion's and also "double perpendicular spring did well" but "The Thrusting Spring the best"[30]. Clearly Hooke was now almost desperately seeking a perfect scheme (despite all his claims of having solved the longitude problem long before) because of the King's threat that he would grant a patent to Huygens' watch unless Hooke could prove

---

[27] Birch, *History*, III, p. 190. Huygens' letter is printed in *Oeuvres Complètes*, VII, p. 422–3. According to Derham (who was eighteen years old in 1675 and presumably drew his information from Hooke later) Huygens' watch "had a longer Spiral Spring, and the Pulses or Beats were much slower ... The Ballance, instead of turning scarce quite round (as Dr Hook's) doth turn several rounds every revolution". (*Artificial Clockmaker*, p. 104). The difference is explained by Huygens' adding a wheel to the verge engaging a pinion on the balance-staff, so that there was a step-up ratio of about 1:5 (*Oeuvres Complètes*, VII, p. 425). This version was sometimes called a *pirouette*. Hooke had already claimed priority over Huygens in the invention of the circular pendulum during the previous year (*Oeuvres Complètes*, VII, pp. 416–8; Gunther, VIII, pp. 105–6).

[28] *Diary*, p. 148. The watch is not described. Presumably it had been made some years before. However, the Paris clockmaker Thuret was able to add Huygens' new mechanism to a watch *in a single day* (*Oeuvres Complètes*, VII, pp. 407–8).

[29] *Diary*, p. 151, 154 (23 March), 155 (26 March), 157.

[30] *Diary*, p. 158 (11 April), 159 (13 and 14 April), 160 (9 May).

Horology and Criticism 271

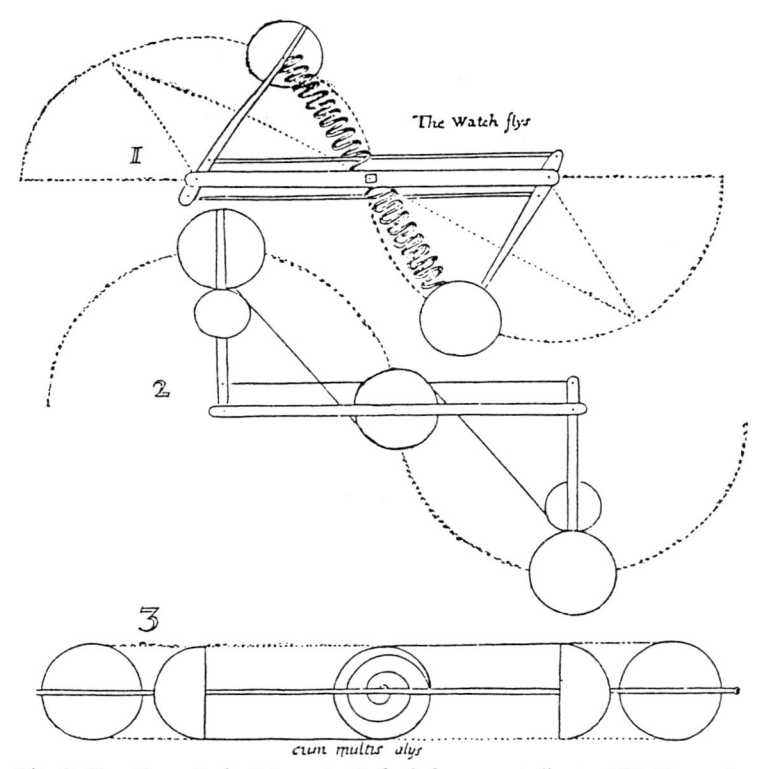

Fig. 3. Gunther, *Early Science in Oxford*, figure preceding p. 299 (*Lampas*).

prior invention[31]. Then a watch with magnets, and a "double pendulum clock" were made by Tompion and shown to the King[32]. Many other expedients are mentioned in the *Diary* during subsequent weeks, until finally the King's watch was sent to him on 26 August 1675 and for a time at least proved satisfactory[33].

---

[31] *Diary*, p. 158 (10 April).
[32] *Ibid.*, p. 161 (21 May), 162 (25 May), 163 (6 June).
[33] *Ibid.*, p. 176. This was by no means the end of the experiments. In the *Diary* for 2 September (p. 178) appears the earliest record of Hooke's Law: "All springs at liberty bending equall spaces by equall increases of weight" which led him to the invention of the "philosophical scales" or spring-balance. The Law was concealed in an anagram of *Ut tensio sic vis* at the end of *Helioscopes* and fully discussed by Hooke in *De potentia restitutiva* (1678; Gunther, VIII, p. 333 ff). It seems fairly obvious that Hooke did *not* deduce his Law as a generalised form of Boyle's Law, nor was it known to him when he first thought of applying springs to the balance of a watch. On the contrary, it was his experiments on watch-springs that suggested the Law to Hooke. Nor was he able to prove from the Law that simple harmonic motion is isochronous (Mary Hesse, *Isis*, 57, p. 435).

Two further accounts of his horological inventions, by Hooke himself, should not be omitted. One, expressed in John Wilkins' *Real Character* symbolism on 28 August 1675, appeared at the end of *A Description of Helioscopes* in 1676. Rendered into English,[34] this statement is a very succint summary of the ideas already found in the Trinity College MS discussed above — twin counter-balances are to be controlled by springs "or other agents" — without any mention of the "cock" or constant-force escapement. The second is a perfectly clear but puzzling passage inserted in *Lampas* (1677), as follows:

> This is a way of regulating both standing Watches, and movable Watches, either for the Sea, or the Pocket, which some ten or twelve years since I shewed the *Royal Society*, when I shewed them my contrivance of the Circular Pendulum... This was by a fly moving Circularly instead of a ballance, whose motion was regulated by weights, flying further and further from the Center according as the strength of the Spring of the Watch had more and more force upon its Arbor. The Weights were regulated from flying out further than they ought to do by the contrivance of a Spiral Spring, drawing both the said Weights to the Center of the motion or fly, in the same proportion as I then demonstrated Gravity to attract the weight of a Circular Pendulum... towards the Center or Axis of its motion.

As there is a sketch to illustrate this description, there can be no question but that this is a third appearance of the "centrifugal governor" device, having nothing to do with the balance and hair-spring mechanism[35].

II. WHAT HOOKE CLAIMED

There can be no doubt that Hooke believed that he had effectively solved the problem of longitude in 1658 or even 1656, and though he had varied and improved his basic ideas since then, he held that his later thoughts in no way invalidated his earlier ones. Everyone else, therefore, was in a general sense a second inventor or a plagiarist, except that Huygens had been first with the marine pendulum clock (but it was useless). Hooke always retained these opinions even though, fortunately or unfortunately, his chronometric ideas were never tested at sea, as Huygens' devices were on several occasions, sometimes with a promising degree of success[36].

---

[34] E. N. da C. Andrade in *Annals of Science*, 1, 1936, p. 12, reprinted in 'Espinasse, *Hooke*, Plate XI.

[35] Gunther, VIII, pp. 197–8. The sketch is on the final plate of *Lampas*. Hooke's demonstration of the proportion of gravity in a circular pendulum (23 May 1666) is in Birch, *History*, II, pp. 90–92 (or Gunther, VI, pp. 265–8). Miss L. D. Patterson (*Isis*, 41, 1950, 304–5) was right to claim that Hooke's demonstration (of the "conatus to the center") relates not to a centripetal force but to the component of gravitational force in the circular pendulum normal to the thread, which Hooke correctly states is proportional to the sine of the angle between the thread and the perpendicular. Alexandre Koyré (*ibid.*, pp. 395–6) rightly asserted that Hooke could deduce nothing concerning the force of rotation from his demonstration.

[36] J. W. Olmsted, "The Voyage of Jean Richer to Acadia in 1670", *Proc. Amer. Phil. Soc.*, 104, 1960, especially pp. 614–20. The tacit assumption sometimes made that Huygens' chronometers were mere fantasies (because Hooke said so) is quite false.

Hooke was convinced that his ideas were continually stolen from him to be exploited by others; finally he levied this accusation against Newton[37]. In 1674 Hooke delivered a by-blow against Huygens at the end of his attack on the Polish astronomer Johannes Hevelius, *Some Animadversions on the First Part of Hevelius his Machina Coelestis.* Hooke complained that Huygens had discussed the circular pendulum in *Horologium oscillatorium* (1673) without recording that he, Hooke, "invented it and brought it into use in the year 1665, and in the year 1666 I communicated it to the Royal Society"[38]. Hooke supposed that Sir Robert Moray had written an account of this to Huygens: "But of this more hereafter, when I examine some other things in that Book, and of finding the Longitude of places, and publish some more certain and practicable ways of doing them"[39]. Apart from the study of the circular pendulum already mentioned (23 May 1666) Hooke did indeed show its mechanical application to a clock which (according to Brouncker) kept time accurately for at least four days (however, this innovation was obviously not applicable to the longitude problem)[40]. It is now known that in this notion Huygens had anticipated Hooke by at least six years, for he illustrated the circular pendulum (corrected to describe a paraboloid of revolution) along with the planar cycloidal pendulum in 1659[41]. Hooke's suspicion of Huygens' plagiarism was accordingly quite unjustified; the only fair verdict on the whole affair is to allow independent invention in both cases, with Huygens the prior in time, if not in communication. Moray, it seems, did not inform him of Hooke's unprinted 1666 discussions and so Huygens could not have acknowledged them.

Hooke repeated these claims of prior invention followed by plagiary on the part of Huygens when the latter made his hair-spring balance known in February 1674/5. To be precise, his claims (expressed with increasing bitterness over the years 1675/6) comprised the following public assertions: (1) that he had been the first to conceive of a spring regulator, about 1658[42]; (2) that he had published his invention in Gresham College lectures of 1664 and imparted it to various Fellows of the Royal So-

---

[37] H. W. Turnbull, *Correspondence of Isaac Newton*, II, 1960, p. 431 (22 May 1686). A. Rupert Hall, "Two Unpublished Lectures of Robert Hooke", *Isis*, 42, 1951, p. 219—230.

[38] Gunther, VIII, p. 37 ff. No writer on Hooke has noted that Hevelins had for many years begged Hooke to have a telescope micrometer made for him in London, at his own expense, so that he could discover its advantages by experience. Hooke studiously ignored this request. (See Hall and Hall, *Oldenburg*, V. pp. 182, 187).

[39] *Ibid.*, p. 105—6. As so often, Hooke did not fulfill his bold promises. See also *Diary*, p. 45 (30 May 1673).

[40] Birch, *History*, II, pp. 97, 105.

[41] *Oeuvres Complètes*, VII, p. 314, note 10, with facing plate, and Hall & Hall, *Oldenburg*, X, Letter 2251, Hooke's work on the circular pendulum has been fully analysed by Miss Patterson, *Osiris*, 10, 1952, pp. 295—301.

[42] E. g. Birch, *History*, III, p. 190; Gunther, VIII, p. 146 (Helioscopes). By implication, Hooke also claims that *no one else* had independently discovered the same thing in the intervening seventeen or eighteen years. As we shall see, this was not the case.

ciety[43]; (3) that clocks or watches incorporating his invention (or part of it) had succeeded[44]; (4) that no one save himself had any right to a patent for the spring-regulated balance[45]; (5) that his invention had been clandestinely communicated to others, who had sought to turn it to their own advantage[46]; (6) that what he had published and others had imitated was nevertheless imperfect without the reserved secret known only to himself[47].

The material upon which an evaluation of these assertions may be based has largely been discussed above. (1) is supported by the facts as we know them, but in proportion as it is a very general claim, so it is imprecise. We have no idea of Hooke's mechanism and cannot identify it (or not) with that later produced by Huygens. (2) is a fair claim, as are Hooke's allusions to Sprat's *History* in justification; but again the vagueness just mentioned re-appears; we do not know whether Hooke explained (or exhibited) a straight spring, a curved spring, a coil spring, a spiral spring of few or many turns, or a centrifugal governor mechanism. Since Hooke (at one time or another) claimed all such applications, it is impossible to test a particular claim for a particular point in time. (3) cannot be proved or disproved, but the evidence is doubtful as regards "success" in a loose sense, negative as regards success in navigation.

When Huygens' letter about the hairspring watch was read to the Royal Society, it was ordered, despite Hooke's protest, that Huygens should be thanked for his communication, "and informed what had been done here; and what were the causes of its want of success"[48]. Hooke was mistaken when he claimed later that the success or otherwise of his watches could not be known to Oldenburg and others[49]. For example, Sir Robert Moray lent Hooke a watch (in summer 1664?) in order that he might give "une espreuve de son invention a nostre president" but when this modified watch was compared by Brouncker with his pendulum clock "il ne trouva point qu'elle alloit si iuste"[50]. It seems likely that Brouncker retained a conviction of the futility of Hooke's scheme, since Hooke bore so strong a resentment against him in later years, noting (for example): "Brouncker a Dog for belying me to the King", the meaning of this perhaps being that Brouncker had refused to confirm the earlier

[43] Birch, *loc. cit.* previous note; Gunther, VIII, p. 149.

[44] Gunther, VIII, p. 207. Hooke did not define what he meant by "succeeded" in this context. Apparently he meant that mechanisms devised according to one or more of his methods performed comparably with a pendulum clock for a few days or weeks. There was never a navigational trial of Hooke's "chronometers", as there were several such trials of Huygens' (note 36 above).

[45] See *Diary*, p. 157 (8 April 1675) and subsequent entiers; Gunther, VIII, p. 208.

[46] Gunther, VIII, pp. 148, 207.

[47] *Ibid.*, p. 148, 150.

[48] Birch, *History*, III, p. 190; the minute was written by Henry Oldenburg.

[49] Gunther, VIII, p. 207; Hooke wanted to have it both ways – to assert that he had published his inventions (hence they had been copied) but also that he had kept them secret, or some part of them secret without which the mechanism actually constructed would be necessarily imperfect.

[50] *Oeuvres Complètes*, V, p. 504; Moray to Huygens, 30 September 1665.

success of Hooke's watches [51]. The most telling evidence against the complete success of Hooke's early spring-regulation devices comes from his frantic endeavour, in the summer of 1675, to devise and test new schemes. Moreover, the first watch he prepared for the King, despite early success, seems to have failed and it went back to Tompion for further improvement[52]. Although the watch delivered to Charles on 26 August was performing excellently on 15 September, by 5 October a change in the weather had caused it to alter[53]. A watch earlier improved for Sir Jonas Moore kept good time but tended to stop[54]. To what extent practical clockmakers like Tompion may have incorporated ideas derived from Hooke into other watches than the half dozen or so noted in the *Diary* is unknown.

One defect in the schemes of Hooke, Huygens and others for applying springs to the balance of a watch or clock is outstanding: the absence of temperature compensation. We now know that no chronometer lacking compensation could prove useful at sea, and indeed this was very strongly suspected then. Hooke himself put it on record that he met with early discouragement on the grounds of "alteration of *Climates, Airs, heats* and *colds*, temperatures of *Springs*, the nature of *Vibrations*, the wearing of *Materials*, the motion of the *Ship*"[55]. He himself seems to have dismissed such difficulties as trivial[56], but Moray among others did not[57]. The problem of temperature compensation was not tackled by such clockmakers as Graham and Harrison till much later, though Tompion can hardly have been unaware of it, Longcase clocks installed in great houses or very solidly constructed observatory buildings would not, perhaps, suffer much variation in temperature thus minimising its effect on time-keeping.

Claim (4) I do not propose to discuss in the legal terms either of the seventeenth or the twentieth century. Hooke certainly defeated the attempt to secure an English patent for Huygens' invention; but he was wrong in supposing his own interest in the spring-controlled balance to be unique. According to Huygens, "Monsieur le Duc de Roanais me parla de la mesme chose et mesme me mena chez l'horloger a qui luy et Monsieur Pascal avoient communiquè chette invention..."[58] Huygens wrote

---

[51] *Diary*, p. 159 (29 April 1675).
[52] *Diary*, p. 157 (7 April 1675); 161 (17 and 19 May 1675).
[53] *Diary*, p. 180 (15 September 1675); 185 (5 October).
[54] *Diary*, p. 170 (24 July 1675).
[55] Gunther, VIII, p. 148.
[56] *Oeuvres Complètes*, V, p. 501; Hall & Hall, *Oldenburg*, II, pp. 551, 553. Hooke, Oldenburg adds, "connoit de la matiere, à ce qu'il dit, incapable de ces ressentimens".
[57] *Oeuvres Complètes*, V, p. 504 (30 September 1665). Huygens too was aware of the effect of temperature on the period of vibration of a spring (*ibid.*, p. 486) hence his preference at this time for the pendulum (the suspension being short and not made of metal).
[58] *Oeuvres Complètes*, V, p. 486 (18 September 1665, N. S.). Artus Gouffier, Duc de Roanez (d. 1696) was well known for his interest in mechanisms. The clockmaker was probably named Martinot or Martinet; see *ibid.*, p. 503 note 4 and IV, 264—5. Huygens' journal for 11 November 1660 mentions Martinot's "ressort au lieu de pendule".

this confession long before he devised a spring balance. We do not know if the Duke and his clockmaker employed a spiral spring, as in the Huygens' and the modern watch, or whether their attempts succeeded in 1660, but then we do not know these facts of Hooke's work either. Again, at the time of the plague in London there was in the city a Frenchman named D'Esson or de Son (of whom more shortly) who seems to have developed the same idea. Another possible inventor of a much later time is Hautefeuille, who caused Huygens much trouble. If Hooke had been less excitable he would not have imagined that his ideas had occurred to no one but himself in the seventeen years after 1658, nor that no one could formulate such ideas without plagiary from himself.

Oldenburg's attempt to gain a patent for Huygens' invention particularly aroused Hooke's fury. "At Sir J. More's. He told me of Oldenburg's treachery his defeating the Society and getting a patent for Spring Watches for himself", reads his *Diary* for 6 March 1675. About a month later he was with Oldenburg and others at the Bear [Inn?] where he "discovered their designe. [Sir] R[obert] Southwell told me of the Kings refusing the warrant for Oldenburg after I had left the King [on the previous day]. I vented some of mind against Lord Brouncker & Oldenburg. Told them of Defrauding"[59]. And so on. Hooke misunderstood Huygens' original offer to the Secretary of the Royal Society; Huygens had written to him: "si vous croyez qu'un privilege en Angleterre pourroit valoir quelque chose, et que ou la Societe Royale ou vous en vouliez tirer de l'avantage, je vous offre volontiers tout ce que j'y pourrois pretendre"[60]. Huygens altready knew that he could not patent his invention in England, being a foreigner, nor draw profit from it, except through nominees[61]. Perhaps it would have been nobler and wiser in Oldenburg to propose the Royal Society as the prospective patentee, but he was certainly within his rights in choosing to act himself and no doubt Brouncker as president so advised him. Oldenburg was an aging man with a young family, without means, who had laboured hard and with little reward for the Royal Society during more than fifteen years. The friendly offer made to him by Huygens was too good resist, and it is a little hard to understand why Hooke was so upset at the Royal Society's loss of a prospective patent right that, in fact, he did not believe Huygens entitled to offer. Curiously enough, Oldenburg could not in any case have been nominated in the patent; he was only naturalized a few months before his death in 1677, although he had then lived continuously in England for almost a quarter century.

As for assertion (5), this was expressed most bitterly by Hooke in the *Postcript* to *Lampas* (1677) where he attacked Oldenburg as one who had "done him injuries" and "made a trade of Intelligence". He even charged Oldenburg with conveying his

---

[59] *Diary*, p. 157 (8 April 1675).
[60] *Oeuvres Complètes*, VII, p. 423.
[61] Or so he had been informed by Moray on 3 September 1664; *Oeuvres Complètes*, V, pp. 116—7.

own geological ideas to Steno[62]. Hooke was confident that Oldenburg had imparted his secret to Huygens at the time when he himself had fled from the London plague to Durdans in Surrey, leaving Oldenburg as virtually the sole representative of the Royal Society in the stricken city. Moray was with the court at Oxford[63]. Modern commentators have been inclined to imagine a conspiracy between Oldenburg, Moray and Brouncker, extending over some fifteen years, in order to disappoint Hooke of his just deserts[64].

Finally, a word should perhaps be added about Hooke's statement that his horological inventions sprang from "an Art of Invention, or mechanical *Algebra* which I was then [1658] Master of"[65]. Dr. Hesse's investigation of this claim led to conclusions that were "largely negative; there is no evidence to suggest that the vibration theory had any direct connection with the invention of the spring-controlled watch, and indeed Hooke nowhere explicitly claimed that it did"[66].

III. WHAT HAS BEEN CLAIMED FOR HOOKE

Despite the many lamentations on behalf of Hooke as the Alexander Selkirk of British science, he was not wanted his Defoes to make him a hero. Perhaps only at the height of Newton-worship in the nineteenth century was Hooke undervalued. Certainly he has always occupied a high place in the history of British horology thanks to Derham, Waller, Robison, Robertson and indeed almost all writers on the subject[67]; recent writers on horology and specifically on Hooke have emphasised his important contributions to this craft[68]. Enough has been said already to show that Hooke had an extremely fertile mechanical brain — even without a perfect "mechanical algebra" — and that potentially he could have made contributions to the art

---

[62] Gunther, VII, pp. 207—8. Hooke's suggestion with regard to Steno's *Prodromus* (which Oldenburg translated and printed in 1671) seems a simple product of paranoia; channels of communication between England and Italy through this period were far too frail to bear any such burden. Hooke's geological speculations do not seem to be anywhere mentioned by Oldenburg.

[63] See Hall & Hall, *Oldenburg*, II and III. Brouncker remained at the Navy Office.

[64] Cf. 'Espinasse, *Hooke*, 63—8.

[65] Gunther, VII, 146.

[66] *Isis*, 57, 441.

[67] John Robison in the article "Watchwork", *Encyclopaedia Britannica*, third edition, Edinburgh 1797; J. Drummond Robertson, *The Evolution of Clockwork*, London, 1931. Miss Patterson cites Robison as authority for the supposed discovery of Hooke's Law at Oxford (denied by Dr. Hesse); it is worth recalling, as a measure of Robison's credibility, that his statement about James Black's contributions to the improvement of the steam-engine were refuted by James Watt himself, and that it was Robison who stated (falsely) that Thomas Newcomen had been in correspondence with Robert Hooke.

[68] Both Miss Patterson and Mrs 'Espinasse assign the anchor escapement, the circular pendulum and the balance spring to Hooke exclusively. Andrade was more guarded (above, note 6). Among historians of horology H. Alan Lloyd was notably cautious about claims on Hooke's behalf (see for example Charles Singer [*et. al.*], *A History of Technology*. III, Oxford 1957, p. 664).

XII

of time-keeping of the highest importance. Although one cannot safely ascribe the anchore-escapement to Hooke in the absence of any positive evidence, it is certainly possible that the spring-balance entered into the watchmaker's repertoire from Hooke, since the "pirouette" of Huygens was not generally adopted; but again this cannot be proved, when all over Europe scientists and mechanics were at work perfecting the general principle of spring-regulation. Hooke's great secret, the "cock" or constant-force escapement, which he still regarded as crucial in 1675, was not (so far as we know) ever communicated or constructed; therefore it was without effect. Others, including Huygens, developed weight- and spring-operated remontoires. As for the circular pendulum, it was never of any practical use.

There remains one part of the Hooke story to consider: the charge against Sir Robert Moray, Henry Oldenburg (Secretary of the Royal Society) and perhaps others that they betrayed Hooke's trust. Here we may well begin with Richard Waller, compiler of the *Posthumous Works of Dr. Robert Hooke* (1705) who quotes a letter he had seen in the archives of the Royal Society written by Moray to Oldenburg on 30 September 1665:

> in which are these words. 'You [meaning *Oldenburgh*] will be the first that knows when his [that is *Huygens's*] Watches will be ready, and I will therefore expect from you an account of them, and if he imparts to you what he does, let me know it; to that purpose you may ask him if he doth not *apply a Spring to the Arbor of the Ballance*, and that will give him occasion to say somewhat to you; if it be that, you may tell him what *Hooke has done in that matter, and what* he intends more'. Although I cannot be assur'd what Oldenburgh wrote to Monsieur *Huygens*, yet is it probable their intimacy procur'd what he knew[69].

Waller, and Andrade following Waller, used this passage to show (what it does not do) that Hooke employed a *spiral* spring even in 1665; Hooke's latest biographer, removing the parentheses employed by Waller, writes simply "Moray tells Oldenburg to ask Huygens" about the regulation of the balance, although Waller himself made it clear that Huygens was not named in the passage he quoted. For a good reason; the letter is not about Huygens at all. Moray's pronoun referred to the M. De Son already mentioned; the paragraph preceding that quoted by Waller begins:

> I pray God Mr de Son may get no harm by his house [which was plague-infected]. I am indeed very hopefull hee shall not, ... and therefore I am confident by Gods favor you are in as little [danger] by the liberty you allow him to converse with you, however I heartily pray the lord God to preserve you.
> You will be the first...[70].

One might wonder how anyone could have supposed that Oldenburg, in plague-ridden London, could have communicated freely or by word of mouth with Huygens, then at The Hague. De Son, "ce diable d'ingenieur qui a fait ce bateau merveilleux, ou plutost chimerique a Roterdam", was a French adventurer, sixty years old, who

---

[69] Waller, *Posthumous Works*, vi; Gunther, VI, p. 15. The emphasis was added by Waller.
[70] Hall & Hall, *Oldenburg*, II, pp. 538−9, from Royal Society MS M 1, no 13. Waller's transcript is accurate as to sense.

had ruined himself constructing an extraordinary catamaran ram-ship, 76 feet long by seven feet beam, propelled by a spring-driven screw! It was never launched, though depicted in contemporary prints[71]. In London De Son made a great impression on Moray, who wrote about him often to Oldenburg and Huygens, while Charles II was delighted by his scheme for a new kind of light chariot. De Son also promised to obviate spherical aberration in lenses, and to perfect the new watches just mentioned. Some communications from him appear in the earliest *Philosophical Transactions*. The whole supposed plot in which Moray and Oldenburg acted as intermediaries between Hooke and Huygens to the former's disadvantage turns out to be a chimaera; read straightforwardly, Moray's concluding sentences are clearly an injunction to Oldenburg to remember Hooke's prior achievement and promises.

Hooke's biographer wrote of the Moray correspondence: "These letters have an unpleasant appearance"[72]. However, she had made only a cursory examination of the letters printed in the *Oeuvres Complètes*, and knew the Moray-Oldenburg correspondence only from Waller's misleading extract. She evidently missed both the illogicality of blaming Oldenburg for "betraying Hooke's invention to Huygens" when it was Moray himself who wrote to Huygens about the balance-spring and the further letter in which Moray explained why he felt free to do so[73]; after relating Hooke's speaking to Brouncker and himself of his invention, under seal of secrecy, and his hopes of a patent, Moray continued:

> Apres quelques uns de nostre Societe layant faire perdre la pensee du profit quil croyoit pouvoir tirer dun privilege (comme de fait les patentes pour les inventions ne sont icy daucun avantage) il est resolu d'en parler dans une lesson publique, et par la, nous ayant franchi de lobligation. Je n'ay pas voulu manquer de vous la communiquer, len ayant mesme averti. J'ay aussi envie de croire que Monsieur de Ronnais vous aura obligé a ne point parler de son invention, puisque vous ne nous en avez rien dit. Mais quoy que cen soit il est bien evident que les deux en peuvent bien estre dits les inventeurs.

Once again the documents themselves remove mystery and remedy paranoia. Moray told Huygens only what Hooke had told the public — as Hooke was himself to recall in later years as evidence of his priority. And what Moray wrote came to Huygens as no surprise, as has been shown already.

Whatever other injustice on the score of prior discovery Hooke may have suffered at the hands of Newton, Steno, Leibniz and many others, on this count at any

---

[71] *Oeuvres Complètes*, V, p. 87 and notes, *Oldenburg*, II, p. 478, note 4 and *passim*.
[72] 'Espinasse, *Hooke*, p. 68.
[73] *Oeuvres Complètes*, V, p. 504. Elaborating the spurious drama further, Mrs. 'Espinasse notes (correctly) that Hooke found two letters from Moray to Huygens "about my watches" by rummaging through Oldenburg's papers after his death (apparently a proper thing to do) and remarks: "With characteristic generosity he did not reopen the controversy [with the deceased Secretary]". Well he might not, since the letters he had found completely exonerate Oldenburg of the (unreasonable) charge of imparting anything improperly to Huygens (or De Son). Since Huygens was a Fellow of the Royal Society almost from its very beginning, Hooke's view that it was improper to communicate to him what occured at its meetings is rather curious, though not unique.

rate it is clear that there was *no* skullduggery with regard to the invention of the balance-spring; indeed, there was no precious secret either. And meanwhile the constant-force escapement remained locked among Hooke's papers, secure from all eyes and quite useless to anyone. The whole story of the unjust reception of Hooke's discoveries in horology seems to rest upon inadequate documentation and the passage from writer to writer of inadequate or downright false traditions. This is the more serious because the whole character of scientific intercourse between socially and intellectually distinguished figures of seventeenth century science has been distorted to make them appear like pickpockets quarrelling over a watch. Priority quarrels are a tiresome concomitant of seventeenth century scientific communication, but historians should not exaggerate them into its principal feature. The real merits of Robert Hooke have been often enough explained, and there is no point in extending them unreasonably[74]. That Hooke *could* have greatly improved the art of timekeeping is beyond doubt; what he *in fact* did is far from clear. Even the balance-spring was unknown to watchmakers in general until publicized by Huygens in 1675; if as Andrade asserted it is "practically certain that Hooke had invented the modern spring-controlled balance wheel by 1665" (and the claim is not unreasonable, though unprovable) nevertheless it was Huygens' public success with a different form that induced Hooke to perfect the device he had (upon this view) kept hidden for ten years, and so it was (upon this same view) Hooke's own fault if he now appeared to most of the world in the role of second inventor. Clearly there is room for differences of interpretation in these episodes of horological history; but historians should be scrupulous in not positively claiming for Hooke (or anyone else) the invention of specific mechanisms, without any evidence at all, and in not attributing the trials and tribulations of Hooke's life to the machinations of powerful enemies which simply exist in the imagination — even if the imagination was Robert Hooke's.

POSTSCRIPT

Lt. Cmdr. Derek Howse has kindly drawn to my attention the (unpublished) allusions to both Huygens' and Hooke's watches in Flamsteed's letters to Richard Towneley (Royal Society MS. 243); he proposes to publish the relevant extracts in *Antiquarian Horology*. In brief, Flamsteed's reports — not savoring of a particular liking for Hooke, it must be said — confirm the views expressed in this paper. Recording (16 March 1674/5) Hooke's claim of priority when first the news of Huygens' new watch reached London, Flamsteed adds "tis certain he had a watch or two made that had the balance moderated by a spring, but it went so ill it was esteemed inferior to the usual contrivances". He describes experimental watches Hooke had made to compete with Huygens': in one (8 June 1675) the balance was controlled by an opposed pair of jack-in-a-box springs (presumably helical); in that made for Sir Jonas Moore (p. 270 above) the balance was controlled by a hair or thread wound round its arbor, the other end of which was attached to a long, flexible spring (15 Nov-

---

[74] As is done, for instance, in the City of Oxford where a large notice is displayed to the public, marking the spot where Hooke discovered the living cell. The claim is meaningless or (in so far as the word *cell* might be taken to imply a science of cytology) downright false.

ember). This watch went irregularly. Flamsteed reports that the watch made for Charles II had two balances with a pair of springs applied to them, but Hooke's fear of plagiary prevented his ever discovering exactly how these springs were arranged. There is no evidence in Flamsteed's letters that Hooke was using a spiral balance spring in the modern manner before the construction of Huygens' watch was known in London and, though he seems to have believed Hooke's watches to be at least as accurate as Huygens', it is clear he did not regard either as rivalling a good pendulum clock for astronomical purposes.

On this, see D. Howse and V. Finch, 'John Flamsteed and the Balance Spring', *Antiquarian Horology*, 9 (1976), 664–73. An ingenious working reconstruction of Hooke's escapement has been made by Michael Wright: see Michael Hunter and Simon Schaffer (eds.) *Robert Hooke: New Studies* (Woodbridge, 1989), pp. 63–118.

XIII

HENRY MORE AND THE SCIENTIFIC REVOLUTION

The relation of Henry More to the Scientific Revolution of the seventeenth century has been a matter of greater interest to historians of philosophy than to historians of science. The same remark might be applied, indeed, to other philosophers who have reflected critically or otherwise upon mathematics and natural science - George Berkeley, to cite another English example. However, the case of More is a little different in that positive influence upon the greatest of English scientists has been more than once confidently claimed for him. The writings of More perhaps most frequently considered by historians of philosophy are his his four letters to Descartes written in 1648-9. Without by any means belittling their importance as indications of contemporary idealist response to Descartes's philosophy, there are good reasons for not giving them great prominence when thinking about More in relation to science. In them More himself gave pride of place to the epistemological and metaphysical problems he found in Descartes's writings; although he does raise scientific objections to Descartes's treatment of the planetary motions, of optics, of magnetism and so forth, not to say of Descartes's fundamental theory of motion (but perhaps this is as much a matter of metaphysics as of science), these do not inhibit him from declaring in later writings that Descartes had constructed as perfect an explanatory mechanism for the universe as anyone could hope to meet with. Difficulties of principle, rather than problems in this or that explanatory model, will permanently trouble More. Then the letters, published by Clerselier in 1657 and by More in 1662, came into the light too late to have had much effect upon English scientific thinking. I have not myself come across any evidence that More's opinions in the letters were read and assimilated - which is not to deny that such evidence may exist. But it may be affirmed that their message was not and is not easy to unravel. Descartes is praised to the skies in general terms by More, who then raises a multiplicity of objections against him. A general tone of acceptance goes with a quiet sapping of the foundations of Cartesian dualism and even (in the passage that provoked Descartes's last caustic reply) a speculation that matter itself is not merely material.

Furthermore, the objections to Cartesianism that More rehearsed in the letters by no means inhibited his proclaiming the merits of this philosophy in his publications at least until 1662. The *Epistola ad V.C.*, More declared, was intended to vindicate Descartes from the giddy charge of atheism. He is the sublime mechanick. His writings should be the subject of a revived Mosaic idea of Nature of which Platonism is the soul. Descartes and More are united in a holy purpose, and

> ... we both setting out from the same *Lists*, though taking severall ways, the one travelling on the lower *Road* of *Democritism*, amidst the thick dust of *Atoms* and flying particles of *Matter*, the other tracing over the high and airey Hills of Platonism, in that more thin and subtil Region of *Immateriality*, meet together nothwithstanding at last (and certainly not without a Providence) at the same *Goale*, namely at the entrance of the holy Bible, dedicating our joint Labours to the use and glory of the Christian Church...[1]

I shall in what follows disregard the letters to Descartes of 1648-9.

The positive influence that More's philosophical poems (1642, 1647) may have exerted in acquainting his reader with the ideas of Copernicus and Galileo as well as Descartes may be less familiar; once again we have no evidence of such readers' reactions. The verses themselves are quite explicit; for example:

> I have the barking of cold sense confuted...
> To show that Pythagore's position's right
> Copernicks, or whatsoever dogma't hight.[2]

Once more, in refutation of mechanical 'proofs' of the Earth's being 'stablished fast by a changeless decree:'

> An arrow shot into the empty aire,
> Which straight returning to the bowman's foot,
> The earth's stability must for ever clear.
> Thus these bad archers do at random shoot,
> Whose easie errour I do thus confute.
> The arrow hath one spirit with this sphere,
> Forc'd upwards turns with it, mov'd by the root
> Of naturall motion. So when back't doth bear
> Itself, still Eastward turns with motion circular.[3]

Less rhetorically, in the *Notes* that accompany the *Philosophical Poems* (1647), that is roughly contemporaneously with the better-known popular books of John Wilkins, More explains in some technical detail, and with the aid of geometrical diagrams, the allusions to astronomy in the texts of his poems. Observe that More had not read Copernicus; he draws his knowledge of the Copernican system from Galileo's *Dialogo sopra i due massimi systemi* (1632) -presumably More read the Latin translation of 1635- and other 'recent' books, such as Philip van Lansberge, *Progymnasmatum astronomiae restitutae* (1619) from which he quotes magnitudes in the solar system:

Distance of the Moon from the Earth at apogee 64 Earth-radii,
at perigee 54 ,, ,,
Distance of the Sun from the Earth
at apogee 1550 ,, ,,
at perigee 1446 ,, ,,

He gives the following distances from the Earth in Earth-radii:

Mars at perigee 556 Venus at apogee 2598
Venus at perigee 339 Mercury at apogee 2176[4]

After giving geometrical representations of the Tychonic and Copernican systems,[5] More remarks of the latter,

> It is plain to any man that is not prejudic'd that this System of the world is more naturall & genuine then that of *Tycho's*. No enterfaring or cutting of the circles as in *Tycho's*, where the course of the Sunne cuts Mars his circuit. No such vast excentricity as there, nor disproportionatednesse of Orbs and motions.[6]

A little later More explains with a diagram what is meant by the phases of Venus and how they furnish evidence for the revolution of this planet (and Mercury) around the Sun. Immediately afterwards he continues with an account of the stations and retrogressive motions of the planets, indicating the superiority of the Copernican treatment though - as is clear from his diagrams - this is a little more difficult to understand than the representation by an epicycle.

In annotations to a short, natural-theological poem entitled *The Philosopher's Devotion* More explains how the daily alternations and seasonal variations of the length of the day and night are brought about, on the assumption of the Earth's daily rotation on its axis and annual revolution about the Sun. More writes that he follows

> *Copernicus* his *Hypothesis* [which] will not merely explane these verses but exceedingly set out the fitnesse and genuinenesse of the Hypothesis it self. Which I will therefore do out of *Galileo* for the satisfaction of the unprejudiced Reader.[7]

Once again, More gives Galileo's diagrams.

A very interesting section of the *Notes* deals in some detail with the theory of tides. [8] The original verses of *Psychathanasia* (Book II, Canto 3, Stanza 56) adopted the Galilean kinematic explanation without question, and More first explains what this involves: the flux and reflux of the sea are due to diurnal and seasonal changes of the speed through space of any point on the Earth's surface.[9] However, More then affirms that the Galilean theory must be wrong, because it makes the annual variations in the tidal movement greatest at the solstices, whereas they are found in fact to be greatest at the equinoxes.[10] Hence he now declares Descartes to be 'far more Succesfull in his Hypothesis' of aetherial pressure as the cause of the tides. This More summarises from *Principia philosophiae* (1644).

Two other points treated by More in the *Notes* and relating to physics are worth mention here. One is a very poor discussion of the well-known problem of the vertical rise and fall of heavy bodies.[11] The other is a note defining *Circulation* (which, it is suggested, might better be called *orbiculation*), a term applied to the diffusion of an effect from the centre as when rings expanding outwards are formed on the surface of water by the splash of a stone:

> In brief, any thing is said to circulate that diffuseth its Image or Species in a round... Such is the diffusion of the Species audible in the strucken Air, as also of the visible Species.[12]

More's *Circulatio sanguinis* is not only one of the earliest poems in praise of Harveian circulation but the one which shows the most familiarity with *De motu cordis*.[13] There is thus some support for More's claim in his letters to Lady Conway to have given instruction in Copernican astronomy. There are also references in the correspondence to his former study of geometry, now largely forgotten, and, perhaps most illuminating of all, to his taking a pupil, her relative Edward Rawdon, through the *Principia philosophiae*, the *Dioptrique* and the *Méteores* of Descartes -'the Machine for making glasses not excepted.'[14] Obviously it is impossible to make a firm inference from these events of 1674 to the teaching More may have given to John Finch and other favoured pupils (not forgetting Richard Ward, More's biographer) during the 1640s and 1650s. But at least one may hazard the frail guess that they took a similar course.

To the best of my knowledge, we have no independent testimony to More's competence in optics. We have, however, much evidence of his distrust of the 'spagyrical' experimental tradition in his attacks upon Thomas Vaughan-despite More's attachment to the Hermes Trismegistus of Ficino, from whom he so often draws his mottoes.[15] It has been suggested that More's mocking attitude to Vaughan gave offence to a powerful group in the later Royal Society: Sir Robert Moray for one, a leading figure among the Founders of the Society, was a patron of Vaughan. On this point, More's early letters to Hartlib are relevant, for they too state More's contempt for 'spagyrical' chemists and clearly display his utter lack of interest in all those well-meaning inquiries and projects to which Samuel Hartlib was devoted. Now Hartlib has long been recognised as an intellectual influence upon some of those who were to found the Royal Society (Boyle, Petty, Oldenburg, to name only three) so that once again More seems to draw himself emphatically away from those who have since been seen as constituting one wing of the new scientific movement. Another Christ's man who was also a correspondent of Hartlib's, Thomas Smith, warned him that in Cambridge the brighter men were so taken up with Platonism 'or other high and aery speculations of

Divinity or Philosophy, that they will scarce vouchsafe to cast a glance on' such things as new discoveries and inventions or any matters outside their own interest.[16]

Of all future Fellows of the Royal Society, only the paradoxical Henry More would describe those Baconians who search for 'usefull experiments for the discovery of Nature' as 'men who dig and droyle like blinde molewarps in the earth':

> ...it would make a dog laugh, to think how highly these low Spiritts, [are] commonly conceited of themselves, and are more easily proud and contemptuous than those, of far and more enlarged facultyes.[17]

For these words and his talk of 'slibber-sauce experiments' More later apologised after receiving an indignant rejoinder from young William Petty, More claiming that he himself reckoned experience the best of knowledge. Yet More is still less than repentant, continuing to assert the pre-eminence of a philosopher like Descartes, for

> ...the first and most generall principles of Nature have more Divinity and Majesty in them than ever to suffer themselves to be Hermetically imprison'd in some narrow neck'd glasse, or like a Jack in a box to astartle the eyes of the vulgar at the opening of a Lidd.[18]

As for any way of

> ...advancing of learning sett on foot, that experimentall knowledge forsooth may flourish like Ivy and *Leucoium* growne out of the cracks and breaches in the walls of ruin'd monasteries, may mine eyes never see that experiment.[19]

It is hardly surprising that Hartlib's attempt to enlist More's aid met with failure. The epistemological difference between the idealist and the empiricist can never be reconciled. It is ironic that the man who twenty-five years later would be the intimate friend and admirer of Francis Mercury van Helmont, from whom he would beg remedies for his ailing kinsfolk, should now complain that the Paracelsians love 'to be tumbling and trying Tricks with the *Matter* (which they call *making Experiments*)... This is that that commonly makes the *Chymist* so pitiful a *Philosopher*.'[20]

The one topic in which Henry More is known to have made experiments himself - which Robert Boyle was to tell him he had better not have published- is hydrostatics: More left hydrostatical apparatus (as well as a globe and mathematical instruments) to friends in his Will.[21] Some experiments were performed with van Helmont at Ragley Hall. To make here a long review of More's objections against Boyle and others in their use of mechanical explanations of buoyancy in fluids and so forth is needless.[22] The plain fact is that More did not comprehend what Archimedes had accomplished two thousand years before. Archimedean hydrostatics, the principles of which Boyle followed, depend upon precise assumptions about the properties of a perfect fluid and the fact of gravity or weight. The former were not in question with More. The latter was, since, in More's view, any phenomenon involving gravity demanded a spiritual explanation. But when More, on more than one occasion, puts forward the following 'experiment' as one that Archimedes and the mechanists cannot solve, one can only be amazed at his naivety: a disk of wood, less dense than water, is made to fit closely but not tightly, to the parallel sides of a cylindrical vessel; when the vessel is filled with water and the disk pressed down through the fluid almost to the bottom, it floats up to the surface although the weight of water pressing down through the narrow circular gap, upon the fluid below the disk, is less than that of the water pressing down upon the disk.[23] This is an inexplicable paradox to Henry More, though it is accounted for by Archimedes.

Against Boyle once again, More showed a similar obtuse inability to comprehend and understand the idea of atmospheric weight and pressure. How can it be asserted, More asks, that the air presses upon us with that force which is sufficient to maintain a column of mercury at a height of 29 inches, when we observe that soft butter is not squeezed flat by it?[24] Boyle actually took the trouble to enclose insects in the bottom of a J-tube to prove that they could survive without harm a total pressure of two atmospheres, in order to confute More's contention (parallel to that about butter) that if the air at the Earth's surface were compressed, the soft bodies of insects would be squashed flat.[25] In his eagerness to vindicate the Spirit of Nature, which by the 1670s had become More's explanation of all phenomena, one material particle being unable without it so much as to impel a second particle by impact, More would not accept the fact that air-particles (for example) might be inherently elastic, like little springs: for such elasticity would imply an active power in mere matter. Now no one would wish to assert that Boyle was necessarily correct in attributing elasticity to air-particles, without by the way feeling under an obligation to offer a mechanical model for their springiness, as a possible hypothesis to account for the elasticity of volumes of air; or to assert that More was necessarily incorrect in wishing to animate the air with a spirit that makes it springy. What seems surprising is that More fails to grasp the point that Archimedean statics or Boyleian pneumatics are not to be refuted by arguments (necessarily incapable of resolution) about the presence or absence of particular properties in the (imagined) material particles composing matter. All that is required is to agree, or disprove, that a bulk of water is heavy or a volume of air is springy. More's supposedly negative experimental illustrations do not cause difficulties for the theories based upon such experiential postulates.

In a well-known letter aimed at Henry Stubbe, More assured Joseph Glanvill in 1671 of his contined support for the Royal Society's endeavours:

> The Philosophy which they aim at, is a more *perfect Philosophy*, as yet to

be raised out of faithful and skilful *Experiments* in Nature, which is so far from tending to Atheism, that I am confident, it will utterly rout it and the *Mechanical Philosophy* at once, in that sense which I oppose, namely, as it signifies a Philosophy that professeth, *That Matter having such a Quantity of Motion as it has, would contrive itself into all those Phenomena we see in Nature*. But this Profession cannot rightly be called the *Mechanical Philosophy* but the *Mechanical Belief of Credulity*.[26]

So far is the Royal Society from favouring the atheistic mechanism opposed by More that Glanvill should

> ...particularly note how serviceable their *Natural Experiments* in *matter* are to the clear Knowledge and Demonstration of the *Existence* of *immaterial Beings*.[27]

Philosophically, though not (as he was aware) methodologically, the positions of the Royal Society and of Descartes do not differ in principle, in More's opinion. Both hold the view that 'all the Vicissitudes of corporeal Nature' arise from alterations in the dispositions of the 'little Bodies or Particles of differing Figures, Magnitudes and Velocities':

> But this thus bounded is not the *Mechanical Philosophy* but part of the old *Pythagorick* or *Mosaick Philosophy*, so far as I can see by any *History*.[28]

Where Descartes was at fault in his 'hasty Presumption' that if

> *Matter* was possesst of so much *Motion* as there is in the World, it would *necessarily* at length contrive it self into all *such Phaenomena*, as we see in the Universe.[29]

A presumption of which the Royal Society is, by implication, innocent.

Thus, not to go beyond general terms, we discover that More's first objection to Cartesian mechanism is cosmogonic: he insists that the world could not have organised itself, supposing the mere injection of motion into matter. The universe must have been formed by a planned and guided process. Sometimes More's language seems to prefigure the words that Newton would employ much later:

> Who causes all the planets not to revolve in one plane (the plane of the Ecliptic)? And also sunspots, not to be in planes at least parallel to the ecliptic? And the Moon itself neither in the plane of the Earth's equator nor in a plane parallel to this? Since [in Descartes' philosophy] these bodies are directed by no internal force but are merely borne round by an external impulse.[30]

This is the language of natural theology, as opposed to the determinism attributed by More to Descartes. In *An Antidote against Atheisme* and elsewhere, More proved himself to be a well-informed and resourceful exponent of its arguments. So far, one may imagine him as speaking with the same voice as Boyle and many other Fellows of the Royal Society.

More's dissatisfaction with Descartes - and, despite his disclaimer, the Royal Society - was by no means restricted to cosmogony. His God was no retiring clockmaker. Some power that is more than mechanical or material is required to maintain the Universe, as well as create it. The great merit of Descartes was that his

> Conceptions concerning the Figure of the Particles of such and such Bodies are exceeding plausible, and probable: amongst which that of the Globuli seems to me so far to surpass all other Hypotheses about Light, that I stand to him close against his most able Opposers on that point in my *Enchiridion Metaphysicum*, so far forth as concerns the Mechanical part of Light and Colours.

Then comes the sting in the next sentence

> But mere Mechanism does not exhaust all those Phenomena neither, as I there prove in a long Chapter on the subject.[31]

What More seems to have surrendered in gross, he often takes back in detail. Even in the precise mechanical details of Nature Descartes is after all far from impeccable. It is hardly necessary to insist upon More's total inability to accept the Cartesian analysis of the animal body as a machine. At an early date More affirms that the soul's movements are as natural

> ... as how the Fire will ascend upwards, or a Stone fall downwards, for neither are the motions of these meerly Mechanicall, but vital or Magicall, that cannot be resolved into meer Matter.[32]

(Another example of the puzzle More found in motion caused by differences in density.) The very 'Motion of Matter is not guided by matter, but by something else,' and in due course More will allege that Descartes's philosophy

> ...fails so palpably even in the general strokes of Nature, of giving any such necessary Mechanicall Reasons of her Phaenomena that it becomes a rotten duck falling to pieces in a man's hand.[33]

By the time of his letter to Glanvill (1671) quoted above, any concession of validity in mechanical explanations of phenomena made by More is specious, nullified by his reiterated declarations that no hypothesis omitting the Spirit of Nature can have value.[34] As men offering particular explanations of effects in Nature, Boyle, Hooke and Glisson occupied positions exactly analoguous to that of Descartes and their a-spiritualist writings were equally at fault, in More's eyes. His criticism of them are fully comprehensible in the light of his a priori commitment to the Spirit of Nature.

One may have a suspicion that Henry Stubbe was not without justification in his invocation of Henry More as a philosopher whose thought ran counter to the mainstream in the Royal Society, and that this very fact lessened his reputation among the Fellows. Boyle and Hooke declared themselves publicly against More's pretensions; Newton's one reference in print to a man sometimes regarded as his close friend was to draw himself away from the hylarchic principle.[35] And it is very striking that the natural theologians of the next generation, some like Richard Bentley writing very much in Newton's shadow, make little or no reference to More's writings, though it may indeed be that they made use of them. In that classic manual of both Cartesianism and Newtonian anti-Cartesianism, *Rohault's System* of *Natural Philosophy*, no friendly reference to that early critic of Cartesian science, Henry More, is to be found. But there is a negative allusion to him. Where Rohault treats of mechanics in Chapter 10, Samuel Clarke observes in his notes:

> Hence it is easie to explain that Paradox, which so much perplexed the famous Dr. Henry Moor, and other learned Men, viz. why a flat round Board, such as a Trencher, when it is put into Water should rise up immediately, though the Weight of the incumbent Water be much greater than that under it...[36]

But at least this proves that, many years after his death, More's polemics against the thriving science of his day were not wholly forgotten, even if his problem is incompetently stated.

It was of course unfortunate for More's later reputation that after 1687 British anti-Cartesianism was overwhelmingly Newtonian. It might be said of More that when he attacked the mechanical philosophy as an epistemology of Nature he was disregarded; and when he specifically attacked the natural philosophy of Descartes his candle was lost in Newton's greater light. Yet the question of More's possible influence on Newton, already addressed by so many writers, is still unresolved.[37] At present I do not mean to discuss in any detail the ideas of absolute space and time advanced by the two men, in part because the treatment of the same subjects by Isaac Barrow in his mathematical lectures at Cambridge (1664-1666) seems so much more close and natural a precedent to Newton's than that of More,[38] and in part because it has not yet been shown that Newton examined the relevant writings of More attentively. It may be noted that Newton's library contained (so far as we know) no copies of *Divine Dialogues* or *Enchiridion metaphysicum*. It is of course known that Newton was considerably influenced by More's *Immortality of the Soul*,[39] and one may in a loose generalisation infer that Newton's anti-Cartesianism was in part inspired by More's; though their criticisms became in time unlike in almost every possible respect.

If unlike, their ideas are nevertheless often parallel. For example, More argued upon metaphysical grounds that the constancy of the quantity of motion in the Universe (according to Descartes) was insufficient to account for the constancy of observed phenomena; Newton argued upon dynamical grounds that motion in Nature could, in fact, be destroyed and so could not ensure the constancy of phenomena. More argued metaphysically against the concept of relative motion upon which Descartes established the theory of planetary vortices; Newton argued dynamically that the motions of bodies in a vortex do not correspond to those consistent with Kepler's laws of planetary motion. Most important, both More and Newton rejected Descartes's idea of a Universe in which the conservation of motion entails the notion that all phenomena result from the continuing partition of motion between particles of matter by their mutual impact, in an eternal game of three-dimensional billiards. For More, the harmonious, perpetual working of the Universe required the constant activity of Spirit. For Newton it required the action of force, a concept which, however, he left somewhat indefinite in terms of the concepts of the science of mechanics, and in terms of natural philosophy barely explained at all.[40] Newton tells us (in a variety of places, that force does not originate from matter, nor is it a correlative of matter; it may be the product of 'active Principles' at work in the Universe; it may be the immediate consequence of God's will, or it may be caused by one or more extremely tenuous and elastic aethers (perhaps in turn actuated by 'active Principles'?)[41]

Despite all the differences of detail, which tend to bring Newton's discussion rather more into the realm of natural philosophy than were the ideas of Henry More, it is clear that both men moved in the same direction, abandoning the simpler version of the mechanical philosophy that had swept the board soon after the midddle of the seventeenth century, the version that Robert Boyle had applied successfully and with characteristic absence of dogmatism to chemistry. This version, which might be qualified as *kinematic*, attributed sensible phenomena to insensible corpuscular motions; but it offered no explanation (or no clear and consistent explanation) of the causes of such motions, or any precise way of defining them. Newton introduced the *dynamic* version of the mechanical philosophy, supposing corpuscles (or particles) to be moved by attractive and repulsive forces according to mathematical law (force varying directly as the distance, inversely as the square of the distance, etc.)[42] An obvious point of distinction is in the treatment of cohesion: for Descartes (curiously) cohesion represents the mutual rest of contiguous particles; others explained it in structural terms (the 'hooks and eyes' type hypothesis); while Newton saw cohesion as a strong, short-range force of attraction between adjacent particles.[43]

Now it is obvious that though More had no idea of force, of dynamics, or of any possible physical solution to the problems he perceived, he did demand the existence in Nature of something other than the motions already inherent in its particles and the particles themselves. He was of course correct in holding that the philosopher cannot properly attribute such properties as elasticity (the prerequisite for Cartesian mechanics and Boyleian pneumatics) to the fundamental properties of matter: one could as legitimately account for the redness of cinnabar in the same way. How could he solve the problem, it being understood that he cannot attribute any sort of activity that might create the effect of elasticity to the particles? More could think only of invoking another agent that is the antithesis of matter, i.e. spirit. Newton agreed that

> God in the Beginning form'd Matter in solid, massy, hard, impenetrable, moveable Particles...these Particles have not only a *Vis inertiae*, accompanied with such passive Laws of Motion as naturally result from that Force, but...are moved by certain active Principles, such as is that of Gravity, and that which causes Fermentation, and the Cohesion of Bodies.[44]

But he devised wholly new classes of agents, forces (or 'active Principles' which are their causes), immaterial agents subject to mathematical laws.

Yet Newton's philosophy of Nature did not cease to be mechanical. As Westfall writes:

> Where the orthodox mechanical philosophy of seventeenth-century science insisted that physical reality consists solely of material particles in motion, characterized by size, shape and solidity alone, Newton now added forces of attraction and repulsion, considered as properties of such particles, to the catalogue of nature's ontology... Physical reality still consisted of material particles in motion, but the ultimate term of explanation was now the force of attraction or repulsion that altered a particle's state of motion.[45]

In this paragraph, Westfall's interpolation of the phrase 'considered as properties of such particles' is in my opinion an error. Newton never thought of forces as properties of particles, that is, as inherent in the matter composing the particles. In a well-known letter to Bentley, quoted elsewhere by Westfall, Newton expressly qualifies such a supposition as absurd. The property that must be attributed to the particles and to the larger corpuscles compounded of them, is a capacity for differential reation to the various forces of Nature. All matter is subject to the force of gravitation. Some matter has a powerful force of cohesion, and is therefore hard. Other matter has almost none and is fluid. Some matter obeys the magnetic force, other matter ignores it. Such behaviour in gross bodies must ultimately be assignable to some differences in the properties of their component particles; for the forces themselves are clearly (for Newton) ontologically distinct from, and independent of, the matter they cause to move.

Needless to say, Newton did not invent the concept of physical force, or always conceive of it in the manner just described. However, in the kinematic version of the mechanical philosophy, force was treated as the product of motion, not its cause; Newton in early drafts eloquently dubs it the 'force of a body's motion'. Thus the dynamic version of the mechanical philosophy, treating force as a cause of motion, reverses the order of cause and effect and requires a new term to describe the 'force' inherent in a moving body manifest when it strikes a second body. It is not surprising that two generations were required to sort out the confusion.

What has Henry More to do with all this, if anything? No obvious relation to him is to be traced in Newton's published writings upon mechanics, or upon the metaphysical foundations of physical science. But in manuscript drafts that precede the *Principia* by twenty years the legacy of More is evident and sometimes acknowledged. To quote Westfall again, in the *Quaestiones quaedam philosophiae* which Newton compiled as a student

> ...the influence of Henry More was particularly strong in those passages intended to refute the possibility of a material order autonomous and independent of spiritual control. Perhaps the influence of More stood behind Newton's further development into violent anti-Cartesianism.[46]

Certainly More strongly impelled Newton towards atomism; he reacted more kindly to Gassendi (via Walter Charleton) than More had done.

It is not surprising that since both men extended the ontology of physical Nature to embrace more than 'mere inert' matter-in-motion, both More and Newton uttered similar protests that they were by no means ipso facto delivering philosophy over to occultism and obscurantism. Their step, both insisted, was calculated to increase real knowledge rather than diminish it. So More in 1662: to look for the ghost in the machine is not

> ...to take sanctuary in an *Asylum* of Fools [and furthermore] to conclude that to be by *Sympathy*, that we can demonstrate not to be by mere *mechanical Powers* is not to shelter a man's self in the *common Refuge* of *Ignorance*, but to tell the *proximate* and *immediate cause* of a *Phenomenon*, which is to philosophize to the height.[47]

Which closely foreshadows Newton in 1715:

> ...must the constant and universal Laws of Nature, if derived from the Power of God or the Action of a Cause not yet known to us, be called Miracles and occult Qualities, that is to say *Wonders* and *Absurdities*?[48]

Or the more familiar apologia in *Opticks*:

> [The Aristotelian] occult Qualities put a stop to the Improvement of natural Philosophy, and therefore of late Years have been rejected. To tell us that every Species of Things is endow'd with an occult specifick Quality by which it acts and produces manifest Effects, is to tell us nothing: But to derive two or three general Principles of Motion from Phaenomena, and afterwards to tell us how the Properties and Actions of all corporeal Things follow from those manifest Principles, would be a very great step in Philosophy, though the Causes of those Principles were not yet discover'd...[49]

My own reading of the last passage is that Newton meant by 'Principles of Motion' not axioms, rules or laws but the same 'active Principles' as are adumbrated at the beginning of this paragraph of Query 31:

> ...such as is that of Gravity, and that which causes Fermentation, and the Cohesion of Bodies. These Principles I consider, not as occult Qualities-...but as general Laws of Nature, by which the Things themselves are form'd; their Truth appearing to us by Phaenomena, though their Causes be not discover'd.[50]

Thus though the epistemologies of More and Newton are similar, their ontologies are not. When More says 'Spirit of Nature' he looks and can look no further. Newton denominates force quantitatively as the cause of motion, and then looks to the Principles (which may or may not be thought as specific as the forces) as the causes of force. Forces are manifest from phenomena. Principles are inferred from the forces. Then what lies behind the Principles (to me, at any rate, wholly obscure entities)? - Not, Newton declares, an hylarchic principle or Spirit of Nature. He looks directly to the will of God. Newtonian forces, writes Westfall, and I agree, were not real, substantive entities in the Universe.[51] In the kinematic version of the mechanical philosophy apparent attractions and repulsions were brought about by undetectable streams of particles; in the dynamic version due to Newton they are brought about by manifest forces exerted by the undetectable, infinite and omnipresent power of God who, with the world as his sensorium, controls and moves all material things within it as our souls control and move our bodies. This is as More would have recognised, a truly Platonic conception.

In the last years of his life Newton introduced yet another idea, that of the electric and elastic spirit[52] which is to be taken as identical with the highly rarifed aether of Queries 17 to 24, added to the English edition of *Opticks* in 1717. *Pace* Hélène Metzger and others,[53] *this* medium is a material one - even if it seems to consist more of immaterial force than of material particle -- and therefore it cannot be identified with More's Spirit of Nature. This notwithstanding, it is certainly analogous to More's spirit in its universality and in its serving as the intermediary of God's action. Perhaps Newton thought of its various roles or functions as constituting what he had already called the 'active Principles.' It is impossible to be precise about such matters, just as it is impossible to decide whether this fresh invention drew Newton closer to More or further from him.

But there is still a further issue about their intellectual relationship to be considered. More was a metaphysician, Newton a natural philosopher - though each strayed into the other's province. It might seem obvious to say that More (like Descartes) begins with metaphysics and looks forward to the establishment of a compatible natural philosophy, while conversely Newton, having constructed a mathematical philosophy, looked backwards in order to establish its metaphysical underpinnings. But this is not biographically true: for we see Newton as a youthful metaphysician as soon as we see him as a mathematician or an experimenter. It would therefore seem bizarre and unhistorical to argue, on the one hand, that Newton was not already conerned about the metaphysical bases of natural philosophy before writing the *Principia* or, on the other hand, that because when he was composing the mathematical preponderance of the book which is devoted to mechanics, he was not directly facing metaphysical issues, his thinking at the metaphysical level must be irrelevant to that work, considered from a scientific point of view. The question relating to Henry More is really quite simple: only if Newton's metaphysical views are irrelevant to the writing of the *Principia* (and, we might add, of *Opticks* too) is it possible to deny to More any possible influence upon the transformation of the mechanical philosophy effected by Newton in these works.

The majority of historians of ideas have been reluctant to banish metaphysical considerations from the mind of the author of the *Principia*. The historical tradition of their discussion bears more strongly on the celebrated Scholium at the opening of the book concerning the concepts of space and time than on Newton's concept and formal treatment of force; but some of the same general considerations are relevant to both issues. Alexandre Koyré, thirty years ago, delared that

> Newton's physics, or, it would be better to say, Newton's natural philosophy, stands or falls with the concepts of absolute time and absolute space [and these are] the selfsame concepts for which Henry More fought his long-drawn-out and relentless battle against Descartes.[54]

Only Stephen Toulmin, obviously reacting against Koyré's chapters on Newton in the same book, has argued for a different interpretation. Toulmin maintains that Newton in the Scholium lays down definitions required for a dynamical system, and is not aiming at metaphysics. He emphasises the point that for Newton the absolutes of time and space are mathematical, necessary for an axiomatic structure rather than for a picture of reality: indeed, the question 'Does absolute space exist?' is absurd. The reader of the *Principia* is not required to tie Newtonian dynamics to the kind of theological superstructure that was added to the concept of absolute space by Henry More and Joseph Raphson:

> The distinction between absolute, mathematical and relative sensible space, time, and motion can be interpreted consistently as a logical rather than a metaphysical distinction, and the theory as a whole justified on purely dynamical grounds.[55]

Further, the thread of Newon's personal intellectual development, and the historical origins of Newton's ideas, 'however suggestive or sympathetic he may have found Henry More's theological bizzareries,' do not entitle us to pronounce upon the validity of Newton's scientific system or to assert that,

'Newton's Physics...stand or falls with the substantial or spiritual Space of the seventeenth-century Neoplatonist theologians.'[56] Toulmin also notes that Newton's language nowhere identifies God and Space so strongly as does that of More, and that Barrow might with greater plausibility be regarded as Newton's antecedent. His cautionary words are worthy of attention, if only because of the tendency in recent years to shine the light on Newton the metaphysician, alchemist and magician to the eclipse of Newton the mathematician and empiricist. It may not be quite just that we should now *uniquely* perceive the Newton that he himself sought to conceal. But Toulmin's article was written when the historical evidence bearing upon Newton's study of More's writings and his composition of early metaphysical sketches was still unpublished. It would seem rash, nowadays, to deny that Newton's mind from first to last was strongly inclined to a religious view of Nature, and that he had no desire to write the natural philosophy of an unreal world, or to write the natural philosophy of the real world in such a way that the deepest questions about its ontology were to be excluded from discussion. There is a sense in which Toulmin may be merely asserting that Newton was wrong to involve God in natural philosophy. But it would be a mistake to think that Newton, just as much as More, did not endeavour to find his way to knowledge of God because Newton also sought for knowledge of Nature.

Von Leyden was surely justified in claiming, in rebuttal of Toulmin's article, that the separation of God and Nature is not to be found in Newton or in Newton's age: Newton was conscious -like all philosophers of his time - that reliance upon reason and natural philosophy alone would leave his system of the Universe in an intellectual vacuum. How could he justify his ontology? To fill the void he was bound to deal with questions of metaphysics and natural theology; in this realm of thought More's ideas had the greatest appeal for him; and these ideas helped him to deal with the concept of force, as well as the concepts of space and time. In Newton's time, though not in ours, the filling of the ontological void might seem to bring strength and plausibility to Newton's system.[57]

Within the last twenty years, discussion has moved from the question of the significance of Newtonian metaphysics, taking their derivation from Cambridge Platonism as being virtually self-evident, to consider the possibility that Newton's concepts of force and (after 1713) aether were derived from Hermetic sources. Westfall has become a strong advocate of this interpretation, but it is not clear to me whether this might be taken to qualify the importance he formerly attached to Newton's reading of More.[58] On the other hand, McGuire has forcefully defended the older view, arguing,

> ...that the development of Newton's scientific thought in relation to the presuppositions of its intellectual orientation can be explained satisfactorily by his response to the thought of the Cambridge Platonists and their rejection of Cartesianism.[59]

52

And more specifically he claims that,

> ... the Neoplatonism of active and passive principles, as they are developed by the Cambridge Platonists, could clearly legitimize the general notion of phenomena that act at a distance but not necessarily the specific, though relatable, Newtonian concepts of attractive and repulsive force.[60]

It is clear that in the above passages 'Neoplatonism' is a term serving especially to describe the writing of Henry More.

I do not mean to enter this debate here, unless to remark that (in my opinion) the thought and language of Newton seem far close to those of More, than to those of the alchemists and other Hermeticists; and perhaps the pretensions or otherwise of Newton to be called an alchemist should not determine the history of the evolution of the concept of universal gravitation.[61] It is hardly possible on the evidence to say that More *dominated* Newtonian metaphysics, or that he handed to Newton the tools for transforming the mechanical philosophy. That he helped Newton to frame his criticism of the established trends of the 1660s and 1670s is more certain. As to the positive influence, we must not forget that Newton, if or when he took anything from More, modified his borrowing to suit his own purposes and mathematical view of Nature, and thereby made it completely his own. Whereas More was always a man looking backwards, and indeed proud of the fact, Newton's was the vision of the future.

1. More, *CSPW*, Preface p. xii.
2. More, *Poems, Psychathanasia*, 3, stanza 44.
3. Ibid., stanza 37.
4. Ibid., 388.
5. Ibid., 389, 390.
6. Ibid., 390-1.
7. Ibid., 401.
8. Ibid., 390-400.
9. Ibid., 391-5.
10. Ibid., 396.
11. Ibid., 385.
12. Ibid., 425.
13. Wallace Shugg et al., "Henry More's *Circulatio Sanguinis*."
14. M. H. Nicolson(ed.), *Conway Letters*, pp. 393,395, 397.
15. F. B. Burnham, "The More-Vaughan Controversy," quotes More's *Observations upon Anthroposophia Theomagica* (1650): 'There never was anything proposed in the world in which there is more wary, subtil and close texture of reason, more coherent unity of all parts with themselves, or more happy uniformity of the whole with the phenomena of Nature' than in the Cartesian philosophy.
16. Charles Webster, "Henry More and Descartes," 365.
17. Ibid.
18. Ibid., 369.

19. Ibid., 371.
20. More, *ET*, 36 in *CSPW*.
21. *Conway Letters*, pp. 481-3.
22. More first made use of some of Boyle's experiments from *New Experiments Physico-Mechanical* (1660) in the 1662 edition of *AA* (in *CSPW*) and again in *Enchiridion Metaphysicum* (1671). Boyle replied to More in *An Hydrostatical Discourse* (1672), which More answered in *Remarks upon Two Ingenious Discourses* (1976). See John Henry's article in this volume.
23. More, *AA*, 44-6 in *CSPW*. Also *EM*, chap. 12.
24. Ibid.
25. Boyle, *Hydrostatical Discourse, in Works*, 3: 622-3.
26. *A Letter from Dr. More to J. G. giving him an Account how M: Stubb Belies him*, in Joseph Glanvill, *A Prefatory Answer to Mr. Henry Stubbe*, 155.
27. Ibid. For further discussion, see Allison Coudert's paper in this volume.
28. *A Letter from Dr. More*, 156.
29. Ibid.
30. More,"Ad Artic. 35": "Qui fit ut Planetae omnes in eodem non circumgyruntur plano (videlicet in plano Eclipticae), maculaeque adeo solares, aut saltem in planis Eclipticae parallelis; ipsaque Luna, aut in Aequatore aut in plano Aequatori parallelo, cum a nulla interna vi dirigantur, sed externo tantum ferantur impetu?" *AT (NP)*, 5: 386.
31. More, *A Letter ... to J.G.*, 156-7.
32. More, *DD*, I: 34, 39.
33. More, *IS*, 275.
34. e.g. *Conway Letters*, p.269.
35. [Isaac Newton], "An Account of the Book entituled *Commercium Epistolicum,*" *Philosophical Transactions*, 29 (1715): 223. Facsimile in A. Rupert Hall, *Philosophers at War: the Quarrel Between Newton and Leibniz* (Cambridge: Cambridge University Press, 1980), 313.
36. *Rohault's System of Natural Philosophy, illustrated with Dr. S[amuel] Clarke's Notes*, trans. John Clarke (London, 1723), 1: 45, note.
37. The *loci classici* are E. A. Burtt, *The Metaphysical Foundations of Modern Science* and Koyré, *Closed World*.
38. *Isaaci Barrow Lectiones Mathematicae XXIII*, (London 1684), translated by John Kirby as *The Usefulness of Mathematical Learning Explained and Demonstrated* (London, 1734). See W. Whewell, *Mathematical Works of Isaac Barrow*, (Cambridge: Cambridge University Press, 1860).
39. J. E. McGuire and M. Tammny, *Certain Philosophical Questions: Newton's Trinity Notebook* (Cambridge: Cambridge University Press, 1983).
40. Richard S. Westfall, *Force in Newton's Physics* (London: MacDonald and Co., 1971).
41. Ernan McMullin, *Newton on Matter and Activity* (Notre Dame and London: University of Notre Dame Press, 1978).
42. Marie Boas Hall, *The Mechanical Philosophy* (New York: Arno Press, 1981; reprint from *Osiris* 10(1952) and , *Isis* 40(1949)).
43. Newton, *Opticks*, 4th ed. (London 1730; reprint New York: Dover Publications, 1952), 388-9.
44. Ibid., 400-1.
45. Westfall, *Force*, 377-8. I first drew attention to More's name in this notebook more than forty years ago, *Cambridge Historical Journal* 9 (1948): 238-50.
46. Westfall, *Force*, 337.
47. More, *CSPW*, Preface, xiv-xv. This quotation gives occasion to remark upon the (to me) strange infrequency of references to Kenelm Digby in More's works. 'Sympathy' for More

embraced what we still call the sympathetic vibration of two strings in resonance - yet another physical phenomenon that he regarded as inexplicable upon mechanical principles.

48. See Hall, *Philosophers at War*, 314.
49. Newton, *Opticks*, note 29, 401-2.
50. Ibid.
51. Westfall, *Force*, 398.
52. *Principia* (1713) *ad fin*.
53. Hélène Metzger, *Attraction universelle et religion naturelle chez quelques commentateurs anglais de Newton* (Paris: Hermann & Cie, 1938), 75, note 6.
54. Koyré, 160.
55. S.E. Toulmin, "Criticism in the History of Science: Newton on Absolute Space, Time and Motion," *Philosophical Review* 68 (1959): 214.
56. Ibid.
57. W. Von Leyden, *Seventeenth-Century Metaphysics*, 259-60.
58. R. S. Westfall, "Newton and the Hermetic Tradition," in A. G. Debus (ed.) *Science, Medicine and Society in the Renaissance* (London: Heinneman, 1972), 2: 183-98; idem, "The Role of Alchemy in Newton's Career," in M. L. Righini Bonelli and W. R. Shea (eds.) *Reason, Experiment and Mysticism in the Scientific Revolution* (New York: Science History Publications, 1975), 189-232.
59. J. E. Mc Guire, "Neoplatonism and Active Principles," 132.
60. Ibid., 104.
61. I hope to make a fuller study of this and other matters briefly considered in this paper, elsewhere.

XIV

HUYGENS AND NEWTON

ON THE TENTH of July 1689 four men set off from Hampton Court for London at seven in the morning, in order to recommend William III to appoint one of them as Provost of King's College, Cambridge, though he was obviously unqualified by statute to fill this office.[1] The supplicant for office was Isaac Newton, Lucasian Professor of Mathematics in the University of Cambridge; one of his companions was Christiaan Huygens, then residing with his brother Constantijn on a visit to England. Christiaan knew England well, and had attended meetings of the Royal Society (of which he was a Fellow)[2] a quarter of a century before; but he had met Newton at the Royal Society for the very first time only three weeks earlier. So for a moment these two giants of seventeenth century physical science were brought face to face together, the Dutchman doing a kindness to the Englishman before their common king and stadtholder.

Let me try to enfold some of the long series of events that culminated in this encounter between Newton and Huygens, events some of which are of far greater importance than this brief meeting. For it would certainly not have occurred without the Glorious Revolution of the previous year, which had brought the younger Constantijn Huygens to London in the service of William III. Christiaan would not have come to James II's England. Then very likely the two men would never have met if Issaac Newton had not published, in the year before the Revolution, the *Philosophiae naturalis principia mathematica*, since it was this great work that brought Newton out of the academic seclusion and the chemical exercises into which he had been plunged for the previous ten years. The world had almost forgotten about Mr Newton of Cambridge, until the astronomer Edmond Halley rediscovered him. The *Principia*, of course, Huygens had already read. Then I think it is possible that he would not have been travelling with Newton but for a certain Nicholas Fatio de Duillier, a young Swiss mathematician, who on his way north had made friends first with Huygens at the Hague, and then with Newton in Cambridge; Fatio was the third man in this mathematical coach (or barge). And of course Huygens would not have been there, probably, if besides being of a noble Dutch family, distinguished son of a distinguished father, he had not been the second best applied mathematician in Europe, Newton being the best. Long before, in 1673, Christiaan Huygens had published his masterpiece, *Horologium oscillatorium*, which Newton knew and admired. I have had the good fortune to examine, far from here, a copy of this book that Huygens presented to Newton, just as Newton in turn was to present the Dutch physicist with a copy of his *Principia*.

Now Huygens came from the great aristocracy of Europe, and Newton was of the smallest class of landed gentry. Moreover, being the senior by thirteen years and a precocious child, Huygens was already renowned throughout Europe when young Isaac was still a schoolboy. In the year of Newton's 'prime of invention', 1666, Huygens was receiving flattering offers from the King of France – or rather his great minister Colbert – which caused him to pass nineteen years of his life as an Academician in Paris. Before this happened, indeed, Christiaan had already visited London twice – while Newton was a Cambridge undergraduate communing with his notebooks – but again we may doubt, I believe, whether the journey with Newton would have taken place had Huygens not been for so long an outstanding member of scientific circles in Paris, because the relations between those circles and the Royal Society were particularly close during the 1660's and 1670's.

You may wonder, when I have said this, what Christiaan Huygens has to do with Anglo-*Dutch* intellectual relations. True, he wrote largely in French or in Latin, he played his academic rôle in the Bibliothèque du Roi of the Palais Royal and he gave technical advice to Louis' great minister. But Huygens was never other than Dutch. Many of his familial letters are composed in the language of his country. He wept over her sufferings. He gloried in her triumphs, intellectual and military. He never lost touch with the able men of his nation, like Antoni van Leeuwenhoek or Nicholas Witsen. And in the end he broke his tie with France. For all that national labels matter in the seventeenth century, we may reckon Huygens a Netherlander, with a deep allegiance to the mathematical and scientific tradition of his own country, despite his long and creative sojourn in Paris. Certainly Huygens was not a man to forget Simon Stevin, nor Willebrord Snell the 'Eratosthenes Batavus', nor Franz van Schooten and Johann Hudde, and the importance of the early followers of Descartes at the University of Utrecht.

Yet when this has been said Isaac Newton was far more narrowly an Englishman than Christiaan Huygens was a Netherlander. He could neither write nor speak French, he never travelled outside England, and he was deeply imbued with that sense of the superiority of the English intellect which (as Huygens complained) made Englishmen unjustly reluctant to recognise the merits of foreigners, claiming all things for their own nation. Before the Revolution he moved little in the great world and few foreigners could claim his acquaintance. Huygens' birthright was an *entrée* to the highest level of international society. His father, the elder Constantijn, 'the most brilliant figure in Dutch literary history . . . the jewel and ornament of Dutch liberty' devoted a long life of diplomatic service to the Republic, was not only Secretary to the Stadtholder but a poet of great renown, and corresponded with all the literary men of Europe. The son, his 'youthful Archimedes', crowned his early reputation as a mathematician by his discovery of the first known satellite of Saturn and his elegant elucidation of that planet's curious structure. We may judge something of his intellectual environment by the reception accorded to the letter addressed to Paris – a city which the young Huygens had visited three years before – wherein he announced his new theory of Saturn; according to the influential Jean Chapelain there were present at the meeting of the Académie Montmor when the letter was read aloud by him (in May 1658) more than forty persons, among them two '*Cordons Bleus* . . . both Secretaries of State, several Abbés of the nobility, several Maîtres des Requêtes, Conseillers du Parlement, officers of the Chambre des Comptes, Doctors of the Sorbonne, several noble amateurs, many mathematicians and numerous men of letters . . .'[3] News of Huygens' investigation of Saturn reached England more slowly, but it was there greeted with no less applause. From Florence Leopold de Medici eagerly sought his correspondence, and his new theory was, of course, also discussed by the great Danzig astronomer, Johannes Hevelius[4].

From this time, with his invention of the pendulum clock following very soon thereafter, Huygens was a public scientific figure, not merely a member of the Royal Academy of Science in Paris, but its acknowledged leader.

I emphasize this point because it is necessary to our understanding of the first controversy between Huygens and Newton, in which the differences between the two kinds of science for which they stood appeared at once. We must remember that Huygens was the senior man, speaking for an established position. His general metaphysics of nature was very close to that of Descartes, certainly he was a 'mechanical philosopher' even to the extent that he seems to have been privately unable to acknowledge the existence of a God. Like Descartes, though not imitating him in detail, Huygens assigned many of the more mysterious phenomena of nature to the operations of an omnipresent aether (if I may use an anachronistic term) which was the real source of what might popularly be called 'forces' or 'attractions' or 'radiations'. So far, then, Huygens went along with the rising tide of Cartesian philosophy or (to speak more broadly) French rationalism. Of course, Cartesian science and philosophy were by no means so firmly and widely established in the early 1670's (when neither Rohault nor Malebranche nor Fontenelle had yet written) as they were to be at the close of the century, but they already constituted the 'advanced' point of view. In his methodology, however, Huygens was neither a Cartesian nor a rationalist of any sort, and here he was much closer in sympathy to the empiricism of the Royal Society. As a mathematical and experimental physicist and as an observational astronomer Huygens had little liking for the hypothetical models so elaborately constructed by Descartes. Virtually every detail of his picture of the physical universe is therefore non-Cartesian to some degree, although his attachment to the fundamental ideas of Descartes meant that he could never attain the revolutionary independence of Newton.

The influence of Descartes had penetrated into England also, where intellectual life during the middle years of the seventeenth century was broadly eclectic, receptive to the various 'modernist' writers of Italy, France and Germany.[5] While there was one declared English Gassendist – the physician Walter Charleton – there was no dedicated English exponent of Descartes, but his influence may be detected in many English scientists, including Newton himself. The English in general and Newton in particular were more strongly inclined towards the atomist variant of the mechanical philosophy than was Huygens, and were strongly inclined to temper their admiration for Descartes' hypothetical models by their awareness of Francis Bacon's precepts and the examples of Gilbert and Harvey. Since in the 1660's (the early years of the Royal Society) Huygens was above all known as a skilled constructor of telescopes and clocks, an able observer and a theorist in mechanics, his position in science seemed comfortably close to that taking shape in England.

In 1669, for instance, he was one of three men (the others being John Wallis and Christopher Wren) invited to lay his analysis of collision phenomena before the Royal Society. Collision, the impact of fundamental particle of matter upon fundamental particle, constitutes the basic phenomenon of Cartesian physics[6]. There is no sign that Huygens and the two Englishmen differed in their awareness of this, nor in their recognition that the laws of collision had been very imperfectly stated by Descartes himself.

Less than three years later, in January 1672, Huygens began to learn of the optical investigations of Isaac Newton, first his construction of a practical, though miniature, reflecting telescope, then his new theory of light and colour. As to the former, Huygens lost no time in making his own trials and soon learned the difficulties of forming in metal a useful optical surface of any size; it is a great pity that he did not continue to attack this problem, as he did that of the construction of large refractors, because he might thus have accelerated the practical introduction of the reflector by some half-century. As to Newton's theoretical investigations, Huygens at once detected in them elements incompatible with his own deepest apprehensions of the universe. To put it crudely, where Huygens was an aetherist, Newton was an atomist. A particulate or emission theory of light is obviously quite irreconcilable with the Descartes-Huygens conception of a universe full of rotating aether. In the former light is a *substance* – and Newton hinted as much in his first optical paper of 1672 – in the latter a *motion*, and we may suppose that Newton preferred the former view because of his strong Epicurean leanings and his conviction that only bodies can travel along straight lines.[7]

The optical controversy between Huygens and Newton furnishes an emphatic example of the limitations of empiricism. By this time (1672) Newton's researches into optics were some eight years old, and he had by him the manuscript of the lectures on the subject that he had given at Cambridge. But as Sabra has pointed out, Newton's first paper contained none of the necessary geometrical optics, nor even clear accounts of his principal experiments. Thus, though it was evident to his readers that Newton believed light to be a substance, and that heterogeneous white light was composed of homogeneous coloured constituents, it was not apparent to them why these conclusions were supposed to follow from the experiments which they only partially comprehended. Huygens did understand that Newton's experiments seemed to show that each coloured ray had a given tendency towards refraction, that is, a blue ray will always be more refracted than a red ray; and so because of this dispersion of the rays of white light (as we call it) the spectral colours are separated out one from another whenever white light is refracted. But Huygens could not agree that this phenomenon entitled Newton to maintain further that 'Colours are not qualifications of light, derived from refractions, or reflections of natural bodies (as 'tis generally believed) but original and connate properties, which in divers rays are divers'. I do not wholly agree with Sabra[8] that it was illogical of Newton to make this claim, for it seems to me that Newton was only saying that we should attribute the same degree of complexity to light before refraction as after refraction; it can hardly be the case that refraction *adds* complexity to simple light while *removing* it from compounded light.[9] Basically, Huygens agreed with this. His criticism was that if white light were so highly complex as Newton supposed – an individual ray for each colour – 'there would still remain the great difficulty of explaining by the mechanical philosophy what this diversity of colours consists of'.[10] It was therefore simpler to postulate only one or two variables in white light, whose modification by refraction might produce the multiple colours. He himself preferred to suppose that the two variables corresponded to 'blue' and 'yellow', and that all other colours, including white, were produced by quantitative intensification and diminution of these two together. Refraction would then be a process distributing the quantities of these two variables. Hence, he maintained, Newton had not discussed a new fact about light, but a very plausible hypothesis. Newton's rejoinders finally led Huygens to complain that Newton maintained his opinion with too much emotion and that he would dispute with him no more.[11]

Huygens saw only those of Newton's optical writings that appeared in the *Philosophical Transactions*, for although besides *Lectiones opticae* the *Opticks* itself was completed in

Huygens' lifetime, neither was printed. Likewise, Newton could have read nothing of Huygens' early work in optics until it was posthumously published in 1703. Huygens had begun his treatise on dioptrics in his youth, in 1652, and introduced his wave-theory into it after the appearance of Newton's paper, that is, in 1672–3;[12] but as everyone knows the wave-theory was first explained to the Académie of Science in Paris in 1678 and printed in 1690 – Huygens sent a copy of the book to Newton. This *Traité de la Lumière* contains nothing on colour and only the barest allusion to Newton's discovery of dispersion as the cause of chromatic aberration in lenses; its subject is the geometry of the propagation of coherent waves, that is of monochromatic light. Huygens' great success was in showing that his geometric construction could account for the position of both the ordinary and the extraordinary ray in the double-refraction of Icelandic spa. But he could not account for *all* the phenomena. In an *Addition* to the original *Traité* (to which I shall return later) Huygens tried to refute the objection which Newton had meanwhile raised (in *Principia*, Book II, Prop. 42) that waves must necessarily 'spread into the shadow'. His arguments are not conclusive; neither he nor Newton realized the significance of diffraction patterns in this context.

Returning the compliment, when he came to publish *Opticks* long after Huygens' death Newton added in the *Queries* an account of double-refraction derived from the *Traité*, but lacking any geometric construction for the extraordinary ray such as Huygens had given. However, Newton's suggestion of assymetries in *all* rays (before and after refraction) provided a better qualitative model of the phenomena, analogous to the latter concept of polarization.

I have necessarily treated these exchanges in a very cursory manner, but even so I hope the difference between two 'styles' of scientific thinking has become fairly apparent. A little closer examination would show, for example, the areas where Huygens employs a mathematical analysis while Newton does not, and vice versa. Note too that Huygens does not deny Newton's discovery of dispersion, though he thinks it a less serious imperfection in lens-systems than Newton did; but it is to him an incidental while to Newton it serves as the determining criterion of a new explanation. Neither experiment nor argument was at this time able to determine crucial issues: does light travel more quickly in water or in air? Is white light compound or homogeneous? Can a wave-train propagate in a straight line without excessive dissipation? If the two parties could not agree to treat all such questions as undecided, it was clearly because (for other reasons) they were committed to their respective 'aetherist' and 'atomist' preconceptions. It is curious that on one point, at least, Newton recognized a potential weakness in his contention for the materiality of light; it would (he recognized) be an adequate model to imagine the various colours differing in frequency and wavelength, so that white would be a mixture of all kinds of vibrations travelling at the same speed. In the last resort his best argument against Huygens' wave-theory was that of Proposition 42, repeated in what became Query 28 of *Opticks*, and of course his universal rejection of the Cartesian aether. But this involved him, and would involve us, in other difficulties which I cannot consider now.

Looking ahead to the eighteenth century one sees the same antithesis – virtually the antithesis between the Aristotelian and the Platonic view of nature – projected far into the future. I need hardly remind you that Newton's materialist idea of light was never completely successful, and that he was compelled to elaborate it by adding an undulatory component. While the English rapidly became convinced Newtonians, on the continent the accuracy of his experiments was doubted into the last years of his life. And long afterwards Euler and others continued to maintain the alternative theory of Huygens, which (with Newton's own undulatory concepts) was in turn taken up by Thomas Young. Note the continuing Platonism of wave-theory; neither Euler nor Young were great experimentalists, and it was a Newtonian, John Dolland, who solved empirically the problem of chromatic aberration. Even in the case of Fresnel the experiments he performed on diffraction were less crucially significant than his mathematical work.

At about the same time as that of which I was speaking just now, that is in 1673, there appeared the book which is universally recognised as the chief production of Huygens' career in science, *Horologium oscillatorium*. In part this is an extension of Huygens' earlier book called simply *Horologium* ('The Clock'), published in 1658, which described the earliest form of his pendulum clock, not yet employing the cycloidal restraining cheeks devised in the following year when Huygens discovered the isochronal property of the cycloidal arc.[13] *Horologium oscillatorium* describes the later clock, and gives elaborate mathematical analyses of the oscillatory and isochronal motion involved in it. Huygens' analysis of the movement of bodies, deriving directly from that of Galileo in the *Discorsi* (1638), goes on to develop considerably greater subtlety, in fact (if we except the theory of collision in which Huygens also had a share, as I have briefly mentioned) Huygens' theoretical mechanics here represents the first important extension of the Galilean science.

Passing over the purely mathematical interest of *Horologium oscillatorium*, one finds that Huygens' dealt with three chief problems in theoretical mechanics: (i) the proof that free oscillation in a cycloidal arc is isochronous; (ii) the determination of the centre of oscillation of a compound (that is, a physical) pendulum; (iii) the determination of the centrifugal force resulting from the revolutions of bodies.[14]

In relation to (i) and (ii), the cycloid and central force, the work of Huygens bears close comparison with that of Newton. As regards (ii), centres of oscillation, I need only remark now that this again illustrates the closeness of Huygens' relation to the Royal Society, for he sent 'coded' forms of these theorems to the Society in 1669 along with his theorems on cycloidal motion.[15] The determination of the centre of oscillation was also investigated by the Society's President, Lord Brouncker.

Now it goes without saying that in these comparisons of the mechanical investigations of Huygens and Newton there is no discrepancy as to the results, but the methods of reaching them are quite distinct. Huygens' attitude of mind is consistently more Platonic, Newton's more Aristotelian, or to be more precise Huygens in general preferred kinematic arguments, Newton dynamic ones. The former, it has been said recently: 'held the very concept of force under suspicion for the occult tendencies he felt to be implicit in it'.[16] And of course to do so was perfectly Cartesian for, when all phenomena were properly to be explained by the impact of subtle particles, to think of matter *attracting* or *repelling* matter (whether the 'force' be gravity, magnetism or electricity) was to invoke an occult notion. Hence for Huygens gravity becomes equivalent to weight; kinematically, we describe the fall of weights by saying that they are uniformly accelerated, but we do not need to invoke gravity as the name of the force which makes bodies weighty. So Huygens' proof that the tautochrone is identical with the 'common cycloid' is concerned only with comparisons of velocities, not comparisons of forces producing accelerations.[17]

How different is Newton's method in *Principia*, Book I, Propositions 51 to 56: here

Newton's point of departure is the magnitude of the accelerating force at each point of a hypocycloid, on the assumption of a centripetal force directed towards the centre of the fixed circle.[18] Then he transforms the fixed circle into a straight line, its centre (now the centre of the Earth) recedes to infinity, the force becomes uniform, and as Newton remarks the situation becomes the same as that discussed by Huygens, since the hypocycloid is transformed into a common cycloid.

It is virtually certain that this dynamical analysis of Newton's was not conceived by him at the time of writing the *Principia*, for it appears already in a single fragment of his devoted to exactly the same subject; whether this fragment was written before Newton had read *Horologium oscillatorium* or not it must surely belong to about the time of the publication of Huygens' book. Here already Newton argues by a comparison of proportionality between lines representing the force of gravity and other lines representing instantaneous rates of acceleration: that is to say, dynamically. Newton's statement that the force at any point P (and therefore the acceleration) is proportional to the distance of P from the centre of the cycloid C is, obviously, tantamount to saying (in our terms) that this is a case of simple harmonic motion (Fig. 3). It is not surprising that Huygens' thoughts exactly paralleled Newton's on this point, though not in *Horologium oscillatorium*, for in a note written, presumably, soon after the publication of that book Huygens states the same relation: the gravity is as the arc-length CP[19]. And though his first demonstration of this is statical, he goes on to a truly dynamical argument employing the term 'incitatio' as a synonym for 'force', a term analogous to the 'conatus' of freely falling bodies towards the centre of the Earth.[20]

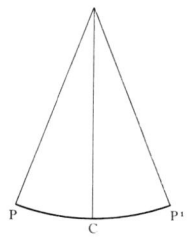

Figure 3 Motion of a pendulum in a cycloid.

Like Newton, Huygens when studying rotary motion introduced the idea of central force; he wrote a treatise *De vi centrifuga* as early as 1659, but this again remained unknown to the world until after he was dead, and in fact Huygens' investigations in this part of mechanics were known to his contemporaries only from the bare summary of theorems appended to *Horologium oscillatorium* in 1673. The reasoning behind these theorems was concealed. Newton of course acknowledged Huygens' priority in the comparison of rotational force with force of gravity, 'in his excellent book on the pendulum clock'.[21] Nevertheless – and this is a point that is generally known – there is an important difference between the conceptions of Newton and Huygens. Both began with the notion that a revolving heavy body – a stone in a sling – acquires an inherent force, 'the force of a body's motion' Newton called it in his earliest notes, by which it strives to fly off from the restricting circle along the tangent;[22] both computed the magnitude of this force by considering the acceleration denoted by the increasing intercepts between the circle and the tangent. But while Huygens always thought of the force accelerating the body away from the centre – at the moment when the sling is released – the mature Newton considered the force required in the opposite sense to retain the body in its circular orbit, that is the inwards pull of the string. Hence Huygens introduced the term *centrifugal* force and Newton in contradistinction spoke of *centripetal* force.

Of course quantitatively we might say from a positivist point of view, there is no difference between the two conceptions, for there is none in the calculations. Like Newton, Huygens attempted to calculate the ratio between the centrifugal force of the Earth's axial rotation and gravity. Like Newton again he was to compute by the same sort of argument the ratio between the Earth's axial and equatorial diameters. And so forth. As Dr. Whiteside has expressed it: 'This continued parallelism of much of Newton's and Huygens' mathematical thought is no accident: many of their contemporaries were educated in the same intellectual tradition and had access to the same published literature, but only James Gregory possibly had the same quality of mind and mathematical ability to explore the subtleties of the new science of continuous motion in time'.[23]

And of course as regards their physical ideas too Huygens and Newton were common heirs of Galileo and Descartes though (as we are discovering) Huygens remained far more faithful to the latter than did Newton. To explore *all* these close parallelisms would be tedious. Consider, as an example, the first two laws of motion as formulated by Huygens and Newton, both of course modelling themselves on Descartes.

NEWTON'S FIRST LAW OF MOTION, 1687

Corpus omne perseverare in statu suo quiescendi vel movendi uniformiter *in directum*, nisi quatenus a viribus impressis cogitur statum illum mutare.

HUYGENS' VERSION, 1675/76

Un corps qui a acquis une certaine vitesse de mouvement, continue d'aller avec cette mesme vitesse s'il n'y a rien qui agisse a diminuer son mouvement, ni rien qui l'incite de nouveau.

NEWTON'S SECOND LAW, 1687

Mutationem motus proportionalem esse vi motrici impressae, & fieri *secundem lineam rectam* qua via illa imprimitur.

HUYGENS' VERSION, 1675/76

Si quelque chose agit continuellement a diminuer le mouvement d'un corps, qui est en mouvement, il perdra peu a peu de sa vitesse. Et au contraire si quelque chose agit continuellement sur un corps en le poussant du costè vers le quel il se meut desia, son mouvement recevra continuellement de l'acceleration.

(*Oeuvres Complètes*, XVIII, p.496)

The observant mind will note that Huygens' version, taken from an unpublished draft, omits the crucial restriction included by Newton (and indeed by Descartes before). I am inclined to believe that Huygens, like Galileo, preserved an attachment to the idea of the 'naturalness' of circular motion, which of course agrees with the idea of centrifugal force being as 'natural' as gravity itself; indeed, as we shall see, for Huygens gravity is the *consequence* of centrifugal force. Again, we may note that Huygens' conception of 'incitatio' – a word as I have remarked unique to himself – is one of generalised mechanical force; he poses the hypothesis that though two incitations may arise from quite different causes, if they accelerate two equal bodies equally they will produce the same motion.[24] In a much more complex and detailed way for which there is no time now we might compare Huygens' and Newton's investigations of resisted motion, which again are closely similar. And so forth.

However, it has been said of Huygens that in his mechanical investigations he distrusted, indeed avoided, dynamics; that he sought to eliminate dynamical concepts (though as we have just seen his very analysis of problems brought them to his mind) in order to reduce all mechanics to statics or kinematics.[25] I think it is possible to exaggerate the importance of this point, not only for positivistic reasons but because (as I have indicated) parallels between Huygens' and Newton's use of dynamical arguments can be found. When Huygens discusses resisted motion, for example, he necessarily argues dynamically, and he does so also in his treatment of the compound pendulum. On the other hand there are examples where he chooses a kinematic argument for preference.

All this would seem less significant if we were not aware that Newton developed a mechanical theory of the lunar and planetary motions, of the tides and so forth which Huygens did not; if, in other words, at least as a procedural step, Newton had not been willing to identify the centripetal force of gravity with an attraction of matter for matter. We know, of course, how strongly Newton insisted that the word 'attraction' was only a *façon de parler*; that he did not mean to say what the cause of gravity was, still less that brute matter could act at a distance on brute matter. Nevertheless, it is clear that Newton could handle centripetal force in a way that Huygens could not handle centrifugal force. Consider the very first proposition of the *Principia*:

> The areas which revolving bodies describe by radii drawn to an immovable centre of force do lie in the same immovable planes, and are proportional to the times in which they are described.

Huygens, of course, never disputed the correctness of Newton's geometrical argument. But equally he would never have formulated such a proposition himself; he would not have conceived of bodies being driven in towards a centre of force; rather they strove always to escape from the centre. The whole physical concept of a centripetal force, of an attraction, was repugnant to Huygens. When Fatio de Duillier wrote to Huygens (in June 1687) an account of the still unpublished *Principia* he confessed, despite the fine propositions he had seen:

> je souhaitterois que l'Auteur vous eut un peu consulté sur ce principe d'attraction qu'il suppose entre les corps celestes.

To this Huygens replied that he did not mind Newton's being anti-Cartesian:

'pourveu qu'il ne nous fasse pas des suppositions comme celle de l'attraction.'[26]

And a few years later, after reading the *Principia* itself and approving so much in it, he restated his own neo-Cartesian view of gravity in his *Discours sur la cause de la pesanteur* (1690). A positivist might say: does this matter? Wouldn't the calculations made by a Newton and a Huygens always agree? This is true; but we may also suspect that Huygens could never have been brought, against his mistrust of attraction, to discover for himself how to make such calculations.

When Newton received from Henry Oldenburg the copy of *Horologium oscillatorium* destined for him, he wrote with his thanks that he had found the book 'full of very subtile & usefull speculations very worthy of the Author'. And alluding to the bare theorems at the end with which we have been concerned, Newton went on: 'I am glad that we are to expect another discours of the *vis centrifuga*, which speculation may prove of good use in naturall Philosophy & Astronomy as well as in mechanicks'.[27] Now it would be as wrong to infer that in 1673 Newton had himself made much progress in the application of mechanics to astronomy, as that he was indebted to Huygens for his knowledge of central forces, but at least we can judge that Newton could already foresee what Huygens *might* have done along that path which he was to follow himself more than a decade later. Huygens did not, in fact, take the kind of steps Newton foresaw as possible and which Newton himself was to take; partly because of his attachment to Cartesianism, partly because he preferred kinematics to dynamics, but partly also because he was personally less vigorous in the last years of his life, because he never completed another major treatise for publication, and partly in the end because he was less inventive in mathematics than Newton. It is not for me to attempt any comparison of the mathematical prowess of these two men, but let us at least clear out of the way any supposition that Newton employed fluxions or the differential calculus in writing the *Principia*. He did not, but he did use closely analogous geometrical methods, and he used his method of series.[28] Huygens too was an immensely capable mathematician, attaining results, notably integrations, by great ingenuity, but he was more restricted than Newton. Allow me to quote the Dutch historian E. J. Dijksterhuis,[29] who emphasises Huygens' strict adherence to the Greek concepts of mathematical rigour:

> Adhering to the habits followed by the Greek mathematicians and especially observed with unwavering consistency by his guiding-star, Archimedes, he allows no trace of the many heuristically fruitful, but logically unaccountable methods that mathematicians will apply in making their discoveries, to be seen in the publication of his results. In particular, every vestige of an unrigorous treatment of infinite processes, as applied with scruple and with notable success in the so-called method of indivisibles, has to be effaced.

Huygens excelled in manipulation of the ancient mathematics; he was its greatest master since Archimedes, but its methods were too cumbersome for contemporary problems in either pure or applied mathematics. The result was that Huygens preferred to investigate by non-rigorous methods and to leave his investigations unpublished because (as Dijksterhuise puts it) 'it meant an ever-increasing self-conquest always to take pains to compose a rigorous demonstration'. As we all know, James Gregory, Isaac Newton and Gottfried Wilhelm Leibniz developed new methods – Leibniz particularly new algorithms – to enable mathematicians to differentiate and integrate readily; but these methods were not demonstrably rigorous and Huygens distrusted them; in any case he learned of them too late for their influence to be effective. Thus, though Huygens demonstrated great ingenuity in the solution of difficult problems in mechanics, his conservative attitude towards rigour both prevented his succeeding with some problems and obstructed publication of his successes. Instead of Huygens, Newton became – as even Leibniz never denied – the first to display the success of new approaches to mathematics in its applications to problems of mechanics. It is curious to reflect that it was indeed applied mathematics – the *Principia* – that forced Newton's work on pure mathematics out into the open.

Time does not permit me to dwell on the last scientific exchanges between Newton and Huygens, which took place in August 1689 as a consequence of the personal meetings with which this lecture began.[30] Newton submitted to Huygens some further explanation of his treatment of motion in a resisting medium in the *Principia*, upon which Huygens wrote critical comments. In this field of rational fluid mechanics – related experimentally to the motion of bodies in air or water – Huygens again preceded Newton by many years (1668 as compared with 1684) but in the end Newton was to outstrip Huygens' analysis, and of course to publish, which Huygens did not do. Again, one feels that Newton had besides greater mathematical power, greater flexibility, where Huygens still retained Cartesian physical preconceptions. Hence, once more, they failed to agree wholly in the rational analysis of a natural phenomenon; nor, by the way, did Huygens agree with Leibniz's views on the same topic. In fact my impression is that in the last years of his life Huygens' sympathies were rather with the Englishman, although he had known the German far better twenty years before in Paris.

Huygens' public reaction to the *Principia* emerged in the *Addition* appended to his *Discours de la Cause de la Pesanteur*. It is almost uniformly flattering to Newton, but Huygens does not conceal the deep division between his physical principles and those of Newton. He did not deny that Newton had propounded true laws of gravitation and in so far as these laws governed celestial mechanics there was no difficulty (as he saw it in substituting for a Newtonian centripetal force acting between the heavenly bodies a Cartesian centrifugal force in the aether driving them towards their centres of revolution. But he could not allow – as Newton did, and made mathematical use of the fact – that such forces between gross bodies were the summation of particulate forces acting between the least parts of matter. For of course interparticulate forces (such as Newton invoked in Book I, Section XII) cannot be explained by Cartesian vortices. In Huygens' words, speaking of the difference in the results obtained by himself and Newton in computing the Earth's axial shortening due to rotation: 'je ne suis pas d'accord d'un Principe qu'il suppose dans ce calcul et ailleurs; qui est, que toutes les petites parties, qu'on peut imaginer dans deux ou plusieurs different corps, s'attirent ou tendent à s'approcher mutuellement. Ce que je ne scaurois admettre, par ce que je crois voir clairement, que la cause d'une telle attraction n'est point explicable par aucun principe de Mechanique, ni des regles du mouvement'.[31]

Here again we have Huygens' distrust of dynamics combined with his distrust of infinitesimal arguments and reinforced by his Cartesian rationalism. Perhaps that means he was a better philosopher than Newton; certainly in seventeenth century terms he was a more orthodox one than Newton, as Leibniz was to proclaim later.

I am sorry too that I have not found time to speak of Huygens' friendship with other Fellows of the Royal Society, and the interactions of his work with theirs. From his early exchanges with John Wallis relating to mathematics in the 1650's, his friendship with Sir Robert Moray and (later) Henry Oldenburg in the 1660's and early 1670's, to his interchanges with Robert Boyle on the subject of pneumatics, Christiaan Huygens was a constant participant in English scientific life. He was esteemed in this country for his discoveries, for his intelligence and empirical skill, and for the fairness of his judgement. Unlike Newton, Huygens was a man without enemies. Though he found the English difficult in social relations, and excessively insular in their intellectual pride, he charmed everyone except Robert Hooke. His own first impressions of English life and manners were less happy. 'I told you' he wrote to his brother Lodewijk from the Hague in June 1661, 'I told you that I did not find my stay in London so charming as you apparently did, since you still manifest so much eagerness to return there. I foresee that we shall have a great dispute about that, for I shall always maintain that the stink of the smoke is unbearable there, and very unhealthy, that the city is ill built, the streets narrow and badly paved, nothing but mean buildings. For when all's said this piazza and all the "common garden" is trifling, nothing to what one sees in Paris. The people there are melancholic, the gentlefolk polite enough but not very sociable, the women very little conversable and not by any means so witty or so lively as in France; but perhaps things were different when you were there, and there is some likelihood that after the re-establishment of the Court one will see some sort of civilized behaviour return. I may say, moreover, that I had to do with very decent people most of whom had travelled in France and elsewhere, who invited me out, dined me and paid for everything most handsomely. I even talked very boldly to those who knew only the language of their country, and made myself pretty well understood'.[32]

In this last respect Huygens was fortunate; for the English were certainly even worse linguists then than they are today. Nor are his criticisms so severe as those of a young Frenchman coming from Caen ten years later, who also contrasts the freedom of social intercourse in France with what he found in England, where if 'one visits ladies they are either dumb or plunged into the utmost solemnity . . . As for the men there is no close acquaintance with them except glass in one hand and pipe in the other, drinking like fish and smoking like dragons'.[33]

The chief topics of scientific interest during Huygens' first visit to London were pneumatic experiments and astronomy. Huygens was compelled to have his best telescope lens sent over from The Hague to London in the diplomatic bag, in order that he might exhibit its powers to the English virtuosi; the instrument was set up in the garden behind Whitehall and the Duke of York with his wife came to inspect the Moon and Saturn through it several times. On the third of May a transit of Mercury occurred which Huygens and others observed in London at the house of the instrument-maker Richard Reeves. There is no doubt that Huygens was impressed by the enthusiasm of the Royal Society group.

During his second visit to London from June to October 1663 Huygens was even more occupied with the Royal Society, of which he then became a Fellow, and where his discovery of the anomalous suspension of mercury – an effect of surface tension – proved of great interest, because it seemed to contravene the idea of atmospheric pressure. In his own letters, however, Christiaan seems more concerned with mastering the technique of pastel drawing employed by the artist Peter Lely. On this longer visit he seems to have found the language more of a barrier; it impeded his enjoyment of the London theatre and discouraged his visits to an extremely gifted lady lutanist. 'Only before certain persons like Mr Moray and Mr Brereton and a few others', he writes, 'do I dare to unfold what I know. I found the latter at Gresham College [that is, the Royal Society] of which he is a member, and I found him become so huge and fat that I hardly knew him . . . I have been to see him at home, where he treated me to his music, which is the most agreeable in the world, for without ever having learned the notes of the harpsichord he plays it with a marvellous confidence, playing nothing but fantasies without any system'.[34] Perhaps this curious music was some compensation for the loss of the fair lutanist, Mrs Warwick.

Sir Robert Moray and Sir William Brereton were old friends from the days of the exiled Stuart court; in his early years as an academician in Paris Huygens became friendly with a young English diplomat in Paris, Francis Vernon. From Vernon we have a poignant glimpse of Huygens' regard for his English colleagues at a moment when, in 1670, the Dutch scientist believed his life coming to an untimely end, with so much unfinished. Calling on him in this condition of desperate illness, Vernon received Huygens' most earnest and solemn entreaty to safeguard certain of his scientific papers:

& thereupon hee reacht out his hand to his breeches which lay upon the bed & tooke out from his Pocquet a little Pacquet sealed & told mee in this Pacquet there are 12 Propositions wch concerne the Doctrine of Motion wth their demonstrations; The anagrams of wch I have formerly sent into England to my Lord Brouncard (a person concerning whom for his great witt & iudgment in Mathematiques I have a long time conceived a very high opinion.) I sent them in those disguised Caracters because It was agreed on between [us,] & iudged by the Royal Society as the most proper way of Proposing those secrets. I gave this Pacquet to you sealed because if it please God that I recover you shall restore it to mee againe in the same fashion that I deliver it to you butt if I die then the seale you shall breake open & the Coppy of the Propositions you shall give to Monsieur Galois Secretaire of the Royall Academie here, the demonstrations there is noe necessity hee should transcribe. There Is one Proposition amongst the rest wch Possibly those in England will not iudge sufficiently demonstrated butt the demonstration of that, I have given fully & at large in some other Papers wch I have left in Monsieur Carcavi's hands. This is what hee said to mee as concerning the sealed Pacquet.

After this Huygens took up another, unsealed, packet of papers inscribed *De Motu per impulsum* which he also gave to Vernon for safe keeping, lamenting that he was not himself in the care of the English physicion Thomas Willis, for the French he said 'have not a right conception of physic', though they were doing their best.

Now I return to Vernon's narrative:[35]

Then hee fell into a discourse concerning the Royal Society in England wch hee said was an assembly of the Choisest Witts in Christendome & of the finest Parts: hee said hee chose rather to depositt those little labours of his wch God had blesst & those pledges wch to him were dearest of any thing in this world, in their hands sooner then in any else. Sooner then of those into whose Society hee was here incorporated & from whom hee had received all demonstrations of a most affectionate civilitie. because hee iudged the Seat of Science to bee fixed there & that the members of it did embrace & promote Philosophy not for interest, not through ambition or a vanity of excelling others, not through fancy or a variable curiosity, butt out of naturall principles of generosity & inclination to Learning & a sincere Respect & love for the truth, wch made him Judge that their constitution would bee therefore more durable because their designes & aimes were soe honourable & that God almighty would give a great stability & blessing to their Labours because hee had inspired them with soe Worthy desires. Whereas hee said hee did foresee the dissolution of this academie because it was mixt wth tinctures of Envy because it was supported upon suppositions of profitt because it wholly depended upon the Humour of a Prince & the favour of a minister, either of wch coming toe relent in their Passions the whole frame & Project of their assembly cometh to Perdition. here hee proceeded to Name severall of the Royal Society for whom hee expresst a singular esteeme the Bishop of Sarisbury, Doctr Wren. Mr Hooke hee termed a man, of a Vast invention & the Bishop of Chester of a most elevated Judgement & a most profound witt & you Mr Oldenbourg hee applauded for a most [*one line crossed out*] and all the whole Society in generall for a most chearfull & unanimous agreement & harmony in the advancing of knowledge wthout wch hee said it was impossible for the most selected body or the most chosen witts long to subsist.

We have no reason to suppose that Vernon's account of these events was materially in error, and I think we may take it as giving a faithful picture of Huygens' opinions of his English colleagues. As we know, Huygens recovered to live another twenty five years; nevertheless he failed to publish the papers on mechanics that he entrusted to Vernon and which (perhaps) we may now read in the *Oeuvres Complètes*. Let us imagine that these papers *had* become known to the world in the 1670's: would the history of science have been materially altered? In the long run, I suppose, not at all. *Horologium oscillatorium* served, in part but only in part, the same function of communication. But it seems to me not unlikely that if Huygens before 1687 had published *more*, Newton would have published *less*. Remember that Newton's was a curious and secretive temperament. We may guess that he was emboldened to write the *Principia* because he was launching into a clear field. Imagine that, on the other hand, Huygens had been the first to occupy this field with his own version of the dynamics of particle motion, of the motions of bodies in resisting media, of the revolution of bodies in an aetherial vortex and his theory of the Earth's shape – would Newton have willingly have confronted Huygens' Cartesian mechanism of the world with his own very different *Principia*? Must we not conclude that in part Newton's success – which induced him to write *Opticks*, moreover – was conditional upon Huygens' reticence?

At any rate, when we imagine these two great men journeying together in July 1689, and talking of mechanics as they must have done, it is obvious who was in the stronger tactical position, for it was Newton who had actually shown the immense power of mathematical principles in natural philosophy. But how easily Huygens might have snatched from Newton not indeed his ideas nor his methods but his right as an innovator in mathematical physics.

NOTES

[1] *Oeuvres Complètes de Christiaan Huygens*, ix: 333, note; xxii: 744. Huygens was in England from 11 June to 24 August.

[2] Huygens was the third Fellow, and the first foreigner, elected (on 23 June) after the election of the Original Fellows on 20 May 1663.

[3] See Harcourt Brown, *Scientific Organizations in Seventeenth Century France (1620-80)* (Baltimore, 1934): 79-84; *Oeuvres Complètes*, ii: 173. A *Cordon Bleu* was not a cook but a member of the Order of the Holy Ghost.

[4] See A. Van Helden in *Notes and Records of the Royal Society*, xxiii (1968): 213-29.

[5] The point is well illustrated by John Wallis's well-known passage on the origins of the Royal Society, conveniently reproduced in Sir Henry Lyons, *The Royal Society, 1660-1940* (Cambridge, 1944): 8-9. See also A. R. Hall and M. B. Hall, *The Correspondence of Henry Oldenburg*, i, passim.

[6] See Hall and Hall, ibid., v: xix, and index, *s.v.* 'Mechanics'; and R. S. Westfall, *Force in Newton's Physics: The Science of Dynamics in the Seventeenth Century* (London, 1971), chap. 4.

[7] See I. A. Sabra, *Theories of Light from Descartes to Newton* (London, 1967), chap. 9.

[8] Ibid.: 249-50.

[9] However, that it did so was certainly the view of Robert Hooke who (in our language) made an analogy between refraction and the transition from smooth to turbulent flow in a fluid.

[10] Hall and Hall, ix: 249.

[11] *Oeuvres Complètes*, vii: 242-44, 302-3; Hall and Hall, ix: 380-84, 674-76.

[12] Sabra, op. cit.: 198-202.

[13] In the first clocks Huygens had restricted the arc of swing of the pendulum by interposing gears

between the verge (carrying the escapement pallets) and the arbor upon which the pendulum crutch was mounted; the same object of restricting the swing was attained more neatly in the anchor escapement. With such restricted circular swings of the pendulum their departure from the cycloid was insignificant.

[14] For the last, see *Oeuvres Complètes*, xviii: 366-68.

[15] See Hall and Hall, *Oldenburg*, vi: 213-18; and *Oeuvres Complètes*, vi: 487-90.

[16] R. S. Westfall, op. cit., note 6: 163.

[17] On the whole question, see Westfall, op. cit.: 162-66; and D. T. Whiteside, *Mathematical Papers of Isaac Newton*, iii (Cambridge, 1969): 390-401, 420-31.

[18] The force varies directly, not as the inverse square, of the distance from the centre.

[19] Whiteside, op. cit.: 390, 423, note 14.

[20] *Oeuvres Complètes*, xviii: 489-90.

[21] *Principia*, Book 1, Prop. 4, Scholium. It is worth noting that, like Newton, Huygens made inertial mass equal to gravitational mass; *Oeuvres Complètes*, xviii: 45.

[22] John Herivel, *The Background to Newton's Principia* (Oxford, 1965): 128-32.

[23] Whiteside, op. cit.: note 17; 423, note 14.

[24] *Oeuvres Complètes*, xviii: 496-8. We may read this as an approximation to $f=ma$ (a result which of course Huygens uses in his mechanical calculations) or alternatively as a *definition* of what equal incitations are. For how could we compare incitations save by observing their effects in accelerating bodies?

[25] Westfall, op. cit., note 6, chap. 4. This contrast between Huygens and Newton is a main theme of this excellent book, to which I am much indebted.

[26] *Oeuvres Complètes*, ix: 167, 190.

[27] Newton to Oldenburg, 23 June 1673; *Correspondence of Isaac Newton*, i: 290.

[28] See D. T. Whiteside, *Journal for the History of Astronomy*, i (1970): 116-38.

[29] E. J. Dijksterhuis, *Centaurus*, ii: 271-72.

[30] See *Oeuvres Complètes*, ix: 32 ff; *Correspondence of Isaac Newton*, iii: 25-40; A. R. Hall, *Ballistics in the Seventeenth Century* (Cambridge, 1952): 145-47.

[31] *Oeuvres Complètes*, xxi: 471.

[32] Ibid., iii: 275-6. From The Hague, 9 June 1661. Covent Garden seems to be meant.

[33] Hall and Hall, *Correspondence of Oldenburg*, viii: 328.

[34] *Oeuvres Complètes*, iv: 365.

[35] Hall and Hall, *Correspondence of Oldenburg*, vi: 503-5.

XV

LE PROBLÈME DE LA VITESSE DE LA LUMIÈRE
DANS L'OEUVRE DE NEWTON

Il est évident que rien n'intéressait Isaac Newton dans le contexte immédiat ou astronomique de la découverte d'Olaus Roemer, car les détails de l'astronomie technique ne le préoccupaient d'aucune façon. Il ne s'occupait ni des éphémérides des satellites de Jupiter, ni de la grandeur de la parallaxe solaire, ni, de ce fait, du problème du trajet de la lumière du Soleil à nos yeux. Contrairement à ce que l'on a dit[1], il n'a jamais rencontré Roemer[2-3], dont il ignora peut-être le nom jusqu'à ce qu'il ait reçu une lettre de Robert Hooke, lui présentant ce dernier comme un observateur, collègue de J.-D. Cassini[4]. Nous ne possédons aucune indication permettant d'affirmer que Newton ait appris la découverte de la vitesse finie de la lumière avant 1684, lorsque Flamsteed lui parla de ce qu'il appelait la "Roemers equation of light" et de son influence sur le calcul des éphémérides des satellites de Jupiter[5].

Cependant, du fait que Newton ne pose aucune question à Flamsteed concernant son indication suivant laquelle la lumière traverse l'*orbis magnus* en dix minutes, il est possible que la découverte de Roemer lui ait été alors déjà connue. Bien entendu, les *Principia mathematica* mentionnent cette même vitesse[6] :

> "Lucem succesive propagari & spatio quasi decem minutorum primorum a Sole ad Terram venire, jam constat per Phaenomena Satellitum *Jovis*, Observationibus diversorum Astronomorum confirmata".

C'est en discutant le mécanisme physique qui produit les principaux phénomènes de la lumière que Newton, dans ses *Principia*, fait mention de la vitesse mesurée de la lumière. Il lui suffit, en effet, de considérer une vitesse finie, quelle que soit celle-ci car, naturellement, on ne saurait ni accélérer ni diminuer une vitesse infinie. D'une façon générale, pour discerner le rôle de la vitesse de la lumière dans la pensée de Newton, il faut examiner ses idées touchant l'essence physique de la lumière, et surtout fouiller dans les manuscrits newtoniens de Cambridge[7].

Commençons par quelques mots sur l'importance capitale de cette vitesse pour la théorie de la lumière au XVIIe siècle. On sait que Descartes, en expliquant dans sa *Dioptrique* la réfraction et la loi dite de nos jours de Snell[8], donne à la lumière une vitesse qui, non seulement est finie, mais qui change en raison inverse de la densité du milieu. Ainsi la réfraction apparaît comme un effet de ce changement de la vitesse de la lumière.

Lorsqu'à Cambridge il présenta, à un public assez restreint et sans doute assez peu apte à l'écouter, son premier exposé scientifique, en suivant l'exemple de son grand prédécesseur Isaac Barrow, Newton introduisit la physique de la lumière d'une façon assez prudente ; c'est-à-dire, en fondant son acceptation de la loi cartésienne sur une vérification *a posteriori* :

> "instrumentis, in istum finem accurate instructis, examinarunt aliqui & veritati (quoad sensum) exacte convenientem adinvenerunt", écrit-il, donc "non dubitamus pro fundamento statuere".

Quant à la démonstration cartésienne *a priori* de la loi, Newton dit seulement qu'elle ne manquerait pas d'élégance si Descartes n'avait pas laissé incertaines les causes physiques sur lesquelles elle reposait[9].

Il est évident que Newton ne veut pas affirmer publiquement que la réfraction est fonction d'une vitesse déterminée de la lumière, soit à la manière de Descartes, soit (peut-être) à celle de Fermat[10].

Bien entendu, dans sa première étude concernant la physique, Newton se montre de façon générale très dédaigneux à l'égard des hypothèses touchant à la lumière et aux couleurs proposées par les philosophes ; la lumière ne se mêle pas à l'ombre pour produire les couleurs ; elle ne se compose ni de globules tournants, ni de vibrations dans l'éther. De telles hypothèses sont en effet si faibles que "non opus est ut Hypotheses ejusmodi refutem, quae ex inventa tandem veritate, sua sponte corruent"[11]. Et quelle est l'hypothèse physique de la lumière que le jeune professeur offre à ses auditeurs ? Aucune : il n'y en a nulle trace dans ses *Lectiones Opticae*.

Il est possible que certains philosophes actuels trouvent assez inquiétant, pour ne pas dire décevant, ce nihilisme de Newton qu'ils qualifieraient volontiers de positiviste. A mon avis, ils comprennent mal le but de la méthode de Newton. Les *Lectiones Opticae* n'avaient pas pour objet de donner une théorie générale de la lumière à la manière de Descartes. Au contraire, Newton nous dit qu'il s'impose la tâche limitée d'approfondir une seule propriété de la lumière :

> "in Dioptrica pedem figo, non ut eam pertractarem de integro, sed tantum ut hanc de natura Lucis proprietatem rimarer primo ; deinde, ut ostenderem quantum ex hac proprietate perfectio Dioptrices impeditur"[12] ;

en fait, cela va sans dire, il s'agit de la variation de la réfrangibilité des rayons colorés. Et la méthode newtonienne pour approfondir cet aspect de la dioptrique consiste à le mathématiser, à créer une science mathématique des couleurs. Newton suggère-t-il à ses auditeurs, que la science physique des couleurs dépasse la responsabilité d'un professeur de mathématiques ? Pas du tout : la réfraction et les couleurs sont tellement entremêlées qu'il est tout à fait impossible de comprendre l'une isolée de l'autre. De même que l'astronomie, la géographie, la navigation sont des sciences mathématiques bien qu'elles traitent toutes de réalités physiques, il en est ainsi pour la science des couleurs quand on la traite *ratione mathematica*[13]. Donc, pour Newton, il suffit de prendre la loi de Snell-Descartes comme un axiome vérifié par l'expérience. Il n'est pas plus nécessaire de la démontrer *a priori* comme conséquence de considérations antérieures qu'il n'était nécessaire à Archimède de démontrer sa définition d'un fluide. Le fait que les théorèmes de cette nouvelle science mathématique des couleurs s'accordent exactement à la réalité physique est le résultat manifeste des expériences successives.

Néanmoins on sait que Newton possédait déjà les idées philosophiques que l'on connût beaucoup plus tard. Même si de telles idées étaient inutiles pour fonder une science mathématique des couleurs, il est cependant impossible que Newton les ait négligées dans le calme de son cabinet de travail. Après tout, le noeud de la théorie newtonienne des couleurs se trouve dans le

XV

fait que chaque rayon coloré, quelle que soit la façon dont il se manifeste, possède une singularité (*discrimen*) qui le distingue de tout autre rayon : cette singularité se révèle aux yeux sous forme de couleur et surtout par une réfrangibilité unique ; mais il est impossible que cette singularité elle-même consiste en couleur ou en angle de réfraction. Newton insiste sur le fait que la singularité existe avant que la lumière ne se soumette à une action réciproque avec la matière telle que la réfraction ou la réflexion ; mais une telle action réciproque est nécessaire comme moyen d'analyse pour faire voir les rayons singuliers. En conséquence la singularité de chaque rayon est antérieure à la réfraction ou à la couleur (qui n'est, en tout cas, qu'un phénomène physiologique). Si l'on veut feindre les hypothèses, il est très facile de deviner que l'idée physique de la lumière (quelle qu'elle soit) doit être modifiée légèrement pour chaque rayon afin qu'il possède une singularité unique. Bien entendu, on pourrait en proposer plusieurs : la rotation des globules selon Descartes, l'obliquité des pulsations selon Hooke, la longueur des ondes proposée plus tard par Newton lui-même. Mais il existe un caractère indépendant de telles hypothèses ; c'est la vitesse. Rien de plus facile que de s'imaginer que les rayons possèdent chacun une vitesse unique et caractéristique.

On sait de nos jours que le jeune Newton qui avait lu la *Dioptrique* de Descartes, avait embrassé cette conception. Dans un cahier de Cambridge il écrit :

> "Remarquez que les rayons qui se meuvent le plus lentement sont plus réfrangés que ceux qui se meuvent plus vite".

Et encore :

> "De là, le rouge, le jaune etc. sont causés dans les corps par l'arrêt des rayons qui vont le plus lentement tandis que le mouvement des rayons plus rapides est très peu retardé ; et le bleu, le vert, le violet [sont faits] par la diminution du mouvement des rayons les plus rapides mais non du mouvement des plus lents"[14].

Il paraît que Newton envisageait déjà une action simplement mécanique ; plus le rayon possède de mouvement, plus grand sera son effet sur un corps soit purement passif (le verre), soit réceptif (l'oeil). Aussitôt après, il aperçoit la possibilité d'une autre variable et il écrit :

> "Soient deux rayons également rapides, néanmoins si l'un est plus petit que l'autre ce rayon-ci aura en proportion un moindre effet que le récepteur puisqu'il a moins de mouvement que l'autre"[15].

NEWTON ET LA VITESSE DE LA LUMIÈRE

Je pense que cette dernière phrase veut signifier une diversité entre les grandeurs ou les masses des globules de la lumière, donc une diversité analogue entre les quantités de mouvement.

Si scrupuleux qu'ait été Newton pour supprimer dans les communications qu'il fit, soit à Cambridge soit à Londres, les idées mécaniques que l'on trouve dans ses cahiers, il en reste cependant des témoignages. Ainsi Bechler a montré que l'analyse de la dispersion dans les *Lectiones Opticae* correspond à l'axiome énonçant que la réfraction typique de chaque rayon est proportionnelle à la vitesse propre de ce rayon[16]. Inutile de dire que Newton présente cette analyse comme purement géométrique, affirmant à ses auditeurs qu'elle "semble différer très peu de la vérité" mais qu'il ne l'avait pas jusqu'alors vérifiée par des expériences[17]. Il est peu vraisemblable qu'un lecteur contemporain n'ait pu déceler l'origine mécanique de cette analyse.

On sait que la première - et pour longtemps la principale - communication publique des idées de Newton concernant l'optique est sa célèbre lettre à Henry Oldenburg de février 1672. Dans cette lettre, en dehors d'une phrase mal formulée qui permet d'entrevoir la préférence constante de Newton en faveur de la conception matérielle de la lumière[18], aucun mot ne lui échappe sur la cause physique de la réfraction ; ce n'est que près de quatre ans plus tard, dans sa célèbre communication de 1675 à la Royal Society sur une *hypothèse* concernant la lumière, que cette situation se modifie et l'*hypothèse* se présente en fait comme assez compliquée[19].

Newton débute, à nouveau, en déclarant que son entreprise n'est qu'une tentative. Il n'est pas essentiel que tout le monde s'entende sur une hypothèse quelconque concernant la lumière ; on peut identifier celle-ci avec un mouvement de l'éther, ou, comme lui-même (de toute évidence) avec des "milliers de corpuscules, inimaginablement petits et rapides, de grandeurs diverses, qui sont projetés des corps lumineux à de grandes distances l'un de l'autre mais néanmoins sans intervalles sensibles de temps, et [qui sont] poussés incessamment par un principe de mouvement" qui leur fait percer l'éther. Mais, en tout cas, il faut lui concéder un éther, qui soit premièrement la *voie* (pour ainsi dire) des corpuscules et le moyen physiologique de transmission des sensations à l'intérieur des animaux, et deuxièmement l'origine des couleurs. Car il nous dit maintenant que les couleurs sont des vibrations de l'éther, justement comme les sons sont des vibrations de l'air et, poursuivant l'analogie, c'est la vibration du corps réfractant ou réfléchissant la lumière qui fait onduler l'éther tout comme la vibration d'un corps sonore fait onduler l'air. Naturellement, ce qui fait vibrer les corps réfringents ou réfléchissants c'est

XV

le choc des corpuscules. Voici d'ailleurs les propres mots de Newton :

> "And now to explain colours ; I suppose, that as bodyes of various sizes, densities, or tensions, do by percussion or other action excite sounds of various tones & consequently vibrations in the Air of various bignesses so when the rayes of light, by impinging on the stif refracting Superficies excite vibrations in the aether, those rayes, what ever they be, as they happen to differ in magnitude, strength or vigour, excite vibrations of various bignesses ; the biggest, strongest or most potent rays, the largest vibrations & others shorter, according to their bigness, strength or power".

On constate que Newton présente une hypothèse à deux niveaux : le premier touchant les corpuscules, dont on ne constate jamais de conséquences directes ; le second, concernant les ondes éthériques, qui créent des couleurs visibles. Sans insister sur d'autres défauts de cette hypothèse, il faut remarquer qu'elle contredit cela même dont Newton a voulu faire l'essence de sa découverte - à savoir que la lumière n'est nullement modifiée par la réfraction.

Dans l'hypothèse de 1675 on voit la naissance de la théorie des "accès" (fits) telle que Newton l'a explicitée dans son "Traité d'Optique" imprimé. Mais m'intéressant ici plus au rayon des corpuscules qu'à l'éther des ondes colorifiques, je souligne de nouveau que Newton hésite entre la vitesse et la grandeur comme trait caractéristique : "bigness, strength or power". En tout cas, il imagine à ce moment là une vitesse finie de la lumière moins grande qu'on ne l'avait proposée jusque là car, dit-il, "nonobstant tout argument que je connaisse jusqu'ici, autant que je sache il est possible qu'une heure ou deux, sinon plus, soient nécessaires à la lumière pour parvenir du Soleil à nos yeux"[20]. On constate combien les idées de ce genre étaient mal précisées avant la découverte de Roemer.

Omettant certaines discussions concernant l'hypothèse de l'éther, considérons pour un instant le rôle qu'ont les globules ou corpuscules de la lumière, qui voyagent si vite depuis le Soleil jusqu'à nous. Newton les considère en premier lieu comme responsables des couleurs en raison de leurs diverses quantités de mouvement, et ceci par un processus physique qui reste mystérieux ; c'est presque comme si les corpuscules *étaient* eux-mêmes des rayons colorés. Mais, en poussant ses idées à un niveau plus complexe et en réfléchissant sur la nécessité d'expliquer les phénomènes périodiques des couleurs, les corpuscules deviennent les causes des ondes éthériques. De ce fait les rayons ne s'inclinent pas en se réfractant à cause de la diversité de leurs quantités de mouvement, mais parce que la densité de l'éther varie graduellement au voisinage des corps appelés solides. Cette hypothèse de 1675 se trouve confirmée dans la lettre de Newton à Robert Boyle de février 1679[21]. On voit cependant que la dispersion qui fait séparer les couleurs ne vient pas de l'éther, mais des singularités des corpuscules ; c'est ce que dit Newton que je cite ici en traduction française.

> "Quant à la cause de ces couleurs et d'autres phénomènes semblables dûs à la réfraction, il faut que les rayons les plus grands ou les plus forts percent la surface réfringeante plus facilement que les autres plus faibles, et par conséquent ceux-là (les plus forts) sont moins détournés par la surface, donc moins réfractés... Et puisque la réfraction ne sert que pour séparer les rayons, et ne change aucunement leur grandeur ni leur force, de là, après avoir été une fois très bien séparés, la réfraction ne saurait changer encore leurs couleurs".

Evidemment ici, presque malgré lui, Newton a réalisé une distinction entre la réfraction (dans notre sens actuel) attribuée à l'existence de l'éther selon son hypothèse, et la dispersion due aux différences de grandeur ou de force des corpuscules.

Il est clair que l'hypothèse de l'éther ne permet pas d'en déduire la loi de Snell-Descartes. Pour cela, en écrivant ses *Philosophiae naturalis principia mathematica* (Liv. 1, Sectio 14), Newton choisit un modèle tout à fait différent. Il rejette la mécanique de l'éther et introduit la mécanique des forces. Depuis les études que ma femme et moi avons publiées, les historiens pensent en général qu'après 1679 environ - après la grande illumination qui se produisit alors dans la pensée mécanique de Newton à la suite des attaques de Robert Hooke - il adopta les concepts de forces attractives et répulsives. Beaucoup plus tard, influencé surtout par les expériences électriques de Hauksbee, il revint aux modèles éthériques qu'il présenta pour la première fois dans les *Quaestiones* de l'*Optice* de 1706[22].

Mais, pour le moment, dans les *Principia*, Newton examine une hypothèse quasi-gravitationnelle : le mouvement des corps très-petits sur lesquels agit une force centripète, dirigée vers les parties d'un corps très grand. On sait qu'il montre l'existence de phénomènes assez proches de ceux de la lumière : réflexion, réfraction, diffraction. Or, il est évident que la force centripète ne peut avoir d'influence sur les corpuscules sans modifier leur vitesse ; il faut donc que les corpuscules possèdent une vitesse déterminée ou finie, et c'est pour cette raison que Newton y mentionne la découverte de Roemer. De plus, on se demande si la force centripète agit également sur *tous* les corpus-

XV

cules du rayon, ou si elle a un effet plus grand sur quelques-uns d'entre eux - par exemple les plus lents - que sur les autres. Dans le second cas, on aurait un mécanisme permettant d'expliquer la dispersion et les couleurs.

De fait, une telle hypothèse ne soulève aucun problème. Comme l'a montré Bechler[23], la forme de la parabole qu'une force constante (comme la gravité) engendre en agissant sur un corps en mouvement - un projectile à la Galilée, comme dit Newton lui-même - dépend de la vitesse du projectile. Galilée le savait aussi. Donc, plus vite se meut le corpuscule, plus aplatie sera la courbure de la parabole ; de là provient la séparation des corpuscules qui provoque la dispersion et les couleurs.

Mais, Newton ne fait aucune mention de tout cela. Pourquoi ? Peut-être parce qu'il avait songé à l'une des conséquences qui résulteraient d'un lien entre la vitesse des corpuscules et les couleurs qu'ils suscitent, conséquence d'ailleurs facile à vérifier. Si les corpuscules de la lumière mettent quelques minutes pour traverser la distance de Jupiter à nos yeux, lorsqu'un satellite disparaît derrière le corps d'une planète, la lumière du dernier groupe des corpuscules les plus lents, c'est-à-dire les rougissants, doit prendre plus de temps que celle des plus rapides, les bleuissants. Donc on devrait s'attendre à voir le satellite rouge à l'instant de l'immersion et, au contraire, à le voir bleu au moment de son émersion. Car, si l'on suppose qu'on peut apercevoir un éclair d'un dixième de seconde, et que la différence de vitesse entre les corpuscules de la lumière n'excède pas un pour cent, un tel éclair coloré doit se manifester même si le passage de la lumière de Jupiter à nos yeux ne demande que dix secondes. Mais Newton n'avait jamais supposé que la lumière puisse se mouvoir aussi vite ; et en fait dès avant 1686 il connaissait déjà sûrement la découverte de Roemer et savait donc que sur une telle distance astronomique la différence entre les corpuscules les plus rapides et les plus lents devrait dépasser quelques secondes de temps.

Il est certain que Newton avait eu de telles idées. Bechler a publié ce passage de brouillon : "Les rayons les plus réfrangibles sont les plus rapides. Car la lumière (parvenant) des satellites de Jupiter est rouge au moment de l'immersion", texte qui pense-t-il, remonte, aux premiers projets du "Traité d'Optique", c'est-à-dire à l'année 1691 environ[24]. Et précisément à cette époque, en août 1691, Newton écrivit à Flamsteed en lui demandant :

> "Lorsque vous faites des observations d'éclipses des satellites de Jupiter, j'aimerais savoir si, au travers de longues lunettes, la lumière du satellite tend au rouge ou au bleu à l'instant qui précède la disparition du satellite,

ou si la lumière devient alors plus rougeâtre ou plus pâle"[25].

Flamsteed lui répondit qu'en fait la lumière du satellite s'affaiblissait avant de disparaître mais qu'il n'avait jamais remarqué un changement de couleur.

On ne sait pas du tout si c'est à cause de ce désaccord d'ordre empirique que Newton abandonna l'hypothèse des couleurs dépendant de la vitesse des corpuscules de la lumière. Certes, Newton n'était pas plus aveugle qu'Augustin Fresnel, qui put vérifier cette même difficulté de l'hypothèse de la vitesse colorifiante :

> "il s'ensuivrait", écrivit Fresnel (5 juillet 1814), "que les premiers rayons qui nous arriveraient après une éclipse de soleil seraient des rayons rouges ; or, d'après un calcul que j'ai fait dans cette hypothèse... il s'écoulerait assez de temps entre l'arrivée des rayons rouges et des rayons violets pour que nous nous aperçussions de la différence de couleur. Mais nous savons par expérience qu'il n'en est rien"[26].

En tout cas, Newton abandonna cette hypothèse et ses brouillons révèlent qu'il poursuivit l'idée des ondes colorifiques d'éther dans sa théorie des "accès", qui apparaissait déjà dans son hypothèse de 1675, et qu'il développera à l'occasion de son "Traité d'Optique". On voit que puisqu'il avait besoin des ondes ou des "accès" comme causes secondaires des couleurs lorsqu'intervenaient des phénomènes de lames minces, il était plus économique de s'en servir dans tous les cas.

Cependant, le problème du mécanisme physique de la réfraction subsistait toujours. Si l'on admet que les couleurs existent telles quelles dans la lumière blanche, il est pour Newton impensable que la réfraction, la dispersion etc. soient produites par des ondes ou des accès. Ces phénomènes doivent être, d'une façon quelconque, créés par la lumière elle-même, c'est-à-dire par les corpuscules. Enfin, puisque la vitesse, comme les ondes, est susceptible de changement, n'est-ce pas la masse du corpuscule qui est la plus constante, la plus sûre ? Voici d'ailleurs ce qu'en dit Newton lui-même dans l'un de ses brouillons publié par Bechler :

> "Les couleurs et les réfractions ne dépendent nullement de modifications nouvelles de la lumière mais des propriétés originales et constantes de ses rayons, et de telles propriétés sont mieux conservées dans les corps en mouvement. Les pressions et les mouvements sont capables de recevoir des modifications nouvelles en traversant des milieux divers, mais les propriétés des corpuscules en déplacement ne sont qu'à peine changées de cette manière. Rien ne convient

> mieux pour la diversité des couleurs et des mesures de réfrangibilité que les rayons soient des corps, de grandeurs diverses..."[27].

Et en effet on trouve cette hypothèse exprimée dans l'*Optice* de 1706, *Quaestio* 21, où Newton commence (employant une phrase qu'il biffa de l'édition anglaise ultérieure) :[28]

> "Les rayons de la lumière, ne sont-ils pas des corpuscules très petits émis des corps lumineux, et réfractés par des attractions particulières par lesquelles la lumière et les corps agissent l'un sur l'autre" ?

et il dit plus loin, de façon précise[29] :

> "D'ailleurs, il n'y a rien d'autre qui soit nécessaire pour la création de toute la variété de couleurs et des degrés divers de réfrangibilité que les rayons de la lumière soient des corpuscules de diverses grandeurs..."

Cependant, une difficulté apparaît alors, on peut même dire une erreur, qu'a analysée Bechler. Newton justifie sa nouvelle hypothèse (*Quaestio* 21 = *Query* 29) en faisant allusion aux *Principia mathematica*, tandis qu'en réalité les propositions de cet ouvrage ne conviennent qu'à l'idée d'une diversité de *vitesses* parmi les corpuscules de la lumière. Il n'est pas possible de séparer les corpuscules d'après leurs masses si la force agit en raison de la masse. Pour cette raison, implicitement, Galilée et les auteurs d'ouvrages de balistique avaient pu supposer que l'angle de tir étant donné, la trajectoire d'un projectile dépend uniquement de la vitesse du projectile, et nullement de sa masse. Par conséquent, si le prisme, par exemple, agit comme un "spectromètre de masse" à l'égard des corpuscules de la lumière, il faut que la force déviatrice du verre soit tout à fait différente de la gravité et, comme la force électrique, indépendante de la masse[30].

Donc on peut dire que Roemer, bien que d'assez loin, est à l'origine du remplacement par Newton d'une hypothèse logiquement exacte mais empiriquement fausse, par une autre hypothèse tout à fait illogique, mais qui sera adoptée par les newtoniens. Certes, on pourrait s'imaginer que Newton ait supposé, presque sans le savoir, une force invariante par rapport à la masse ; mais il n'en dit pas un mot. Tout au contraire, fait plus grave, dans l'édition latine de l'*Optice* (1706) il posa une force réfringente en raison *inverse* des masses : plus les corpuscules sont petits, plus la force les attire[31]. Je traduis ici ce passage de son texte latin[32] :

> .... en ce qui concerne ces corps, qui sont du même genre

NEWTON ET LA VITESSE DE LA LUMIÈRE

et de la même vertu, plus l'un d'eux est petit, plus est forte, par rapport à sa grandeur, sa force attractive. Celle-ci est reconnue plus forte dans les petits aimants, au regard de leur poids, que dans les grands. Car les particules des petits aimants, puisqu'elles sont plus proches entre elles, conjuguent plus aisément leurs forces en une seule. Aussi, puisque les rayons lumineux [Newton entend par là des corpuscules] sont de tous les corps - ce que nous savons - les plus petits, on devra s'attendre à les reconnaître comme ayant les forces attractives les plus puissantes. Qu'il en soit probablement ainsi, pourra être déduit de la règle suivante. L'attraction d'un rayon de lumière, par rapport à sa quantité de matière, est à la gravité que quelque projectile a par rapport à la même quantité de sa propre matière, en raison composée de la vitesse du rayon lumineux à la vitesse du projectile, et de la flexion ou courbure de la ligne que décrit le rayon dans le lieu de réfraction à la flexion ou courbure de la ligne que décrit le projectile. Cela, bien entendu, si l'inclinaison du rayon sur la surface réfringente est la même que celle que le projectile a sur l'horizon.

En fait Newton veut exprimer que :

$$f/g = c/v \cdot R/r$$

où f est la force attractive du rayon, g la force de la gravité terrestre, c la vitesse de la lumière, v la vitesse d'un projectile quelconque, R la courbure de la trajectoire du projectile, r la courbure du rayon lumineux.

Or, en effet, si la trajectoire du projectile est une parabole, la quantité v exprimée en pieds par seconde devient égale à R : donc on a :

$$f/g = c/r$$

Posant, d'après Roemer, que le passage de la lumière à nos yeux exige sept minutes, et que la parallaxe solaire est égale à dix secondes, Newton calcule la vitesse de la lumière $c = 10^9$ pieds / seconde, environ. Postulant la courbure du rayon $(1/12) \cdot 10^{-5}$ pieds, on a une proportion de $12 \cdot 10^{14}$ à 1, ou, ainsi que Newton écrit dans l'*Optice*, la force attractive des corpuscules de la lumière est au moins 10^{15} fois plus grande que celle de la gravité.

> "Une force si grande dans les rayons, ajouta-t-il, ne saurait qu'accomplir des effets énormes dans les particules de la matière, avec lesquels ils sont unis pour composer les corps".

Hélas ! Il y a une erreur manifeste. On savait depuis longtemps, et Newton lui-même l'avait démontré dans sa jeunesse, que l'expression correcte de la force centripète est proportionnelle à $\underline{v}^2/r$ et non à $\underline{v}/r$. Donc, on aurait dû exprimer la proportion précédemment citée sous la forme :

$$\underline{f}/\underline{g} = (\underline{c}/\underline{v})^2 \cdot \underline{P}/\underline{r} = 4 \cdot 10^{22} \quad \textit{quamproxime}.$$

Et, en effet, Bechler a remarqué que Newton avait fait une telle correction[34].

Nous ne pouvons suivre ce dernier auteur dans l'étude des diverses formulations de cette hypothèse que l'on trouve dans les brouillons de Newton à Cambridge. Notons cependant que lorsqu'il prépara l'édition finale de son *Opticks* (1717) Newton biffa complètement ce passage de la *Quaestio* 22 que nous venons d'examiner, le reste de la *Quaestio* 22 devenant la *Query* 30 de cette édition anglaise. On sait que Newton ajouta à celle-ci huit questions nouvelles touchant aux fonctions de l'éther ; dont la *Query* 21, où il reprend à nouveau l'idée rejetée de la *Quaestio* 30. Voici ce texte dans la traduction de Marat :

> "Comme l'attraction a plus d'énergie dans les petits que dans les grands aimants, eu égard à leur masse ; que la gravité est plus grande aux surfaces des petites planètes qu'aux surfaces des grandes, eu égard à leur masse ; et que les petits corps sont beaucoup plus agités par l'attraction électrique que les grands corps ; de même la petitesse des rayons de lumière peut extrêmement contribuer à l'énergie de la puissance qui les rétracte. Ainsi, en supposant que l'éther soit composé, comme l'air, de particules qui tendent à s'écarter les unes des autres... et que ses particules soient incomparablement plus petites que celles de l'air ou même que celles de la lumière ; l'excessive petitesse de ces particules peut contribuer à la grandeur de la force, en vertu de laquelle elles s'écartent les unes des autres... ?" (J.P. MARAT, *Optique de Newton*, traduction nouvelle. Paris, 1787, p. 205).

Mais cette fois, l'idée apparaît dans le contexte de l'hypothèse de l'éther. Faisant une deuxième volte-face complète et rejetant absolument la physique des *Principia*, Newton revient à ses idées de 1675 et 1679[35] ; il admet un éther plus dense dans les espaces vides qu'à l'intérieur des corps, éther élastique qui comprime les corps de ses régions les plus denses aux moindres, et qui, d'une façon semblable, détourne la lumière. Mais il est passionnant de voir comment Newton a interverti ses calculs dans lesquels entre la vitesse de la lumière. L'analogue d'une force extrêmement puissante de petite étendue est l'élasticité extrêmement puissante de l'éther. Ici Newton fait appel à la théorie des ondes. Dans les *Principia* (Liv. II, Prop. 48) il avait démontré que la vitesse $\underline{v}$ des ondes se propageant dans un milieu est proportionnelle à la

NEWTON ET LA VITESSE DE LA LUMIÈRE

racine carrée de E/d, où E est l'élasticité de ce milieu, d sa densité.

Alors, si l'on pose c la vitesse de la lumière, v celle du son dans l'air, E_1, E_2, d_1, d_2 les élasticités et densités des milieux respectifs, on a :

$$c/v = \sqrt{(E_1/E_2) \cdot (d_2/d_1)} = 7 \cdot 10^5.$$

Ici Newton suppose la vitesse du son égale à 1140 pieds par seconde, la parallaxe du Soleil à douze secondes, et le temps de passage de la lumière à sept secondes et demie, donc la vitesse de la lumière à $8.1.10^8$ pieds/seconde, d'où la proportion $7.10^5 : 1$. Il en résulte que :

$$E_1 = 5.10^{11} \cdot (d_1/d_2) \cdot E_2 \;,$$

ainsi que l'écrit Newton.

Peut-on voir ici une solution désespérée ? En vérité, il semble que oui. Finalement Newton n'a pas pu admettre l'idée d'une dualité de forces, c'est-à-dire l'existence d'une force gravitionnelle où la masse d'un petit corps n'entre pas dans les calculs et celle d'une force de petite étendue qui serait inversement proportionnelle à la masse. Pour nous accoutumés, dans la tradition pourrait-on dire de Boscovich, à la multiplicité des forces, Newton peut nous paraître trop scrupuleux ? Mais, ainsi que Bechler nous le rappelle, il faut songer que pour Newton, la croyance au principe de *Natura sibi semper consona* - c'est-à-dire à l'analogie entre les macro-phénomènes et les micro-phénomènes - était très profonde, même sacrée. Quel autre principe d'inférence possédait-il ?*

Un mot pour conclure. On a vu que Newton, élève peut-on dire de Descartes, a toujours cru à la vitesse finie de la lumière, et recouru éventuellement à cette idée. La découverte de Roemer lui a donné plus de confiance, et lui a conféré aussi le pouvoir de quantifier ses hypothèses. C'est tout. La mesure de la vitesse de la lumière, sa quantification, n'ont rien changé dans l'essor de ses pensées.

---

*Extensio, durities, impenetrabilitas, mobilitas & vis inertiae totius, oritur ab extensione, duritie, impenetrabilitate, mobilitate & viribus inertiae partium ; & inde concludimus omnes omnium corporum partes minimas extendi & duras esse & impenetrabiles & mobiles & viribus inertiae praeditas. Et hoc est fundamentum Philosophiae totius. *Principia*, Liv. III, Regula Philosophandi III, ajouté à l'édition corrigée de 1713, p. 358.

NOTES

1. I. Bernard COHEN, "Roemer and the first determination of the velocity of light" *Isis*, v. 31, 1940, p. 343.

2. Thomas BIRCH, *History of the Royal Society*, t. III, London, 1757, p. 482.

3. Joseph EDLESTON, *Correspondence of Sir Isaac Newton*, London, 1850, p. lxxxv ; Newton visita sa mère, malade, le 15 mai 1679.

4. H.W. TURNBULL (ed.) *The Correspondence of Isaac Newton*, t. II, Cambridge, 1960, p. 298 (cette édition sera citée ci-après sous la forme *Correspondence*, t. X, p. y).

5. *Ibid.*, p. 404.

6. *Principia*, Book I, Prop. 96, Scholium.

7. Pour l'histoire de ces ms., voir D.T. WHITESIDE, *The Mathematical Papers of Isaac Newton*, t. I, Cambridge, 1967, p. xvii - xxxvi.

8. Dans les *Lectiones Opticae*, (London, 1728, p. 36), Newton attribue à Descartes la première découverte de cette loi. Voir aussi *The Unpublished First Version of Isaac Newton's Cambridge Lectures in Optics, 1670-72, a facsimile of the autograph... with an introduction by D.T. Whiteside*, Cambridge University Library, 1973, p. 71.

9. *Lectiones Opticae*, p. 36. Deux études très importantes de Zev Bechler traitent de la vitesse de la lumière dans les spéculations newtoniennes : (1) "Newton's Search for a Mechanistic Model of Colour Dispersion : A suggested Interpretation", *Archive for History of Exact Sciences*, v. 11, 1973, p. 1-37 ; (2) "Newton's law of forces which are inversely as the mass : a suggested interpretation of his later efforts to normalize a mechanistic model of optical dispersion", *Centaurus*, v. 18, 1974, p. 184-222. Ces deux études m'ont été très utiles.

10. Le principe de moindre temps de Fermat nous est très bien connu (voir par exemple A.J. SABRA, *Theories of Light from Descartes to Newton*, London, 1967, Ch. V) mais je pense que Newton l'ignorait.

11. *Lectiones Opticae*, p. 145 sq., 235-6 ; 1er Ms, p. 19 sq., (v. n° 8 supra).

12. *Lectiones Opticae*, p. 3 ; 1er Ms, p. 2.

13. Le passage continue : "Imo vero cum horum accurata scientia videatur ex difficillimis esse quae Philosophus desideret ; spero me quasi exemplo monstraturum quantum Mathesis in Philosophia naturali valeat ; et exinde ut homines Geometras ad examen Naturae strictius aggrediendum, & avides scientiae naturalis ad Geometriam prius addiscendam horter ; ut priores suum omnino tempus in speculationibus humanae vitae nequaquam profuturis absumant, neque posteriores operam praepostera methodo usque navantes, a spe sua perpetuo decidant : verum ut Geometris philosophantibus & Philosophis exercentibus Geometriam, pro conjecturis et probabilibus quae venditantur ubisque, scientiam Naturae summis tandem evidentiis firmatam nanciscamur". Premier MS., f. 23 ; *Lectiones Opticae*, p. 152-3.

14. "Note yt slowly moved rays are refracted more then swift ones...Hence redness & c are made in bodys by stoping ye slowly moved rays without much hindering of ye motion of ye swifter rays, & blew, greene & purple by diminishing ye motion of ye swifter rays & not of ye slower". A.R. HALL, "Sir Isaac Newton's Note-

book", *Cambridge Historical Journal*, t. 9, 1948, p. 247-8, citant le Ms : Cambridge University Library MS. Add. 3996.

15. "Though 2 rays be equally swift yet if one ray be lesse yn ye other that ray shall have so much less effect on ye sensorium as it has lesse motion yn ye other".

16. *Lectiones Opticae*, p. 62-67 (Pars I, Sect II, XLII) ; 1er Ms, p. 85-6. See D.T. WHITESIDE, *The Mathematical Papers of Isaac Newton*, Cambridge, 1967 -, t. III, p. 466-70 and BECHLER, *op. cit.* (1), p. 4-5.

17. *Lectiones Opticae*, p. 64 ; 1er Ms, p. 86.

18. *Correspondence*, t. I, p. 100 : "These things being so, it can be no longer disputed... whether Light be a Body". Plus tard, Newton s'efforça d'affirmer que même l'hypothèse ondulatoire suppose que la lumière est matérielle, c'est-à-dire l'éther.

19. *Ibid.*, Letter 146, surtout p. 376 *sq*, décembre 1675. Il faut remarquer que l'hypothèse apparaît dans les pensées de Newton au moins dès avant juin 1672, car il en fait mention dans sa première réponse à la critique de Robert Hooke (*Correspondence*, t. I, p. 174 ; BECHLER, *op.cit*, (1), p. 6). Ici Newton proportionne l'effet du rayon à la quantité de mouvement : les vibrations de l'éther varient "as they are excited by the said cospuscular rays of various sizes and velocities".

20. *Ibid*, p. 378.

21. *Correspondence*, t. II, p. 289.

22. Voir Marie BOAS et A. Rupert HALL, "Newton's Mechanical Principles", *Journal of the History of Ideas*, t. 20, 1959, p. 167-178 ; *Unpublished Scientific Papers of Isaac Newton*, Cambridge, 1962, surtout p. 183-213. L'étude des idées newtoniennes a été beaucoup avancée par MM. Guerlac, Herivel, Westfall, Whiteside etc. voir par exemple l'excellent exposé de R.S. WESTFALL, *Force in Newton's Physics*, London, 1971, surtout p. 377 *sq*. Sur Hooke et Newton, voir l'étude capitale d'Alexandre KOYRÉ : "An Unpublished Letter of Robert Hooke to Isaac Newton", *Isis*, t. 43, 1952, p. 312-337.

23. BECHLER, *op.cit.* (1), p. 17.

24. *Ibid*, p. 22.

25. NEWTON, *Correspondence*, t. III, p. 164 : "When you observe ye eclipses of ♃ satellites I should be glad to know if in long Telescopes ye light of ye Satellit immediately before it disappeares incline either to red or blew, or become more ruddy or more pale than before."

26. Augustin FRESNEL, *Oeuvres complètes*, Paris, 1868, t. II, p. 821, cité in BECHLER, *op.cit*, (1), p. 36.

27. BECHLER, *op.cit*, (1), p. 33, citant Cambridge University Library Ms Add. 3970, f. 291r.

28. *Optice*, London, 1706, p. 315 ; *Opticks*, London, 1717, *Query* 29, *ad init*.

29. *Ibid.*, p. 317.

30. BECHLER, *op.cit*, (1), p. 33-37.

31. Cf. BECHLER, *op.cit,* (2).

32. *Optice,* p. 320-321, *Quaestio* 22 (= *Query* 30, *Opticks,* 1717).

33. Il y a une petite faute d'impression ou de calcul (cf. BECHLER, *op.cit,* (2), note 7).

34. *Ibid.,* notes 8,9.

35. "I suppose this aether pervades all gross bodies, but yet so as to stand rarer in their pores then in free spaces,& so much ye rarer as their pores are less". *Correspondence,* t. II, p. 289 ; 28 febr. 1679.

XVI

LEIBNIZ AND THE BRITISH MATHEMATICIANS
1673–1676

Leibniz arrived in London for the first time on 24 January 1673 (Old Style). It was nine months since he had likewise made his first journey to Paris, where he had become acquainted with Christiaan Huygens and enraptured himself with his early studies on the summation of series[1]. Even though he had profited by Huygens' guidance in Paris, Leibniz had still read very little mathematics, and his ignorance tended to lead him to undervalue the significance of what had been accomplished already. In particular, when he arrived in London he had no knowledge of English mathematicians unless we reckon among them Thomas Hobbes, to whom the English mathematicians proper were scarcely cordial[2], and of course he could not be expected to know that one of the greatest mathematicians of all time was then at work in Cambridge, as this was a fact of which only a couple of Englishmen at most then had any inkling. His correspondence with Henry Oldenburg, Secretary of the Royal Society, carried on for some two and a half years before his first arrival in London, is of a general philosophical and mechanical character. To Leibniz Oldenburg wrote letters very different from those which he sent to Sluse, for example. The only mathematical allusion in Oldenburg's reply to Leibniz's first letter was a purely bibliographical one to Barrow's recently published optical and geometrical lectures as works "greatly valued by readers of acute judgement"[3]. Equally casual are Leibniz's allusion to

---

[1] This lecture is based on the work of some of the many scholars who have devoted themselves to seventeenth century mathematics and especially Leibniz the mathematician, beginning with C.I. Gerhardt (1816–99), whose editions have been relied upon for more than a century. Among later mathematical students of Leibniz J.E. Hofmann has been outstanding; I have made constant use of his *Leibniz in Paris, 1672–76*, Cambridge 1974. The most useful works on his great British contemporaries are H.W. TURNBULL, ed., *James Gregory Tercentary Memorial Volume*, London 1939; C.J. SCRIBA, *James Gregorys frühe Schriften zur Infinitesimalrechnung*, Giessen 1957, and D.T. WHITESIDE, ed., *The Mathematical Papers of Isaac Newton*, Cambridge 1967 –. I am very grateful to Dr. Whiteside for his constructive comments on the first draft of this lecture.

[2] HOFMANN, *Leibniz in Paris*, 7 note 31 (cited hereafter as HOFMANN).

[3] A. RUPERT HALL and MARIE BOAS HALL, *The Correspondence of Henry Oldenburg*, Madison and London 1965 – , VII, 111; 10 August 1670 (cited hereafter as OLDENBURG, *Correspondence*).

Cavalieri's infinitesimals and his inclusion of the names of Wallis and Mercator among a list of Londoners whose opinions of the *Hypothesis physica nova* be solicited[4]. Whether because the opinions transmitted to him by Oldenburg were insufficiently encouraging, or because of his increasing involvement in other interests (including his diplomatic career) the correspondence between Oldenburg and Leibniz lapsed in the autumn of 1671, and was not renewed throughout the latter's first stay in Paris. Thus Oldenburg and the other Londoners would have known nothing of Leibniz's new preoccupation with series.

On the other side, and this is a fact essential to the understanding of what follows, Leibniz's correspondent Henry Oldenburg (about whom in general I need add nothing to what my wife has said yesterday) was no mathematician. He had considerable sympathy with Leibniz's generalising ambitions in natural philosophy, with his interest in chemical arcana and mechanical inventions, and with his endeavours to refine the mechanical philosophy although, like most of the English, distrustful of Leibniz's strong leaning toward the speculative rather than the empiricist method. Even so, one observes Oldenburg treating Leibniz not so much to stimulating, critical discussion as to the kind of general intellectual news-letter which many correspondents welcomed. When specifically mathematical issues occurred between him and his correspondents — as with Huygens and Sluse, for example — Oldenburg leaned heavily on the expertise of Brouncker, Wallis and Collins, whose letters or comments he either transcribed in quotation, or adapted for his own use. Oldenburg was unlikely therefore to be a very sensitive detector of the new facet to Leibniz's intellect that had appeared in Paris, nor was he immediately well qualified to act as a guide and informant to Leibniz of the state of English mathematics, though of course he could name a number of leading figures. He was certainly not equipped to bring out the merits of talented but obscure English mathematicians like Thomas Baker and Francis Jessop[4a].

The senior among these was William, Viscount Brouncker, first and present President of the Royal Society. His main work — isolated successes in infinite fractional expansions — had been done in the late 1650s and now, entering old age, he was much involved in public business, especially that of the Navy Board. Although still sometimes consulted by Oldenburg on mathematical points, he was rather out of touch with active currents. To a large extent this was also true of the major established figure on the English mathematical scene, John Wallis, who had also done his best work and been most closely in touch with continental mathematicians before the Restoration. By the 1670s his correspondence was

---

[4] Ibid, VII, 487, 1 March 1671; VIII, 24, 29 April 1671.
[4a] See NEWTON, *Correspondence*, II, 89–90 and OLDENBURG, *Correspondence*, X, passim. Jessop's paper on the rectification of the cycloid is in Royal Society MS. I(i), no. 165.

virtually confined to Oldenburg and Collins; he had no knowledge of the unpublished work of James Gregory and of Newton before 1676.

For several years, therefore, Oldenburg's chief mathematical adviser and informant had been John Collins, a senior clerk in the government service, a man evidently of great industry and great enthusiasm, but of limited intellectual horizons. He tended towards the xenophobia with which, perhaps justly, the proud island race was widely credited at this period; magpiefashion, he was fascinated by what seemed to him splendid examples of mathematical insight to the exclusion of other developments which a sounder critical sense might have valued; and he saw progress in mathematics as lying in the solution of problems rather than in the attainment of new conceptions. Above all he concentrated on general methods for resolving higher-order equations. As against the undoubted narrowness of Collins' mathematical competence, however, must be set his assiduity in encouraging both Gregory and Newton (not that either of these acute minds profited directly from anything Collins could contribute) and in giving at least a restricted publicity to their achievements.

Of the English mathematicians upon whom Collins reported from time to time to Oldenburg, other than Gregory and Newton, the most notable was John Pell, whom Leibniz met during his first visit to London failing, however, to "awaken the slightest sympathy" in the heart of "this morose, rather melancholic sixty year old"[5]. Pell had undoubtedly been an active intellectual of the Commonwealth period when his reputation and activity were highest and he had composed his *Idea of Mathematics* as one manifesto (among many) of the spirit of the victorious movement[6]; like Collins he had but a partial knowledge of the work of modern mathematicians. His work on the approximate numerical solution of equations was of great interest to Collins, but as this never matured, and Pell shows no signs either of flexible receptivity or of outgoing influence on others, it is difficult to give him a place of much significance in this story, save as a (probably deliberate) source of humiliation to Leibniz. The meeting took place at Robert Boyle's house[7]. Leibniz spoke of his "method of forming the terms of any ... series whatever from a certain sort of differences that I call g e n e r a t i v e ... " that is the method of successive differences. As Leibniz's highly elaborate letter of explanation and exculpation to Oldenburg makes plain[8], he was astonished to find what seemed to himself a wholly new discovery regarded by some one else as part of the current literature of mathematics. Pell seems to have been a trifle frigid in responding that "this was already

---

[5] Hofmann, 26.
[6] CHARLES WEBSTER, *The Great Instauration,* Oxford 1975, 354, 356, 358.
[7] Or rather that of his sister, Lady Ranelagh, where Boyle dwelt; Oldenburg lived in the next house but one in Pall Mall, Westminster.
[8] 3 February 1672/3; OLDENBURG, *Correspondence,* IX, 438–447. Something in the overwrought tone of this document must be put down to Leibniz's sensitivity, as well as to Pell's blunt coldness.

in print, reported by M. Mouton, Canon of Lyon, as the discovery of François Regnauld of Lyon ..." inferring (apparently) that Leibniz's want of scholarship was a serious defect. Having consulted Oldenburg's copy of Mouton's book[9], Leibniz accepted the fact of his non-originality with reasonably good grace, perhaps indeed conceding almost too much, for whereas Mouton used differences for subtabulation Leibniz meant to employ them for interpolation. We have no reason to believe that this story, painful to Leibniz as it was, was given any wide circulation or affected Oldenburg's opinion of him. But it was to be brought up against Leibniz in future years.

Leibniz was really more preoccupied with his calculating machine than with mathematics proper during this first London visit; I say no more on that score. One feels that Leibniz, after a rough handling from the Fellows of the Royal Society (other than Oldenburg and, in all likelihood, Boyle)[10] can have carried away no very favourable impression from this visit. Yet it had the positive result of initiating a mathematical correspondence between himself and Oldenburg. In his first letter to Oldenburg after regaining Paris, Leibniz asked about English success in reducing higher-order equations, posed some of Ozanam's problems and also mentions the names of Pardies and Bertet. In reply he received, as Latinised by Oldenburg, a pretty typical Collins mathematical news-letter, with bibliographical queries about Fermat's remains, de Beaune's *De angulo solido* and Desargues' *Leçons de Tenebres* with, more to the point, Collins' reference to Kersey's forthcoming book for English work in algebra and a brief account of interpolation methods, after which he set Leibniz the problem of ascertaining the sum of a finite number of terms in a musical progression (one of the form $\frac{1}{a+b} + \frac{1}{a+2b} + \frac{1}{a+3b} + \ldots$). It is perhaps typical of Collins' over-exuberance that he claimed a general method for making such a summation exactly; whereas Newton (from whom Collins derived it) made it clear that any method was approximate to any desired limit[11].

Hot upon this Leibniz received — transmitted this time by Oldenburg in English — an even longer and more miscellaneous narration of British mathematics[12]. The two obvious first points to emphasise about this document con-

---

[9] GABRIEL MOUTON, *Observationes diametrorum solis et lunae apparentium*... Lyon 1670. See WHITESIDE, *Mathematical Papers*, IV, 4–5; OLDENBURG, *Correspondence*, IX, 439, 444; HOFMANN, 26–29.

[10] "... a man to be counted among the greatest of the race, and one whom humanity will one day wish to immortalise in marble" as Leibniz wrote of him in his first letter to Oldenburg after leaving London (8 March 1673 N.S.; OLDENBURG, *Correspondence*, IX, 488, 494).

[11] OLDENBURG, *Correspondence*, IX, 549–553; 556–62; HOFMANN, 32–33 and H.W. TURNBULL, ed., *Correspondence of Isaac Newton*, I, 16–19, 68 (cited hereafter as NEWTON, *Correspondence*).

[12] Printed for the first time in OLDENBURG, *Correspondence*, IX, 563–7; it is analysed and discussed by Hofmann, pp. 36–45. Hofmann seems to me to exaggerate its interest.

cern its incoherence and its superficiality. It purports initially to be a summary of Kersey's *Algebra*, goes on to a series of bibliographical jottings, largely inaccurate, and ends up with a number of vague boasts such as the following (coming immediately after a paragraph on conics): "Mr. Newton solves all equations not exceeding the ninth degree by the aid of a constant cubic parabola, which being once described never varies..." There follows more on conics, Desargues and Pascal, then again: "As to solid or curvilinear geometry, Mr. Newton hath invented (before Mercator published his *Logarithmo-technia*) a general method of the same kind for all curvilinear figures, the straightening of curves, the finding of the centres of gravity (etc.) ... with infinite series for the roots of adfected equations, easily composed out of those for pure powers". Collins simply does not attempt to follow any line of argument or method of exposition — he seems indeed incapable of such an orderly treatment — nor does he attempt to elaborate the sense or meaning of anything of which he, so to speak, shows Leibniz the label. How much he could have learned by applying careful thought to this epistle must be an unsolved question; there is no reason to suppose that in fact he paid attention to more than a few points in it.

The last point I make about it is that it is the sort of communication (if such it can be called) with which Collins had been briefing Oldenburg for a number of years. He had helped the secretary prepare just such news-letters for Sluse in recent years[13]. The same character appears also in Collins' letters to Gregory, though there mitigated by other content of richer mathematical detail and more sustained discussion. Hence Leibniz was not treated in any special way by Collins, nor (I believe) was Collins emphatically significant on the eminence of English mathematical achievement, as Hofmann has suggested. In other words, whatever Leibniz made of it, this was the pretty normal Collins treatment of a foreign correspondent. And things might have continued along this rather dim track, had it not been for Leibniz's own personal development. The latter part of the year 1673 was to witness (in Hofmann's words) Leibniz's transformation from a tyro to a nearly mature mathematician[14]. By the end of that year, or early in 1674, Leibniz had achieved his arithmetical quadrature of the circle (the equivalence, $\frac{\pi}{4} = 1 - \frac{1}{3} + \frac{1}{5} - \frac{1}{7} \ldots$) which had been "written up" by November 1674; indeed, Leibniz's late-spring 1673 letters to Oldenburg already manifest his rapidly increasing talents in this area[15].

---

[13] See OLDENBURG, *Correspondence*, VI, Letters 1283, 1424 (especially the reference to Newton in the former, p. 227); VII, Letter 1649, and VIII, Letter 1906.

[14] HOFMANN, 45.

[15] Ibid., 59; CHRISTIAAN HUYGENS, *Oeuvres Complètes*, VII, 247 (loan to Leibniz of his own *De circuli magnitudine inventa* and JAMES GREGORY'S *De vera circuli quadratura*, 30 December 1673) and 393–5 (comment on Leibniz's paper on his quadrature, 7 November 1674 N.S.). One should perhaps emphasise here that Leibniz's discovery of the $\frac{\pi}{4}$ series owed nothing to Huygens' inspiration or example, but was rather based as to its method of termination (here I draw upon D.T. Whiteside) upon the Roberval/Fermat tradition — prob-

The transformation of Leibniz into a serious and highly original mathematician, one who "was concerned to acquire not facility in calculation or a mere catalogue of results, but basic insights and methods", characteristics developing rapidly into "a unified passion for knowledge"[16] took place in Paris, very much in the context of French mathematical history, and specifically under the influence of Huygens[17]. After May 1673 no correspondence passed between Leibniz and England until 5 July 1674, when Leibniz again wrote to Oldenburg. Thus during a critical period — perhaps the most critical period — of his mathematical metamorphosis Leibniz was immersed in a French environment, and wholly isolated from that of England. I do not mean, of course, that he did not read the books of British mathematicians. Besides the continental writers — Grégoire de Saint-Vincent, Descartes (his geometry in the great edition of Frans van Schooten), Pascal, Honoré Fabri and Sluse, Leibniz certainly read at least part of Wallis (especially the *Arithmetica infinitorum*), James Gregory (*De vera circula et hyperbolae quadratura*, 1667) and Barrow — it is known indeed that he had bought during his first visit to London a number of British mathematical books, including Nicholas Mercator's *Logarithmotechnia* (1668), Gregory's *Exercitationes geometricae* (1668) and Barrow's *Lectiones opticae et geometricae* although he studied none of these works attentively while in London nor, it seems, for some little while thereafter[18]. At Huygens' instigation he carefully examined Gregory's contention that an analytically constructable quadrature of the circle is impossible, in opposition to the view that Huygens had taken in 1654. Leibniz seems to have satisfied himself that Gregory's demonstration of the impossibility was incomplete, but no demonstration of his to that effect seems to be recorded and it is doubtful if he could have attained one at this time[19]. A third work of James Gregory's also known to Leibniz at this time was *Geometriae pars universalis* (1668) but he as yet possessed neither this nor the *Vera quadratura*.

Gregory, who had studied at Padua with Stefano degli Angeli, was (after Newton) by far the most learned and fertile British mathematician of this period; Hofmann remarks that "much more of Gregory's work' was taken over by Isaac Barrow "into his more famous *Lectiones geometricae* ... than has hitherto been suspected"; and D.T. Whiteside adds that we "are only now beginning to realise the extent and depth of his influence, mathematically and

ably as transmitted through GREGORY'S *Geometria pars universalis* of 1668 — and as to its method of division upon MERCATOR'S *Logarithmotechnia* of the same year.
[16] HOFMANN, 48.
[17] See the three autobiographical narratives conveniently summarised in *Oeuvres Complètes*, VII, 245–7, notes.
[18] HOFMANN, 75, note 59; OLDENBURG, *Correspondence*, IX, 595, 599.
[19] HOFMANN, 64, especially note 6. It is not clear here whether Leibniz shared Huygens' conviction that a geometrical quadrature is possible, or whether he shared Gregory's view (while recognising Gregory's failure in the mathematical demonstration of it).

scientifically, upon Newton"[20]. He was a thorough master of the whole theory of infinitesimals down to his own time, and provided (in *Geometriae pars universalis*) "a systematic exposition of elementary calculus techniques which he freely admits are largely reworkings and generalisations of approaches pioneered by others"[21]. After his return to Scotland Gregory's continuing mathematical fertility is almost uniquely recorded in his letters to John Collins — to whom he communicated results but not methods — and has only become fully apparent in recent decades. He dealt with a wide range of calculus problems, matured rapidly his understanding of infinite series (including the general binomial expansion) and developed powerful methods of interpolation. Much of this work was in parallel to that of Newton, some of it in advance of Newton. But because, after 1669, Gregory's only mathematical contact with the outside world was through Collins, his influence was incomparably less than Newton's. Nevertheless, Leibniz learned much from the books that Gregory published in 1667–68, and (during his second visit to London) he had an opportunity to see the material of Gregory in Collins' hands.

Gregory also worked on the method of tangents[22], as of course did Newton. Neither published his methods. The critical date here so far as Leibniz is concerned, is January 1673, when Henry Oldenburg published in the *Philosophical Transactions* the method of tangents of René François de Sluse, communicated to him by letter just a week or two before[23]. This had already been read to the Royal Society. Now Sluse's rule was far from new, though new to print — he calls it "[methodum] qua tot ante annos usus sum" — but it appeared more general than any stated hitherto. At any rate, Sluse's tangent-rule aroused Newton, who replied to Collins (somewhat egocentrically):

"it pleased me not a little to understand that [the foreign mathematicians] are fallen into the same method of drawing Tangents with me. What I guess their method to be you will apprehend by this example . . . "

After explaining his own procedure, Newton then assures Collins:

"This is one particular, or rather a Corollary of a Generall Method which extends itself without any troublesome calculation, not only to the drawing [of] tangents to all curve lines whether Geometrick or mechanick, or however related to streight lines or to other curve lines but also to the resolving other abstruser kinds of Problems about the crookedness, areas, lengths, centres of gravity of curves &c. Nor is it (as Huddens method de maximis et minimis & consequently Slusius his new method of Tangents as I presume) limited to equations which are free from surd quantities. This method I have interwoven with that other of working in equations by reducing them to infinite series."[24]

This letter naturally remained in Collins' possession, and was by him copied for Oldenburg to send to Sluse, who however did not receive it (owing to the

---

[20] Ibid., 70; *Dictionary of Scientific Biography*, I, 474, col. 2; V, 529, col. 1.
[21] D.T. WHITESIDE, "James Gregory", in *D.B.S.* V, 527, col. 1.
[22] OLDENBURG, *Correspondence*, VII, 360–67, 372–76.
[23] Ibid., IX, 386–96; *Phil. Trans.* no. 90 (20 January 1672/3), 5143–47.
[24] To Collins, 10 December 1672, NEWTON, *Correspondence*, I, 247–8; Oldenburg to Sluse, 29 January 1673, OLDENBURG, *Correspondence*, IX, 427–8, 588, 618–9.

loss of the first copy sent) until April 1673. Permit me to state categorically that Newton's method could only have become known to Leibniz from Sluse (which we have not the least reason to suppose) or from Collins (whom he did not meet before his second visit to London in 1676). Sluse's tangent-rule on the other hand was published both by word and in print, and indeed we may confidently believe that Leibniz was actually present when Sluse's letter was read at a meeting of the Royal Society on 29 January 1673[25]. It is not in dispute that Sluse's rule and Newton's are substantially though not formally, the same, though Sluse's rule was limited to "geometric" curves and expressions free from radicals and fractions. Newton, in writing to Oldenburg later, claimed no more than this, writing:

"it seems to me that he [Sluse] was acquainted with it [the tangent-rule] some years before he printed his Mesolabum [1668] and consequently before I understood it. But if it had been otherwise yet since he [Sluse] first imparted it to his friends and the world, it ought deservedly to be accounted his. As for the methods they are the same, though I believe derived from different principles. But I know not whether his principles afford it so general as mine, which extends to equations affected with surd terms, without reducing them to another form"[26].

Newton was of course conscious — I think it heightened his sensitivity to this whole issue of the tangent-rule — that his version of the rule was (as we see him insisting) a detached fragment from a whole new corpus of mathematical thinking. It was, in fact, extracted from Problem 4 of his 1670–71 tract *De methodis serierum et fluxionum*[27]. But — as we now know — the context in which Newton placed his tangent-rule was very different from that in which Leibniz, having apparently paid little attention to Sluse's rule in London during early 1673, later in that year or perhaps in 1674 perceived its importance. It is intrinsically implausible that Leibniz would have had to wait until 1676 to learn of the Newton-Sluse rule, and Hofmann has marshalled the documentary evidence to show that in fact he became acquainted with it in Sluse's paper during 1673, at which time also he achieved the crucial recognition that the inverse method of tangents and the method of quadratures are the same thing.

Thus, although this is not at all the kind of issue on which I mean to insist, it is emphatically clear that on the first and original point of indebtedness which Newton attributed to Leibniz — acquisition while in London on his second visit of the tangent-rule from the four year old letter to Collins — Newton was mistaken. Leibniz's own insistence that he had taken the tangent-rule from Sluse seems to be fully borne out by the evidence, as well as the inherent likelihood of the circumstances.

In the past it was widely assumed — at least by Anglo-Saxon writers like J.M. Child[28] — that Isaac Barrow provided an open entrance to the theory of

---

[25] HOFMANN, 72; THOMAS BIRCH, *History of the Royal Society*, III, London 1757, 74.
[26] Newton to Oldenburg, 23 June 1673, *Correspondence*, I, 294.
[27] WHITESIDE, *Mathematical Papers* (see note 1), III, 15, 120–33.
[28] J.M. CHILD, *The Early Mathematical Manuscripts of Leibniz*, London 1920.

tangents for both Newton and Leibniz. Modern scholars, with deeper information, have refuted this notion; Hofmann, so far as Leibniz is concerned, Whiteside for Newton[29]. Barrow was presumably original in his method of "generating figures by motion" — so much Newton allowed him; however, a great deal of the *Lectiones geometricae* consists of what Whiteside has called "a systematic generalisation of tangent, quadrature and rectification procedures gathered by Barrow from his reading of Torricelli, Descartes, Schooten, Hudde, Wallis, Wren, Fermat, Pascal, and above all James Gregory."[30] In fact modern studies emphasise, rather than depreciate, the strong dependence of English mathematical writings in the 1660s on the strong, earlier continental tradition, partly mediated to mathematicians like Barrow and Gregory by their English predecessors of the 1650s — Neile, Wren and Wallis. Similarly, in this vein, Hofmann points out that if Barrow was the first to publish the characteristic triangle in a formal work, it had been known to a dozen mathematicians previously (including, among the British, Wren, Neile, Wallis and Gregory), Leibniz learned of it from Pascal's letters, not from Barrow. Equally, the improved concept of indivisibles was developed in Italy and France before it was known in England.

Barrow seems, indeed, an inappropriate figure to have been selected — by overemphasis of Newton's own tendentious statements — as the forefather of the calculus. Recent opinion is that the *Lectiones geometricae* were little read even within the select group of readers capable of understanding them. Newton himself never acknowledged deep indebtedness to Barrow; Whiteside has qualified as a "myth" the tradition that Newton was Barrow's pupil and protégé[31]. If Newton had no real need of Barrow, how much less strong was his impact on Leibniz likely to be!

Hofmann believed that Leibniz made no close study of the *Lectiones geometricae* before 1675, when his attention may have been directed to them by Tschirnhaus[32]. At the time between his first and second visits to England, when Barrow's book would have been most valuable to Leibniz, it was really too difficult for him, and furthermore it was a book neglected by his chief mentor Huygens. As for various technical suggestions indicative of Leibniz's direct indebtedness to Barrow's work — for example, those made by Child — these only seem plausible in ignorance of the achievements of Barrow's predecessors and collapse before a more searching inquiry; Leibniz's sources were the same as Barrow's.[33] Thus Leibniz's own insistence that his mathematical ideas were not moulded by Barrow seems not merely inherently plausible, but is fully confirmed by the documentary evidence.

---

[29] HOFMANN, 74–8; *Dictionary of Scientific Biography*, I, s.v. "Isaac Barrow".
[30] *D.S.B.*, I, 474, col. 2.
[31] Ibid., I, 475, col. 1.
[32] HOFMANN, 76, note 61.
[33] *D.S.B.*, I, 474, col. 2–475, col. 1.

As the point is of some importance, let me quote one of Leibniz's last autobiographical statements on this issue, written to the Abbé Conti in March 1716:

"... si quelqu'un a profité de M. Barrow, ce sera plus tôt M. N. qui a étudié sous luy que moi qui (autant que je puis m'en souvenir) nay veu les Livres de M. Barrow qu'à mon second Voyage d'Angleterre, & ne les ay jamais lû avec attention, parce qu'en voyant le Livre je m'apperçus que par la consideration du Triangle Characteristique (dont les cotez sont les Elements de l'Abscisse, de l'Ordonnée & de la Courbe) semblable a quelque Triangle assignable, j'etois venu comme en me jouant aux Quadratures, Surfaces & Solides dont M. Barrow avoit remply un Chapitre..."[34]

Leibniz is too cavalier: he did acquire the *Lectiones* on his first visit to England, as we have seen, and he did — later — devote some time to their study; but the essence of his statement is correct. And when Leibniz goes on to add, in the next sentence:

"... je ne suis venu a mon Calcul des Differences dans la Geometrie qu'apres en avoir vû l'usage (mais moins considerable) dans les nombres..."[34]

here again he makes a fundamental, important, and valid claim to the difference between his route to the calculus and that followed by Newton; a route of his own along which Barrow could not have been a guide.

As against this, Newton seeing only the prior publication of Barrow's *Lectiones*, the obvious generic similarity between Barrow's and Leibniz's methods, and the slight reason to suppose that Leibniz was already an inventive and generalising mathematician by 1674, long before his second visit to England, convinced himself and for ever repeated that Leibniz had done no more than turn Barrow's method into a new algorithm with a new symbolism; thus in a draft of 1714:

"Dr. Barrow published his method of tangents in the year 1670, and that very candid gentleman the Marquis de l'Hôpital, in the Preface of his Analyse [des Infiniment Petits] represents that Dr. Barrow stopped at fractions and surds, & where Dr. Barrow left off Mr. Leibniz began. His method of tangents is the same as Dr. Barrow's except that he has changed his [Barrow's] letter a and e into the symbols dx and dy, and (being admonished by Mr. Newton's letters of 10 December 1672, 13 June 1676, and 24 October 1676) taught how to avoid fractions and surds"[35].

Further, as the allusion to the Marquis suggests, the lineage from Barrow to Leibniz was equally apparent to exponents of the calculus unprejudiced in Newton's favour. Tschirnhaus drew attention to it in 1678, and so again did Jakob Bernoulli in 1691 when he declared that the obscurities in Leibniz's own treatment would not trouble one who had mastered the calculus of Barrow (calculum Barovianum), upon which Leibniz's was founded and from which Leibniz's differed only in point of notation and greater convenience. The Newtonians did not let slip the opportunity to use such sentiments against Leibniz himself[36].

I have dwelt on the question of Leibniz's knowledge of Barrow at some length because though itself neutral in the Leibniz-Newton issue, since Leibniz

---

[34] NEWTON, *Correspondence*, VI, 310.
[35] Ibid., 86.
[36] HOFMANN, 77; NEWTON, *Correspondence*, VI, 138.

might have learned a great deal from the *Lectiones geometricae* and still gone on to develop the calculus in total independence of Newton, nevertheless, for those who chose to see it so, it was a first step into a false Leibnizian historiography, a step even his friends admitted. If Leibniz, the tyro, knew at first only what he learnt from Barrow, and began by a trifling reworking of Barrow, was it not the more likely (especially as no word of his debt to Barrow was acknowledged) that he had also borrowed his first real improvement of Barrow, that is, the treatment of fractions and surds? For, said the Newtonians, this too was open to his eye, as open as the *Lectiones geometricae*.

If it had only always been clear that Leibniz did n o t profit from Barrow, then the next accusation — that he needed further help to get beyond Barrow — would have seemed the less plausible.

To return now to Leibniz's direct relations with England. Busy as he was, he did not reply to Oldenburg's last letter before July 1674. Mathematical news is even then only a small component in a long letter; he tells Oldenburg in some detail of his success in making a rational quadrature of a particular cycloid-segment and adds:

"Others of my theorems are of considerably greater importance, of which that especially is most wonderful by means of which the area of a circle or some given sector of it may be exactly expressed by a certain infinite series of rational numbers. But I also possess certain analytical methods, extremely general and far-reaching, which I esteem more highly than particular theorems however exquisite."[37]

Oldenburg's reply perished. Accordingly, Leibniz wrote again in October[38], composing a fairly ordinary mathematical newsletter, except that he emphasises, indeed overemphasises, the importance of his own work on Ozanam's Diophantine problems and reiterates his statement about the circle-series, to which he now adds the arc--sine series, all in somewhat flamboyant terms: "Whoever has hitherto sought the exact quadrature of the circle has not so much as opened a path by which one might hope to be able to arrive at it, I would dare to state that this has now first been done by me."

Alas! Leibniz was once again to be disappointed. His discoveries had been anticipated by both James Gregory and Isaac Newton, though neither had published[39]. Every one, in fact, worked in ignorance of the achievements of others; there is no foundation for the *Commercium Epistolicum* insinuation that Leibniz had earlier knowledge of the British work on series via Sluse; there is no known route by which this could have been, nor could Sluse have transmitted what he did not know. On the other hand, there is no doubt that Oldenburg's dampening reply (December, 1674)[40] was perfectly justified:

---

[37] OLDENBURG, *Correspondence,* XI, Letter 2511; HOFMANN, 58—59, 80—81.
[38] OLDENBURG, *Correspondence,* XI, Letter 2550; HOFMANN, pp. 94—98.
[39] Mercator, too, seems to have attained a similar success.
[40] OLDENBURG, *Correspondence,* Letter 2576, HOFMANN, pp. 99—100.

"What you relate about your success in the measurement of curves is very fine, but I would regret your being unaware (ignorare te nolim) that the method and procedure for measuring curves have been extended by Gregory, as also by Newton, to any curve whatever, whether mechanical or geometrical, even the circle itself; in so much that if you have given the ordinate of any curve, you can by this method find the length of the curved line, the area of the figure, its centre of gravity, the solid of revolution, its surface whether erect or inclined, and the segment of revolution of the solid of revolution, and the converse of these; and, moreover, given the quadrature of any arc, to compute the logarithmic sine, tangent or secant, without the natural ones being known, and conversely."

As to Leibniz's claim — somewhat incautiously expressed in the October letter — that the circumference of the circle could be exactly expressed by the sum of a series, Oldenburg reminds him of Gregory's continuing confidence in the production of a proof that this is impossible. Hofmann has already remarked on the greater coolness of this letter, full as it is and perfectly courteous. The truth is that in his three main areas of interest hitherto — natural philosophy, mechanics, and mathematics — Leibniz had failed to impress the British. The vehemence of his claims was more evident than the solidity of his achievement. Oldenburg needed to be friendly, but very cautions; his temperament, experience and situation all bade him to obey the British inclination towards scepticism of bold claims, especially those made by foreigners. Hooke, in an unpleasant way, and Wallis in a more amiable way, were always ready to launch out against absurd foreign pretensions, and the continental — Newton optical debate was going on at this very moment. Worse, Huygens himself was temporarily estranged from the Royal Society in London by the dispute over the first rectification of a geometric curve[41]. Oldenburg may well have known of Leibniz's close mathematical association with Huygens; though such an association might well be seen in England as a kind of guarantee that Leibniz would claim nothing absurd — nor had he done so — still it reinforced the need to tread very delicately. Above all, the claims of the British mathematicians themselves must not go unrecorded, as had happened with poor William Neile in 1657 over the rectification of the semicubic parabola.

Unfortunately, Leibniz was not quite convinced by Oldenburg's word that the British had made as much progress as himself[42]. To the end of his life he could not reconcile himself to this loss of priority. At the time when the dispute about the discovery of the calculus rose to its height, after the publication of the *Commercium epistolicum* in 1712, Leibniz wrote to Johann Bernoulli: "I now hear for the first time that my discovery of the magnitude of the circle is to be attributed to [James] Gregory also ... Newton himself praised my discovery at the time when it was imparted to Oldenburg, and admitted that my own way of discovering it was an original one. Therefore he did not then know of Gregory's discovery."[43] And shortly afterwards, in drafting the notorious *Charta Volans*,

---

[41] HOFMANN, Chapter 8; OLDENBURG, *Correspondence*, vols. X, XI, passim.
[42] Cf. HOFMANN, p. 100.
[43] NEWTON, *Correspondence*, VI, p. 7; 17 June 1713.

XVI

Leibniz and the British Mathematicians

Leibniz attempted to rebut the false and unjust charge that he himself had stolen the quadrature of the circle by an infinite sum of rational terms from the British mathematicians with the allegation that the British themselves — Wallis, Hooke, Newton and the younger [David] Gregory — were ignorant for 36 years of what James Gregory had achieved, and had acknowledged Leibniz himself as the discoverer of that series. Indeed, Leibniz continues (no doubt relying on memory's blandishments) Newton himself "admitted in a letter that (so far as he knew) this method of series was not yet employed by others (ab aliis nondum usurpatam)"[44]. Alas again for the elderly philosopher; Newton had made no such admission in the letters of 1676, and on the contrary had taken some trouble to display before Leibniz at that time the rich accomplishments of the British[45]. Let us not insist on the mistakes that both Newton and Leibniz made in later years; my only point now is that Leibniz obviously never clearly understood that even yet, with his rational quadratures and ones by rational series, he was not quite at the limits of mathematical knowledge in 1674, even in this one area — and there were of course many other areas of mathematics into which he had not yet ventured.

We now come to the point in time where, after the interval commencing with his departure from London in March 1673, Leibniz's direct and indirect relations with London once more became voluminous and significant; that is, I have now to consider the year and a half (roughly) from April 1675 until the time when Leibniz began his new career at the court of Hanover; in this period Leibniz discovered his new calculus, visited London for the second time, and received two famous letters from Newton. The mass and complexity of the mathematical detail involved is very considerable and I can only skate over the surface of specialist historians' investigations to convey some idea of their generally accepted conclusions.

Leibniz reiterated allusions to his progress in mathematics aroused Collins and Oldenburg to send Leibniz in April 1675 a very long, rambling and confused document attempting to be a survey of the frontiers of mathematical achievement as Collins saw them at that time[46]. More serious, no doubt, than defects in transcription and translation (from Collins' English to Oldenburg's Latin) were the limitations of Collins' own mathematical equipment and attitude; notably his own partial comprehension of the work of Gregory and Newton in so far as this had been imparted to him during the last six or seven years, notwithstanding his great enthusiasm for their successes. We have to recall also that in this, as in other communications of the period, the object was as much to state

---

[44] Ibid., 17, 21 note (12).
[45] There is certainly no concession of priority in his reply to Oldenburg on 13 June 1676; NEWTON, *Correspondence*, II, 21, 29.
[46] OLDENBURG, *Correspondence*, XI, Letters 2641, 2642.

a claim as to diffuse the mastery of new knowledge and methods. Newton's own letters later were far more rich and instructive.

Collins started by giving (without explanation or demonstration) Gregory's latest series for π, of which he had learned nearly five years before, and Newton's series for deriving the arc from the sine and the sine from the arc. He makes it clear that this work, and much else which I need not detail, had been done years before, that the method of series had been extended to the resolution of equations, and that Gregory had willingly decided to leave it to Mr. Newton "to make the first discoveries of this new method of infinite series to the world". He then plunges into the "doctrine of equations", with the usual futile references to Pell and Dulaurens. Collins also outlined work by Gregory and Newton on intersecting conics, and of Newton on the generation of a general conic[47].

One may agree with Hofmann both that Collins' information gave Leibniz a "considerable stimulus" to the further study of fundamental problems in algebra, and that the paper contained no direct enlightenment, either as regards algebra or the treatment of series[48]. To this extent the later Newtonian interpretation of Collins' letter was mistaken. But there were equally many hints and indications which a more mature mathematician than Leibniz could have taken to heart and developed — if he had merely addressed himself to reconstructing the achievements of Gregory and Newton. But Leibniz was far too immersed in his own thoughts to do this — a fact of which the Newtonians were not aware, and would not have credited. The subsequent correspondence concerning algebra and especially the general resolution of cubic equations I gladly pass over; it was frustrated by the mistaken assertions of minor mathematicians on both sides of the Channel, and though the names of Gregory and Newton appear here and there, this is largely an arid desert where the only glitter comes from fools' gold. There was a good deal that Leibniz did not understand, much of which was of no value to him, but much also that it would have profited him to understand[49].

Equally tenuous and negative was Leibniz's next, indirect contact with London through Tschirnhaus, who was in England from early May to mid August. Tschirnhaus was a highly accomplished algebraist, keen, ambitious, and highly energetic. He plunged eagerly into mathematical discourse and wrote several letters to Oldenburg about matters that excited him. But among the British mathematicians he met only Collins (of course) and Wallis — from whom he perhaps took a hint about imaginary numbers back to Leibniz[50] — he had no immediate knowledge of the investigations made by Gregory and Newton. And he was at least as much eager to impress as to learn. Probably he picked up

---

[47] HOFMANN, 131—2.
[48] HOFMANN, 139.
[49] See ibid., chapter 11; the documents are in OLDENBURG, *Correspondence*, XI.
[50] HOFMANN, 175—6.

little more about British mathematics than was already known to Leibniz from Collins' news-letters[51]. He did, apparently, study Barrow's geometrical lectures with care, but impressed no respect for them on Leibniz when the two Germans were in close communion on mathematical matters during the summer of 1675. All this ground too has been very ably covered by our lamented colleague Joseph Hofmann, who concluded that while this Parisian association with Tschirnhaus was of advantage to Leibniz's development as a mathematician, because his friend was very skilful and studious in algebra, if also uncritical, yet Leibniz learned nothing crucial from Tschirnhaus, and certainly nothing which Tschirnhaus had brought over from Britain[52]. If I understand part of his argument aright, it is that Tschirnhaus was unable to absorb and admire the new infinitesimal methods that were taking shape in Leibniz's own mind; indeed, he rejected them, and, being deeply immersed in his own algorithms, took no interest in the new analysis. This certainly seems to indicate that he would have been a highly unlikely vehicle for the transmission of new, British infinitesimal methods to Paris, had he come across them. His letter to Oldenburg of early July 1675 shows how full he still was, some time after his arrival in London, of his own methods and their excellence[53].

And now we reach the critical point in this review, the date of Leibniz's first entrance into his new calculus.

After his "Tschirnhaus" summer, in which the two young Germans devoted much study to the papers of Pascal and other French mathematicians of mid century, Leibniz broke his long silence to write to Oldenburg on 18 December 1675 a long flattering, and extremely cordial letter in which he summarised his mental activity of recent month. He reports various things I have already mentioned; he writes about Boyle, which leads him into a long passage on his philosophical intentions wherein he pays Boyle a very elegant compliment ("Boyliano itaque more semper philosophabuntur homines, nostrum aliquando ad finem perducent..."); he turns to Collins, and the reduction of equations again, Cardan's rule and Schooten's which he says fails with imaginaries like $\sqrt{-1}$. He adds more about his own hopes concerning imaginary numbers and irrational roots. Finally, he promises Oldenburg his unique instrument for constructing all equations geometrically and his quadrature of the circle by a

---

[51] There is a specific statement by Oldenburg in a letter to Leibniz (30 September 1675, OLDENBURG, *Correspondence,* XI, Letter 2754): "as regards the rectification of any arc of circle Tschirnhaus can impart to you a method discovered by our Gregory which Collins imparted to him when he was with us" (see HOFMANN, 171, note 33).

[52] Leibniz himself wrote to Oldenburg (18 December 1675, OLDENBURG, *Correspondence,* Letter 2804): "In sending Tschirnhaus to me, you acted as a friend, for I much delight in his company and recognise an outstanding capacity in this young man; promising important new discoveries, he has actually shown me not a few things in analysis and geometry which were indeed extremely elegant whence I easily judge what may be expected from him".

[53] OLDENBURG, *Correspondence,* Letter 2698.

rational series "which I have imparted to the geometers here [i.e. Huygens] more than two years ago". Further, he goes on, he had lately made a successful new attack upon ("aditum reperi felicem") another geometrical problem of which he had hitherto quite despaired, of which he would say more when leisure permitted; all he had done needed putting in proper order[54]. Hofmann takes this intractable geometric problem to be that of inverse-tangents, to which Leibniz had recently returned with success. The success was due, of course, to his new calculus and notation, still in its infancy. Leibniz was, as Hofmann remarks, still making many mistakes in the use of his new mathematical methods. But since October 1675 the differential calculus had been in being, and furnished with powerful techniques, and Leibniz was already thinking about the manner of publication. The development was traced from his private materials by Leibniz in his unpublished *Historia et Origo calculis differentialis,* by Gerhardt and other nineteenth century historians, and most recently by Hofmann[55].

After this point, once Leibniz had devised his new notation and an algorithm for handling his method of differentiation (thought methods of integration came considerably more slowly) it might seem as though all else must be anti-climax. This is not quite the case. It is true that Leibniz had formulated the calculus long before the termination of his connection with the British mathematicians — indeed, before his direct relationship with Newton commenced — yet he was still, for all that, a very partially read and expert mathematician. It might be still the case that he owed important debts to others for the maturation of his concepts and methods.

Before attempting any judgment on this issue, I will briefly summarise the ways in which Leibniz could have learned anything more of British mathematics. First, there is the Latin letter, now lost, sent by Oldenburg to Tschirnhaus in May, 1676. It is clear that this letter differed a good deal from Collins' English model for it, which survives[56]. Starting from Collins' criticism of Descartes' achievements in mathematics, it is yet another long, rambling statement of what the British have recently done, with little or no information as to methods and a large number of blunders as to fact and significance. Pell, Gregory and Newton are the main "contemporary" figures[57]. Of the references to Newton the most important is an account of Newton's tangent-method — which, it is likely, was not given in full — and a bare announcement of his success in performing quadratures and rectifications by the method of infinite series. Hofmann regards this letter as unimportant, not unjustly describing Collins as a pygmy between

---

[54] Ibid., ad finem. This passage was not quoted in the *Commercium epistolicum* (1712). It is an omission, against Leibniz, of which he might well have complained. See HOFMANN, p. 195.

[55] Chapter 13.

[56] Royal Society MS. *Commercium epistolicum,* 25; partially printed in NEWTON, *Correspondence,* II, 15–17; analysis by HOFMANN, 202–8.

[57] Gregory was already dead.

giants. Shortly afterwards, in response to Tschirnhaus's reply to this letter, Collins assembled in the form of extracts from James Gregory's letters to himself the so-called "Historiola", to which he also added an account of Pell's work.

These papers were never sent to Leibniz, who did however examine them while in London during October. Instead, Collins prepared an "Abridgement" dated 14 June 1676, and which was approved by Newton (to whom there were brief allusions)[58]. Meanwhile, though the correspondence between Newton and Oldenburg for this period has vanished, we know from a memorandum that Oldenburg was interesting Newton in Leibniz's mathematical ideas and was surely encouraging him to compose his *Epistola prior* (13 June 1676)[60]. Oldenburg himself incorporated the "Abridgement" into a Latin letter to Leibniz dated 26 July 1676 and added to it a copy of the *Epistola prior*[61].

Collins' fairly elaborate account of the late work of the great Scottish mathematician (who had died in the previous autumn) gives a highly impressive picture of what Gregory had achieved in dealing with power-series and algebra. Its object was to show how far the British had advanced beyond Descartes. At the same time, Collins was not able to give proofs or much more than bare results, since Gregory had concealed his working from him. His report on Pell covers the same ground as before on the treatment of equations, which Pell had so far refused to divulge in example or detail.

Newton's paper, very cautiously composed in order to express his achievements succinctly and clearly, and not entering into derivations and proofs, is very different. Newton's initial phase of mathematical success was over; publication of his work was still in the future. It was ten years since he had written his first tract on fluxions, to be succeeded by *De analysi per aequationes infinitas* and *De methodis serierum et fluxionum; De analysi* had actually been examined only by Barrow and Collins while *De methodis* was seen by no one before 1684. Meanwhile, Newton had launched out into other fields of natural philosophy, into optics, and (privately) into chemistry. As Collins remarked to James Gregory in October 1675, Newton like Barrow seemed now already to find mathematical speculations "nice and dry if not somewhat barren"[62]. Within a year Newton's correspondence with both Collins and Oldenburg ceased. It required fresh personal stimuli from Hooke and Halley to bring about New-

---

[58] Royal Society MS. *Commercium epistolicum*, 30, 13 June 1676; see HOFMANN, chapter 15. Brief extracts from the "Historiola" and "Abridgement" are printed in NEWTON, *Correspondence*, II, 18–20, 47–49.
[59] NEWTON, *Correspondence*, II, 7.
[60] NEWTON, *Correspondence*, II, 20–32.
[61] Ibid., 54–5 (not the transmitted text); C.I. GERHARDT, *Der Briefwechsel von G.W. Leibniz mit Mathematikern*, I Band, Berlin 1899, 169–179.
[62] NEWTON, *Correspondence*, I, 356.

ton's return to mathematics in the *Principia philosophiae* which was followed by the composition of *De quadratura curvarum*.

It is a strange fact that Newton's two letters, addressed to Oldenburg at his request for the benefit of Leibniz, were not only the fullest exposition of his mathematical ideas ever deliberately written for a reader up to this time, but closed his correspondence on mathematical topics for a number of years. Why did Newton take so much trouble, at Oldenburg's request, in satisfying the curiosity of a young German of whom he knew nothing? His doing so is certainly inconsistent with the conventional view of Newton as secretive and uncommunicative. We know that the direct occasion for the writing of the *Epistola prior* was Leibniz's request for further enlightenment about series expansions imparted by Collins to the young Dane Georg Mohr in May; this request, as we have seen, Oldenburg transmitted to Newton. All Newton himself offers by way of explanation of his exposition is that since Leibniz wants to know what the English have discovered, "I have sent you some of those things which occurred to me in order to satisfy his wishes"[63]. One may choose with Hofmann to see Newton rather carefully safeguarding his own priority, or with Whiteside to see him proceeding with exceptional generosity[64]. The puzzle is made the stranger because Newton was already tired of the altercations following his optical publications, to which Newton refers in the last lines of the *Epistola prior*[65].

The letter is full of technical mathematics with which I cannot deal, nor shall I attempt to compare Newton's mathematics with Gregory's and weigh their respective impacts on Leibniz. All I need convey now, I think, is the double point that the *Epistola prior* contains nothing of which Leibniz had not heard in outline already, and that although Newton now provided more details and examples than Leibniz had received previously he was — inevitably in terms of sheer space one might think — far from completely open and explicit. Newton's new methods are not satisfactorily explained; in Hofmann's view (perhaps too extreme) "everything was done to prevent Leibniz from, as it were, improperly penetrating the world of Newton's thought" and he goes on to note specifical-

---

[63] Ibid., II, 20.

[64] HOFMANN, 225–6; WHITESIDE, *Mathematical Papers*, IV, 666. The latter prints (ibid., 28) a draft in which Newton offers further details "in usum calculatorum ... quibus siquos noveris ... communicare possis"

[65] Surely Hofmann is too cynical in suggesting that Newton deliberately added this comment to prevent Oldenburg's sending his original to Leibniz. It is in any case most unlikely that the secretary would have allowed so important an original to go out of the Society's possession. Equally, Hofmann makes much of the fact that in the "Newtonian" tradition the sending of the *Epistola prior* is dated 26 June 1676 (a mistake for 26 July), bolstering the argument that before replying Leibniz had some six weeks in which to modify Newton's series so as to be able to claim them as his own. In fact, Leibniz acknowledged the *Epistola prior* very hastily, two days after receiving it. But I do not believe myself that these matters of priority were so urgently in the minds of either Newton or Leibniz in 1676.

ly that "nothing was said of the central problems — nothing of his [Newton's] methodus fluxionum or the differential equations into whose solution by power series Newton already possessed considerable insight."[66] Two points should be made here. The first is that Hofmann, writing nearly thirty years ago, exaggerated the development of the direct and inverse method of fluxions that had taken place by 1676; as of course it suited Newton's book to exaggerate it in much later years. Notably, as regards the "solution of differential equations by power series" the *De quadratura curvarum* was not yet written; as we shall learn from Dr. Whiteside's seventh volume of Newton's mathematical papers shortly, he began work on this tract only in December 1691. Therefore, perhaps, there was less of a finished kind to communicate with respect to fluxions than Hofmann supposed; and secondly one may wonder whether such complete candour as he looked for was usual, or even practical within the framework of a learned correspondence. One may set beside Newton's fluxions anagram in the *Epistola posterior* that of Huygens relating to his spring-regulated escapement of the previous year. However this may be, it is certainly clear that Leibniz really was not even yet able fully to appreciate and profit from the hints that Newton did set before him now and in the *Epistola posterior*[67]. In this respect his use of Newton's material was much inferior to James Gregory's.

We now know that the *Epistola prior* was long in transmission to Leibniz, and that his letter of acknowledgement was composed promptly and in haste. Again, I shall not repeat the summary of Leibniz's results as stated in this letter which others have already provided. Obscurities and imperfections in it were as much due to haste and to clumsiness in Leibniz's presentation arising from his inexperience as to any conscious desire to lead Newton astray.[68] In fact we may be sure that Leibniz's was an honest and genuine letter, and surely Newton received it as such. The charges levelled against it in 1712 and later by Newton himself were quite false, misconceptions produced by the evil atmosphere which by then existed and springing in part, it must be said, from Leibniz's own provocations.

In the letter Leibniz congratulates Newton on his unprecedented success with the method of series. One sees taking clearer shape the conviction already present in his mind that Newton's method of series had nothing to do with his own method of differences, of which, evidently, he found no vestige in the *Epistola prior*. Accordingly, his requests for further enlightenment relate in no way to what he saw as his own province of mathematics, but wholly to Newton's: he sought enlightenment on the genesis of the binomial theorem (which he had greatly admired in Newton's letter), on the resolution of algebraic equations,

---

[66] HOFMANN, 230. His analysis of the *Epistola prior* is in Chapter 16; WHITESIDE'S, in *Mathematical Papers*, IV, 666–70.

[67] Cf. WHITESIDE'S comment, ibid., 13.

[68] But the opinion in HOFMANN, 234, note 11 and 237 is different.

and on the inversion of series. Thus Leibniz and Newton fell into opposite, but complementary misunderstandings. Leibniz believed (in one sense, quite rightly) that Newton was ignorant of his own precious secret, because his route of advance and Newton's were utterly distinct. Newton believed — later — that Leibniz had penetrated his secret and used it against himself, when really Leibniz had indeed employed only his own methods.

But what did Newton think of Leibniz in the summer of 1676? It is hard to decide. It is clearly Hofmann's view that Newton was always secretly suspicious of Leibniz and hostile towards him. Quickly realising that Leibniz was clever, he could not see that Leibniz had produced anything essentially new. What he had written seemed like a reconstruction of Newton's own work.

I quote Hofmann's most telling sentence: "That there was here no independent invention, not even a rediscovery, but simply an attempt at plagiarism seemed certain to Newton when Leibniz asked him to explain again more explicity the decisive points in his letter, namely his methods of series-expansion and series-inversion." Hence Newton meant by his second letter to end Leibniz's game and put an end to discussion with an unworthy opponent[69]. Once again Newton's editor D.T. Whiteside has implicitly presented an opposite view: Newton's reticence on vital mathematical issues was not, he suggests, so much due to mistrust of Leibniz as to native caution. "What prevented Newton on this occasion from being more explicit on the subject of his fluxional insights was, almost certainly, lack of self-confidence and the memory of the hail of criticism he had had to endure when he made public his equally novel theory of light a few years before. In all other respects the tone of Newton's letter is one of friendly helpfulness . . . "[70].

In my view cynicism, like guilt, needs to be proved and innocence should be assumed. I agree with Whiteside in judging Newton's *Epistola posterior* to be like the letter from Leibniz to which it was a response, wholly innocent. When Newton writes that "very great things" are to be expected of Leibniz, when he remarks at its close that the "letter of the most excellent Leibniz fully deserved that I give it this more extended reply", and when a few days later he writes (as it were privately) to Oldenburg of Leibniz's "goodness and ingenuity", I think he quite straightforwardly meant what he said[71]. I do not believe he was double-dealing. After all, in both these letters he did what was natural and expected, that is, he went back and used after reworking it the material in the tracts he had by him. We know that he devoted six weeks to the composition of the *Epistola posterior* — knowing what work was to Newton, that is a very large

---

[69] Ibid., 260.
[70] *Mathematical Papers*, IV, 673.
[71] NEWTON, *Correspondence*, II, 111, 129, 162. Whiteside justly draws attention to Newton's apology here for severity in handling Leibniz's "oversights" (partly in fact due to Collins, for example the "hujus-ludus" mistranscription).

intellectual effort. Would he have made such an effort against an "unworthy opponent", as Hofmann puts it? Would not Newton simply have refused to have more to do with Leibniz, treating him as later he treated Hooke? And why, in any case, should Newton think of Leibniz at this time as an "opponent" at all?

Hofmann's account is based on the premise that the bad impression that Leibniz seemed to make on Pell in 1673 was universally diffused in England. I do not think it was so. It did not affect Oldenburg. I cannot believe that it ever reached Newton, who can only have learned the story of Mouton long afterwards. We know that in 1687 — after Leibniz's first calculus publication — Newton took an unsuspicious view of his achievement. I think this reflects the view that Newton had formed, from the little he knew of Leibniz, in 1676. Certainly Leibniz, as sensitive a mortal as ever was, found nothing to distress him in what Hofmann has called the "unmistakable tone" of the *Epistola posterior,* with which he was on the contrary delighted[72]. That Newton let the correspondence drop after Oldenburg's death is explicable enough without introducing any notion in his mind of Leibniz's guilt.

As is well known, the *Epistola posterior* only reached Leibniz's hands in June 1677, long after his settlement at Hanover. There remains one issue, therefore: what did Leibniz learn about English mathematics during his second visit to London in October 1676? The record is clear; in that he did go over the Gregorian "Historiola" and the Newtonian transcripts collected by Collins. Remember that these included a complete copy of Newton's mathematical notebook (now Cambridge University Library MS. Add. 4006) and a complete copy of the 1666 tract on fluxions besides *De Analysi,* that is, in essence the whole "calculus" part of what Dr. Whiteside has collected in the first volume of his *Mathematical Papers* was at least potentially open to Leibniz's inspection. At least, it is hard to believe that Collins did not offer to put all these in Leibniz's hands. However, the message has been clear for over a century, even though Leibniz's annotations made while in London have not yet been completely published: Leibniz took nothing from these London papers relative to his calculus, now formulated for over a year. His excerpts from *De Analysi,* for example, related only to series-expansion and he disregarded Newton's discussion of infinitesimals altogether, for the obvious reason, Hofmann remarks, that they offered nothing new to Leibniz[73]. Hence the private record must, in Whiteside's words finally "clear Leibniz of any lingering suspicions still felt by any ardent Newtonian supporter that he made good use of his chance to annex for his own purposes the fluxional method briefly exposed there"[74].

---

[72] Ibid., 212, 231.
[73] HOFMANN, 279; WHITESIDE, *Mathematical Papers,* II, 170. Leibniz's annotations from *De Analysi* are printed ibid., 248—59.
[74] *Mathematical Papers,* 170.

My sketchy review has done no more than indicate the trend of scholarship for more than a century, and a conclusion we may now regard as definitively established. There is no doubt that "calculus" methods originated independently in several minds at about the same time by reflection on the body of mathematical knowledge and technique that had been assembled by circa 1660. That, as between Newton and Leibniz, the former was first to achieve a "breakthrough" there can be no possible doubt. That the latter failed for ever to perceive Newton's achievement, or understand it, and therefore owed nothing to it, is equally clear. For the ordinary historian the honours must therefore be equally divided, and we may leave the specialist historians of mathematics to consider the relative depths and subtleties of individual mathematical writings [75].

One point, discussed in my last few paragraphs, remains undecided. While there is an obvious deep sense in which the calculus quarrel was inevitable, given two inventors, partial communication and imperfect mutual comprehension, was the priority dispute already potentially in existence in 1676? Did Newton really always see himself as Leibniz's "opponent"? Was Newton indeed always as xenophobic as John Wallis — curiously, perhaps the English mathematician from whom Leibniz profited most — though certainly less xenophobic than Wallis would have him be? This must be a matter of personal judgement; for myself, I do not believe that the priority dispute existed even potentially before 1684. After Leibniz had made his public claim — in his own eyes, to his own knowledge, a perfectly just claim — to complete and unparallelled originality in the discovery of the calculus, of course the dispute existed in potentia. To my mind, however, reluctant as I am to differ from so great an authority as Joseph Hofmann, it is not to be taken as self-evident that Newton nourished the seeds of enmity towards Leibniz from 1676 onwards. And of course nothing that Newton wrote or did after 1711 — and he wrote and did much that was reprehensible, as Leibniz had also — can prove that he did carry this blackness in his heart all those years.

---

[75] Cf. Christoph J. Scriba 'The Inverse method of tangents: A dialogue between Leibniz and Newton (1675–1677)', *Archive for History of Exact Sciences*, II, 1964, pp. 113–137.

XVII

NEWTON IN FRANCE: A NEW VIEW[1]

The story of the penetration of Newtonian science into France is a complex one which, despite the distinction of the historians from Pierre Brunet[2] (or should one say Voltaire?) onwards who have treated it, has not yet been fully told. It is doubtful if it *can* be fully told as a personal story rather than as an episode in Anglo-French scientific relations. For to the French (and to the Germans, Italians...) Newtonian science appeared as a subspecies of English science; they do not refer (as we may do) to "Newtonians" but to "Englishmen"; they linked Newton as a mathematician with Barrow, and as an experimental philosopher with Boyle. When continentals complained in the early eighteenth century of the chauvinism of Newton's English followers they specifically likened it to that displayed by Wallis fifty years before, and qualified chauvinism as a particularly English weakness. Moreover, by these early years of the eighteenth century Newton himself had played a role in Anglo-French scientific discussions for almost half a century. The problems posed by Newton, as they became more and more acute in France through the second and third decades of the new century, were not new problems nor ones devoid of historical precedent.

What is so special about the reception of Newton's work in France, and Franco-Britannic scientific relations generally? I do not mean to indicate that it would not also be worthwhile to examine Anglo-Germanic or Anglo-Italian scientific relations systematically, and Newton's place in them. Quite the contrary. But in the cases of the relations between Englishmen and Italians or Germans in this period there exists an air of deference of the continental to the English which slightly cloys the atmosphere. The Italian or German was all too conscious of the fissiparity of his political history; all too aware of the weak territorial and political base of his honoured, though decayed, universities and scientific patronage. Impressed by the multitude of scientific books that poured from Britain, over-awed by the social grandeur of those like Robert Boyle who engaged in the scientific labours of the Royal Society or at least gave them countenance, and wrongly assuming that the adjective *Royal* implied wealth, power and rich patronage, they were all too ready to see themselves as humble followers of the British example.[3] Or should I not rather write Franco-Britannic example? For my point here is that the English and French were the only equals, and therefore the only rivals. Only they, in the seventeenth century, possessed national scientific societies with kingly patronage, finance, and institutions. (As we all know, the Parisians were indeed far better off than the Londoners in all material respects.) Only the French and the English took part in organized research—sometimes co-operative research. Only in the French and English languages were widely-circulated journals of broad scientific interest published, from which other editors freely transcribed.[4] And what is nearer to the heart of the matter, only the French and the English engaged in a close, continuous and voluminous intellectual skirmish whose terms far exceeded those of Newton's life. At any rate, it seems to me evident that there was no similar relationship between the intellectuals of Britain and those of other countries.[5] The skirmish of which I write was far from limited to science or to science and philosophy; it embraced literature, theology, historiography and indeed almost every subject about which books are written, or lectures delivered. While one may roughly define the core of the debate as being (so far as science is concerned) Cartesianism during Newton's youth and Newtonianism in his late years, argument between the English and French in fact touched on almost every aspect of methodology and theory in every active area of science, from astronomy through mechanics to zoology. And the skirmish was fought on at least two readily distinguishable levels—in the air and on the ground, as it were. The debate might be about the most universal intellectual principles, as between Henry More and Descartes at one end and Leibniz and Samuel Clarke at the other; or if such examples seem too airily metaphysical, between Huygens and Newton after the publication of the *Principia*. (To forestall any possible doubt, allow me hastily to express my recognition that neither Huygens nor Leibniz was French by nationality, for what that concept was worth in the seventeenth century; but both can, I hold, be taken as ardent proponents of French science.) Such debates, to which we might further add that between Spinoza and Boyle though its *casus belli* is a great deal more specific,[6] frequently found their way into the gravity of print. At another level, where John Wallis was a doughty champion, the argument was very much more personal, turning not on such things as the ideas of God, spirit and matter but rather on who had done what first, who had been more right, and (more broadly) what kind of science was (judging by its fruits) the more accurately prolific. Some of this debate was published contemporaneously also, for example in Wallis's two collections of *Commercia epistolica*,[7] but a great deal was not.

Thus a complete analysis of Newtonianism in France should be founded upon an understanding of this multi-valued intellectual skirmish which, alas, we do not yet possess either. My present objective is much more limited: using the work that Dr Laura Tilling and I have done in preparing for publication[8] the final three volumes of the *Correspondence of Isaac Newton*[8] to approach the question: what did the French know and think of Newton during the third phase of the assimilation of his work into French science?

To define what I mean by "third phase": the first stage of Newtonianism in France, obviously, extends from 1672 when a non-trivial product of Newton's pen first appeared in print to 1699 when he was chosen as an *associé étranger* of the Académie Royale des Sciences. The second phase covers the years 1699–1713, during which Newton seems to have taken little interest in the distinction the French had thrust upon him, and to have made no effort to promote his work in that country. The *Principia* certainly found readers in France during these years (though no attempt has yet been made to examine them as a group), and by 1713 such principal figures of the Académie Royale des Sciences as the Abbé Bignon, Fontenelle and Varignon were ready to express the most profuse admiration for Newton's achievements in their letters to him. Newton seems to have presented no copies of *Opticks* (1704) nor of *Optice* (1706) to the Académie of which he was a member, though presentation copies found their way to individual Frenchmen.[9] The third phase, however, extending to the publication of Maupertuis's *Dissertation sur les figures des astres* in 1732, an event commonly taken to signalize the beginning of Newton's triumph in France, opens with Newton's deliberate and persistent efforts to mend fences with the French, starting with the presentation of some copies of the *Commercium epistolicum* (1712).[10] These were soon followed by the second edition of the *Principia* (1713); the Abbé Varignon was elected FRS in 1714 *in absentia*, three other members of the Académie, visitors to London, in 1715.

Now where should we turn first for information on the reception of Newtonian science in France if not to the magisterial work of Pierre Brunet, *L'introduction des théories de Newton en France au XVIIIe siècle*? It is true that this work is almost half a century old and was left incomplete, but no successor of similar scope has replaced it. However, the reader of Brunet's book soon realizes that the manuscript archives and correspondence collections remained closed to him, and indeed his special view of the problem led him to attach little importance even to some of the evidence in print. Although he chose a title of a very general form, Brunet was concerned almost entirely with the introduction of Newtonian celestial mechanics into France; that is to say his "Newton" is the author of the *Principia* not of the *Opticks*, and the fate of the *tourbillons* is very much the core of his story. The Newton who was in controversy with Leibniz and the Bernoullis over the discovery of the calculus—surely the context in which Newton's name was best known in France at this time—is not discussed by Brunet either. This is understandable, if not perhaps wholly defensible, in the modern approach to historical studies, but what of the omission of *Opticks*, when it is very well known that this work was published at Paris, in French, in 1722; the only scientific work of Newton's to be published in French in his lifetime, more than thirty years before the *Principia*? Granted that *Opticks* is a lesser work than the *Principia*, still it is hardly a trivial book in the history of science, and we cannot suppose Newtonian influence so dichotomized that the influence of the lesser work is of no significance in relation to the reception of the greater. Brunet treats as the first Newtonian writings in France those of Maupertuis, commencing with the *Discours sur la figure des astres* (1732). Yet by this time the *Optiques* had been available in French for ten years, under the most august auspices as we shall see, prefaced by the following declaration from the pen of the eminent mathematician and academician, Pierre Varignon:[11]

> Il m'a paru que ce Traité [d'Optique sur les couleurs de M. le Chevalier Newton], par le nouveauté des choses qu'il découvre, par les surprennantes expériences dont ces nouveautés y sont appuyées, & par la profonde capacité que son illustre & sçavant Auteur y fait paroître, comme depuis long-temps par tout ce qu'on a vû jusqu'ici de lui, méritoit fort d'être traduit en notre langue.... Ainsi je suis persuadé que l'Impression de cette Traduction Françoise fera d'autant plus de plaisir, qu'elle repandra davantage les connoissances merveilleuses dont ce Traité est rempli.

This was written in April 1720, as Varignon informed Newton at the time,[12] and prefaced with the other usual *privilèges* to the very beautiful Paris edition of 1722. I cannot believe that Varignon's strictly superfluous expression "comme depuis long-temps par tout ce qu'on a vû jusqu'ici de lui" is either a mere empty compliment or the fruit of carelessness, at a time when Varignon himself was acting as an intermediary between Newton and Johann Bernoulli. On the contrary, I think that Varignon weighed his words carefully, and meant to indicate clearly that in his view Newton's contributions to mathematics and mechanics, made long before, were no less estimable than his book on optics which had only become known to the world at large, and to Frenchmen in particular, within the last few years.

I do not here enter on the question whether Varignon, who died in December 1722, was ever converted from the *tourbillons* to universal gravitation, nor consider whether such a change of hypothesis would have been important to him. But I would certainly argue that the question of Newtonianism is much wider than this single issue of the Cartesian *tourbillons*. If one reads the letters that Varignon wrote to Newton there is no doubt of his immense respect for Newton as a man, equalled only by his admiration for Newton as a natural philosopher. When thanking Newton for the copy of the second edition of the *Principia* presented to him, Varignon recorded his anxiety to obtain a copy of the book as soon as it appeared and continued:[13]

> This burning eagerness had been aroused in me by the first edition of this exquisite book of yours, which I had read with exceedingly great pleasure, wondering always at the supreme strength and sharpness of your genius, with which you unlock the door of nature, penetrate into her inmost recesses, and most skilfully demonstrate by reasoning derived from a sublime geometry laws which no one who was not most acute could perceive, which you have discovered there.

XVII

NEWTON IN FRANCE 237

Thereafter the relations between Newton and Varignon became highly cordial. Admittedly, the Frenchman would not allow that either Leibniz or Johann Bernoulli were knaves or fools, but equally he recognized that Newton possessed a valid claim to the prior, independent and fertile discovery of the calculus. The two men exchanged portraits and after Varignon's death Newton had an engraved printing-plate made in London from his portrait of Varignon, which he proposed to send to Paris in order that a proposed memorial edition of Varignon's correspondence (in which Newton agreed that his own letters might appear) could be adorned by an engraving of him. Unfortunately, the project came to nothing.

These exchanges alone (and I shall describe others in a moment) are enough to indicate that the story of French attitudes to Newton is a good deal more involved than Brunet's rather too simple account of a 'paradigm revolution' in the 1730s might suggest. It seemed worth while to examine the story afresh, if not in enormous detail. Since Brunet's time, Professor I. Bernard Cohen has published a long article on Newton in France,[9] and I have had the advantage also of reading an excellent paper on the reception of Newton's optical work by Professor Henry Guerlac, which is still unpublished. Professor Cohen draws attention to two main points. The first I have already mentioned, namely that Newton, after his election as *associé étranger* in 1699, appears to have taken no interest in the honour done him by the French Academy, to have acknowledged this honour in no way, and to have communicated with the Académie not at all, so far as we know, before 1713. In the first years of the eighteenth century the main avenue of communication between the Royal Society and the Académie des Sciences was between the former's Secretary, Hans Sloane, and Etienne-François Geoffroy;[14] and when Sloane in turn was elected *associé étranger* (1709), Geoffroy pointedly asked him whether he would be willing to submit himself to the rules imposed equally on foreign and French academicians, that they should do all in their power to advance science and add lustre to the Academy by their work, and impart to the Academy from time to time the results of their researches. The *associés* were expected, literally, to be 'corresponding members'. I say 'pointedly' because in a later letter (2 June 1711 N.s.) Geoffroy directly stated that "Mr Newton despised (*méprisoit*) the mark of distinction" intended by his election as an *associé*.

Professor Cohen seems to share this opinion of the French academicians, but I am not sure that he is wholly right to do so. Note that (as Geoffroy admitted) Newton was never asked if he wished to be elected an *associé*; he was presented with the *fait accompli*. It is likely (for the documents do not survive) that he was also never informed of any duties of maintaining a correspondence and so forth expected of him. Newton was not one to thrust himself uninvited into that sort of rôle. Furthermore, he had consciously abandoned scientific and mathematical research; how neatly the connection is brought out by James Gregory writing in 1699: "Mr Neuton is lately made a member of the royal Academy of Paris. ... Mr Neuton is more backward from printing than ever being now the chief officer of the Mint of England. So that we begin to dispair of any of his things, more than we have, in his lifetime".[15] Had Newton been told that his duties as *associé* required him to make reports of his scientific research from time to time, he would certainly have replied that he was now a full-time servant of the Crown.[16] Nor did he have published work to offer to the French Academicians, with the exception of *Opticks*; the other 'Newtonian' works before 1713 were published by others, like William Whiston, William Jones, and Joseph Harris; in the case of the former Newton deplored the (inadequate) publication of his *Universal arithmetick* and would surely have stopped it if he could.

In any event, whether or not Newton attached little significance to his election to the French Academy is not at all the same question as to ask about the significance attached to Newton's work in France, and the latter is (to my mind) much more important. The correspondence between Sloane and Geoffroy, for example, makes it quite plain that far from being blindly prejudiced against everything that came from the island of atoms and attraction, the French even in the Académie itself were eager to learn as much as possible about the accomplishments of English science, now as in the past. The implications for the Cartesian/Newtonian debate of Geoffroy's interest in Hawksbee's experiment proving a difference in refraction between air and vacuum are obvious enough. However, as a warning not to read too much into such interest one may note Geoffroy's remark (in a letter of 1715) that "attraction seems to take us back to occult qualities" even though he goes on to admit that Newton used 'attraction' simply to indicate an effect whose cause was not understood.[17] Postponing *Opticks* again, there are many hints in the Newtonian correspondence of a passionate French interest in his writings, and commitment to his scientific principles, whereas Brunet's attention to printed books causes only the opposite to appear. For example, as early as 1714 Father Charles-René Reyneau was writing letters to the English mathematician William Jones which, if not flatulent adulation (and I do not know why this should be), must be judged to express a measure of conversion to Newtonian science:[18]

> J'ai une ardeur extrême de voir tout ce qui vient de ce grand homme [Newton] à qui on doit tant d'utiles découvertes, persuadé que j'y trouverai toujours de quoi profiter.... J'avais vû, dans la première edition du sçavant et profond ouvrage des Principes de la Philosophie Naturelle les belles applications qu'il fait de ses méthodes à découvrir tout ce qu'il y a de plus caché dans la nature...

and much more of the same sort, general praise certainly but containing some internal evidence that he really had read the *Principia* and admired it.

A more obscure Newtonian, perhaps worthy of a little further investigation, is Louis-Jean Levesque de Pouilly. Of his history in general I can only quote what was written long ago in the *Nouvelle biographie generale*;[19] he was born in 1691 at Reims, and after studying there he went to Paris, where he devoted himself to mathematical studies. I quote:

> Un des premiers en France, il s'efforça d'expliquer l'admirable ouvrage des *Principes*, publié avec tant de succès par Newton, mais qui dans sa forme sévèrement géometrique était peu accessible au public. Le travail de Levesque fut communiqué à [Nicolas] Freret, qui conçut du jeune auteur une idée fort avantageuse...

and assisted him when, later, he deserted mathematics in favour of literature. Whether or not Levesque de Pouilly was a Maupertuis *manqué*, I can add that he certainly addressed a letter to Newton on 14 July 1717.[20] Unfortunately this bears on nothing more interesting than methods of determining the difference in longitude between two meridians, but it contains again general expressions surely indicating more than polite respect. These methods, Levesque writes, are no more than pretext for addressing himself to Newton:

> vous ayant l'obligation d'un bien aussy grand que la connoissance du vray... car enfin, grâces a vous, il est permis presentement d'estre initié aux mysteres de la nature et admis a la connoissance de ses secrets les plus caches. mais il n'en est point de vos decouvertes comme de ces systemes fameux qui ne sont appuyes que sur des conjectures, et qu'il est facile de renverser par d'autres conjectures. c'est sur des fondemens inebranlables que vous aves elevé ce magnifique édifice de votre philosophie. les yeux des ignorans n'en appercevront jamais toutes les beautes. mais ceux qui s'y connoistront le regarderont toujours avec etonnement comme le chef d'oeuvre et la merveille de l'ésprit humain. de ce grand nombre d'hommes qui sont penetrés d'admiration pour vous, j'ose me flatter que personne ne l'est plus que moy.

Despite the existence of more powerful and better-known exponents of Cartesianism in France at this time, it is not surprising that at least a few young Frenchmen gave their allegiance to Newton; what *is* surprising is that we as yet know so little of them. Another, much more familiar, was the enigmatic Jacques-Eugène d'Allonville, chevalier de Louville, astronomer by profession (if one may use the phrase) but a writer on mechanics also. It is perhaps not wholly coincidental that two of his papers in mechanics were against the Leibnizian concept of *vis viva*. The extraordinary thing about Louville, who visited London in 1715 in order to observe the solar eclipse of that year, met Newton, and became a Fellow of the Royal Society, is that he based his most important work—a study of the Earth's orbit—upon a naïve exposition of Newtonian gravitational conceptions without ever mentioning Newton's name, and indeed setting these conceptions forward as though they derived from Kepler. It seems necessary to quote at some length from his "Construction et théorie des tables du soleil" (1720):[21]

> Ce n'est que depuis fort peu de tems que l'on a découvert une loi générale des mouvements des Plànetes; c'est la fameuse Hypothèse de Kepler, qui rend à présent l'Astronomie aussi simple qu'elle étoit embarrassée auparavant.

Now this sounds straightforward enough; presumably Louville means to allude to Kepler's discovery that the planetary orbits are elliptical. What is extraordinary is the immediately following passage in which Louville makes this discovery, not a derivation from observations, but a deduction from mechanical principles:[22]

> Cette hypothèse est fondée sur un principe si simple, qu'on ne peut presque pas douter que ce ne soit celle qu'a suivi la Nature dans la composition de l'Univers. Elle ne suppose qu'une simple pesanteur dans les Planètes qui les porte vers le Soleil, comme les corps pesants sont portés vers le centre de la Terre. Cette pesanteur compliquée avec un mouvement en ligne droite, que leur aura imprimé le Créateur de l'Univers en les créant, leur fait décrire les Courbes que nous leur voyons parcourir....

And Louville goes on to explain that when the centre of gravity or focus is infinitely remote (as we suppose it to be when considering the motion of projectiles on the surface of the Earth) the curve produced is a parabola, as Galileo first demonstrated, but when the centre or focus is not at infinity the curve becomes an ellipse. Surely, one thinks uncomfortably, this is Newton disguised as Kepler? One's suspicion is confirmed on meeting not only the Newtonian idea that a missile projected high enough and fast enough above the Earth's surface would become a satellite, but the following explanation of how the natural rectilinear motion of the planets is converted into a closed orbital motion because it is

> compliquée avec une autre force qui les rapproche continuellement du Soleil à mesure qu'elles s'en éloigneroient en suivant la ligne droite, les oblige de circuler dans la circonférence d'une ellipse ou ovale; or il ne faut, pour produire cet effet, qu'une force semblable à la pesanteur qui soit plus petite à une plus grande distance du Soleil, & plus grande à une plus petite dans la raison réciproque des quarrés des distances. Cela supposé, on démontre geometriquement que la Planète sur laquelle agiront ces deux différents mouvements, doit circuler perpétuellement dans la circonférence d'une Ellipse.[23]

XVII

NEWTON IN FRANCE   241

The implication of Louville's memoir that these phrases summarize the work of Kepler is really quite farcical. I cannot believe that Louville was so misinformed; it must be that he is being deliberately disingenuous. Of course there may have been something in Newton's *Principia* of which we are ignorant to which Louville had some objection of principle. But it is more likely that his disingenuity was born of discretion, just as his rejection of the *tourbillons* is most discreet:

> Voilà donc l'Astronomie rendue bien simple, & délivrée de tous les embarras qu'y avoient mis les anciens Astronomes; plus de déférents, pas même de fluides, qui voiturent les Planètes ... tout est réduit à la simple composition des deux mouvements dont nous venons de parler, que nous voions tous les jours, par expérience, agir sur les corps que nous jettons en l'air.[24]

Louville does elsewhere[25] refer specifically to the 'savant Traité' of Newton on *Analysis per quantitatum series, fluxiones, ac differentias* as published by William Jones in 1711 and it is possible that he was also involved in the story of the establishment of Newton's *Opticks* in French science. This is the opinion of Henry Guerlac in a study of this question written with his customary penetrating erudition, and to this matter of the *Opticks* I now turn, for regrettably our correspondence, so far, has thrown little fresh light on the mysterious Louville or on other early French students of the *Principia*.

Pierre Coste, the translator of Newton's *Opticks* into French, provided in his preface to that work a useful account of the French reaction to Newton's experiments on light and his theoretical views of colour derived from them, which Professors Cohen and Guerlac have considerably amplified.[26] As Mr Lohne has emphasized,[27] Newton's descriptions of his various experiments (especially before *Opticks* appeared) were sparing and obscure. From the first his procedures and his manner of describing what he saw were misunderstood. It was difficult to duplicate his results; few if any Englishmen in the seventeenth century tried to do so. It was unfortunate for Newton's reputation that in France Edmé Mariotte did attempt the task of repeating the experiments, and with typical self-assurance proclaimed, in 1681, the view that Newton's optical experiments were false, and his theory no more worthy of attention than his experiments;[28] Mariotte had obtained differently coloured rays from what he took to be a pure colour issuing from the prism. Since Mariotte's reputation as an experimenter was supreme, the effect of his failure was devastating and for thirty years Newton himself published nothing further to alleviate Mariotte's hostile criticism. However, in 1705 Sloane sent his correspondent Geoffroy a copy of *Opticks*—of course in its first English edition. Geoffroy had visited England years before and apparently knew the language reasonably well, though he and Sloane corresponded in French.

Geoffroy then prepared a French *précis* of the book, which he proceeded to read to the Académie *seriatim* at no fewer than ten sessions between August 1706 and June 1707. The manuscript of this French précis still exists and has been described at some length by Bernard Cohen;[9] it covers the whole book but not the appended *Queries*.

However, Geoffroy's enthusiasm—so we must interpret the events, I think—did nothing to remove the substantial doubt: were the material facts truly as Newton reported them? A second attempt at duplication in France by Philippe de la Hire (perhaps as a consequence of Geoffroy's exposition, for the date does not seem to be recorded) also failed to vindicate Newton.[29] Hence there was still grave doubt. Meanwhile, *Opticks* itself—but now surely the *Optice* of 1706—had won over another powerful figure. Henry Guerlac has shown, from the Leibniz correspondence, that in the Summer of 1707 Malebranche went off for a country holiday with a copy of *Optice*.[30] The result is reflected in the xvith *Eclaircissement* appended to the sixth edition of *La recherche de la verité*, published in 1712. In the previous edition (1700), Professor Guerlac writes, Malebranche had repeated his own earlier views concerning light and colour, now, however, in 1712, Malebranche described how the vibrations created in the eye by the *matière subtile* reflected from a body may arouse the sensation of "quelqu'une des couleurs simples homogènes ou primitives, comme le rouge, le jaune, le bleu &c", or, if the vibration is more complex, of "les autres couleurs composées, & même la blancheur qui est la plus composée de toutes, selon les divers mélanges des rayons". And Malebranche understood that not only colour is associated with each different vibration, for they "font des refractions differentes. Mais il faudroit voir sur cela les expériences qu'on trouvera das l'excellent ouvrage de M. Newton".[31]

As with Louville, distinctly Newtonian concepts are embedded by Malebranche in a Huygenian neo-Cartesian context, with the aid (perhaps) of some misunderstanding by Malebranche of what Newton meant when he wrote of periodicities in optical phenomena.[32] Malebranche remained staunchly an aetherist; indeed, he declared (after assuring his readers that what he had just explained should not be considered "comme des conjectures ou des vues generales insuffisament prouvées" since it was intended to make sense of the "principales expériences que M. Newton, ce sçavant Géometre & si renommé en Angleterre & par tout, a faites avec une exactitude telle que je ne puis douter de la verité") that it was his "principale vue dans cet Eclaircissement... de faire voir que toute la Physique dépend de la conoissance de la matière subtile".[33] For the *tourbillons* of this matter constitute tangible substances, and "la source du mouvement n'est que dans cette matière invisible, que quelques personnes très-scavantes d'ailleurs, comptent pour rien...".[34] Malebranche can hardly have failed to know that Newton was among them.

Whether or not Malebranche was also aware of the attachment to a corpuscular or emission theory of light then and since widely attributed to

Newton does not appear; but the contrast in scientific methodology between his experimentally-based treatment of light in *Opticks* and Malebranche's use of it to bolster an undulatory theory totally alien to Newton's conceptions is evident and piquant enough; and this may be said without making Newton a positivist or ignoring his own preconceptions. Malebranche's attitude towards Newton is sharply defined in a quotation taken by Henry Guerlac from a letter of (probably) 1707:

> Although M. Newton is not a physicist, his book is very curious and very useful to those who have the right principles in physics, and he is moreover an excellent mathematician. Everything I believe concerning the properties of light fits all his experiments.[35]

If Malebranche, from 1707 or 1708 onwards, was broadcasting the empirical merits of *Opticks*, it is nevertheless certain that he had not repeated Newton's experiments himself. It is possible that the next attempt to verify them in France made (as we again learn from Pierre Coste's prefaces to *Optiques*) by Dortous de Mairan—then a very young man—in 1716 and 1717 was stimulated by Malebranche. Certainly Dortous was very much a Malebranchiste (he was never a Newtonian, and wrote against Newton's theory of the Earth in 1720) and he, like the great Oratorian philosopher, made his confidence in the experiments of *Opticks* widely known from 1716 onwards.[36] However, it is equally likely that Dortous's verification, like the later ones, was stimulated by the French scientific expedition to England in 1715. The solar eclipse of April in that year was visible in London, but not in Paris. Claude-Joseph Geoffroy, younger brother of Etienne-François, Pierre Rémond de Monmort and the Chevalier de Louville whom I have already mentioned made the trip to London to observe it, but also (as the letters from the elder Geoffroy to Sloane make plain) to see something of English experimental science at the Royal Society;[37] they were particularly eager to see repeated Hawksbee's vacuum experiments and those of Newton on light and colours. Hawksbee, however, was dead by this time, his place as experimental demonstrator to the Royal Society having been taken by John Theophilus Desaguliers.

Now already, some nine months before the French visit (that is, in July 1714), Desaguliers had begun a series of experimental verifications of Newton's optical discoveries, repeated before a group of Fellows of the Royal Society and described in the *Philosophical transactions*,[38] where his paper is preceded by a note on the mistaken procedures used long before by the "Gentlemen of the English College at Liege", Mariotte and others who had sought to obtain the "primitive Colours of Light", procedures which in turn had given rise to doubts about the accuracy of Newton's results, voiced most recently in the *Acta eruditorum*.[39] It was this last criticism—springing from so

Leibnizian a source and treating Mariotte's deceptive experiment as decisive —that had impelled Newton to ask Desaguliers to repeat the *experimentum crucis*.[40] Thus Desaguliers was well aware of the need to be "particular in mentioning such things as ought to be avoided in making the Experiments" of Newton, especially as "some Gentlemen abroad [had] complained that they had not found the Experiments answer, for want of sufficient Directions in Sir *Isaac Newton's Opticks*; tho' I had no other Directions than what I found there".[41]

Desaguliers, then, was already prepared to satisfy the curiosity of "Monsieur *Monmort* and others of the *Royal Academy of Sciences*" as to the reality of Newton's optical experiments when they arrived in London, and presumably this was successfully done in the spring or summer of 1715.[42] It is a reasonable guess that the Frenchmen were all afterwards convinced of the truth of Newton's reports by what they themselves witnessed. Certainly Louville was, as we have seen, strongly inclined towards Newtonianism; Pierre Rémond de Monmort had been in friendly contact with Newton for several years, and Geoffroy Cadet was (we shall see) man-midwife to the first repetition of Newton's optical work in France. "We can conclude", writes our colleague Henry Guerlac, "without serious risk of error, that it was the report of the Academicians, informed of the precautions that had to be observed, that led to the first recorded instance of a successful repetition of these famous experiments in France".[43] This opinion is, I believe, wholly correct.

However, it is only from a fuller reading of the Newtonian correspondence than Guerlac could make that there emerges a full picture of the formation of a group of Frenchmen eager to promote Newtonian experimental science in Paris. The leaders of this group were two different, powerful and unlikely figures, whose names have not yet been mentioned, Henri-François Daguesseau, the Chancellor of France, and the Cardinal de Polignac. Who first proposed a republication of Coste's Amsterdam translation of *Opticks* in Paris is not known; possibly it was the bookseller François Montalant but his later lethargy suggests that the real impulse originated elsewhere. Examination of the Amsterdam, 1720, text was entrusted by the *garde des sceaux*, Fleuriau d'Armenonville, to Pierre Varignon, who not only wrote the *Approbation* already quoted but undertook to see the book through the press. Unfortunately, the letter of the Summer of 1720 in which Varignon explained the business details to Newton is not extant; his subsequent letters are filled with complaints about the slow progress of the edition. Varignon shared his troubles with Fr. Reyneau, who in turn had a friend (unnamed)[44] with access to the Chancellor, Henri-François Daguesseau. For so long as he retained office, that is, until February 1722, a powerful force to promote the edition was available; in fact the whole Daguesseau clan seems to have taken the cause of *Optiques* to heart, and to have attended demonstrations of the principal experiments. Newton wrote him a letter of thanks for his intervention on behalf of the French *Optiques*, which is lost, though Daguesseau's reply survives.[45]

Daguesseau of course was a great advocate, no man of science. More interesting is the Cardinal de Polignac, a member of the Académie Royale des Sciences since 1714; indeed Dortous de Mairan in his *Eloge* describes him as one of its most enthusiastic supporters. In the present context it is curious that Polignac was also a fervent Cartesian: "Le Newtonianisme, tel qu'il le concevoit", wrote Dortous, "lui avoit toûjours paru dangereux par sa conformité avec les points fondementaux de la Physique d'Epicure".[46] The elegist also reports that the Cardinal drafted some lines on the optical experiments of Newton for his pro-Cartesian poem *Anti-Lucrèce*, but these had disappeared before its posthumous publication.[47] Nevertheless, it was certainly the Cardinal de Polignac, as Coste confirms, who was the chief instigator of the repetition of Newton's experiments by Fr. Sebastien and who (according to Montucla) paid for the expenses involved.

From the names listed by Pierre Coste, from the correspondence, and in few other hints, then, it appears that quite a large group of Frenchmen was forming who had knowledge of, and were concerned for the wider understanding of, Newton's work. A very few by 1720 like Louville, Levesque de Pouilly and just possibly Fr. Reyneau either accepted the Newtonian theory of universal gravitation already, or at least extended towards it a benevolent neutrality. Others, like Malebranche, the Cardinal de Polignac and Dortous de Mairan definitely continued to support the *tourbillons* of Descartes, but nevertheless accepted the experimental reality of the work described in *Optiques*, though how far they even now went along with Newton's interpretation of the experiments must be regarded as highly uncertain. For we must not confuse the truth of the experiments reported by Newton with the validity of the theories he propounded. According to Coste, in his revised preface to the Paris 1722 *Optiques*, these famous experiments on light were first successfully duplicated in Paris in 1719 by Fr. Sebastien [Truchet] "& depuis quelquetemps par M. [Nicholas] Gauger, lesquels en presence de plusieurs personnes très-intelligentes, ont verifié la plupart . . .".

Coste's footnotes indicate that the spectators with Fr. Sebastien included besides the Cardinal de Polignac and Varignon, M. Jaugeon and M. Jussieu; with Gauger were the Chancellor and his relations, M. de Lagny, and Fr. Reyneau. (In his first-edition preface Coste had also listed Fontenelle as a witness, probably mistakenly.) Now it might seem that with these events and the publication of the *Optiques* at Paris in such prestigious circumstances the position of the work in French science would henceforth be secure. But once again correpondence shows that, beneath the surface, situations are often more complex than they seem. We have one surviving letter from Fr. Sebastien to Newton, probably written after the appearance of the Amsterdam translation in 1720, but possibly two years later with reference to the Paris edition.[48] The exact date is not highly significant, nor perhaps the degree of enthusiasm manifested for the book by Fr. Sebastien. What is significant is that Fr. Sebastien reports that the description of Newton's optical experiments was taken from an English *Opticks*, with M. Geoffroy (presumably Claude-Joseph) acting as translator. The success of the repetition by Fr. Sebastien is, in his letter, stated by implication rather than in explicit words; what is clear (since he devotes a separate sheet to it) is his formal rejection of Newton's primary physical assumption in optics; that white light is heterogeneous, consisting of homogeneous, variously coloured rays, each signalized by its own distinct angle of refraction. Fr. Sebastien does not deny the facts of refraction and dispersion, but he supposes the phenomena to arise from the fact that the rays coming from the periphery of the sun travel farther, and are weaker, than those travelling from its centre; the stronger rays have a greater inertia and therefore are less refracted than the weaker: "Ergo radii majore vi donati sese suo in statu conservant diutius quam qui sunt debilioris".

Humanum est hypotheses fingere. Newton had set himself against the evasion of his 'doctrine of colours' by others' hypotheses in the 1670s and repeated his formal condemnation of hypothetical arguments at intervals since—in *Opticks* as in the *Principia*. But in vain. Fr. Sebastien Truchet was the latest, after Malebranche, Huygens, Hooke and others, who had striven to create yet another new framework of ideas for Newton's facts. Fr. Sebastien might lament his lack of opportunity to meet Newton face to face which religion denied him, and flatter Newton as 'physicorum omnium nostræ ætatis longe Principem' but, like nearly all his compatriots, he was still far from being a convinced and thorough Newtonian, if to be a Newtonian was to adopt certain scientific concepts, certain patterns of scientific argument and certain quite precise theoretical explanations—if, one might say, to become a Newtonian required that one ceased to be a Cartesian.

To admit that *Opticks* is an important book was indeed one step towards accepting the *Principia* as important; to recognize the genius of Newton was another step towards understanding his intellectual creation. On this point we may be sure that by 1720 French science was ready to pay full tribute to Newton's status; so Fontenelle, no Newtonian, nevertheless could write to him, and I think sincerely:[49]

> The Académie Royale des Sciences has instructed me to thank you very humbly for the French translation of your *Opticks* which it received yesterday from M. Varignon; you know what the whole of the learned world of Europe thinks of a work so original, so ingenious, so worthy of yourself, but the Académie (which numbers you among its members) is conscious of its merits, and praises it, with a more particular concern.

To this Fontenelle added a personal postcript:

Take it well, Sir, that to the thanks of the Académie I add my own for the copy which I received from you; I cannot sufficiently express my sense of the honour done me by a man such as yourself, when he remembers me in so obliging a way. Even if you only knew my name, I should be proud of the fact and would reckon it an extreme happiness that it had reached you. . . .

And so forth. As Henry Guerlac has rightly emphasized, French recognition of the achievements of Newton in mathematics and experimental physics increased rapidly after 1715, and matured with the publication of the Paris *Optiques*. From that point the Académie was genuinely proud to claim Newton as a member. But Brunet was equally right in holding that in mechanical and physical *theory* the transfer of French allegiance had hardly begun by 1720. Until then we have no solid evidence that the reception of Newton in France was other than positivist—he was meritorious as a geometer and an experimenter, not as a natural philosopher. Newton did not possess the true principles of Malebranche's physicist. And important as this positivist welcome to Newtonian in France certainly was, we must distinguish it from the dawning sense (still to follow later) that Newton's works contained the true principles of science.

REFERENCES

1. An earlier version of this paper was read to the British Society for the History of Science on 8 July 1975.
2. Pierre Brunet, *L'introduction des théories de Newton en France au XVIIIe siècle. Avant 1738* (Paris, 1931). No continuation was published.
3. While recognizing the inappropriateness of these sentences to define the attitudes of Leibniz and his associates during the latter part of Newton's life, I think they depict ones which were universal during his youth and still common among Europeans at the time of his death.
4. What of the *Acta eruditorum*? Not in its Latin language alone, but in its style, this journal seems to me very different from the *Journal des sçavans*, the *Philosophical transactions*, and the *Mémoires* of the *Académie Royale des Sciences*.
5. The plausible exception is Holland (see, for example, Rosalie J. Colie, "Spinoza and the early English Deists", *Journal of the history of ideas*, xx (1959), 23–46; idem, "Spinoza in England, 1665–1730", *Proceedings of the American Philosophical Society*, cvii (1963), 183–219).
6. See A. Rupert Hall and Marie Boas Hall, "Philosophy and natural philosophy: Boyle and Spinoza", in *L'aventure de l'espirit: Mélanges Alexandre Koyré* (Paris, 1964), ii, 241–56.
7. See John Wallis, *Commercium epistolicum de quæstionibus quibusdam mathematicis nuper habitum* (Oxford, 1658); and *Opera mathematica* (Oxford, 1693–99).
8. Vol. v (1709–13) is due to appear in the present month of August 1975; vol. vi (1713–18) is in proof, and vol. vii is well advanced in preparation.
9. See I. Bernard Cohen, "Isaac Newton, Hans Sloane and the Académie Royale des

Sciences" in *L'aventure de la science: Mélanges Alexandre Koyré* (Paris, 1964), i, 61–116.
10. Newton, *Correspondence* (ref.8), vi, Letter 1004 (7 June 1713 N.S.).
11. *Traité d'optique ... par M. le Chevalier Newton. Traduit par M. Coste sur la seconde edition angloise ... Second edition francoise, beaucoup plus correcte que la premiere* (Paris, 1722), "Approbation". The publication of this edition (based on the French translation first published at Amsterdam in 1720) figures largely in Newton, *Correspondence*, vi (ref. 8).
12. Newton, *Correspondence* (ref. 8), vii, Letter 1338 ([May], 1720).
13. Newton, *Correspondence* (ref. 8), vi, Letter 1024, 5 December 1713 N.S. My translation from Latin.
14. See G. R. de Beer, "The relations between Fellows of the Royal Society and French men of science when France and Britain were at war", *Notes and records of the Royal Society*, ix (1952), 244–9; Jean Jacquot, "Sir Hans Sloane and French men of science", *ibid.*, x (1953), 85–98 and *Le naturaliste Sir Hans Sloane (1660–1753) et les échanges scientifiques entre la France et l'Angleterre* (Les conférences du Palais de la Découverte, série D, no. 25, 1954). Cohen, *loc. cit.* (ref. 9).
15. Newton, *Correspondence*, iv (Cambridge, 1967), 311; 29 May 1699.
16. See Newton to Flamsteed, 6 January 1699; *Correspondence*, iv (ref. 15), 296.
17. I do not quite follow I. Bernard Cohen's comment (*loc. cit.* (ref. 9), 102) that by comprehending Newton's (overt) use of the word 'attraction' Geoffroy "shows himself to have been a thorough-going Newtonian". Geoffroy's own words are: "les experiences [de Hauksbee] nous ont paru fort curieuses, mais on a bien de la peine a s'accoutumer au terme d'attraction, qui semble nous ramener aux qualités occultes" (*ibid.*, 100).
18. S. P. and S. J. Rigaud, *Correspondence of scientific men in the seventeenth century* (Oxford, 1841), i, 265; Newton, *Correspondence* (ref. 8), vi, Letter 1116; 23 November 1714 N.S. Reyneau's letter acknowledged the gift of Jones's *Analysis per quantitatum series, fluxiones ac differentias* (London, 1711).
19. Vol. xxxi, 35.
20. Newton, *Correspondence* (ref. 8), vi, Letter 1248.
21. *Mémoires de l'Académie Royale des Sciences* for 1720 (Paris, 1722), 35–84.
22. *Ibid.*, 36.
23. *Ibid.*, 36–7.
24. *Ibid.*, 38.
25. *Mémoires de l'Académie Royale des Sciences* for 1722 (Paris, 1724), 133. Newton(?) presented a copy of the *Analysis* to the Académie des Sciences through Louville in the spring of 1714 (Newton, *Correspondence*, vi (ref. 8), Letter 1248).
26. Strictly, Coste wrote two prefaces, for that in the second, Paris, 1722, edition of *Optiques* (ref. 11) differs markedly from the preface to the Amsterdam, 1720 edition.
27. J. A. Lohne, "Experimentum crucis", *Notes and records of the Royal Society*, xxiii (1968), 169–97.
28. Edmé Mariotte, "De la nature des couleurs", in his *Essays de physique* (Paris, 1679–81). See J.A. Lohne, *loc. cit.* (ref. 27), 186 and Henry Guerlac, "Newton in France: The delayed acceptance of his theory of color" (typescript), 24–26. What seems to be the same account of Newton's theory appears in Mariotte's *Traité des couleurs* (*Oeuvres* (Leyden 1717), i, 226–7). Mariotte puts forward the evidence in favour of "l'hypothèse nouvelle et fort surprenante" of

XVII

NEWTON IN FRANCE 249

Newton, then that which is contrary, namely his own experiment in which the light at the extremity of the violet part of the spectrum of one prism was passed through a slit one-sixth of an inch in diameter; then the ray thus formed was shone through a second prism and displayed both yellow and red after refraction. Thus the second prism had modified the violet ray and so (Mariotte declared): "l'ingenieuse hypothèse de Monsieur *Newton* ne doit point être reçue".

29. Guerlac, *op. cit.* (ref. 28), 41–42.
30. *Op. cit.* (ref. 28), 39–43.
31. N. Malebranche, *De la recherche de la verité, ou l'on traitte de la nature de l'espirit de l'homme, et de l'usage qu'il en doit faire pour eviter l'erreur dans les sciences* (sixth edition, Paris, 1712), 330.
32. *Ibid.*, 361, col. 1. It is the simple (and, as it happens, correct) assumption of Malebranche that "chaque rayon conserve ensuite la même promptitude dans ses vibrations". That there is only a determined number of such rays (of constant frequency and constant angle of refraction) is certain from Newton's experiments. "Car de même que lorsqu'on devise harmoniquement une octave ... il ne peut y en avoir qu'un nombre determiné de tons; il ne peut aussi y avoir qu'un nombre determiné de rayons simples. Aussi M. Newton ... a trouvé que le rang des couleurs simples étoit harmoniquement divisé". Malebranche thence concludes that the red rays, being refracted less, have a lower frequency of vibration, while the blue rays, more markedly refracted, have a higher frequency.
33. *Ibid.*, 361–2. The passage continues: "que cette matière n'est composée que de petits tourbillons, qui par l'équilibre de leurs forces centrifuges, font la consistance de tous les corps; & par la rupture de leur équilibre qu'ils tendent sans cesse a rétablir, tous les changemens qui arrivent dans le monde".
34. *Ibid.*, 362.
35. Guerlac, *op. cit.* (ref. 28), 41. See André Robinet (ed.), *Malebranche*, tome xix: "Correspondance, actes et documents, 1690–1715" (Paris, 1961), 771–2; Malebranche to P. Berrand [1707]: "Quoique M. Newton ne soit point physicien, son livre est tres curieux et tres utile à ceux qui ont de bons principes de physique, il est d'ailleurs excellent geometre. Tout ce que je pense des proprietez de la lumiere s'ajuste à toutes ses experiences".
36. On Dortous and Newton's optics see Guerlac, *op. cit.* (ref. 28), 29–36.
37. See I. Bernard Cohen, *op. cit.* (ref. 9), 98–102.
38. J. T. Desaguliers, "An account of some experiments of light and colours, formerly made by Sir Isaac Newton, and mention'd in his *Opticks*, lately repeated before the Royal Society", *Philosophical transactions*, xxix, no. 348 (1715), 433–47; idem, "A plain and easy experiment to confirm Sir Isaac Newton's doctrine of the different refrangibility of the rays of light", *ibid.*, 448–52. See Lohne, *op. cit.* (ref. 27), 189–90 and Guerlac, *op. cit.* (ref. 28), 47–58.
39. October 1713, 447, particularly mentioning the difficulty raised by "ingeniosissimo *Mariotto*, rerum naturalium scrutatore indefesso nec infelici".
40. *Philosophical transactions*, xxix, no. 348 (1715), 435.
41. *Ibid.*, 447.
42. This confirmation for the French delegation is mentioned in *ibid.*, 435 and by Coste in his prefaces.
43. *Op. cit.* (ref. 28), 67.
44. Possibly the Chancellor's relative, the Abbé Daguesseau.

2—HOS * *

45. Newton, *Correspondence* (ref. 8), vii, Letter 1369.
46. Dortous de Mairan, *Eloges des Académiciens de l'Académie Royale des Sciences morts dans les années 1741, 1742 & 1743* (Paris, 1747), 90.
47. *Ibid.*, 79.
48. Newton, *Correspondence* (ref. 8), vii, Letter 1350.
49. *Ibid.* Letter 1402.

The reader may now consult Henry Guerlac, *Newton on the Continent*, Ithaca & London, 1981.

INDEX

Académie Royale des Sciences:
　XVII 233–4, 236–8, 244–5
Andrade, E.N. da C.: X 219; XII 278, 280
Angeli, Stefano degli: XVI 136
Angot, Pierre: X 221–2
Archimedes: XIII 41–2
Aristotelianism: I 242; VI 169
Aston, Francis: VIII 35
Auzout, Adrien: XI 47

Bacon, Francis: XIV 47
Baker, Thomas: XVI 132
Barrow, Isaac: I 239, 246; VIII 31; XI 39,
　41–3, 45; XIII 51; XV 180; XVI 131, 136,
　139, 140–41, 145, 147; XVII 233
Bartholin, Erasmus: X 221
'Basil Valentine': IV 114, 128
Beaune, Florimond de: XVI 134
Bechler, Zev: XV 183, 186–8, 190–91
Becke, David von der: IV 127
Bentley, Richard: V 297–8, 300–302;
　VII 136, 144; VIII 30, 42, 46; XIII 47
Bercé, M. de: XI 47
Berkeley, George: XIII 37
Bernoulli, Jakob: XVI 140
Bernoulli, Johann (I): V 292, 294–6, 301,
　317–20; VIII 32, 45; XVI 142;
　XVII 236–7
Bernoulli, Nicholas: V 295n, 296; VIII 45
Bertet, Jean: XVI 134
Bignon, *Abbé* Jean Paul: XVII 235
Birch, Thomas: X 219
Boyle, Robert: I 243; II 27–8, 35–7;
　IV 114, 118–20, 126, 139; VI 167–9;
　VII 131, 133; IX 14; XII 270; XIV 55;
　XV 185; XVI 134, 145; XVII 233–4;
　and More: XIII 41–2, 46
Brahe, Tycho: XIII 39
Brereton, *Sir* William: XIV 56
Brewster, *Sir* David: I 246; II 27, 36;
　IV 113; VIII 30; X 219, 250
Brouncker, William *Viscount*: XII 264–5,
　273–4, 276–7; XIV 50; XVI 132
Brunet, Pierre: XVII 232, 235, 237–8, 246

Cajori, Florian: III 64

Cassini, J.D.: XIV 179
Catalogue of the Portsmouth Collection:
　IV 119
Charles II, *King*: XII 270–71, 274, 279
Charleton, Walter: XIII 48; XIV 47
Cheyne, George: VIII 30
Child, J.M.: XVI 138–9
Clarke, Samuel: VII 137–8, 143; VIII 30,
　46; XVII 234
Clerselier, Claude: XIII 37
Cohen, I. Bernard: V 291; VI 178; VII 136;
　VIII 33–4, 41; XI 51; XVII 237, 241–2
Collins, John: IV 120; VIII 31; IX 14;
　XI 41–3, 45, 50, 53; XVI 132–3, 134–5,
　137–8, 143–7
Conduitt, John: I 245; IV 113
Conti, *Abbé*: VIII 30; XVI 140
Copernicus, Nicholas: XIII 38–9
Coste, Pierre: XVII 241, 243–5
Cotes, Roger: V 293–4, 298–302; VI 132;
　VIII 30, 33, 42–6, 47–9
Cudworth, Ralph: VIII 46

Daguesseau, H.-F.: XVII 244
De Morgan, Augustus: VIII 48
Derham, William: X 220; XII 277
Desaguliers, J.T.: XVII 243–4
Desargues, Girard: XVI 134–5
Descartes, René: VI 168–9; X 221–2, 226;
　XIV 46–7, 52; XV 180, 182; XVI 136,
　146; and More: XIII 37–8, 40, 43–6;
　XVII 234; and Newton: I 240, 243;
　II 35–8, 40, 43; VII 133, 137; VIII 37
De Son, M.: XII 276, 278–9
Dijksterhuis, E.J.: XIV 54
Dollond, John: II 43
Dortous de Mairan, J.B.: XVII 243, 245
Double refraction: X 221, 224
Dugas, René: III 62, 68
Duillier: *see* Fatio

Earth, figure of: X 225–9
Edleston, Joseph: V *passim*; X 219
'Espinasse, Margaret: XII 261n, 264n,
　268n, 279
Euler, Leonhard: XIV 50

Fabri, Honoré: IX 13–19; XVI 136
Fatio de Duillier, Nicolas: V 291–3; VIII 42; XIV 45, 53
Fermat, Pierre de: X 221–2; XV 180; XVI 139
Ficino, Marsilio: XIII 40
Finch, John: XIII 40
Flamsteed, John: VIII 31–2, 41, 48; XV 179, 186–7
Fontenelle, B. Le B. de: XIV 47; XVII 235, 245–6
Forbes, R.J.: IV 114–15, 117
Franklin, Benjamin: VI 172
Fresnel, Augustin: XV 187
Fromanteel, J. and A.: XII 262

Galilei, Galileo: III 70; VI 167–8; XIII 38–9; XIV 52; XV 186; XVII 240
Gassendi, Pierre: XIII 48; XIV 47
Gauger, Nicolas: XVII 245
Geoffroy, Claude-Joseph: XVII 243–4, 246
Geoffroy, Etienne-François: XVII 237–8, 241–2
Glanvill, Joseph: XIII 42–4
Glauber, J.R.: IV 126
Glisson, Francis: XIII 44
Graham, Thomas: XII 275
Gravitation: I 241; III 62–71; X 224–7
Gregory, David: V 292, 301; VIII 42
Gregory, James (I): XI 41, 44–5; XIV 52, 54; XVI 133, 135–7, 139, 141–4, 146–7, 149, 151
Gregory, James (II): XVII 238
Grimaldi, F.M.: IX 13–19, 20, 22; X 222
Guerlac, Henry: XVII 237, 241–4, 247
Gunther, R.T.: X 219, 220

Hall, Chester Moor: II 43
Halley, Edmond: III 62–4, 68; VIII 30, 33–42, 47–8; XIV 45; XVI 147
Harris, John: II 36; IV 113; VIII 30; XVII 238
Harrison, John: IX 14
Harrison, William: XII 275
Hartlib, Samuel: XIII 40–41
Harvey, William: XIV 47
Hauksbee, Francis: IX 21; XVII 238, 243
Helmont, F.M. van: XIII 41
Henshaw, Nathaniel: IX 14
Hermes Trismegistus: XIII 40
Hesse, Mary B.: XII 267n, 277
Hevelius, Johannes: XII 273; XIV 46
Hobbes, Thomas: XVI 131
Hofmann, J.E.: XVI *passim*

Holmes, *Sir* Robert: XII 263
Hooke, Robert: II 30, 34; III 64; VI 168; VII 132–3; VIII 32–3, 38; IX 13–15, 17, 19, 22; X 219–30; XI 46–8, 52–3; XIV 55, 57; XV 179, 185; XVI 142, 147, 151; and horology: XII 261–81
Hospital, *Marquis* de l': V 292; XVI 140
Hudde, Johann: XIV 46
Huygens, Christiaan: I 250; and horology: XII 261–2, 265, 266, 268–70, 272–9; XVI 149; and Leibniz: XVI 131–2, 142, 146; and Newton: III 62–3, 68; V 291–4, 300, 301; VI 236; IX 14; XIV 45–58; XVII 234; *Discours de la Pesanteur*: X 224–7; *Traité de la Lumière*: X 220–24
Huygens, Constantijn (I): XIV 46
Huygens, Constantijn (II): XIV 45

Jaugeon, M.: XVII 245
Jessop, Francis: XVI 132
Jones, William: VIII 29, 30, 32; XVII 238, 241
Jourdain, P.E.B.: X 219
Jurin, James: XI 55
Jussieu, Antoine de: XVII 245

Keill, John: V 296–7; VIII 46–7
Kepler, Johannes: XI 56; laws: III 69; XIII 46; XVII 240–41
Kersey, John: XVI 134–5
Keynes, *Lord*: IV 113, 115; VII 136
Kinckhuysen, Gerard: XI 41–5, 53, 60
Koyré, Alexandre: V 291; VI 177; VII 136–7; XIII 50

Lagny, M. de: XVII 245
La Hire, Philippe de: XVII 242
Lansbergen, Philip van: XIII 38
Leeuwenhoek, Antoni van: XIV 46
Leibniz, Gottfried, Wilhelm: V 292–6, 300–301; VII 137–8, 144; VIII 29, 31–2, 41, 45, 46; XII 279; XIV 54; XVI 131–52; XVII 234, 237
Lely, *Sir* Peter: XIV 56
Levesque de Pouilly, Louis-Jean: XVII 239, 245
Locke, John: IV 118; VII 131
Loggan, David: XI 50
Lohne, J.A.: XVII 241
Louville, J.-E. d'Allonville de: XVII 239–45
Lucas, Anthony: XI 52

INDEX

McGuire, J.E.: XIII 51
Machin, John: VIII 30, 47
McKie, Douglas: IV 114–17
Magalotti, Lorenzo: XII 269
Maignan, Emmanuel: X 221–2
Malebranche, *Fr.* Nicole: XVII 242–3, 245–7
Mariotte, Edmé: XVII 241, 243–4
Maupertuis, P.L.M. de: XVII 235–6
Mercator, Nicholas: XVI 135–6
Metzger, Hélène: XIII 49
Mohr, Georg: XVI 148
Moivre, Abraham de: VIII 30
Monmort, Pierre Rémond de: XVII 243–4
Montalant, François: XVII 244
Moore, *Sir* Jonas: XI 45; XII 270, 275, 276
Moray, *Sir* Robert: XI 47, 51; XII 265, 268, 273–4, 277–9; XIII 40; XIV 55–6
More, Henry: I 243; VII 133; VIII 46; XIII 37–52
More, Louis T.: I 246, 249; II 27
Mouton, Gabriel: XVI 134, 151

Neile, William: XVI 142
Newall, L.C.: IV 113–14, 119
Newton Humphrey: IV 113
Newtonianism: XVII 233–47
Newton, *Sir* Isaac:
— and alchemy: IV 113–19
— and France: XVII 233–47
— and gravitation: III 62–71
— Hooke upon: X 224–7
— and Huygens: XIV 45–58
— and Leibniz: XVI 133, 135, 137–52
— Manuscripts of (C.U.L. Add.): *3958*: VII 132; *3965*: VII 133; *3970*: VII 133; *3973*: IV 120, 142; *3975*: II 27–36; IV 119–52; *3985*: III 62–71; *3996*: I 239–50; *4000*: I 239n, 240–41, 246; II 36–43; *4003*: VII 133; *4005*: VII 133
— and mathematics: I 240; V 294–301; XIV 54–5
— and mechanical philosophy: VI 167–78; VII 131–44; XIII 46–9; XIV 47
— on mechanics: V 291–326; XIV 51–5
— on metals: IV 133–48; X 220–21
— on metaphysics: VII 137–8, 143–4; VIII 46; XIII 49–52
— and More: XIII 43, 45–7
— on natural philosophy: I 242–5; VI 167–78
— *Opticks*: VI 171–2; VII 135–7, 140–41; VIII 30; IX 19; XI 49; XIII 48–9; XV 187–91; XVII 235–6, 241–7

— on optics: I 245–50; II 27–43; VIII 31–2; IX 13–23; XI 39, 44–54; XIV 47–50; XV 180–91
— *Principia*: V 291–326; VI 167–78; VII 131–4, 139–40, 142; VIII 29–49; IX 20; XIV 45, 54–5; XV 179–80, 185, 190; XVII 236, 238–41
— student reading of: I 241–2

Oldenburg, Henry: VIII 29, 31–2; IX 13; XI 39, 44–7, 49, 51–3; XII 269, 274, 276, 278–9; XIV 53, 55, 57; XV 183; XVI 131–8, 141–52

Paget, Edward: VIII 39
Pardies, *Fr.* Gaston Ignace: X 221–2; XI 47–8; XVI 134
Pascal, Blaise: XVI 135–6, 139, 145
Pell, John: VII 133, 146–7, 151
Pemberton, Henry: VIII 30, 33, 45–7
Petty, *Sir* William: IX 13; XIII 41
Pitt, Moses: XI 42–3, 53
Polignac, *Cardinal* de: XVII 244–5

Raphson, Joseph: XIII 50
Rawdon, Edward: XIII 40
Reyneau, Charles-René: XVII 238, 244–5
Richer, Jean: X 227
Roannais, *Duc* de: XII 275–6
Robertson, J.D.: XII 277
Roberval, G.P. de: VI 167–8
Robinson, Bryan: VII 135
Robison, John: XII 277
Roemer, Ole: X 221; XV 179, 184–6, 188–9, 191

Sabra, I.A.: XIV 48
St. Vincent, Grégoire de: XVI 136
Scarborough, *Sir* Charles: XII 270
Schooten, Franz van: I 240; XIV 46; XVI 136, 139, 145
Shapiro, Alan E.: IX 21
Sloane, *Sir* Hans: XVII 237–8, 241, 243
Sluse, R.F. de: VIII 29; XVI 131–2, 135–8, 141
Smith, Thomas: XIII 40
Snell, Willebrord: XIV 46; XV 180–81, 185
Sotheby Catalogue: IV 113, 116
Southwell, *Sir* Robert: XII 276
Spinoza, Baruch: XVII 234
Starkey, George: IV 118, 120
Steno, Nils: XII 277, 279
Steuwer, R.S.: IX 20, 21
Stevin, Simon: XIV 46

Stubbe, Henry: XIII 42, 44

Taylor, F. Sherwood: IV 114–17
Tilling, Laura: XVII 234
Tompion, Thomas: XII 262, 264, 270–71, 275
Toulmin, Stephen: XIII 50–51
Towneley, Richard: XI 43; XII 264
Truchet, *Fr.* Sebastien: XVII 245–6
Tschirnhaus. E.W. von: XVI 140, 144–7
Turnbull, H.W.: III 62, 70, 71; XI 40, 52

Varenius, Bernhard: XI 39, 40, 46, 55–61
Varignon, Pierre: XVII 235–7, 244–6
Vaughan, Thomas: XIII 40
Vernon, Francis: XIV 56–7
Vigani, Francis: IV 128
Waller, Richard: X 219–20; XII 262, 277–8

Wallis, John: I 240; VI 168; VIII 41; X 224–5, 228–9; XI 43; XIV 47, 55; XVI 132, 136, 139, 142, 152; XVII 233–4
Ward, Richard: XIII 40
Ward, Seth: XIV 57
Westfall, Richard S.: IX 17; XIII 47–9, 51
Whistler, Daniel: XII 270
Whiston, William: VIII 30; XVII 238
Whiteside, D.T.: VIII 31, 35, 38; XIV 52; XVI 136, 139, 148–51
Wilkins, John: XIII 38; XIV 57
William III, *King*: XIV 45
Willis, Thomas: XIV 57
Witsen, Nicholas: XIV 46
Wren, *Sir* Christopher: VIII 33; X 255; XIV 47; XVI 139

Yarworth, William: IV 119